# PREFACE

THE last few years have witnessed, in French and German speaking lands, a marked revival of in est in the person and work of Calvin. The publica n of the monumental edition of his writings, under editorship of a distinguished succession of Strass ig theologians, has been accompanied and followed the studies of Kampschulte, Cornelius, Lefranc, ng, Müller, Wernle and Choisy, and has its crown the great work of Doumergue, now more than half npleted. The resources thus freshly placed at the posal of the historian are ample excuse for a new graphy of Calvin in English; and the writer would ke grateful acknowledgment of his indebtedness to labours of the scholars he has named.

n a volume limited in size and scope by conformity the requirements of a series, as this necessarily is, ne selection as to the weight of emphasis is impera in describing a career so full of incident, of con versy, and of far-reaching influence as that of Cal . The writer has chosen therefore to lay special ght on Calvin's training, spiritual development, and structive work rather than on the minutiae of his

CALVIN AT 53. FROM AN ENGRAVING BY RENÉ BOYV

# JOHN CALVIN

## THE ORGANISER OF REFORMED PROTESTANTISM

1509—1564

BY

WILLISTON WALKER

TITUS STREET PROFESSOR OF ECCLESIASTICAL HISTORY IN YALE UNIVERSITY

G. P. PUTNAM'S SONS
NEW YORK AND LONDON
The Knickerbocker Press

# PREFACE

THE last few years have witnessed, in French and German speaking lands, a marked revival of interest in the person and work of Calvin. The publication of the monumental edition of his writings, under the editorship of a distinguished succession of Strassburg theologians, has been accompanied and followed by the studies of Kampschulte, Cornelius, Lefranc, Lang, Müller, Wernle and Choisy, and has its crown in the great work of Doumergue, now more than half completed. The resources thus freshly placed at the disposal of the historian are ample excuse for a new biography of Calvin in English, and the writer would make grateful acknowledgment of his indebtedness to the labours of the scholars he has named.

In a volume limited in size and scope by conformity to the requirements of a series, as this necessarily is, some selection as to the weight of emphasis is imperative in describing a career so full of incident, of controversy, and of far-reaching influence as that of Calvin. The writer has chosen therefore to lay special weight on Calvin's training, spiritual development, and constructive work rather than on the minutiæ of his Genevan contests, or the smaller details of his relations to the spread of the Reformation in the various countries to which his influence extended. Enough has been said on these topics, however, the writer hopes,



892.

to make evident the nature and course of Calvin's principal controversies, and to indicate the character and the wide scope of his connection with the Reformation movement as a whole.

The writer desires to express his gratitude for most valuable suggestions and assistance, especially in procuring illustrations for this volume, to Rev. Dr. Eugène Choisy and to Rev. H. Denkinger-Rod, of Geneva, respectively President and Curator of the *Société du musée historique de la Réformation* of that city; and to Rev. Nathanaël Weiss, Secretary of the *Société de l'histoire du Protestantisme français* of Paris.

YALE UNIVERSITY,
January 1, 1906.

## CONTENTS

# Contents

## ILLUSTRATIONS

[1] Rev H Denkinger-Rod writes under date of April 2, 1903. "I would remark that there is no painting or engraving regarding which one can affirm that it was taken from life. Calvin was too busy during his life-time to find leisure to pose for an artist But as he inspired great admiration in his pupils and in all who approached him, it is more than probable that, without his knowledge, sketches were made which served as models for woodcuts or medals executed in his life-time or soon after his death."

# BIBLIOGRAPHICAL NOTE

THE pathway of the student of Calvin's life and writings and of the literature which has to do with him has been made easy by several elaborate bibliographies. Best of all is that prepared by the late Alfred Erichson, the most recent editor of Calvin's Works, for the concluding volume of the series,[1] and also issued separately in convenient and revised form as *Bibliographia Calviniana* [2] A useful list is that given in the second volume of *The Cambridge Modern History* [3] Older, and therefore less valuable, but with brief critical estimates of the worth of the several authors cited, is that of Philip Schaff in the seventh volume of his *History of the Christian Church.*[4]

All earlier collections of Calvin's Works, as a whole, have been superseded by the noble edition, *Joannis Calvini Opera quae supersunt omnia*, begun in 1863 and completed in fifty-nine volumes in 1900,[5] under the able editorship of the Strassburg scholars, Johann Wilhelm Baum, Edouard Cunitz, Edouard Reuss, Paul Lobstein, Alfred Erichson, and their associates. This series includes in volumes i -xa. Calvin's theological treatises; in volumes xb.-xx. letters by Calvin and relating to him; in volumes xxiii -lv his homiletical and

[1] *Opera*, lix 462-586 He died April 12, 1901.

[2] Berlin, 1900.

[3] Pp. 779-783, London and New York, 1904.

[4] Pp. 223-231, 681-686, New York, 1892.

[5] Braunschweig. They constitute volumes xxix.-lxxxvii. of the *Corpus Reformatorum*. A sketch of the execution of the task, by Erichson, is given in the *Bulletin de la société du Protestantisme français*, xlix. 613 (1900).

exegetical works. This edition is cited as the *Opera* in the notes of the present volume.

The correspondence contained in the *Opera* is supplemented by the carefully annotated series of *Correspondance des réformateurs dans les pays de langue française*, of which nine volumes were issued by Aimé Louis Herminjard,[1] until the work of this admirable scholar was interrupted by death The later volumes of Herminjard's work had the advantage of publication subsequent to the corresponding sections of the *Opera*, and the writer has therefore cited them in references to Calvin's letters where they thus present the fruits of further investigation.

The larger portion of Calvin's theological and exegetical writings are accessible to the reader who knows English only, in the *Works of John Calvin*, published in fifty-two volumes, 1843–1855, at Edinburgh by the "Calvin Translation Society." The *Institutes* have been often translated; most worthily by Henry Beveridge for the series just named A selection of Calvin's letters collected by Jules Bonnet was printed in English translation in part at Edinburgh, in 1854, and as a whole, in four volumes, as *Letters of John Calvin*, at Philadelphia, in 1858 The edition should be used, however, only in comparison with their more critical presentation in the *Opera* or in the collection of Herminjard.

The earliest lives of Calvin, by his friends, Beza and Colladon, originally published in 1564, 1565, and 1575, may be found in volume xxi. of the *Opera*. That of Beza, of 1575, is printed, in English translation by Beveridge, in *Calvin's Tracts* in the edition of the "Calvin Translation Society "[2]

Of important modern biographies, the earliest in date and

[1] Geneva, 1866–1897 The series ends with the year 1544. Herminjard died at Lausanne, December 11, 1900.

[2] I xix–c, Edinburgh, 1844

the amplest in learning up to its time was that by the pastor of the French Church in Berlin, Paul Henry, *Das Leben Johann Calvins des grossen Reformators*, in three volumes, Hamburg, 1835–1844 Highly eulogistic and the fruit of great industry, it was, for its epoch, the ablest defence as well as the fullest biography of the Genevan reformer, but is now largely superseded by later publications. A maimed translation into English (lacking most of the notes and appendices which give much of value to the original) was put forth by Henry Stebbing, in 1849[1]

Diametrically opposite in purpose, and lacking all claim to regard as a serious attempt to ascertain the facts of history, was the intensely polemic and unscrupulous *Histoire de la vie, des ouvrages et des doctrines de Calvin*, of the partisan Roman Catholic, Vincent Audin, published at Paris in two volumes in 1841. An English translation, by John McGill, was issued at London in 1843 and 1850

In 1850, the English historian, Thomas Henry Dyer, published at London his *Life of John Calvin*, in a single substantial volume. Based largely on a careful independent study of Calvin's correspondence, and on the work of Henry, it differs much in tone from that of the Berlin biographer Dyer's attitude toward Calvin is critical, not to say severe, but the volume is one of much merit. It discusses Calvin's origins and early history with brevity; but details his Genevan controversies with thoroughness

In 1862 and 1863, Félix Bungener published a popular history, *Calvin, sa vie, son œuvre, et ses écrits*, in two volumes at Paris, which, though well written, added little to the existing knowledge of its subject. It was immediately translated into English, and appeared at Edinburgh in 1863.

More thorough in its workmanship, and in fact one of

[1] London and New York.

the best of the older biographies of Calvin, was *Johannes Calvin, Leben und ausgewahlte Schriften*, by Ernst Stahelin, a pastor in Basel, published at Elberfeld in two volumes, in 1863. Stahelin's attempt to estimate Calvin's personal characteristics was peculiarly successful.

The work of Jean Henri Merle d'Aubigné, Professor in the Free Church Theological Seminary at Geneva, the first volume of which appeared, in 1863, under the title *Histoire de la réformation en Europe au temps de Calvin*,[1] deserves mention chiefly because of its enormous circulation, especially in English-speaking lands. Its account of the Genevan Reformation extends to 1542. Though based on much use of documentary sources, it is essentially partisan, paints its portraits without shade, and makes constant sacrifices to dramatic effect

A biography of a much more satisfactory nature was that of the Old-Catholic Professor of the University of Bonn, Friedrich Wilhelm Kampschulte, *Johann Calvin, seine Kirche und sein Staat in Genf* The first volume of the three planned by the author appeared in 1869; the second was complete at the time of his death on December 3, 1872, but, though intrusted to his friend, Professor Carl Adolf Cornelius, of Munich, was not published till 1899,[2] and then under the editorship of Dr. Walter Goetz of the University of Leipzig. The third was never begun Though undoubtedly unsympathetic and too much inclined toward a critical estimate of the reformer, and not a little influenced by the Galiffes [3] who regarded Calvin as a foreign usurper in Gene-

[1] Paris, 1863–1878 Eng tr London, 1863–1878; New York, 1870–1879

[2] Both at Leipzig.

[3] Jacques August Galiffe and Jean Barthélemy Gaifre Galiffe, of Geneva, father and son, maintained with much learning the thesis that Calvin was a foreign intruder who introduced into Geneva, before

van affairs, Kampschulte's volumes, incomplete as they are, by accuracy of scholarship and acquaintance with the events in which Calvin bore a part, are still indispensable to the student.[1]

In Amédée Roget, Professor in the University of Geneva, that city possessed a capable historian of its affairs. His *Histoire du peuple de Genève depuis la réforme jusqu'à l'escalade*, in seven volumes, 1870–1883, covers the period from 1536 to 1567,[2] and therefore embraces all of Calvin's Genevan activity. Remarkably impartial, and essentially objective in its treatment, it gains high value from its constant citation of the Genevan archives, with which the author was thoroughly familiar

In 1888, a brilliant young scholar of France, now Professor in the Collège de France at Paris, Abel Lefranc, published at Paris a study of Calvin's youth of great significance, *La jeunesse de Calvin.*

Four years later, the late Professor Philip Schaff gave, as the principal content of the seventh volume of his *History*

his time free, a system of tyranny. The chief works of the elder Galiffe were, *Matériaux pour l'histoire de Genève*, Geneva, 1829; and *Notices généalogiques sur les familles genevoises*, *Ibid.*, 1836 Of the younger, *Quelques pages d'histoire exacte* (trials of Perrin and Maigret), in the *Mémoires de l'Institut national genevois*, for 1862; and *Nouvelles pages d'histoire exacte* (trial of Ameaux), *Ibid*, for 1863. They represent, in modern times, the opposition of the old-Genevan families to Calvin

[1] The writer, while recognising Kampschulte's predisposition to severity of judgment, believes Doumergue's criticism of him too unfavourable (ii. 717–721), and even Doumergue declares: "For Catholic historians, it is certain that Kampschulte and Cornelius have given proof, in regard to Calvin, of a remarkable impartiality"; though regarding that "impartiality" as inadequate.

[2] Published at Geneva Roget intended to carry his work further, but was interrupted by death on September 29, 1883

*of the Christian Church*, a careful sketch of Calvin's career and significance, marked by his well-known merits and limitations [1]

In his *La théocratie à Genève au temps de Calvin*, published at Geneva in 1897, a Genevan pastor and scholar, Rev. Dr. Eugène Choisy, has presented a brief but very valuable discussion of the principles which underlay Calvin's Genevan policy.

A cyclopædia article of more than usual merit was that of the late Professor Rudolf Stahelin in the third (Albert Hauck's) edition of the *Realencyklopädie für protestantische Theologie und Kirche* [2]

Calvin's conversion, earliest theological writings, and indebtedness to previous reformers have been subjected to searching and rewarding investigation by a pastor of Halle, August Lang.[3] The discussion has been continued in papers of high importance by Professor Karl Müller of Tübingen,[4] and Professor Paul Wernle of Basel.[5]

In 1899, Kampschulte's friend and fellow Old-Catholic, the late Professor Carl Adolf Cornelius [6] of Munich, gathered the studies which he had made preparatory to the intended completion of Kampschulte's unfinished work,

[1] New York, 1892

[2] III 654–683, Leipzig, 1897. He died March 13, 1900.

[3] *Die ältesten theologischen Arbeiten Calvins*, in the *Neue Jahrbücher für deutsche Theologie*, for 1893, Bonn, pp. 273–300; *Die Bekehrung Johannes Calvins*, in the *Studien zur Geschichte der Theologie und Kirche*, Leipzig, 1897, i 1–57; *Der Evangelienkommentar Martin Butzers*, Leipzig, 1900 He has also written on Calvin's household life, and relations to Luther and Melanchthon.

[4] *Calvins Bekehrung*, in *Nachrichten von der königl Gesellschaft der Wissenschaften zu Göttingen*, for 1905, pp 188–255

[5] *Noch einmal die Bekehrung Calvins*, in the *Zeitschrift für Kirchengeschichte*, xxvii 84–99 (1906)

[6] Died February 10, 1903.

with other monographs, into a volume entitled *Historische Arbeiten, vornehmlich zur Reformationszeit*,[1] in which, quite in the spirit of that scholar, with similar thoroughness and command of accessible sources, he discussed Calvin's journey to Italy and his Genevan work to 1548 On this period Cornelius is indispensable to the student[2]

The year of the publication of Cornelius's discussions, 1899, witnessed the issue of the first volume of the remarkable biographical undertaking which is to constitute a monument not only to the Genevan reformer, but to its laborious author, Professor Émile Doumergue, of the Theological Faculty of Montauban Of the five volumes proposed, three have appeared,—the second in 1902 and the third in the closing weeks of 1905. The first carries Calvin to the publication of the *Institutes*, the second to his recall to Geneva, while the third is devoted to a description of the city and of his home and surroundings. No such elaborate biography has been planned of any other leader of the Reformation as this entitled *Jean Calvin: les hommes et les choses de son temps*;[3] and its beauty and interest is enhanced not merely by abundant photographic reproductions, but by drawings of high artistic merit by Henri Armand-Delille. In elaborateness of discussion, in amplitude of treatment, it leaves little to be desired. The most conspicuous criticism to be passed upon it is that it is everywhere a defence of its subject. Professor Doumergue is above all a worshipper of his hero, but a very painstaking worshipper, who

[1] Leipzig.

[2] Most of these studies were first published in the *Abhandlungen der königlichen Akademie*, Munich, 1886–1895.

[3] Published at Lausanne. The size is a quarto almost as large as a sixteenth century folio. The first volume contains 648 pages; the second, 829, and the third, 734.

is undoubtedly led into occasional exaggeration by his enthusiasm. His critical judgment is sometimes impaired, also, by his desire to win the utmost of biographical result from his sources, and to present Calvin in the most favourable light. For the student of Calvin the work is, nevertheless, of much value, and the writer can but express his indebtedness to its author and his hope that the labours now so far advanced may be carried without interruption to their intended conclusion.

A brief summary of Calvin's work, marked by deep insight into its ruling purposes and spiritual significance, is presented in the chapter by Principal Andrew Martin Fairbairn of Mansfield College, Oxford, entitled *Calvin and the Reformed Church*, in the second volume of *The Cambridge Modern History*, issued in 1904 [1]

No bibliographical note, however limited, would be complete without mention of the *Bulletin historique et littéraire* issued by the *Société de l'histoire du Protestantisme français* of Paris, now under the efficient management of Rev Nathanael Weiss, and in the fifty-fifth year of its publication (1906). Scattered through its pages may be found many discussions, documents, and reviews of high value to the student of Calvin.

[1] Pp. 342–376, London and New York.

JOHN CALVIN

# CHAPTER I

## CALVIN'S SPIRITUAL ANTECEDENTS

CALVIN belongs to the second generation of the reformers. His place chronologically, and, to a large extent, theologically, is among the heirs rather than with the initiators of the Reformation. At his birth Luther and Zwingli were already twenty-five years of age, Melanchthon was about to take up a student's career at the University of Heidelberg, and Henry VIII. had just begun his eventful reign. None of these leaders had entered, indeed, upon his reformatory work; but the thorough development of the Reformation in Germany and in German-speaking Switzerland was achieved before Calvin reached the activities of manhood. Yet, in spite of his lateness in point of time, Calvin must be ranked among the most influential leaders in the gigantic struggle of the sixteenth century. He could not have done his work had not Luther and Zwingli gone before; but he was far more than a builder on other men's foundations. That work had its antecedents and was made possible by many predisposing influences. A brief glance, therefore, at the state of the land in which Calvin grew to manhood may be of service as exhibiting the soil and the atmosphere in which his early intellectual and religious life was nurtured.

The kingdom of France, at the beginning of the

sixteenth century, had many claims to eminence among the states of Christendom. In consciousness of national unity, in efficiency of governmental organisation, and in consequent influence on the politics of Europe, it could challenge favourable comparison with any of its contemporaries. Not so world-wide in the activities of its inhabitants as the newly significant kingdom of Spain, then feeling the fever stimulus of the great discoveries which marked the close of the fifteenth century, its growth was more natural, solid, and unforced than that of its portentous southern rival. Though the neighbouring kingdom of England could show the forms at least of more popular governmental institutions, the physical strength of England was reckoned far inferior to that of France. The great Holy Roman Empire, rich in commerce, cities, and soldiers, was much less able to use its strength than France by reason of its divisions and its lack of a national spirit. Though far from having attained the organic development of a modern state, France, in the early sixteenth century, was, with the possible exception of England, the most advanced of any European kingdom on the road toward modern national life.

The national tendencies characteristic of the French monarchy of that age had conspicuous embodiment in Francis I. (1515–1547), contemporary with whom Calvin was to do the formative portion of his work. A ruler of unbounded military ambition, anxious to win for France the post of highest influence in Europe, his personal charm, ready wit, eloquence, tact, and appreciation of scholarly and artistic merit gave him served popularity. His social talents attracted a lendid court; but his easy morality and entire want personal religion or of ethical seriousness unfitted m to appreciate the fundamental significance of the gantic religious struggle which convulsed Europe ring his reign. France, under him, had an aggressive, ough largely unsuccessful, military policy, a brilliant urt, and a high degree of national unity and internal osperity.

The relations between the French Church and the onarchy had for centuries been close and cordial to degree hardly equalled elsewhere in Europe. Church d King had aided each other against the nobility. hile thoroughly orthodox, as the middle ages underood orthodoxy, and bitterly opposed to "heretics" at me like the Cathari and Waldenses, the French urch felt a greater hostility toward extreme papal aims than was general in other branches of Western ristendom. It possessed a strong sense of corporate ity, and of national or "Gallican" rights, which even e Papacy ought not to infringe. But the growing rength of the crown was leading to increasing control the sovereigns over the Church, and this control was cidedly strengthened when, in 1516, Francis I. and eo X. entered into the famous Concordat. The King as henceforth to nominate to the higher administrave and monastic posts in the realm. To the sovereign e Concordat brought a firmer grasp on the French hurch; to the Papacy it secured an increase in revenue. ut though the rights of the Church were thus in a easure sacrificed, it was exempt from many papal interferences and exactions that bore heavily on other lands. There was not, therefore, in France that popular hatred of the Roman *curia* which was so widespread in Germany and there made possible the rapid growth of the Lutheran revolt.

It would be an error to suppose, however, that the spiritual state of the French Church was superior to that existing in lands where the crown enjoyed less influence. The same evils of externalism in the conception of religion, of emphasis on acts done, penances performed, pilgrimages accomplished, and indulgences won, rather than on the inward state of the soul and on the ruling purpose of the life, existed in France that were to be found elsewhere in Latin Christendom; and whatever of criticism may justly be passed upon the Roman Church of this period as a whole attaches equally to that of France. The growth of the power of the monarchy brought far less aid to the spiritual interests of the French Church than did a similar increase of royal authority south of the Pyrenees to that of Spain, since no French sovereign of the fifteenth or sixteenth centuries manifested a religious zeal comparable with that of Isabella of Castile or even with that of the emperor, Charles V. The French kings enjoyed the control of the Church which their share in the appointment of its prominent officers afforded. They appreciated its possibilities as a source of revenue. They were ready enough to oppose changes which would in any serious way alter a fabric so useful to them. But they gave to political considerations the chief weight in ecclesiastical appointments; and the great evils of the possession of office by the morally unfit and the heaping up of benefices in the hands of favourites,[1] who, however well intentioned, could give them no adequate spiritual care, continued to flourish unrelieved by any counter acting influence from the throne. France, as a whole, seems to have been fairly well content with its religious situation at the beginning of the sixteenth century, and, as compared with Germany or Spain, its sense of the need of betterment was undeveloped.

Foremost among the intellectual forces of France was still to be placed the University of Paris. That eminent seat of mediæval learning, to which all other universities of northern Europe looked up as their archetype, had enjoyed high academic fame since the beginning of the thirteenth century. Within its walls Aquinas, Bonaventura, Duns Scotus, William of Occam, d'Ailli, and Gerson had taught. Its repute as a centre of theologic instruction had, indeed, been considerably dimmed by the beginning of the sixteenth

[1] Henry C Lea, in *The Cambridge Modern History*, i 659, gives a striking instance of pluralism contemporary with Calvin's life. Jean, son of Duke René II of Lorraine, was born in 1498 In 1508, he entered into possession of the revenues of the bishopric of Metz; 1517 saw him bishop of Toul, 1518 brought the addition of Térouanne, 1521 added Valence and Die, 1523 Verdun In 1524, he became archbishop of Narbonne. The year 1533 added the archbishopric Reims and made him primate of France In 1536 he became bishop of Alby, and the next year archbishop of Lyons He then gained the bishoprics of Mâcon, Agen, and Nantes. Several of these posts he resigned to relatives; but many he continued to hold till his death in 1550. And, in addition, he was in possession of the "abbeys of Gorze, Fécamp, Cluny, Marmoutiers, St. Ouen, St. Jean de Laon, St. Germer, St. Médard of Soissons, and St. Mansuy of Toul."

century, but was still great. Its theological faculty, known popularly as the Sorbonne, from the large concentration of its instructors in the College founded in 1253 by Robert de Sorbon, regarded itself, and was widely reputed, of unimpeachable orthodoxy. Nor was it wanting in courage and independence. Its opposition to the Concordat, as recently as 1516, bore witness to the jealous concern of the University for the liberties of the French Church. But it was, nevertheless, on the whole a hindrance to progress. It stood strongly opposed to innovations in learning or in doctrine. Not that it wholly neglected the new learning that was crossing the Alps from Italy. Greek had been taught within its walls, though for a brief period, as early as 1458. In 1508, new interest in the Attic tongue had been awakened by the coming of Girolamo Aleandro, afterwards famous as an opponent of Luther at Worms. But, in spite of this measure of approval, the friends of classic studies felt that the University was hostile to them, that its dominant spirit was scholastic, and its methods antiquated. Its leaders looked upon Greek as the "language of heresies," and they condemned the teachings of Luther in terms of the utmost abhorrence.[1]

Yet, in the early years of the sixteenth century, the new learning was rapidly winning its way in France. In 1507, the printing of books in Greek was begun in

[1] See the letters of Henri Lorit and Valetin Tschudi in A. L Herminjard, *Correspondance des réformateurs dans les pays de langue française*, i. 31, 38; Abel Lefranc, *Histoire du Collège de France*, pp 60–63, 68

Paris, and two years later the leader of native French Humanists, Jacques Le Fèvre, already famed for his studies on Aristotle and in mathematics, published his exposition of the Psalms which Luther was to use in his early years of teaching at Wittenberg. Among many distinguished pupils of Le Fèvre, none was more eminent for scholarship than Guillaume Budé, whose *Commentary on the Greek Language*, of 1529, gave him a European fame To Budé's influence with Francis I. was due the establishment, in 1530, of the Royal Lecturers (*Lecteurs royaux*), at Paris, to give instruction in Greek, Hebrew, and mathematics, wholly in the spirit of the Renaissance, and with a zeal for the new learning that roused the hostility of the Sorbonne From this royal foundation the Collège de France was to grow Indeed, under the reign of Francis I., the new learning had become distinctly fashionable. The King was conspicuously its supporter, and the roll of scholars, architects, and artists who found in him a patron is an ornament to his reign. Even more committed to the support of Renaissance men and methods was Francis's elder sister, Marguerite d'Angoulême, whose increasing liberalism was ultimately to carry her into real, though not publicly announced, sympathy with Protestantism.[1] In Marguerite men of liberal ideas, generally, had a determined defender; and she afforded to many efficient protection, especially after her marriage, in 1527, to Henri d'Albret, King of Navarre, had put her at the head of a little court at

[1] Abel Lefranc, *Les idées religieuses de Marguerite de Navarre*, Paris, 1898, p 123

Nérac. With Francis, however, support of the new learning was based on admiration for humanistic scholarship rather than on conviction, and it ceased whenever the new leaven threatened the constitution or the doctrine of an organisation so useful to the French monarchy from a political and financial point of view as the French Church.

It was true in France, as elsewhere in Europe, that the new learning was leading to criticism of the existing state of the Church. From its standpoint the Sorbonne was amply justified in its opposition. The spirit of the Renaissance was that of a return from the scholarship of the later mediæval period to the sources. Begun with a revived interest in the writers of classical antiquity, it soon led men to investigate anew the sources of religious truth, and to go back of d'Ailli, Occam, Scotus, and Aquinas, to Augustine, and, even further, to the New Testament. The attempted return did not usually involve any hostile intention toward the established Church. Men like Erasmus, Ximenes, or Reuchlin believed that sound learning, the study of the Scriptures and of the Fathers, and earnest opposition to the superstition, ignorance, and maladministration rampant in the Church would effect all that was necessary for its betterment. They had no wish for revolution. In France this humanistic spirit of reform had its conspicuous embodiment in Le Fèvre, who, both by reason of his own services to the cause of religious awakening and the disciples whom he aroused to similar or even greater zeal, deserved the first place among the religious leaders of his native country in the generation that preceded Calvin, and prepared the way for Calvin's more positive work.

Born at Étaples in Picardy about the middle of the fifteenth century,[1] Jacques Le Fèvre was early attracted to Paris, where he learned Greek of a fugitive from Sparta, George Hermonymus. A journey to Italy, in 1488–1489, quickened his humanistic zeal, and his religious spirit was no less manifest in a sympathy with the mystical type of piety. A little man, modest, kindly, gentle, of a life that did honour to his priestly vows, he won friendship by his personal qualities as much as he attracted admiration by his zeal for scholarship. His disciples were destined to the most various parts in the Reformation struggle; but they seem to have held him in singular affection. Among those who honoured him as their teacher were Guillaume Briçonnet, sprung from one of the eminent noble houses of France, and to be bishop of Meaux; Guillaume Budé, instrumental, as has been seen, in the establishment of the Royal Lecturers; François Vatable, one of the first teachers of Hebrew on that foundation and to be Calvin's instructor; Gérard Roussel, the later confessor of Marguerite d'Angoulême, and bishop of Oloron, for a time Calvin's friend; Louis de Berquin, destined to die at the stake for his Protestant faith; and Guillaume Farel, to be the fiery preacher of

[1] The usual and more probable date is "about 1455," *e g* G. Bonet-Maury in Hauck's *Realencyklopädie für protestantische Theologie*, v 714, but Professor E Doumergue, *Jean Calvin, les hommes et les choses de son temps*, Lausanne, 1899, *seq*, i. 539–541, has an interesting argument favouring the conclusion that at his death, in 1536, he was 100 years old.

Evangelical doctrines in French Switzerland, and Calvin's intimate associate.

It was by reason of Briçonnet's appointment as abbot of the great Parisian monastery of St. Germain-des-Prés, in 1507, that Le Fèvre came to make that religious foundation his home for the next thirteen years. There, aided by its noble library, he turned to the study of the Bible in a singularly fresh spirit. In 1512, he published a Latin translation of and commentary upon Paul's Epistles which shows clearly the development of his thought. Le Fèvre did not break with the Roman Church as an organisation,—that he never did. He still held to many of its characteristic doctrines. Yet, five years before Luther's theses, he had come to deny the justifying merit of good works, to hold salvation to be a free gift from God, to doubt the doctrine of transubstantiation, and to imply a belief in the sole authority of the Scriptures.[1] But these assertions, though clear, were the utterances of a quiet, scholarly mystic, who saw no incongruity between his views and a cordial support of the Church as it then existed; and it is no wonder that few perceived what he failed to see. His book made no sensation; and he continued his peaceful career, holding with ever-increasing firmness the affection of his friends and pupils, and gaining, through the good offices of Briçonnet, the regard of Francis I. and of Marguerite.

Meanwhile Luther was beginning his reformatory

[1] For discussions, from somewhat divergent points of view, of the extent of Le Fèvre's Protestantism, see Herminjard, *Correspondance*, i. 239, and Doumergue, *Jean Calvin*, i. 81–86, 542–551.

work in Germany, and, by 1519, that land was filled with the noise of the battle. His books soon reached France. The Sorbonne, under the lead of its syndic, Noël Béda, condemned his views in April, 1521. Criticisms of the Church which had passed well-nigh unnoticed now appeared dangerously "Lutheran." Le Fèvre himself came under suspicion. In 1517 and 1518, he had put forth a scholarly study denying the identity of Mary Magdalene with Mary, the sister of Lazarus and the Mary who anointed the Saviour's feet. In itself, this might seem an academic question; but it denied the current teachings of the Church, it practically asserted the right of private Biblical interpretation, and it was an invasion by one who was only a master of arts of a field thought to be fittingly open only to a doctor of theology. Under the suspicion which the rise of Luther had instilled, Le Fèvre was now attacked by Béda, and his opinion on the problem of the Marys was condemned by the Sorbonne about seven months after it had denounced the Saxon reformer.

About a year before the condemnation of his book, however, Le Fèvre had left Paris for the friendly home of Briçonnet, who, since 1516, had been bishop of Meaux. The bishop was a worthy disciple of Le Fèvre in purpose. He saw the need of reform, and held the humanistic belief that a return to the sources—the study of the Bible and the preaching of Biblical truth—would right the evils of the Church. He perceived no need of revolution, nor did he, any more than Le Fèvre, grasp the seriousness of the situation But he was willing to do much more than most humanists to use the remedies in which he believed; and in his reformatory convictions and his efforts alike, he had the powerful sympathy of Marguerite. He now began the work in earnest. Under his encouragement and that of Marguerite, Le Fèvre published, in 1523, a translation of the New Testament which grew by 1530 to a version of the whole Bible. This was, indeed, far from being the first translation of the Scriptures to be made or printed in France; but those that had gone before had been marked by the abbreviations and modifications popular in the middle ages. Le Fèvre now gave a careful version of the Vulgate, enriched here and there by comparison with the Greek.[1] Though in no sense a great translation, Le Fèvre's work undoubtedly furthered extensive reading of the Scriptures in France.

Briçonnet was inaugurating, meanwhile, an active campaign of preaching in his diocese, aided by Roussel, Vatable, Farel, and Michel d'Arande, all of whom had caught their inspiration from Le Fèvre; but he soon found himself in great difficulties. By the champions of the existing order he was looked upon as little better than a Lutheran. On the other hand, the new preaching could not be confined to simple expositions of the Scriptures. The humanistic reformatory course was one almost impossible to hold in practice, save as an individual attitude. Farel inveighed against the Papacy,

[1] Reuss and Berger in Hauck, *Realencyklopädie*, iii 126–131; Doumergue, i. 98; *The Cambridge Modern History*, ii 283 The New Testament had been printed in French at Lyons about 1477; and the whole Bible, modified as above mentioned, at Paris about ten years later.

GENERAL VIEW OF NOYON
(Reproduced by permission of Georges Compiegne, Noyon.)

and was probably dismissed by Briçonnet in 1523. But iconoclastic acts, wholly distasteful to Briçonnet, Roussel, and most of his friends, soon occurred. In December, 1524, Jean Le Clerc, a wool-carder of Meaux, tore a copy of a papal bull from the cathedral door and affixed instead a declaration that the Pope was Antichrist.[1] Briçonnet denounced the acts of Le Clerc and his possible associates in January, 1525;[2] but the political situation soon made his position impossible. The great defeat of the French at Pavia, in February, was followed by the captivity of the King in Spain, whither Marguerite went to join him in August The Parlement of Paris was now able to oppose Briçonnet unhindered. His preachers were forbidden and Le Fèvre's translations ordered burned.

Briçonnet felt that the situation was beyond his solution. He was not a man of the highest courage; but had he been more daring than he was he might well have thought that his mild reformatory efforts had resulted in attempts more revolutionary than he anticipated or relished. He now issued, on October 15, 1525, two synodical decrees[3] condemning Luther's doctrines and books and deploring the "abuses of the Gospel" by those who denied purgatory and rejected prayers to the saints. His reformatory work at Meaux was over. The same month Le Fèvre and Roussel

[1] He was whipped and branded at Paris. On July 22, 1525, he was burned at Metz for the destruction of a shrine

[2] Letter to the clergy of Meaux, Herminjard, i 320.

[3] Herminjard, i. 153, where they are dated 1523, though with hesitation. On the true date see Doumergue, i. 110.

were compelled to fly for safety to Strassburg; bu Briçonnet himself continued in possession of his offic till his death in 1534. Fortunately the royal favou followed the fugitives On his return from Madric in 1526, Francis recalled them. To Le Fèvre he gav the post of teacher to his children and librarian of th Château of Blois. Here the aged scholar laboured o his translation of the Bible, but the growing tension c the ecclesiastical situation led the ever-kindly Ma guerite to effect his transfer to the safety of her cou at Nérac in 1530, and there Le Fèvre died six yeai later. Roussel did further work as a reformatoi preacher in France, and, as will be seen, influence Calvin at a crisis in that reformer's history; but h was even more of a mystic quietist than Le Fèvr Like Le Fèvre and Briçonnet, he saw the need c reform, without desiring or appreciating the necessit of revolution, or being willing to pay the cost.[1] Aide by Marguerite, he accepted the bishopric of Oloroi and died about 1552, in good repute for fidelity in th spiritual administration of his diocese.

Yet if Le Fèvre, Briçonnet, and Roussel were thu disposed only to a humanistic type of reform that d not break with Rome, and proved inadequate to tl struggle, there were those who entered into the spii of the German revolt and wished to effect a simil revolution in France. Most of these radical reforme were from the mercantile and wage-earning classes; b a few men of learning and rank were to be found amoı

[1] Letter to Farel, August 24, 1524, Herminjard, i 271

them. Of Le Fèvre's stormy pupil, Guillaume Farel, something has already been said, and there will be abundant occasion to speak further of him in this narrative. The most eminent in station among the early uncompromising reformers of France was Louis de Berquin, a noble of Artois, and, like Farel, a disciple of Le Fèvre. A man of dignified bearing, scholarly attainments, and high character, Berquin won the friendship of Marguerite and Francis I., and became a member of the royal council. A little later he gained the rather timid regard of Erasmus.[1] A translator of Erasmus and Luther, and himself a writer in favour of reform, he was an object of attack from 1523 onward; but was at first saved by the friendship of Marguerite and of her royal brother. That favour Francis I. failed to extend to Berquin at last, probably because he became convinced that Berquin's attack on so useful an institution as the crown found the French Church to be was too serious; but his end came in death by fire on April 16, 1529, on condemnation by the Parlement of Paris,—a sentence hastily passed and executed to prevent possible interference by the King. When a nobleman of such connections and influence was thus made to suffer, it was evident that scant mercy could be expected from the French courts by heretics of lower social rank. In the death of Berquin French Protestantism of the thorough-going type lost its most conspicuous representative. Yet he cannot be called a leader. He

[1] His story is well told by H M Baird, *History of the Rise of the Huguenots*, i. chap iv. For Erasmus's estimate, see Herminjard, ii. 188

was no organiser. He seems to have had little missionary force. He fought largely alone; and he left the reform movement little stronger save for the courage of his example.

The vast majority of the radical reformers of France were, however, from the humbler walks of life, and their conduct in many instances was such as to exasperate rather than attract. Iconoclastic excesses, such as had been exhibited at Meaux, were repeated in many places, notably at Paris in 1528. The Gallic spirit is more impulsive than the German, and though iconoclasm was common enough in many lands during the Reformation age, it showed its injudicious, aggravating face nowhere more plainly than in France, where the image-breakers, instead of representing, as in some lands, a popular revolution, were but a handful as yet among a hostile and angered population.

By 1530, the French reform movement, in both its types, was slowly and somewhat irregularly growing. Its humanistic form appealed to men of culture. Where the new learning had penetrated, in the court and among student circles, there was not a little sympathy with such efforts as Le Fèvre had led. A critical attitude toward mediæval doctrines and practices, that yet did not break with Rome, was extensive, especially among the younger race of scholars. The radicals found little sympathy among the humanistic reformers. If the latter were inadequate to their task, the former were as yet incapable of widely commending their cause. The great lack of the French reformatory movement was a leader whose controlling mind could knit its scattered and divergent forces. Such a leader must appeal to the world of scholarship, and yet go further in opposition to Rome than the humanists had done. He must be as firm as the radicals in hostility to the Papacy, and yet be able to show that iconoclastic excesses were incidental, not characteristic. He must present a type of theology congenial to non-German religious thought. Such a leader it was to find for the first time in Calvin. That the intellectually and politically divided forces opposed to Rome, or to Roman abuses, not merely in France, but ultimately in Switzerland, the Netherlands, Scotland, and to a large degree in England, also, were knit into spiritual unity; that the theology of the Reformation was given an interpretation congenial to the non-German mind; and that a great type of ecclesiastical organisation was developed in which the churchly independence characteristic of Romanism, but forfeited by most of the reformers, was preserved, and combined with a lay participation in church government unknown to the Latin Church, were to be the results of his work.

## CHAPTER II

### CHILDHOOD AND EARLY STUDENT DAYS

THE venerable episcopal city of Noyon lies on the little river Verse, about a mile above the entrance of that short-coursed tributary into the much larger Oise, and some fifty-eight miles to the north-northeast of Paris. Its situation is one of no marked strength to resist military attack under the conditions of mediæval and even of sixteenth century warfare; but its chief natural advantage has always been the great fertility of the surrounding soil. Never a place of large population,[1] it has yet had a distinctive character. First known as a station on the Roman road from Reims to Amiens,[2] probably in the fourth century of our era, it gained ecclesiastical distinction when, about the year 531, St. Médard transferred his see thither from the town which was afterwards to be known as Saint-Quentin, and inaugurated a succession of bishops that continued at Noyon till the French Revolution brought it to an end. The significance of the city in the eighth century is attested by the coronation there, in 768, of Charlemagne as joint king of the Franks; and it is almost certain that Noyon beheld the similar

[1] At present 7443 inhabitants

[2] Many of the facts in this paragraph are due to Abel Lefranc's *Histoire de la ville de Noyon*, Paris, 1887, and to Doumergue's *Jean Calvin*, vol. i.

THE PLACE AU BLÉ, NOYON

(The roof of the "Maison de Calvin" is to be seen immediately in the rear of the white building at the extreme left.)

(Reproduced by permission of Georges Compiègne, Noyon.)

consecration to royal office of Hugh, the first sovereign of the Capetian line, in 987. The political developments of the twelfth century brought about the comparatively peaceful organisation of its citizens into a commune, in 1108 or 1109; but by the end of the next century, the power thus obtained had largely slipped from the grasp of the burghers, and authority had either been regained by the ecclesiastics, or passed into the hands of officers representing the rapidly growing might of the King. The commune persisted in name, however; and in the time of Calvin still chose burghers to its fellowship, and elected a mayor and councillors, to whom some vestiges of authority still clung.

In the early years of the sixteenth century, as throughout the middle ages, Noyon presented the aspect of a very clerical town. The absence of any considerable trade or manufacture, which then even more than now marked the little city, left the field the more open for the development of its ecclesiastical interests, and the architectural evidences of this priestly dominance give a distinct quality to the appearance of Noyon even at the present day, when the bishopric that there had its see has ceased for more than a century. Its dignified though rather heavy and sombre cathedral, built during the middle decades of the twelfth century, combines the strength of Romanesque architecture with some of the graces of the Gothic style which was then just developing in the region. It yet stands a witness to the zeal and sacrifice of those who erected it. But, besides this imposing monument of mediæval piety, Noyon still preserves a graceful thirteenth century Chapter-house wherein the canons of the cathedral once transacted their business; while the library, of sixteenth century construction, and still remaining fragments of the bishop's house, attest the now vanished dignity of its prelates. That secular rights were not utterly forgotten is evidenced by the quaint Renaissance City Hall, built in 1486, and on which, as upon the other structures of which mention has been made, Calvin's eyes must often have rested.

In the sixteenth century, Noyon's most conspicuous resident was its bishop, by office one of the twelve peers of France, and in his dual capacity as count and spiritual lord the largest landed proprietor of the region. The occupant of this honoured post from 1501 to 1525, and therefore during Calvin's boyhood, was Charles de Hangest,[1] sprung from a family eminent among the nobles of Picardy. His successor was his nephew, Jean, whose episcopate of fifty-two years extended beyond Calvin's death, and whose stormy nature involved him in quarrels with his chapter over so trifling a matter as his right to wear a beard; while his indifference to the religious questions of the day laid his soundness in the faith open to suspicion.[2] Rivalries were, indeed, far from uncommon between the bishops at Noyon and the fifty-seven canons who constituted its assertive and tenancious chapter,—a body possessed of much landed property and ancient rights, and able to contend for its claims oftentimes on equal and sometimes on

[1] On the family of Hangest see A Lefranc, *La jeunesse de Calvin*, Paris, 1888, p 186, and Doumergue, i 536

[2] Doumergue, i 18.

superior terms. And, besides these two ecclesiastical powers that centred round the cathedral, Noyon was marked by its parish churches, its well-endowed monastic establishments, and other abundant evidences of the presence and importance of churchly interests Education, moreover, had been remembered; and Noyon possessed an ancient school founded by Canon Robert Lefèvre in 1294,[1] of which Calvin was himself to be a pupil, nicknamed that of the *Capettes*, from the dress which distinguished its beneficiaries. Altogether, judged by sixteenth century standards, Noyon must have been a pleasant place in which to live for those in the service of the Church or laymen not dependent on a trade. It had its own local interests and debates, besides the questions that forced their way in from the great world outside. Its proportion of men of some education and of assured position must have been large. Even if its controversies were often petty, they must have stimulated intelligence.

Geographically, Noyon belonged to Picardy, and its inhabitants exhibited the characteristics of the Picard race. Eager, controversial even to fanaticism, enthusiastic, dogmatic, and persistent, they have fought on all sides in the controversies by which France has been divided, but have never been lukewarm or indifferent. They are capable of producing men of leadership and ready to carry principles to logical consequences. A territory that has given birth to Peter the Hermit, the philosophers Roscelin and Ramus, and the revolutionists Desmoulins and Babœuf, to mention no others, was a

[1] Lefranc, *Jeunesse*, p. 12.

land where the reformatory ideas of the early sixteenth century could not fail to find response;[1] and Picardy contributed significant names, besides that of Calvin, to the list of French religious reformers. Le Fèvre, Olivétan, Roussel, and Vatable were among its sons. It was then true, as an eleventh century bishop of Noyon[2] had declared of the land in his day, that it was a "country fertile in warriors and in servants of God."

The family of which Calvin was to come was one rising in worldly success and in the social scale during the closing years of the fifteenth century. Its roots did not run back to Noyon itself, but to the little neighbouring village of Pont-l'Évêque, where the Cauvins—for so they spoke the name—had long had their home, and whence they went forth to the exercise of their ancestral occupation as boatmen on the Oise.[3] Calvin's grandfather, whose Christian name seems not to have been preserved, is said to have added the cooper's trade to that of riverman;[4] or possibly he may have undertaken the more sedentary occupation when years counselled a life of less exposure than that on the water. But his sons, of whom it seems uncertain whether there were two or three,[5] were all ambitious of a larger place in

[1] Compare Lefranc, *Jeunesse*, pp 23–25, Doumergue, i 4

[2] Rathbod II, bishop 1068–1098, see Lefranc, *Hist de la ville de Noyon*, 27.

[3] The facts have been gathered by Lefranc and Doumergue.

[4] So Le Vasseur, *Annales de l'église de Noyon*, Paris, 1633; Doumergue, i. 5.

[5] The matter is discussed by Doumergue, i 6, 7 It seems more probable that Richard and Jacques were son and grandson of the cooper-boatman of Pont-l'Évêque, rather than both sons.

the world, or at least of membership in a more populous community, than their father had enjoyed. One of these sons, Richard, and a second, also, Jacques, if there were really three of them, found a home in Paris, and there followed the iron-worker's trade.[1] The remaining son, Gérard, whose story most concerns us, established himself in Noyon before 1481,[2] as a man of professional employment rather than as a manual labourer like his ancestors and brothers. Here his skill in legal and administrative business soon won him standing; and to the post of one of the registrars of the government of Noyon which he had attained by 1481, he added gradually the duties and emoluments of solicitor in the ecclesiastical court, fiscal agent of the county, secretary of the bishopric, and attorney of the cathedral chapter. By 1497, he was reckoned sufficiently one of the leaders of the Noyon community to be admitted a member of its somewhat exclusive *bourgeoisie* and thus given a political stake in the city. We may readily credit the statement of Beza[3] that he was a man of judgment and ability, and he must have been of attractive personal qualities, also, for he won the friendship of that powerful family of Hangest which was the most influential noble house of the region, and which gave two bishops in Gérard Cauvin's lifetime to the Noyon diocese. This friendship, in turn, may well

[1] See a genealogy of Calvin, from the Dupuy Collection, in the National Library at Paris, in Henry, *Das Leben Johann Calvins*, Hamburg, 1835–1844, iii. 174.

[2] His name first appears in a legal document of September 20, 1481, Le Vasseur, p. 1170; Lefranc, *Jeunesse*, p. 2.

[3] *Life*, in *Opera*, xxi. 121.

have helped his early rise; and, as the quarrel between the chapter and the younger of these prelates waxed fierce, may have been no inconsiderable source of the troubles of his later years.[1]

Here at Noyon, at some uncertain date, but not improbably about the time of his admission to the *bourgeoisie*, Gérard Cauvin married Jeanne Le Franc, the daughter of a well-to-do retired innkeeper, Jean Le Franc, who, having prospered in business in Cambrai, had settled at Noyon, and was received into its *bourgeoisie* in 1498, where he soon attained the distinction of membership in the city council.[2] Of the mother of the future reformer little is known. In spite of attempted, and wholly baseless, detraction by later religious partisanship, she seems to have been a woman marked by earnest piety of the Roman type, and she lived in local tradition as possessed of unusual beauty. Her influence on the training of her children was brief, however, for she died before any of them reached maturity, though the year is not known. Her husband married again; but the personality of this step-mother of the reformer is yet more shadowy than that of his mother. It is probable that she died before Gérard Cauvin, and even the name of this second wife has perished.[3]

[1] A suggestion due to Principal A M Fairbairn, *The Cambridge Modern History*, ii 350

[2] The facts regarding the Le Francs have been investigated by Abel Lefranc, *Jeunesse*, pp. 5-7

[3] Le Vasseur, p. 1152. There is no mention of her in the probate proceedings after the death of her husband given, *Ibid*, p 1169, and quoted by Lefranc, pp 201-203. She was a widow when she married Gérard Cauvin.

COURT OF THE "MAISON DE CALVIN"
(The second story-room on the left is not improbably that in which Calvin was born)
(Reproduced by permission of Georges Compiègne, Noyon)

Gérard Cauvin and his wife, Jeanne, lived in a comfortable house on the lively Place au Blé, where the dwelling of the Le Francs, from which the bride had come, was also situated. Though the greater part of this home of the Cauvins has long since been replaced by other structures, it seems probable that an inner portion still remains, so that it is quite possible that the room in which the future reformer first opened his eyes on the world may yet be seen by the visitor to Noyon.[1] Within its walls, five sons, apparently, were born to Gérard and Jeanne Cauvin,[2] three of whom grew to maturity. Antoine and François died in childhood. Charles, the eldest of the sons who reached manhood, ran his brief career in priestly orders at Noyon and in its vicinity to its tragic end in 1537, as there will be occasion to note. The youngest son to grow up to man's estate, who was also the second who bore the name Antoine, was to accompany his brother, John, to Geneva, and was to live there, a respected citizen, in spite of much distress caused to him and to his relatives by the scandalous conduct of his first wife, till his death, February 2, 1572. Besides these sons, Gé-

[1] Lefranc, in *Le bulletin de la société de l'histoire du protestantisme français*, for 1897, pp 371–376, Doumergue, i 9 It is known as the "Maison de Calvin"

[2] Nicolas Colladon, in his *Life of Calvin* (1565), *Opera*, xxi 53, gives to Calvin four brothers As the name "Antoine" is ascribed to two of them, one then living and another dead in childhood, many have seen in this repetition a confusion on Colladon's part, and have reckoned Calvin's brothers as three instead of four, *e g* Lefranc, *Jeunesse*, p. 7, Doumergue, i 22, but there is nothing uncommon in the repetition of a beloved name, the first bearer of which had been removed by death, and therefore no real ground to doubt Colladon's accuracy.

rard Cauvin had two daughters, both apparently by his second wife, and therefore John's half-sisters. One of them, Marie, like her brothers John and Antoine, ultimately made her home in Geneva, where it would seem she married. The other half-sister, whose name is unknown, became the wife of a resident of Noyon.[1]

John Calvin, to give the familiar Anglicised form of his name, was the second of the sons of Gérard Cauvin and Jeanne Le Franc to grow to maturity.[2] Born on July 10, 1509, he was taken for baptism, doubtless speedily thereafter, to the little church of Sainte-Godeberte, to the parish of which his parents belonged and which then stood in the Place au Blé opposite the

[1] John Calvin, in his will of April 25, 1564, left a bequest to "Jeanne daughter of Charles Costan and of my half-sister on the paterna side"; French version, *Opera*, xx 300 The Latin version, *Ibid* xxi 163, is less definite, calling her simply *affinis*, but the Frencl is earlier and was printed by Beza in the year of Calvin's death Th reference to "Maria Paludana," in Calvin's letter of January 18 1532, in which Herminjard (*Correspondance des réformateurs*, ii 397 saw a Latinised form of the name of a supposed husband, is probabl not to her Marie was more probably unmarried when she came t Geneva with Calvin in 1536, and her marriage to Charles Costa was probably during Calvin's first stay in the city; though of th nothing is certainly known See Doumergue, iii 676–679 For th nameless sister, see Lefranc, pp 8, 183 That both were half-sister is made probable by the absence of mention of them in the legal pro ceedings instituted by Charles, John, and Antoine Calvin regardin the disposition of the property of their late mother *Ibid*, pp. 202 205, Doumergue, iii 678 That Calvin had a sister Catherine, wh became the wife of William Whittingham, dean of Durham, as ofte alleged, is an error Doumergue, iii 666–675

[2] According to the genealogy from the Dupuy Collection, Henry, ii 174, John was the third son All other authorities place him seconc See Lefranc, p 8

Cauvins' home. Here he had as godfather Jean de Vatines, one of the canons of the Noyon cathedral; and it is possible that he received his Christian name out of compliment to this sponsor whose place in the little episcopal city was undoubtedly one of dignity. Of the events of his boyhood only scanty memorials have been preserved. Gérard Cauvin was ambitious for his sons. He was determined that they should have the best education that was in his power to obtain for them; and, therefore, Charles, the eldest of the boys, was sent by his father to the endowed school known as that of the *Capettes*, of which mention has already been made. Thither John and Antoine followed him in due course; and, though his later fame may have coloured the tradition, one can readily believe that the impression which existed two or three generations later was correct, that even here John Calvin manifested so eager a spirit and so retentive a memory as to give him an easy superiority over his youthful schoolfellows.[1]

Quite as influential in the development of the boy's life as this instruction in the schoolroom of the *Capettes* were the friendships which he formed with his contemporaries among the sons of the noble family of Hangest, notably with those of Louis de Hangest, lord of Montmor, and of his brother, Adrien, lord of Genlis.[2] To Claude, son of the nobleman last named, Calvin was,

[1] So Papire Masson, writing about 1583, *Elogia*, Paris, 1638, ii. 409; and Jacques Desmay, between 1614 and 1621, *Remarques considérables sur la vie et mœurs de Jean Calvin*, Rouen, 1621 See, also, Doumergue, i. 35

[2] On the members of this family see Lefranc, *Jeunesse*, p 186, and Doumergue, i. 536.

years later, to dedicate his first book, when Claude had become abbot of Saint-Éloi at Noyon. With Joachim and Ives, and a brother of theirs whose name is now lost, sons of the seigneur of Montmor, Calvin stood in intimate school fellowship, and his relations to these households of Montmor and Genlis seem, indeed, to have been much closer than merely those of the schoolroom. To Claude he could later gratefully describe himself as "a child brought up in your house, initiated with you into the same studies." [1] Such an association was doubtless in large part a result of the high estimate in which Calvin's father was held by the family of Hangest; but not wholly so, for neither of John's brothers seems to have enjoyed this friendship in a similar degree, so that some share in its growth must be ascribed to the attractive qualities of the boy himself. Yet it was as no dependent on the bounty of those higher in station that Gérard Cauvin encouraged or the boy fostered a relationship which the early death of his mother may have rendered even more homelike and attractive. His education, as Beza definitely affirms, was at his father's charges; [2] and he never forgot the relative simplicity of his own origins, describing himself in the dedication from which quotation has just been made as "a man of the people," in contrast to the noble house whose friendship he enjoyed. Of the value of that friendship to the future reformer there can be no question. It probably determined his father to send him to the University of Paris; and it certainly gave to

[1] *De Clementia*, in *Opera*, v. 8.
[2] *Life*, of 1575, in *Opera*, xxi. 121.

Calvin an acquaintance with the ways of polite society such as few of the reformers enjoyed, in an age when the gulf between the manners of those in high station and of the mass of the people was far greater than at present.

Though Gérard Cauvin was too independent by nature to permit his sons to solicit the gifts of friendly noblemen, he had no hesitation in employing his influence with the bishop and chapter of Noyon to procure for them appointments to lucrative ecclesiastical positions as a means of aiding their studies. This was a not infrequent practice, and conveyed to the popular mind little of the impression of an abuse that would now attach to it, when it is remembered that the youthful recipients of office were not themselves of age or position to discharge the duties thus nominally assumed, but were compelled to have the actual service performed by those in clerical office and of maturer years who would be willing to undertake the labour for a fraction of the stipend. Gérard Cauvin first procured this means of support for his eldest son. On February 24, 1519, Charles was put in possession of a chaplaincy attached to the altar of *La Gésine* in the cathedral of Noyon,—a charge which he exchanged, in November, 1520, for a similar post in the same church. The nineteenth of May, 1521, saw the same office which Charles Cauvin had received two years before bestowed on his brother, John, who still lacked nearly two months of having reached twelve years of age when thus given an ecclesiastical charge. He doubtless received the tonsure,—the only sign of membership in a clerical order which Calvin ever attained in the Roman Church,—but there could be no question of ordination of the youthful incumbent, whose connection with the office was purely financial. Chief of the revenues which it brought its schoolboy holder were taxes in grain, payable by the neighbouring territories of Voienne and of Eppeville (Espeville). To this benefice in the Noyon cathedral, John Calvin added, on September 27, 1527, the pastorate of Saint-Martin de Martheville,—a curacy which he exchanged, on June 5, 1529, probably for family and pecuniary reasons, for that of Pont-l'Évêque, the ancestral home of the Cauvins. His claim on the altar of *La Gésine* John relinquished, on April 30th, of the year last mentioned, in favour of his younger brother, Antoine; but resumed it again not quite two years later, on February 26, 1531.[1] In this matter all three brothers received similar advantages, Charles becoming pastor at Roupy in 1527, and Antoine at Tournerolle about two years later. With the income thus provided John Calvin and his brothers were enabled to carry on their studies and make their star in life.

This wish to do the best possible for the educatio of his children doubtless was the prime moving caus that induced Gérard to send John to the University c Paris in August, 1523, when the boy had just passe

[1] Extracts from the Registers of the Chapter are given by Lefran *Jeunesse*, pp 194–201, see also *Ibid*, pp. 9–12, and Doumergue, 37–39 On these dates see Karl Müller, *Calvins Bekehrung*, in t' *Nachrichten von der königl Gesellschaft der Wissenschaften Göttingen*, for 1905, pp 220–222

his fourteenth birthday. But certain special considerations made the parental decision easy at the time. The plague was raging in Noyon,[1] rendering that city an unsafe place of residence. His three friends of the house of Montmor were going to the University under the charge of a tutor, whose instruction and guidance, all insufficient as it proved,[2] he could share; and the residence of an uncle, Richard, gave the boy the certainty of friendly supervision during the trying beginnings of his student life. It may well have been agreeable to Gérard's independent spirit that his son, while enjoying the advantages of study and companionship with his noble friends, should not be in any way indebted to their father's bounty for his living, but should find a home with his uncle, near the church of Saint-Germain l'Auxerrois, separate from that in which they were domiciled.

To the boy of fourteen the transfer to Paris brought almost complete separation from the city in which his childhood had been spent. Thenceforward he was to be rarely and but for brief sojourns in Noyon; but his interest in the fortunes of the town and of its inhabitants always continued keen, and his relations to the friends who still lived there show the depth and permanency of his affection for the city of his nativity.

The University of Paris, in which Calvin now became a student, had long been reputed, as has already been noted, the most eminent seat of learning in Europe.

[1] Lefranc, *Jeunesse*, p. 13.

[2] Calvin calls him "*homo stolidus*," Letter to Cordier, *Opera*, xiii. 6.

It had not maintained its ancient leadership in the world of thought. In the educational transition which the rise of the new learning was effecting, it had clung for the most part to the older methods which humanism would revolutionise, and even these traditional conceptions of education were inefficiently applied. Doubtless the scorn of the humanists for its teaching, its prevailingly mediæval Latinity, and its hair-splitting dialectics was not wholly deserved; but it had a very considerable basis of truth. Yet an institution that was, through one of its instructors, to develop Calvin's Latin style, and by its classrooms was to train his dialectic skill, cannot have been without strength even in its comparative decay. Though it prevailingly resisted the new learning, Calvin was to find a representative of that classic revival within its walls. In general, however, the intellectual outlook of the University of Paris was unquestionably mediæval.

Judged by modern standards, the University was a seat of secondary as well as of higher instruction.[1] Its Faculty of Arts, under which the student began his course, was divided, according to the nativity of those under instruction, into the four "nations" of France Germany, Normandy, and Picardy. Above this Faculty of Arts were the higher Faculties, or, as we should now say, graduate schools, of Theology, Law, and Medicine,—that first named being of great strength for Paris was primarily noted as a seat of theology and philosophy, while the two latter were weak. Thes

[1] Doumergue has treated the University with great wealth of detail, i. 49–77.

"nations" of the Faculty of Arts were administrative divisions,—the work of the students being chiefly carried on in "colleges," in which a great portion of the student body also lived. These colleges in origin were charitable foundations to aid indigent scholars, but had extended by the time of Calvin to the University as a whole. In many of these colleges the life of the student was marked by an asceticism in food that now seems almost incredible,[1] while the filth, the severe hours of study and recitation, beginning at five in the morning, and extending with but four hours' intermission for food and play till eight in the evening, and the constant employment of corporal punishment, made his lot a hard one from the point of view of modern education. To a certain extent, as an out-student, living in the home of an uncle, Calvin must have been protected from the temptations and spared the more trying physical experiences that then beset student life, and there is no evidence that he ever regarded his way as peculiarly difficult; but the path to knowledge must have been a painful one at best.

The preparation in Latin, already gained by Calvin at Noyon, was but a beginning, insufficient to enable him to enter any class higher than the fourth,[2] in which the rudiments of the language were studied. But here a piece of great good fortune awaited him. Though still, and for some time to come, under the direction of the unsatisfactory tutor who had guided him and his friends the Montmors, and had accompanied them to

[1] Compare Doumergue, i 68–73

[2] *Opera*, xiii 525

Paris, he now became a student in the comparatively inconspicuous Collège de la Marche, where Mathurin Cordier then served as one of the two "regents in grammar." Moreover, Cordier, who had been teaching the first, or most advanced, class with success, disgusted with the insufficiency of current grounding in Latin, had, in the year of Calvin's coming to Paris, taken up voluntarily the instruction of the comparative beginners of the fourth class.[1]

To be under Cordier's tuition was to enjoy the best introduction to the study of Latin that France had then to offer. About forty-four years of age when Calvin became his pupil, Cordier had been as a young man a priest in Rouen, of which region he was probably a native,[2] but for ten years he had taught at Paris. Convinced that the prime task of the teacher, especially of young scholars, is to arouse interest for study in his pupils, he put aside, in large measure, the formal and arbitrary methods of instruction then generally in vogue. To make the language live in the thought of the pupil, rather than to fill the young student's mind with a mass of mechanically acquired detail, was his aim. That it should be accomplished, he devoted great attention to the acquisition of a correct and elegant conversational use of the ancient tongue. He strove to weed out current barbarisms, of which student usage afforded only too plentiful illustration. His kindly spirit, no less than his clear pedagogical insight, led him to oppose the constant use of the rod, and to urge

[1] *Opera*, xiii 525

[2] He was from Normandy or le Perche, Doumergue, i. 537.

the establishment of familiar and friendly relations between teacher and scholars, whose moral development, no less than whose intellectual training, the teacher, he held, should regard as a duty. Not a little of this kindliness of relationship to his young pupils by which Cordier effectually put into practice his enlightened ideas of education was the fruit of his simple, unaffected piety of heart.[1] A lovable, as well as a very helpful, man, he may well have aided in the religious, as he certainly did in the intellectual, development of the boy who now came under his moulding influence and found in him a teacher to admire and reverence. Calvin always remembered with affection this instructor under whom he began his student days at Paris; and ascribed to Cordier his initiation into effective methods of study.[2] When, in turn, thirteen years later, Cordier found France dangerous ground for the Protestant sentiments which he had then embraced, he followed his former pupil to Switzerland, was welcomed by Calvin, taught at Neuchâtel, lived in Geneva, and died in the latter city, in the same year as Calvin, at the advanced age of eighty-five

Calvin's stay at the Collège de la Marche, and consequent training under Cordier, was but for a few months at most. His studies were still regulated by the tutor who directed him and his three friends of the house of Hangest; and by what Calvin seems afterward to have regarded as the tutor's caprice he was transferred

[1] His ideas were set forth in his *De Corrupti Sermonis Emendatione*, of 1531, see, also, Doumergue, i 60, 61.

[2] *Opera*, xiii 525, 526.

to the Collège de Montaigu.[1] It may have been true, however, that his father's intention that he should be fitted for a career in the Church, and the wishes of the canons of Noyon, by whose favour he held the benefices that defrayed the expenses of his student days, were factors in the decision, for Montaigu was a much more ecclesiastically flavoured, as well as more noted, college than La Marche.[2] The college of which Calvin now became a member bore the name of Pierre de Montaigu, bishop of Laon, by whom it had been reconstituted in 1388, seventy-four years after its foundation by Gilles Aiscelin, archbishop of Rouen; but its fame in Calvin's day was primarily due to the work of Jean Standonch, by whom it had been brought to a flourishing condition, and given a series of rules of exceeding ascetic and scholastic strictness which were completed in the year of Calvin's birth.[3] Erasmus had been one of its scholars half a generation before Calvin entered its halls, and Ignatius Loyola was to follow immediately after Calvin's departure. Nor was the head of the Collège de Montaigu in Calvin's student days in any way unworthy of its fame. Its principal for many years had been Noel Béda, a conservative theologian of power, the determined enemy of all modifications of Roman doctrine or usage. In 1521, he had led the onslaught on Le Fèvre which had resulted in the condemnation by the Sorbonne of that mild-tempered scholar's criti-

[1] *Opera*, xiii. 526.

[2] Lefranc, *Jeunesse*, pp 63, 64, makes this suggestion.

[3] Félibien, *Histoire de Paris*, v. 726–740, compare Doumergue, i 66–73.

cism of the current identification of Mary Magdalene with Mary, the sister of Lazarus, and with the woman "which was a sinner." Not content with this achievement, Béda, five years later, attacked Le Fèvre and Erasmus in print;[1] and showed the courage of convictions which were bringing upon him, by reason of their extremely reactionary character, the hostility of King Francis I., and at a later period (1533) were to lead to his exile from Paris. It was no weak or insignificant champion of mediæval scholarship and theology that ruled the Collège de Montaigu while Calvin was numbered in its student body.

Calvin's immediate instruction in the classroom on his entrance into the Collège de Montaigu was from an unnamed learned Spaniard, the vehicle being of course the Latin tongue, for the use of French was not permitted in the college. So effectively did the work supplement what had already been begun under Cordier that Calvin soon surpassed those who had been his companions in the preliminary studies of grammar and rhetoric; and was promoted,[2] doubtless as the result of the successful passage of the examination then required, to what were regarded as the more important disciplines of philosophy and dialectics, which constituted the backbone of the course then pursued under the Faculty of Arts. Any calculation of the date of this event is, of course, conjectural; but if, as is probable, Calvin followed the philosophical course for the three years and a half then considered its normal

[1] Herminjard, i. 78, 402, 436.

[2] Beza, *Life*, of 1575, *Opera*, xxi. 121.

length,[1] his promotion from grammatical studies would have occurred in the autumn of 1524, a little over a year after his entrance to the University. Such facility in the mastery of Latin reveals the young scholar as giving brilliant promise not merely of success in the usual student career of the University, but of conspicuous humanistic attainments as within his ultimate grasp. Of his course in the college little can be definitely affirmed. The institution was famous for its learned disputations, and there is every reason to believe not merely that Calvin's own powers of argument were developed and strengthened by these intellectual wrestling-matches, but that he soon came to excel in argumentative force as he had already in linguistic ability. The discipline thus undergone must have been of great value in training those keen powers of logical analysis and constructive reasoning of which he was afterwards to make remarkable use. Here, at the Collège de Montaigu, his course of study continued till the close of 1527, or, more probably, the opening weeks of 1528, when he would naturally attain the rank of licentiate of arts. That he received this degree is not a matter of record; but without it he could not have entered upon the higher studies that he then immediately began.[2]

If it is impossible to recover many details of Calvin's early student career, we are fortunately not in ignorance as to some of the friendships he then continued or

[1] Bulæus, *Hist Univ Paris*, v 858-859

[2] Herminjard, ii 279, note. He is described as a "magister" in the records of the Noyon Chapter of April 30, 1529, Lefranc, *Jeunesse*, p. 197.

formed which throw some light on his character at this critical period of his life.[1] With the three boys of the Hangest family he had come to the University, and the friendship begun in Noyon remained steadfast. There is no evidence that any of them was conspicuous for scholarship, and two of the three were to die early in the profession of arms; [2] but to their cousin, the third of the group,[3] Calvin was warmly to dedicate his first book, as has already been noted. A younger brother of the two first mentioned was, years later, to throw in his lot with Calvin at Geneva, and the family of Hangest was to contribute a number of its representatives to the Protestant cause.

Besides these companions of his boyhood home, Calvin became intimately acquainted, at Paris, with the household of Guillaume Cop,[4] first physician to the King and an eminent member of the Faculty of Medicine. A Swiss from the liberal and humanistic city of Basel, Cop enjoyed the friendship of Erasmus and Reuchlin, and was not merely of high fame in his

[1] The subject is discussed by Lefranc, *Jeunesse*, pp 67–71, Doumergue, i 75–77; and Fairbairn, *The Cambridge Modern History*, ii 351

[2] Joachim and Yves were killed at the storming of Saint-Pol in 1537 Lefranc, *Ibid*, p 68

[3] Claude, then abbot of Saint-Éloi at Noyon

[4] Haag, *La France Protestante*, 2nd ed, iv. 615–617 Calvin's letter of June 27, 1531, to François Daniel, Herminjard, ii. 346, shows that his acquaintance with the Cops did not begin with his second stay at Paris, and therefore probably dates back to this undergraduate period Müller (*Calvins Bekehrung*, p 203) thinks that Nicolas Cop may have first met Calvin in Orléans or Bourges, or the Cops and Calvin may have been brought together by Wolmar.

profession, but possessed of considerable interest in letters.[1] The elder two of Cop's four sons were perhaps too[2] old to be well acquainted with the student from Noyon, but to Nicolas, the third of these brothers, Calvin was attached by the closest ties of friendship Four years Calvin's senior, and of such brilliant scholarly attainments that he received a professorship of philosophy, in 1530, in the Collège Sainte-Barbe of the University, Nicolas Cop was to be associated with Calvin in the crisis of his own scholarly career, on terms of intimacy the exact extent of which there will be occasion later to examine. With the fourth of Guillaume Cop's sons, Michel, Calvin was almost as closely associated as with Nicolas; and this friend was later to follow Calvin to Geneva, and enter the Reformed pastorate. A further close acquaintance of Calvin's Parisian student days was one whom he may have met at Noyon while a schoolboy, Pierre Robert, who bore the scholastic nickname of Olivétan. Older by a few years than Calvin, he was not only a fellow-townsman from Noyon, but the son of one who, like Gérard Cauvin, was a solicitor in the ecclesiastical court, and linked to Calvin by family relationship.[3] Of his later relations to

[1] Erasmus called him, in 1498, "*Musarum cultorem*," *Letters*, ed Le Clerc, iii. 1, 26.

[2] This has been disputed, Herminjard, ii 348, Doinel, *Bulletin* xxvi. 176; Doumergue, i 75

[3] Just what the relationship was it is impossible to say, but Beza and Colladon witness to the fact, *Opera*, xxi 29, 54, 121 On him in general see Herminjard, ii 451, v 228, 280, Lefranc, *Jeunesse*, 28, 99–104; Doumergue, i 117–125, Bonet-Maury in Hauck's *Realencyklopädie für prot Theologie*, xiv. 363.

Calvin's religious development there will be not a little to be said; but the fact of his friendship may now be noted in trying to form some picture of Calvin's circle at the University.

Besides the more intimate friends already mentioned, it is probable that Calvin's membership in that portion of the student body known as the "nation" of Picardy would bring him into close touch with all students or instructors of prominence who regarded his native region as their home. But, as these relations are inferential rather than a matter of proof, it is easy to insist upon them too much[1] It is evident, however, from such friendships as have been described, most, if not all, of which were now formed, that the young student at Paris must have been of more than ordinary attractiveness and charm To win the regard of such a man as Cordier, to hold the affections of young noblemen like those of the house of Montmor-Hangest, who assuredly were under no obligation to continue a friendship had it proved irksome, above all to gain the goodwill of a family of distinguished station and scholarly eminence like that of Cop, bespeak unusual winsomeness in a student of relatively humble birth, with little save himself to offer. Nor is the quality of his friendships less illuminative as to his personal character. To attract a Cordier or the houschold of a Cop certainly indicates a nature attuned to the better and finer side of life. No student of low impulses, or unrefined tastes, or of a misanthropic, uncompanionable

[1] Lefranc, *Ibid.*, pp. 68, 69, and Doumergue, i. 76, give the names of some into relations with whom he was probably brought.

disposition, could have won the permanent regard or made the lasting impression that Calvin did upon those whose friendship it was an honour to possess.

Yet legend, reflecting it may be the severer traits of his later life, has ascribed to the student Calvin a censoriousness of judgment in his relations to his companions, and an unsociability of temper, that, if true, would paint for us a very different portrait of the young scholar whose experiences at the University of Paris have just been reviewed. A story, credited by Le Vasseur [1] to Calvin's brilliant renegade one-time friend and disciple, but afterward enemy and calumnist, François Baudoin (1520–1573), relates that his fellow-students called him "the accusative case," because of his denunciatory spirit. It is unnecessary, however, to weigh the question of Baudoin's degree of truthfulness, as the statement is not to be found in his own published controversy with Calvin, and has no real foundation. A degree of plausibility is given to it, it is true, by Beza's declaration regarding the friend whose biography he was writing that, as a student at Paris, Calvin was not merely very religious, but a strict censor of all vices among his associates (*severus omnium in suis sodalibus vitiorum censor*).[2] Student life, as is abundantly witnessed not merely by the satires of Rabelais, but by the sober letters of Erasmus and of many less distinguished scholars, was apt in that day to be lawless and vicious enough; and an earnest,

[1] *Annales de l'Église de Noyon*, Paris, 1633, p 1158; see also Kampschulte, *Johann Calvin*, i. 225, and Doumergue, i 73–75

[2] *Opera*, xxi 121

religious, and scholarly youth, of refined tastes, such as Calvin was, could have had little sympathy with its cruder excesses. But that he was misanthropic, of unfriendly spirit, or was regarded by his associates with aversion, there is no adequate evidence. The facts point to an opposite conclusion, and he appears at the completion of his course under the Faculty of Arts, in his nineteenth year, a student of high personal character, great linguistic and dialectic promise, able to make and keep friends whose interest in him must have been primarily due to the attractive qualities of head and heart which he revealed to them. The report of his successes at the University must have pleased his old patrons, the canons of the cathedral at Noyon, for in September, 1527, they added to his ecclesiastical holding the curacy of Saint-Martin de Martheville. The increase in his income was considerable, and the purpose which impelled the gift can have been naught else than a desire to aid a brilliant young fellow-townsman in his studies, for the relations of Gérard Cauvin to the chapter were already such that the benefice cannot have been given for the father's sake. Certainly the young student from Noyon was well treated by the friends who had known him in his boyhood town and, in turn, must have possessed qualities which commanded their regard.

## CHAPTER III

### UNCERTAINTY AS TO HIS WORK IN LIFE

THE completion, late in 1527 or early in 1528, of what would now be called in America his undergraduate course under the Faculty of Arts, brought Calvin face to face with the question of his life-work and the consequent further direction of his studies. The time for technical preparation for a profession had come. His father had long intended him for the Church and had strongly desired that he should specialise in theology;[1] but the father now insisted with equal positiveness that he should turn to the study of law. It was an age in which those expert in legal knowledge and practice had become the chief recipients of important civil offices from the crown, and a successful lawyer was well-nigh certain of high distinction. The Church had long since ceased to be the path to royal favour that it had been in the middle ages. An ambitious father, and certainly Gérard Cauvin deserves so to be described, may well have regarded the law as offering the "surest road to wealth and honours".[2] Gérard Cauvin, though an officer of the Church, was concerned wholly with its secularities and in no sense

[1] Calvin in Preface to *Commentary on the Psalms*, *Opera*, xxxi 22; Colladon and Beza, *Lives*, *Opera*, xxi. 54, 121.

[2] Beza (*Ibid.*), gives this as his reason; Calvin (*Opera* xxxi 22), speaks only of wealth.

a clergyman. Had he received a full legal education, such as his clever son might now enjoy, could he not have risen to yet higher "wealth and honours"?

But whatever weight these considerations may have had with Gérard Cauvin, other reasons, of a more personal nature, seem to have had their share in affecting his decision so radically to alter his son's prospective career. His own relations to the Chapter at Noyon had been rapidly changing for the worse.[1] The precise cause is difficult fully to define. It may have been pecuniary embarrassment leading to mishandling of trust funds which aroused the antagonism of the Chapter. His conduct in this respect was certainly irregular and blameworthy. But the case cannot have been very serious in the amount involved at least, since his sons had, apparently, little difficulty in persuading the Chapter that they could adjust it after his death. One suspects that Gérard Cauvin and the Chapter had other grounds of quarrel than merely pecuniary questions, and that the matters of accounting were demanded and refused in a spirit of ill-will on either side. If this was the case, the most probable explanation is to be sought in Gérard Cauvin's devotion to the family of Hangest. Charles de Hangest, who had held the bishopric of Noyon since 1501, was a man of high character, much practical insight, and skill; but, on his resignation in 1525, he was succeeded by his nephew, Jean de Hangest, older brother of Calvin's friend and fellow-student, Claude. Jean was, indeed, too young to

[1] The pertinent records are given by Lefranc, *Jeunesse*, pp. 196–199; see also *Ibid*, pp. 15–22

enter on the full duties of his office for several years, during which he travelled and studied. He was arbitrary, rather petty, and quarrelsome, to say nothing of suspicions entertained at a later time as to his orthodoxy; and it was not long before his relations to the Chapter were strained As an ardent supporter of the house from which the new bishop-elect sprang, Gérard Cauvin may have shared in his unpopularity with the Chapter. However this may have been, the records of the Chapter show that on June 27, 1527, Gérard Cauvin was ordered to make an accounting as executor of the estate of Nicolas Obry, a deceased chaplain of the cathedral at Noyon. This he failed to do; and on May 15, 1528, he was again directed to make returns on this estate, as well as on that of Michel Courtin, who had held a similar office. His refusal led to repeated action by the Chapter, and ultimately to his excommunication. He was under the ban at the time of his death, and it was only at the intercession of his sons that his body was allowed burial in holy ground. One thus in open quarrel with the ecclesiastical authorities of his city would certainly be disposed to see in some other profession than the service of the Church the best road of advancement for his son.

How the young student himself regarded the change of plans thus effected is a question not altogether easy to answer. His earliest biographers, Beza and Colladon, affirm that his mind had already been turned from scholastic theology and that he had begun to read the Scriptures and feel that the Roman worship was superstitious, thanks to the influence of his friend and relative, Pierre Robert Olivétan.[1] But Calvin's own statement regarding his entrance upon the study of law[2] implies that he did so in obedience to his father's wishes rather than from any desire of his own.

The decision that Calvin should study law led to a change of Universities, for Paris had no teacher of jurisprudence worthy to be compared with Pierre Taisan de l'Estoile, the leading lawyer of France,[3] who had been an ornament of the Faculty of the University of Orléans since 1512, and was now forty-eight years of age. A man of strongly conservative opinions, of profound learning, and thorough Catholic orthodoxy, the death of his wife had led him into clerical orders, while continuing his professorship, and, in February, 1528, just as Calvin was about to go to Orléans, he had been urgent in demanding repressive action against the rising Protestants at the Council of Sens.[4] The jealousy of the University of Paris, proud of its theologic eminence, had prevented the establishment of chairs of divinity at Orléans, with the result that law was there vigorously cultivated, no less than eight "doctors," of whom l'Estoile was by far the most noted, being charged with its exposition.

In sharp contrast to the clerical, and often ascetic, atmosphere of the University of Paris, such as had surrounded Calvin at the Collège de Montaigu, the

[1] *Opera*, xxi 29, 54, 121 The fact or the extent of the influence thus ascribed to Olivétan will be discussed in considering Calvin's conversion.

[2] *Opera*, xxxi 22, see, also, Kampschulte, i 226

[3] Beza, *Opera*, xxi 121, 122

[4] Lefranc, *Jeunesse*, p 72, Doumergue, i. 130.

University of Orléans had the repute of being a delightful and rather easy-going place of study;[1] and certainly this unascetic atmosphere, and the advanced character of his own studies, permitted Calvin to regulate his life more as he might wish than had been possible in the undergraduate days and under the severer discipline of the Collège de Montaigu at Paris. Yet if Calvin was now released from the stricter rules imposed on undergraduate life at Paris, he was strenuous far beyond what was wise in his employment of his own time. Nicolas Colladon recorded,[2] in 1565, that those then living who had known Calvin at Orléans remembered that, after a very light supper, he often studied till midnight and then waking early in the morning would lie abed recalling and thinking over what he had learned the evening before. Undoubtedly, as Beza,[3] as well as Colladon, points out, these protracted vigils strengthened his remarkably retentive memory as well as greatly enlarged his erudition, but they also gave rise to the dyspepsia[4] which ever after pursued him, and was the prime cause of the ill health of his later life Brilliant as a student, his keen and ready powers of argument, his clearness of analysis, and charm of diction won him distinction in debate, and his repute was speedily such that on several occasions he took the place of one or another of his instructors, who found themselves unable to meet their classes.

[1] Lefranc, (*Jeunesse*, p. 74), compares it to Heidelberg, Jena or Göttingen

[2] *Opera*, xxi. 55

[3] *Ibid*, 122.

[4] "*Ventriculi imbecillitatem contraxit*," says Beza, *Ibid*

While thus winning reputation by his success in the study of law, Calvin found time, however, for the development of his knowledge of the classics. The humanistic spirit of the age strongly moved him. His intercourse with Cordier and the Cops at Paris must have served as a powerful antidote to the scholasticism of Béda and the Collège de Montaigu. That interest in letters now probably attracted the friendship of one to whose stimulus Calvin was to owe much,—Melchior Wolmar. A German by nativity, having been born, in 1496, in Rothweil, a town of Würtemberg, Wolmar had studied at Bern, Freiburg, and Paris, where he was greatly distinguished, being first on the list of Licentiates of Arts.[1] His religious opinions, which were, apparently, inclined to Lutheranism, made Paris an uncomfortable place of sojourn,[2] and he established a boys' boarding-school in the freer atmosphere of Orléans, of which the nine-year-old Theodore Beza became one of the pupils in 1528. To Wolmar, Calvin subsequently owed his initiation into Greek literature. His possible indebtedness to this kindly German teacher for his religious development will be discussed later in our story, but to Wolmar, no less than to Cordier, Calvin looked back with grateful recollection as to one who had been powerfully influential in his scholarly development.

Busied with the law course and continuing doubtless his studies in the field of letters, Calvin's days at Orléans can have left him little leisure. But even

[1] Herminjard, ii 280, 281, note

[2] Bulæus, *Hist. Univ. Paris*, vi. 963.

when thus burdened, he was no hermit. Though his intimate circle of acquaintances at Orléans seems to have been limited, a warm attachment united him to those friends whom he came to know at this epoch, François Daniel and François de Connam, fellow-students, and a somewhat older young lawyer, Nicolas Duchemin, with whom he lodged during part, at least, of his stay at the University. Connam was from Paris, where his father was one of the Masters of the Chamber of Accounts. Daniel was a well-to-do native of Orléans, having two brothers and several sisters, who formed a pleasant family circle into which Calvin was welcomed. To these friends Calvin's earliest surviving letters were addressed, and in them he expresses himself in terms of warmest affection[1] His relations were evidently more than a common interest in the same studies, which was doubtless the connecting link with which the acquaintances began, and though their separate walks in life, and the fact that these friends remained in the communion of the Roman Church, led to the cessation of this correspondence after a few years, Calvin improved an opportunity to do a service to a son of François Daniel, as an occasion to renew the correspondence with the father, in 1559 and 1560, on the old friendly footing.[2]

Though Calvin thought highly of the instruction given by Pierre de l'Estoile, his interest was aroused by the reports that became current among the students at Orléans of the teaching given by the great Italian jurist

[1] E g *Opera*, xb 3, 9–30

[2] *Opera*, xvii 585, 681, xviii. 16

Andrea Alciati (1492–1550), who had begun his work in the University at Bourges on April 29, 1529.[1] Just when he made his transfer thither is unknown, but the very probable suggestion has been made by one of his most recent biographers that the autumn of 1529 saw him matriculated at Bourges and in Alciati's class-room.[2] His friend Daniel made the same change of Universities; and the satisfaction of his stay there was doubtless much enhanced when Wolmar removed thither, also, late in 1530. The University of Bourges was a comparatively recent foundation, having been privileged in 1463 and 1464. It had greatly declined; but under the fostering care of Marguerite d'Angoulême, mistress of the duchy of Berry, of which Bourges was the capital, able teachers, like Alciati and Wolmar, were being induced to settle there, an atmosphere of considerable intellectual and religious freedom prevailed, and the scholastic reputation of the University was rapidly rising. Alciati, in particular, was a real reformer in juridical science. Law was not for him, as for l'Estoile, a mere dry matter of arbitrary detail; it was capable of explication by great general principles, and of illumination by history and literature. In his teaching it became a science rather than a mere mass of knowledge. Such a training must have been of the highest value in supplementing the teaching which Calvin had received at Orléans. Yet, contrary to one's presuppositions as to what would have been the case, Calvin preferred the severely churchly and rather medi-

[1] *Opera*, xxi 55, 122, Doumergue, i 141–143.
[2] Doumergue, i. 141.

æval instructor at Orléans to the brilliant innovating Italian at Bourges. In the controversy that sprang up between their partisans his friend, Duchemin, published a defence of l'Estoile, and Calvin contributed to the volume a brief preface,—his first writing to appear in print.[1]

Calvin's work seems to have gone forward at Bourges on the same lines as at Orléans, and he now began with Wolmar the study of Greek.[2] His time was still divided between the law and literature, and he regarded anything that took him from his studies with impatience. But an event of no little significance occurred in the spring of 1531. Calvin had been in Paris, probably during vacation, in March of that year, and had thence apparently gone to Noyon, either for a visit or summoned by bad news from home. From his native city he wrote to his friend Duchemin under date of May 14th that he was detained by the illness of his father, which, though at first not hopeless, was now evidently fatal.[3] Twelve days later Gérard Cauvin's death occurred. The baldness with which he announces the news to his friend gives the reader a sense of shock.

[1] Duchemin's work was written in 1529, and published in 1531 at Paris under the title *Antapologia adversus Aurelii Albucii Defensionem pro And. Alciato contra D. Petrum Stellam*. Calvin dated the Preface from Paris March 6, [1531], and saw the book through the press for his friend. The Preface is given in Herminjard, ii. 314–318, also *Opera*, ix. 785.

[2] Calvin's dedication of his *Commentary on II. Corinthians* to Wolmar in 1546, *Opera*, xii. 364, 365, makes it evident that it was but a beginning. On the time see Beza, *Life*, of 1564, *Ibid.*, xxi. 29, 30; and Müller, *Calvins Bekehrung*, pp. 194, 201.

[3] *Opera*, xb. 8, Herminjard, ii. 332.

COURT AND STAIRWAY OF THE "MAISON DE CALVIN" IN NOYON.
(Reproduced by permission of Georges Compiègne, Noyon.)

The contrast between the bare statement of his father's approaching mortality and his address to Duchemin as "my friend, dearer than my life," is striking Yet it must be remembered, in partial explanation at least, that Calvin had seen little of his father since he left home, a boy of fourteen, nearly eight years before, and there can have been no very deep sympathy between the highly studious, sensitive, cultivated young lawyer and his ambitious, acquisitive, self-made father. Yet he owed a great debt to Gérard Cauvin, whose highest and most unselfish desire seems to have been to secure for his sons advantages which he had not enjoyed.

The death of Calvin's father removed from him the parental pressure that had kept him to the study of law; but not till that course had been substantially, if not wholly, completed, for a legal document of February 14, 1532, describes him as *licentié ès loix*,[1] and this degree may have been obtained some months earlier. An obscure passage in a letter written by his friend François Daniel in the previous December implies that Daniel, at least, had hopes that Calvin might obtain some appointment befitting his legal talents from an unnamed bishop, probably his acquaintance, Jean de Hangest, bishop of Noyon. But, meanwhile, within a month of his father's death, Calvin had betaken himself to Paris, and now devoted himself to the study of the classics, with all the zeal of an eager disciple of the "new learning." Many reasons have been given for this change of the scene of his studies. It is

[1] Le Vasseur, *Annales*, p 1169, Lefranc, *Jeunesse*, p. 202.

certain that his pursuit of the law was due to his father's desires rather than to his own, and it has been suggested that he recoiled from public conflicts at the bar;[1] that he found no suitable opening as a lawyer,[2] or that he wanted to give himself to the solution of personal questions, primarily those of religion.[3] A sufficient reason may be seen, however, in his desire to avail himself of the revolution in teaching that had just taken place at Paris. Moved by Guillaume Budé and by Guillaume Cop, both earnest humanists, Francis I. had appointed in March, 1530, a group of "Royal Lecturers," to give instruction in Greek, Hebrew, and Mathematics. This event, which, as has already been noted, is regarded as the foundation of the Collège de France,[4] was of capital significance in the history of French education. It was the triumph of the "new learning," which thus made a place for itself such as it had never before possessed in France. And who would be more willing to avail himself of the privileges thus offered by the royal bounty than a student whose interest in Latin had been awakened by a Cordier, and who had found time amid the exactions of a course in law to pursue Greek with a Wolmar?

At Paris Calvin now lodged in the Collège Fortet, opposite his familiar Collège de Montaigu.[5] Under the

[1] Henri Lecoultre, in the *Revue de théologie et de philosophie*, Lausanne, for 1891, p 53

[2] A. Lang, *Die Bekehrung Johannes Calvins*, Leipzig, 1897, p. 8.

[3] Doumergue, i 196

[4] *Ante*, p. 7.

[5] Lefranc, *Jeunesse*, p 89.

guidance of the marvellously wide-read "Royal Lecturer," Pierre Danès, he pursued eagerly the study of Greek, and with Danès's colleague, François Vatable, he began that of Hebrew.[1] Engaged in congenial studies, his life in Paris must have been very pleasant, in spite of the ill health from which he occasionally suffered. He was in constant communication with Duchemin and Daniel, and saw them from time to time in the city. His younger brother, Antoine, was a resident of Paris. For Nicolas Cop he had a warm friendship. It was an agreeable and a relatively large circle of young humanists and jurists of which Calvin now made a part. But, while Calvin thus rejoiced in a circle of friends so considerable that the mere visits of greeting filled four days on his arrival in Paris,[2] his nature was sensitive and exacting, and he seems to have been quick to feel any real or fancied want of friendliness on the part of those dear to him.[3] Yet, aside from these occasional slight lacerations of a somewhat demanding friendship, and the limitations due to his uncertain health, Calvin's chief worry in this relatively unburdened portion of his life must have been caused by the affairs of his older brother, Charles, who had remained at Noyon. So negligently did Charles discharge his duties as Calvin's business representative in the collection of income due from the Parisian students' ecclesiastical holdings, and in the settlement of

[1] Doumergue, i. 205, A J Baumgartner, *Calvin hébraïsant*, Paris, 1889, p 14

[2] *Opera*, xb 9

[3] See Lefranc, *Jeunesse*, pp 95, 96; *Opera*, xb. 11, 13, 21, 26, etc.

their father's estate, that Calvin, on one occasion at least, had to borrow from Duchemin,[1]—a thing evidently galling to his pride to do.

Charles's financial slowness was a lesser cause of anxiety, it may be believed, than the difficulties into which he fell with the Chapter at Noyon, which began before the death of Gérard Cauvin, and continued in growing aggravation till his own decease.[2] The cause seems at first to have involved no question of religious opinion. Excited, it may be, by the discussions arising from his father's quarrel with the Chapter, though of this there is no definite proof, he had a personal encounter with Antoine Tourneur, a beadle of the Noyon cathedral, regarding which event the Chapter ordered an investigation on February 11, 1531. Only two days later he was again under discipline for having struck one of the clergy. By this act the quick-tempered young man incurred excommunication; and this was his condition when his father died, also excommunicate. Apparently he made no attempt to remedy it; but treated the Chapter with contempt, procuring ordination to the subdiaconate in spite of his want of ecclesiastical standing. On September 15, 1531, when his brother John had been in Paris engaged in humanistic studies for about three months, Charles was forbidden entrance to the cathedral by the Chapter,

[1] *Opera*, xb 17

[2] The matter has been discussed by Lefranc, *Jeunesse*, pp 18–21, 197–201, 210, where extracts from the registers are given Doumergue, i. 22–25. On the dates, see Müller, *Calvins Bekehrung*, pp. 220–223

with which he continued in full quarrel. So the matter remained during the rest of John Calvin's student days, but in May, 1534, a month of great importance in the younger brother's life, as there will be occasion to see, Charles was accused of a heretical opinion, regarding which such secrecy was observed that it is impossible to say how far his revolt against the Roman Church may have gone. In its maintenance Charles persisted; and at his death, October 31, 1537, he refused the Roman sacraments and was, in consequence, buried beneath the gallows at Noyon. Charles Cauvin's "heresy" did not manifest itself till after his brother had broken with the Roman Church; it was quite as probably due to John's influence over him as in any way a cause of John's adhesion to Protestantism. He seems to have been of coarser fibre than his more famous brother. He had none of John Calvin's capacity for leadership. And his earlier, and more personal, quarrels with the Noyon Chapter, which occurred while John was still a student, show the contentious rivalries of administrative jealousy in a small city, or at most a filial participation in his father's quarrel, rather than the presence of deep religious conviction such as was to lead John Calvin to his break with Rome.

During these months at Paris in the latter half of 1531 and the beginning of 1532, Calvin had not only been studying Greek and Hebrew under Danès and Vatable, he had been hard at work upon his first book,—his *Commentary on Seneca's Treatise on Clemency.*[1]

[1] It bore the title of *L. Annei Senecae, Romani Senatoris, ac Philosophi Clarissimi, Libri duo de Clementia, ad Neronem Cæsarem*·

Calvin's attention seems to have been called to the theme by Erasmus's edition of Seneca's works, published in 1529, in which the great humanist has expressed a critical, and, as it seemed to Calvin, a too disparaging, judgment of the Roman Stoic Philosopher.[1] All the eagerness of a young scholar's enthusiasm—the author was not yet twenty-three—went out to it, as it came from the press in April, 1532. The expense, which he had paid from his own pocket, had been a heavy draft upon his means, and he sought the good offices of his friends to secure the distribution of copies in influential quarters, and to let him know its reception.[2] The impression upon the scholarly world which his volume might make, was to him a matter of great, and natural, concern. Calvin's *Commentary* is a work of one hundred and fifty-six pages in quarto. Beginning with the dedication to his boyhood companion and student friend, Claude de Hangest, to which reference has already been made, there follows a short life of Seneca, "compiled from good authors," and then a series of brief chapters, each having at its head a consecutive section of the text of Seneca's essay, but being made up chiefly of notes on the passage quoted. These comments are of all kinds, explanatory, historical, critical, exegetical; but chiefly philological and philosophical, and illustrative by constant quotation of the linguistic usage

*Joannis Calvini Noviodunaei Commentariis Illustrati.* Paris, 1532 It is printed in *Opera*, v. 1-162

[1] *Opera*, v 6, 7 Henri Lecoultre has a very valuable discussion of the whole work, *Revue de théol et de philos*, Lausanne, 1891, pp. 57-77

[2] *Opera*, xb. 19-22.

of the Roman philosopher. From the point of view of scholarship the young author had nothing to fear. Written in a Latin style of singular clarity and brilliancy, with not a little of the lawyer's sense for lucid presentation and cogent argument, his book showed a range of reading almost marvellous in a man of Calvin's years. This impression of precocity is but intensified when it is remembered how comparatively recently he had begun the study of Greek. The text is illuminated by citations from fifty-six Latin and twenty-two Greek classical writers, seven Fathers of the Church, and the humanists of his own age.[1] Many of these references are to a number of works by the same author; for instance to thirty-three of the orations, treatises, and letters of Cicero, or to five of the plays of Terence. Certainly those long hours of study and reflection at Orléans and Bourges, and of work under the "Royal Lecturers" at Paris, had had their abundant fruitage in the erudition of which the young humanist revealed himself so easily the master. Nor is the work less remarkable for its maturity and poise of judgment. There is in it almost no suggestion of a youthful effort. Perhaps an exception is to be seen in a slap at his former teacher, Alciati,[2] whom he and his friend Duchemin had criticised; but the opinions expressed are, almost universally, those of one who seems to have thought long and wisely.

Conspicuous throughout the volume are Calvin's

[1] Lecoultre, *op cit.*, pp 76, 77, gives an approximately full list, and remarks, (p. 59), "*c'est en effet un puits d'érudition,*"

[2] *Opera*, v. 146.

high sense of moral values, and conception of the sinfulness of conduct not in accordance with them. His sympathies are drawn to the Roman writer who laid such stress on moral action. It is because Seneca is so conscious of the importance of right ethical principles in human life that Calvin is attracted to him. Clemency and justice, he holds, are virtues of the first order; and, however exalted the prince or magistrate, it is only as he illustrates them in his conduct that he proves himself the friend and not the enemy of those whom he judges or rules. Moreover, with all his sympathy for Seneca, Calvin has sufficient independence sharply to criticise the Stoic philosophy. He finds its insensibility abhorrent to the general sentiment of mankind. It is human, he declares, to be affected by grief, to feel, to resist, to receive consolations, to shed tears. The individual isolation of Stoicism he dislikes. Even to follow conscience is not sufficient, if such following leads a man to neglect the good name and welfare of his neighbour,—a doctrine which Calvin declares to be the teaching of "our religion," that is, of Christianity Here, then, is the treatise of one who knows and admires the world of classical antiquity, but who feels the compelling force of moral law, is desirous to apply it to his own age, and is convinced that union and mutua dutifulness, not isolation, even that of individualistic philosophic rectitude, are the proper conditions of mankind.

Did Calvin have any purpose in writing this remarkable treatise beyond that of illuminating an author who he felt, had not been rightly appreciated, and winning for himself, in so doing, an honourable name in the world of scholarship? From the time that Papire Masson wrote his sketch of Calvin (about 1583)[1] to the present there have been those who have asserted that a further purpose was to move Francis I. to a more kindly treatment of his Protestant subjects. This is the view of Henry,[2] and, in a modified form, of Doumergue.[3] On the other hand, Kampschulte,[4] the Strassburg editors of Calvin's works,[5] Lecoultre[6] and Fairbairn,[7] see in it no evidence of any such ulterior or disguised purpose. In that conclusion the writer must agree. Had it not been for Calvin's later history no one would probably have seen in this noble Commentary more than the work of an unusually high-minded, ethically strenuous humanist. Nor would one have looked upon its author as specially interested in religious problems. The Bible is cited but three times, and then in a relatively incidental manner. It may be too much to say, with one of the most careful of recent students, that Calvin then knew only the Vulgate;[8] but it is not unwarranted to affirm with him that the Bible had no such attraction for the youthful commentator on Seneca as was possessed by the great writers of classical

[1] *Elogiorum*, pars secunda, Paris, 1638, p 403, Doumergue, i 214, 529

[2] *Das Leben Johann Calvins*, i 52–55

[3] I 215, 216

[4] I. 238.

[5] *Opera*, v xxxii

[6] *Op cit*, p 72

[7] *The Cambridge Modern History*, ii 352.

[8] A Lang, *Die Bekehrung Johannes Calvins*, p 29, but comp. Doumergue, i 219

antiquity. There is no impression that can be traced unmistakably to the burning religious controversies of the hour. If Calvin was interested in them at the time that he wrote this volume that interest does not appear in its pages.

Calvin's life during the months immediately following the publication of the *Commentary* just considered is difficult to trace in detail; but one or two features are fortunately made evident by letters and documents which have survived. The correspondence with his friend, Daniel, shows that in May, 1532, Calvin was planning soon to make the journey to Orléans, and to bring with him a copy of the Bible,—possibly Le Fèvre's translation, which had been printed at Antwerp late in 1530.[1] Had these letters been all the evidence, a stay at Orléans longer than a brief visit would hardly be conjectured. But documents in a legal action dated May 10 and June 11, 1533,[2] show not merely that he was then at Orléans, but that he was holding the office of *Substitut Annuel de Procureur* for the nation of Picardy,—one of the ten "nations" in which the students of the University of Orléans were organised, and composed of course of those from Calvin's native region of France. As annual representative of the Attorney, or, more properly, Proctor, of the Picard students, Calvin presumably remained some months at Orléans, and as he was present at a meeting of the Cathedral Chapter at

[1] *Opera*, xb 20-22, Herminjard, ii 388, 418-421, Hauck's *Realencyklopadie für prot Theologie*, iii 130, 131

[2] Doinel, *Le bulletin de la Soc de l'histoire du Prot français*, for 1877, pp. 174-9; Lefranc, *Jeunesse*, pp 105, 203, 204.

Noyon on August 23, 1533, when prayers were ordered on account of the plague,[1] and had settled once more in Paris by the following October,[2] the supposition seems well-nigh certain that he prolonged his stay and spent a year, from the early summer of 1532 to that of 1533, once more as a student at Orléans. It was probably further discipline in the law that attracted him, for the opportunities to continue his humanistic studies were much better at Paris. It has been suggested that he desired the degree of doctor, he may have wished to be with his friends Daniel and Duchemin; but all is conjecture. The only fact that can be confidently affirmed is that Calvin had not yet found his life-work, and some reasons why this discovery was not easy at this time will appear in the consideration of his conversion. The law and the path of classic scholarship he had tried successively and alternately. He had greatly distinguished himself in both; but he was not yet satisfied in his own mind. He had not yet come to peace with himself as to what his path in life should be.

It was while serving as a representative of the Picard students of the University of Orléans that Calvin became engaged in his official capacity in a curious lawsuit illustrative of surviving mediæval conditions. A count of Beaugency, having recovered from a severe illness, three-quarters of a century before Calvin's sojourn, had then attributed his cure to the favour of St. Firmin, a missionary martyr of the seventh century,

[1] Doinel, Lefranc, *Jeunesse*, p. 200.

[2] *Opera*, xb 27-30

often called the "Apostle of Picardy." In recognition of the blessing received,[1] he had acknowledged himself the vassal of the saint for certain properties near Beaugency. Of the revenues thus pledged by the count, a portion came ultimately to be paid to the "nation" of Picards at Orléans, which held St Firmin in reverence as its patron Payment was due annually on January 13th, in the form of a *maille d'or de Florence,* that is a medal or specially struck coin of a fixed weight of gold, bearing the fleur-de-lis as well as an image of John the Baptist. It was of no great intrinsic value, but its reception was the occasion of a much prized and rather Bacchanalian student festival in which Picardy was duly glorified with oratory and feasting. For some reason, payment was refused in January, 1533, and a legal action, which ultimately proved successful, was therefore begun by the Picard students before the Parlement of Paris, authority being given by successive meetings of the "nation" under Calvin's chairmanship. The expenses were in part paid by a tax on the students, but in part, also, by the sale of two silver vases which belonged to the "nation" and were not improbably used in the services of the Church of Nôtre-Dame des Bonnes-Nouvelles which it regarded as its headquarters. The full legal record of the authorisation of this sale still exists;[2] but an absurd and slanderous legend, after Calvin had become an

[1] For the whole matter, see Bimbenet, *Mémoires de la Société des Antiquaires de Picardie,* x 393,-474, Lefranc, *Jeunesse,* 105, 106, 203, 204, Doumergue, i 299-304

[2] Doinel, *Bulletin,* etc, for 1877, p 179, Lefranc, *Jeunesse,* p 203.

object of attack, and was no longer living so that a reply was impossible from him, twisted this clear transaction into a story that he abused his position at Orléans to steal a silver chalice belonging to the Picard nation, in order to pay the personal expenses of a long journey.[1]

While other positive intimations of Calvin's life during the last half of 1532 and the first seven months of 1533 are lacking, save the important legal records just considered which show his presence and official position in the University of Orléans, a letter of Calvin's has been preserved, undated as to the year, but written, apparently from Noyon, on a September 4th, to the eminent German reformer, Martin Bucer (1491–1551) of Strassburg, commending to that theologian's favour a French refugee who "could no longer bow the neck to that voluntary bondage which even yet we bear."[2] This epistle was assigned to the year 1532 by Conrad Hubert in the sixteenth century, and this traditional date, which was followed by the older historians, was retained, though with much hesitation, by the Strassburg editors of Calvin's works. It has a recent though cautious defender in Professor Doumergue.[3] If this view is correct, we have not merely an additional indication as to Calvin's whereabouts during the period in question; but what is vastly more important, clear proofs of his relations to the great Strassburg reformer,

[1] Jacques Desmay, *Remarques . . . sur la vie . de Jean Calvin*, published at Rouen, in 1621, reprinted in Cimber and Danjou's *Archives curieuses de l'histoire de France*, v. 393; Doumergue, i. 303

[2] *Opera*, xb. 22–24.

[3] I 297–299, 556.

and of his own Evangelical opinions, as early as September, 1532. But weighty reasons serve to throw doubt on the correctness of this dating. The letter itself, as the Strassburg editors pointed out,[1] implies a previous intimacy, of which there is no proof if 1532 be the date; and its tone is strikingly, and one may say from the point of view of that age shockingly, familiar, if used by a youthful student toward a scholar of European reputation. Herminjard would, therefore, put it in 1534, or possibly 1533,[2] and Lefranc accepts the former date;[3] but whatever may be urged as possible in view of Olivétan's relations to Bucer, or Calvin's later indebtedness to Bucer's theological writings, it seems difficult to the present writer to avoid the conclusion reached by Lang, that while we cannot certainly fix the date of this letter as 1534, it must unquestionably be considerably later than 1532.[4]

When we next encounter Calvin after his presence in the meeting of the Chapter at Noyon, on August 23, 1533, of which mention has already been made, he is settled once more in Paris, and is writing to his friend, François Daniel, at Orléans, under date of the twenty-seventh of the following October. Calvin had come to Paris at an interesting juncture. The year was one of hope in the history of the reformatory movement in France as none previous had been and

[1] *Opera*, xb 23.

[2] Herminjard, iii 204, Doumergue, i 557.

[3] *Jeunesse*, p 46.

[4] *Die Bekehrung Johannes Calvins*, pp 16, 17 Müller (*Calvins Bekehrung*, pp 245–253) inclines to put it in 1538, or possibly from Nyon, on Lake Geneva, in 1537, 1542 or 1543–1547.

none for a long time to come was to be. And of the hope Paris was the centre. Under the kindly patronage of Marguerite d'Angoulême, who represented her brother, the King, in his long absence from the capital, the humanistic reformers of the school of Le Fèvre were in high favour, and their opponents had some reason to fear that this goodwill would lead to the countenancing of teachers of a much more radical policy. Calvin's letter[1] shows him deeply interested in the discussions of the capital, among which the religious questions of the hour had large place. He is evidently on cordial terms with Gérard Roussel, the intimate disciple of Le Fèvre, who, like his master, was never to break with the Roman Church outwardly, but who was far enough removed from its dominant spirit. Roussel, whom Marguerite d'Angoulême had long admired for his mystical piety and humanistic conceptions of reform, had been secured by that Queen and her husband, the King of Navarre, in the absence from Paris of Francis I., as Lenten preacher for 1533 His sermons had led to that outbreak of hostility on the part of the theologians of the University which King Francis had checked in May by banishing Béda and his associates, the representatives of an unbending Roman conservatism which the King was willing for the time being to oppose in the interest of fashionable humanistic learning.[2] Calvin could now speak of

[1] *Opera*, xb 25–30 For the general situation see Bourrilly and Weiss, *Jean du Bellay, les Protestants et la Sorbonne*, in the *Bulletin*, lii 193–231 (1903)

[2] Herminjard, iii 54–61

Roussel as "our G.[érard]," and circulate his writings confidentially.[1] It must have been with keen satisfaction that Calvin was able, in this letter, to refer to his friend Nicolas Cop as "now rector" of the University, an office to which Cop had been chosen only seventeen days before; and Calvin unquestionably shared the pleasure of his humanistic friends, Roussel and Cop, when, just as he was writing, the interference of the King had compelled the conservatives of the University to disavow any intention to condemn Marguerite d'Angoulême's *Le miroir de l'âme pécheresse*.[2] Five days after this letter, Cop pronounced his rectorial address in the Church of the Mathurins, using possibly, though hardly probably, the words of Calvin; and giving utterance to sentiments of an unmistakably Evangelical character, drawn from Protestant sources.[3] With his friend Calvin undoubtedly sympathised. It is evident that by this first of November, 1533, Calvin, whether in his own estimate a Protestant or merely an earnest humanistic reformer of the school of Le Fèvre, had come to religious convictions generally associated with Protestantism, and had been mastered

[1] *Opera*, xb 26, Herminjard, iii 105

[2] An expression in Calvin's letter has given rise to much perplexity He said, "*Visum est statui pessimum exemplum eorum libidini qui rebus novis inhiant,*" etc (*Opera* xb 27) Those "who gape after new things" are regarded by Herminjard, Lecoultre, Stähelin, and Doumergue as the reformers If so, it is hard to explain Calvin's remark, in view of his evident sympathy with Roussel and Cop. Müller (*Calvins Bekehrung*, p 198) interprets them more truly as a criticism of those who were "making trouble," *i e* of the conservatives by whom the reformers were opposed.

[3] This address will be considered in the next chapter.

by an interest in religion of which there is no evidence in his *Commentary on Seneca* or in his earlier correspondence. Whether he then knew it or not, and probably he had yet little conception of its significance, Calvin had found his life-work. This crisis properly challenges the questions of Calvin's religious development and of the nature of that transforming experience which he himself styled his "conversion." [1]

[1] *Opera*, xxxi. 21.

# CHAPTER IV

## RELIGIOUS DEVELOPMENT AND CONVERSION

IN approaching the subject of the religious development and conversion of Calvin a theme of much difficulty is encountered. Not that the final result is in any way obscure. No religious leader of the Reformation age stands more clearly defined than he in all the traits of the spiritual character of his maturer years. But the process by which Calvin passed from the status of a student supported by funds drawn from Roman ecclesiastical foundations, and reckoned as of the Roman clergy even if in no clerical orders, to that of a leader of Protestantism, is exceedingly difficult to follow in detail, partly by reason of Calvin's own reticence in regard to all that concerned his inward experiences, partly because his earliest biographers unintentionally, but none the less effectively, distorted the facts of his early religious life, and partly, also, in consequence of the varying interpretations which modern historians have placed on such scanty indications of the stages of his spiritual development as have survived. Nor are those who have recently treated of the matter at one as to what they understand by his "conversion." Is that to be regarded as implying simply his attainment of views now considered distinctive of Protestantism; or can nothing be properly given that name that does not involve a deliberate separation from the

Roman communion? The answer given to this question makes not a little difference in the dating assigned to this crucial episode in Calvin's religious history.

Calvin's most distinct account of his spiritual development was written in middle life, and occurs almost incidentally in the Preface to his noble *Commentary on the Psalms*, published in Latin in 1557, and in French the year following. It is at nearest almost a quarter of a century later than the experiences that it pictures. The struggles of the writers of the Psalms, especially of David, recall to him his own combats, and induce him to compare his own trials with those of the Jewish poet-king.[1]—

It is true that my estate is much humbler and lower [than David's], and there is no need that I should stop to demonstrate the fact, but as he was taken from caring for beasts and raised to the sovereign rank of royal dignity, so God has advanced me from my humble and lowly beginnings so far as to call me to this most honourable office of minister and preacher of the Gospel From the time that I was a young child, my father had intended me for Theology, but afterwards, because he perceived that the science of Laws commonly enriches those who follow it, this hope caused him promptly to change his plan That was the reason why I was withdrawn from the study of Philosophy, and why I was set to learning Law. Though I forced

[1] *Opera*, xxxi 21–24 The Latin and French versions are there given in parallel Both are thought to be from Calvin's pen I quote from the French

myself to engage faithfully in it in order to obey my father, God finally made me turn about in another direction by his secret providence.

And, in the first place, because I was so obstinately addicted to the superstitions of the papacy that it was very hard to draw me from that deep slough, by a sudden conversion He subdued and reduced my heart to docility, which, for my age, was over-much hardened in such matters Having consequently received some taste and knowledge of true piety, I was forthwith inflamed with so great a desire to reap benefit from it that, although I did not at all abandon other studies, I yet devoted myself to them more indifferently Now I was greatly astonished that, before a year passed, all those who had some desire for pure doctrine betook themselves to me in order to learn, although I myself had done little more than begin. For my part, I commenced to seek some hiding-place and means of withdrawing from people, since I have always loved quiet and tranquillity, being by nature somewhat shy and timid; but so far was I from succeeding in my wish that, on the contrary, all retreats and places of retirement were as public schools for me. In short, while I have always had this aim of living privately without being known, God has so led me and guided me by various vicissitudes that He has never let me rest in any place whatever, but, in spite of my natural disposition, He has brought me forth into the light, and, as the saying is, has thrust me onto the stage [1] And, in fact, when I left the land of France I came to Germany of set purpose to the end that there I might live in some inconspicuous nook as I have always wished.

[1] An English equivalent is lacking for Calvin's expression "*et fai venir en jeu, comme on dit*"

Earlier in date of composition, though much less definitely of a biographic character, are certain passages in Calvin's brilliant *Reply to Jacopo Sadoleto*, of 1539 The Roman cardinal had pictured a Catholic and a Protestant as rendering account of their religious principles and motives before the bar of God's judgment, to the decided disadvantage of the reformer.[1] Calvin takes up the same figure and puts into the mouths of a Protestant minister and of a common member of his flock most skilful defences of Protestant principles, written with consummate literary art and by no means to be considered wholly autobiographic,[2] yet of such spiritual earnestness and verisimilitude that they are undoubtedly to a considerable extent drawn from his own religious experience.

Called to answer before God, the minister may make reply:[3]—

They charged me with two of the worst of crimes,—heresy and schism. And the heresy was that I dared to protest against dogmas which they received. But what could I have done? I heard from Thy mouth that there was no other light of truth which could direct our souls into the way of life than that which was kindled by Thy Word. I heard that whatever human minds of themselves conceive concerning Thy Majesty, the worship of Thy Deity, and the mysteries of Thy religion, was vanity. I heard that their introducing into the Church instead of Thy Word,

[1] *Opera*, v 379–381

[2] Lang, *Bekehrung*, pp. 31–36, but comp. Doumergue, i. 347–350.

[3] *Opera*, v. 408; Henry Beveridge's translation, *Tracts*, Edinburgh, 1860, i. 50.

doctrines sprung from the human brain, was sacrilegious presumption. But when I turned my eyes towards men, I saw very different principles prevailing. Those who were regarded as the leaders of faith neither understood Thy Word, nor greatly cared for it. . . They had fabricated for themselves many useless frivolities, as a means of procuring Thy favour, and on these they so plumed themselves that, in comparison with them, they almost condemned the standard of true righteousness which Thy law recommended —to such a degree had human desires after usurping the ascendancy, derogated, if not from the belief, at least from the authority, of Thy precepts therein contained. That I might perceive these things, Thou, O Lord, didst shine upor me with the brightness of Thy Spirit; that I might comprehend how impious and noxious they were, Thou dids bear before me the torch of Thy Word; that I might abominate them as they deserved, Thou didst stimulate m soul.

The solemn justification ascribed to the layman b Calvin bears fewer marks of the author's personal struggles. Some of its touches, especially regarding th Bible, reflect the experience of the "common man o the people" rather than that natural to an inquisitiv student at Paris and Orléans. But it would seem t be the order-loving, legally trained, precedent-seekin Calvin that speaks for himself in these words :[1]—

When, however, I had performed all these things [*i e.* ha sought forgiveness for sin in accordance with the teaching of the Roman Church], though I had some intervals c

[1] *Opera*, v. 412; *Tracts*, i 56

quiet, I was still far off from true peace of conscience, for, whenever I descended into myself, or raised my mind to Thee, extreme terror seized me—terror which no expiations nor satisfactions could cure And the more closely I examined myself, the sharper the stings with which my conscience was pricked, so that the only solace that was left to me was to delude myself by obliviousness. Still, as nothing better offered, I continued the course which I had begun, when, lo, a very different form of doctrine started up, not one which led us away from the Christian profession, but one which brought it back to its fountain-head, and, as it were, clearing away the dross, restored it to its original purity. Offended by the novelty, I lent an unwilling ear, and at first, I confess, strenuously and passionately resisted; for (such is the firmness or effrontery with which it is natural to men to persist in the course which they have once undertaken) it was with the greatest difficulty that I was induced to confess that I had all my life long been in ignorance and error. One thing, in particular, made me averse to those new teachers—viz. reverence for the Church But when once I opened my ears, and allowed myself to be taught, I perceived that this fear of derogating from the majesty of the Church was groundless For they reminded me how great the difference is between schism from the Church and studying to correct the faults by which the Church herself was contaminated.

A hint as to one of Calvin's earliest acquaintances with Protestant discussion, and as to a difficulty which operated with others to set him in opposition toward Protestant claims, appears to be contained, also, in the following passage from his *Second Reply to Westphal*, published in 1556, many years after the experience to which it refers:[1]—

For when I was beginning to emerge from the darkness of the papacy, having gained a slight taste of sound doctrine I read in Luther that nothing was left of the Sacraments by Œcolampadius and Zwingli save bare and empty figures I confess that I was so alienated from their books that I long abstained from reading them. Afterwards, before I undertook to write, they moderated something of their former vehemence, having discussed together at Marburg so that the thicker fog was somewhat scattered even if it was not yet fully clear weather.

The implication would seem to be that Calvin had run across one of Luther's discussions of the Supper before the Marburg Colloquy,—that is before October 1529.

From Calvin's positive statements regarding his religious experience several conclusions may with confidence be drawn. It is evident that he regarded his "conversion" as the sovereign work of God. Nothing less he felt, than divine power could have wrought the change which he recognised as having taken place in him. It had been brought about by an immediate and transforming intervention of God himself. Nothing stood or could stand between his soul and God. Equally plain is it, also, that this transformation in the fundamental habit of his mind by a power outside himself had been, in his apprehension, "sudden." It had been a change of view no less unlooked for than supernatural

[1] *Opera*, ix. 51.

in its origin. And it is clear, too, that, within the year following this experience, Calvin had become a leader in Evangelical, or at least humanistically reformatory, circles in the community in which he was. This publicity, to whatever extent it may have reached, was distasteful to him, and he would have preferred a life of literary ease; but the same divine power that had effected the initial transformation in him, now, as it seemed to him, forced him into conspicuity and increasing leadership. If to these positive details drawn from his Preface to the *Commentary on the Psalms* the less certainly autobiographic intimations of the *Reply to Sadoleto* may properly be added, it is clear that this "sudden conversion" had as an important factor—probably as its central experience—the recognition of the Scriptures, and of the Scriptures alone, as the very voice of God. God speaks, and he can but listen. And this speaking for Calvin is through the Word,—not through the Church, or even primarily within, though it will be found that in his developed theology Calvin gives weight to the inward testimony of the Spirit. This strenuous conviction regarding the absolute and exclusive divine authority of the Scriptures, characteristic of the Reformation generally, but held by Calvin more clearly, perhaps, than by any other of the reformers, is the logical outcome of that return to the sources which was the ground-note of the Renaissance. With most of those who had thus far sought a betterment of religious conditions in France its full significance was but dimly apprehended; with Calvin it was fundamental. But one can well believe that, before his order-loving mind could feel that only in the Scriptures is final divine truth to be found, Calvin had to struggle with that "reverence for the Church" and sense of the sanctity of accepted views of the Sacraments which were part of his race-inheritance. His lawyer-grasp must have a document on which to base its deductions. The authority must be tangible and objective, and this he found in the Scriptures, but before he could deny to the Roman Church any authoritative interpreting function, or reject its long series of precedents and decisions, he must needs pass through a struggle the outcome of which seemed to him the intervention of a power no less than that of God. It is fair, also, to infer from the *Reply to Sadoleto* that a sense of sinfulness and of the inadequacy of the common mediæval theories of the way of salvation, ending in glad acceptance of relief from the burden through the way known as justification by faith alone, was an integral part of the experience which he called his "conversion." In a measure, at least, his pathway was similar to that of Luther; though a comparison to Augustine would perhaps be truer.

But, if the general features of Calvin's religious development are thus made at least presumptively plain by his own statements, very weighty questions yet remain unanswered. When and where did this great transformation occur? Who were the human instruments, if any, in it? Was its power that of a revolution in the whole spiritual man leading to immediate action; or was it a sudden energising of a will thus far lacking strength to put into vital practice convictions already long held as intellectual verities? To these queries most various answers have been and are still given by competent scholars.

According to the representations of Calvin's friends and oldest biographers, Beza and Colladon,[1] Calvin's transition to Protestantism began with the influence of his relative, Pierre Robert Olivétan, and was already so advanced by the time that he entered on the study of law at Orléans, early in 1528, as to be an important factor in that decision to substitute jurisprudence for theology Influenced by Olivétan, the youthful Calvin began the study of the Scriptures and withdrew himself, in a measure at least, from the Roman worship. According to their representation, this must have happened before Calvin was nineteen years old. Arrived at Orléans, Calvin vigorously continued his study of the Bible, and made himself a leader among those seeking religious reform. While a student at Bourges he preached at Lignières, and on coming to Paris, where he wrote his *Seneca*, he became acquainted with all the reformers there, and his relations with Estienne de la Forge, the noble Evangelical merchant who was to seal his faith by martyrdom in 1535, and with Nicolas Cop, are cited as examples of this reformatory activity.

A modification of this interpretation of the beginnings of Calvin's Protestantism was presented by the Catholic historian, Florimond de Ræmond.[2] Anxious to find in

[1] *Lives*, of 1564, 1565, and 1575, in *Opera*, xxi. 29, 54, 55, 121, 122.

[2] *La naissance, progrès et décadence de l'hérésie*, Paris, 1605, p 882. The author died in 1601

Germany rather than in his native land the source of Calvin's "heresy," he affirmed that its initiation was due to Melchior Wolmar at Bourges. Among more modern historians, Henry was firmly of the opinion that Wolmar was the prime human factor in Calvin's conversion.[1] It is easy, moreover, to combine the report of Beza with the representation given by Ræmond, and to hold, as Merle d'Aubigné and many other historians have done, that Olivétan began and Wolmar ably continued the Evangelical development of the reformer.

Within the last third of a century, and especially during the last twenty years, Calvin's statements, the affirmations of his earliest biographers, and such hints as can be derived from his letters and the *Commentary on Seneca* have been subjected to much patient scholarly analysis. Yet the conclusions reached exhibit great variety of critical deduction.

To the Old-Catholic German historian, F. W. Kampschulte, writing in 1869, the "traditional view" seemed "wholly erroneous that Calvin had been completely won for the Reformation during his university years, and had even stood forth with great success as its defender and furtherer."[2] The evidence of the letters shows the contrary. Kampschulte reaches the conclusion[3]—

> We recognise that Calvin long found himself in a state of uncertainty and vacillation regarding religious questions.

[1] *Leben Johann Calvins*, i 38 (1835).
[2] *Johann Calvin*, i 233
[3] *Ibid.*, pp. 240, 241.

His earlier dependence on the religion of his fathers had been shattered by the impressions which he had received during his university days, as well as by his theological studies. The former peace was gone; the forms and spiritual remedies of the Catholic Church no more gave him full satisfaction. What he experienced in his family was not fitted to strengthen him in the faith of the Church. His father died, excommunicate. His older brother, Charles by name, although a clergyman, fell into conflict with the spiritual authorities and was laid under ecclesiastical censure by them. One of his nearest relatives, Robert Olivétan, was devoted to the principles of religious innovation, and early sought, it is said, to win him for them. It was hard permanently to withstand so many points of attack. . . There were already in the capital and elsewhere actual congregations of Evangelical believers, who had wholly broken with churchly tradition and were ready to pledge property and life for their new religious convictions. At Paris Calvin came into close relations with some of them, notably with a respected and well-to-do merchant, de la Forge, whom he extolled in his later writings. Should he have less courage than these men, and persist in his determination to lead a quiet life? Without acting against his conscience he could not. . . . It is difficult to determine the date of this decisive change Yet we shall not think ourselves in error if we place it in the second half of the year 1532

Twelve years after Kampschulte published his volume, a Dutch scholar, Allard Pierson, put forth the most radical criticism of the accepted view of Calvin's conversion yet offered,—a criticism that has secured comparatively few followers.[1] Not only does he deny to

[1] *Studien over Johannes Kalvijn*, Amsterdam, 1881, pp 58–109.

6

Calvin the authorship of Cop's inaugural discourse of November 1, 1533, but he finds no certain proof of Calvin's Protestantism before August 23, 1535,—the date of the Preface to the *Institutes*.

In 1888, Abel Lefranc, now Professor in the Collège de France at Paris, presented in his remarkable study of Calvin's youth an interesting modification of the traditional view, and supported it with great learning. His investigations marked a decided advance in the knowledge of Calvin's family and early environment. Calvin's transition to Protestantism, he concluded, was a very gradual process, however sudden in its decision at the end, for which the way was prepared by his native surroundings and family experiences.[1] His father's excommunication and his elder brother's breach with the Noyon clergy aroused in Calvin the spirit of protest which was natural to the Picard character, and had its illustration in Le Fèvre, Roussel, and others from the same territory. To these influences were added the positive Evangelical exhortations of Olivétan from 1528, onward, and that young reformer, who had had to seek protection in Strassburg by May of the year just mentioned, was the cause, Lefranc held, of a gradual and mysterious propagation of reformed ideas at Noyon, which soon won such following that the Chapter did not dare too vigorously to oppose it. But while the way was made ready for Calvin's Protestantism by the influences that came from his native city, as well as by the experiences of the University, it was long before he became fully an adherent of the new faith, or

[1] *Jeunesse*, pp 21, 24, 31, 37, 39, 41, 97-99, 112, etc.

could engage in a "great stroke" in its behalf such as Cop's Address, Calvin's authorship of which Lefranc fully accepts—

> The[1] truth is that, long before inclined by his own nature, prepared by his education, the situation of his family, his relations, his studies, he did not declare himself openly a Huguenot until the time when all these circumstances unitedly forced him to do so almost against his will, and when, so to say, he could no longer do otherwise.
>
> Calvin's decisive conversion was above all a question of logic and reflection, in which sentiment had no part. . . In all probability, and as far as it is possible to determine so intimate a growth of ideas, this change must have taken place in the second half of the year 1532

Two years after Lefranc, in 1890, Henri Lecoultre, a young Swiss scholar, now no longer living, took up the problem once more.[2] In criticism of Lefranc he rejected the thought of any direct influence tending toward Protestantism upon Calvin derived from the family or early environment at Noyon Gérard Cauvin's troubles were pecuniary, not religious; Charles Cauvin's "heresies" did not appear till 1534; nor is the existence of a Protestant movement in Noyon demonstrable before that year, by which time Calvin was a decided adherent of Evangelical views. Possibly Gérard Cauvin's insistence that his son should study law may have been, in its consequences, a step of high importance toward ideas of reform; but it was in no

[1] *Jeunesse*, pp. 41, 97, 98

[2] *Revue de théologie et de philosophie*, Lausanne, 1890, pp. 5–30.

way so intended by the father. But Lecoultre agrees with Lefranc in admitting the influence of Olivétan and the Calvinistic authorship of Cop's Address. With Lefranc he holds that Calvin was long intellectually convinced of the truth of Protestant doctrine before being willing to break with the Roman Church, but he differs from the scholar just named in refusing to see conclusive evidence of that conversion in any act earlier than Calvin's formal breach with the ancient communion by his resignation of his benefices in May, 1534:[1]—

What was the day of that sudden conversion? What was its immediate occasion? We do not know, perhaps we may never know. But its meaning need not be doubtful, it is neither a conversion of intellect, nor a conversion of feeling, but a conversion of will It did not give him conviction regarding Protestant dogmas,—that he possessed already; it did not inspire in him a warm interest for the things of the kingdom of God,—he was already filled with it, it made vital an arrested resolution to conform his conduct scrupulously to his convictions, and to break all connection with the errors which he had already abjured in the depths of his heart The first external evidence of this conversion, the first at least known to us, is a sacrifice of which Calvin never boasted, and of which Theodore Beza seems to have had no knowledge The archives of Noyon prove that on May 4, 1534, Calvin resigned, in his native city, all his ecclesiastical benefices This act, the natural consequence of which was voluntary exile, was needed to make of Calvin a real Protestant, for genuine Protestantism

[1] *Revue de théologie et de philosophie*, Lausanne, 1890, pp 27, 28

does not consist only of the doctrines of justification by faith and of the supreme authority of the Scriptures. It implies, as its name indicates, an energetic protest, formulated in the name of these doctrines, against ecclestiastical abuses of every kind.

The careful sketch of Calvin's life by the late Rudolf Stähelin, printed in 1897,[1] without entering as deeply into the question as the discussions just cited, expresses disbelief in his authorship of Cop's Address, and concludes, in view of Calvin's letter written on October 27, 1533, of which some account has been given,[2] that the future reformer "cannot have come to the break with the Catholic Church . . . before the first months of the year 1534."

But during the same year that Stahelin's biographical article appeared, a no less able German-speaking scholar, August Lang of Halle, published one of the most thorough investigations of the circumstances of Calvin's conversion yet attempted.[3] In Lang's opinion, as in that of Lecoultre, influences from Noyon can have had little direct connection with Calvin's conversion. And, furthermore, the allegations of Beza and Colladon, made much of by Lefranc and accepted by Lecoultre, regarding the instrumentality of Olivétan, Lang regards as resting "on very unsafe ground." Wolmar's share in Calvin's religious transformation is quite as unsupported. Calvin thanked him for initiation into

[1] Hauck's *Realencyklopädie für protestantische Theologie*, iii. 654–683

[2] *Ante*, p. 67.

[3] *Die Bekehrung Johannes Calvins*, Leipzig, 1897.

the knowledge of Greek,—he said nothing regarding any indebtedness to his old teacher for religious instruction. In fact, as a student Calvin exhibited no special interest in religion. His letters and the *Commentary on Seneca* show that "the Bible is still a closed book for Calvin because his heart does not beat for it. We must, therefore, lay aside all attempted explanations which would place the beginnings of the conversion of the great Biblical theologian in his student years as thoroughly astray. Before the year 1532, and we may go yet further, to perhaps the middle of 1533, the religious question is as good as non-existent for him." But a "change first appeared in the second half of the year 1533"; and it had its most conspicuous early manifestation in Cop's Address, Calvin's authorship of which Lang strongly defends. That transformation is best explained as occasioned by the activity of the reform party in Paris in 1533, and especially by the acquaintance of Calvin with Gérard Roussel, who, though never breaking with the Roman Church, was preaching doctrines to all intents Protestant. It is inconceivable also, Lang thinks, that a man of iron will and strenuous conscientiousness, as Calvin always was, could have remained for years intellectually convinced of the truths of Protestantism and yet not subject his action to his conviction, as Lefranc and Lecoultre would have it. His was no mere conversion of the will. Calvin's own statements that he "was obstinately addicted to the superstitions of the papacy," and that his "heart was over-much hardened," [1] show that both

[1] See *ante*, p. 49.

intellect and will were active in the transformation. "As soon as his understanding was convinced, the newly-won knowledge must almost of itself arouse the will to eager activity." To Calvin, his conversion appeared the direct work of God, the results of which were "the certainty that God speaks in the Scriptures, and the recognition that all truth is contained in them; and that therefore their study and their dissemination are the worthiest object of the talents and zeal of a man's whole life." This conviction made of the humanist a Bible theologian.

The problem has not, however, rested with the solution that Lang has offered, for the traditional view, in a somewhat modified form it is true, has found a defender of great learning and force in Émile Doumergue, Professor of the Theological Faculty at Montauban in France, the first volume of whose monumental biography of Calvin appeared in 1899.[1] To Doumergue the statements of Beza and Colladon as to Calvin's Evangelical beginnings carry great weight. Olivétan initiates him into Evangelical principles as early as 1528. This was Calvin's "sudden conversion." It was, indeed, but a beginning; but it led Calvin to the study of religious questions, and to read, for instance, the Lutheran exposition of the Lord's Supper earlier than the Colloquy at Marburg (1529). At Orléans and even more at Bourges, Calvin came into contact with Wolmar, and, though Calvin speaks only of Greek as the subject of their study, it is probable that they read the Greek Testament together,

[1] See i 116, 117, 181–183, 337–352.

and inconceivable that they could do so without religious instruction being given by the teacher to the pupil. Wolmar's influence Doumergue views as "decisive." It confirmed and greatly extended the work begun by Olivétan. And Doumergue furthermore holds that Calvin's statement, "Before a year passed all those who had some desire for pure doctrine betook themselves to me in order to learn,"[1] refers to his student days at Orléans and to his friends there like Daniel and Duchemin, at whose instance it may be believed he preached, not as a Protestant, but as a reformatory Catholic, at Lignières. Evidence of Calvin's interest in religion Doumergue sees in his citation of the Scriptures and of the Fathers in the *Commentary on Seneca* as well as in his purchase of a Bible for Daniel; and he thinks there would have been a good many more such tokens had not Calvin's correspondence been searched after the Address of Cop. But Calvin's religious development appears to Doumergue gradual, taking him through the stage of the partial Protestantism of a Le Fèvre; and it was not till the views were reached that are shown in Cop's Address, in Calvin's authorship of which Doumergue is fully confident, that his conversion, suddenly begun years before, was evidently completed. The termination of the gradual process of Calvin's conversion by his arrival at the full Protestant position Doumergue would place apparently in the months immediately following the publication of his *Commentary on Seneca*,—that is, in 1532.

[1] *Ante*, p. 72.

Calvin's conversion still proves a theme rewarding study, and in 1905, an elaborate monograph appeared from the pen of Professor Karl Muller[1] of Tubingen, not only discussing the whole subject anew, and with much dissent from Doumergue, but subjecting the claim that Calvin wrote Cop's Address to a painstaking examination leading to its denial. Müller holds it as probable that Olivétan influenced Calvin in the direction that Le Fèvre represented as early as Calvin's undergraduate days, and brought him into connection with Evangelical circles at Orléans. Wolmar, in Muller's opinion, may later have been the agent through whom Calvin was led during his second or third stay in Paris into association with similar reformers there. But his "sudden conversion," Muller believes, may have taken place in connection with the Roman services held on account of the pest in which he shared in Noyon on August 23, 1533, when he may have seen the inconsistency of his principles with participation in Roman worship. The chief element in that conversion he regards as a submission of Calvin's will to that of God.

Yet the discussion has not rested here, for in the early part of 1906 Professor Paul Wernle of Basel has taken it up,[2] examining principally the sources of Beza and Colladon's *Lives of Calvin.* He concludes that their assertions regarding Calvin's religious development

[1] *Calvins Bekehrung*, in *Nachrichten von der königl. Gesellschaft der Wissenschaften zu Göttingen*, pp 188–255

[2] *Noch einmal die Bekehrung Calvins*, in the *Zeitschrift für Kirchengeschichte*, xxvii. 84–99.

are simply their interpretations of the scanty allusions in Calvin's own writings, and that almost nothing of original value on this question is to be derived from them. In his opinion we have no direct knowledge of Calvin's religious history during his studies in law at Orléans or Bourges, nor can any connection of Wolmar or Olivétan with that development be proved from the sources at our disposal.[3] Wernle inclines to Muller's association of Calvin's "conversion" with the inward questionings aroused by participation in the Roman service of August, 1533, at Noyon.

It must be clear that a main cause of the wide divergency of these conclusions regarding the time and nature of Calvin's conversion is to be found in the scantiness of the evidence. Calvin's own reticence, to say nothing of the remoteness of the time at which he wrote from the events to which he cursorily alludes, the even greater removal in point of time of his earliest biographers, and the fragmentary remains of his correspondence, leave much room to conjecture and give but an imperfect foundation for the erection of a structure of solidly buttressed historical facts. To the present writer none of the careful interpretations just cited is wholly satisfactory; but he can offer his own attempted reconstruction only with the consciousness that it is equally tentative and fallible.

[3] Wernle would trace Beza's statement regarding Olivétan's influence simply to Calvin's allusion to his acquaintance with that reformer as "*vetus nostra familiaritas*" in his Preface to Olivétan's translation of the Bible (*Opera*, ix 790)

It would seem that Calvin's family experiences must have done not a little to loosen the hold of the Church upon him, even if it be thought that Lefranc has claimed too much. To have a father and a brother fall into open conflict with the ecclesiastical authorities, even though the causes were only financial and disciplinary, must certainly have disposed a boy just passing into manhood toward an attitude of criticism. This need not have gone far, but it must have left the mind in some degree open to discussion of the claims of the establishment with which his relatives were in controversy, even though that controversy was with a local Chapter and in no sense with the Church as a whole. Furthermore, the statement of Beza and Colladon that Calvin's initiation into Reformed sentiments was effected by Olivétan is so definite that it must reflect the impression prevalent among Calvin's friends during his later life, and have some probable basis in fact. Mistake here is far less likely than regarding the date and extent of Calvin's early religious activity. The long acquaintance of Calvin with Olivétan is witnessed by Calvin's own description, in 1535, of their friendship as *vetus nostra familiaritas*.[1] It is difficult to find a place for this influence later than 1528, except on the improbable supposition that it was by letters of which we have now no hint, written after Olivétan had fled from Orléans to Strassburg in the spring of that year.

[1] Preface to Olivétan's French Bible, *Opera*, ix. 790. This seems to the writer a sufficient justification for Beza's conclusion even if it is, as Wernle believes, only Beza's conjecture from the phrase itself

Supposing Olivétan's influence to fall in Calvin's early days at the University of Orléans, it came at a time when the young scholar was not merely escaping from the severities and mediævalism of the Collège de Montaigu into greater liberty of advanced student life, and the more humanistic atmosphere of Orléans, but at a season when Gérard Cauvin's difficulties with the Chapter at Noyon had developed and that ambitious father had determined that his son should exchange theology for law. The statement of Beza that Calvin turned to the study of law partly because of opposition to the old Church, receives, however, no confirmation from Calvin's own writings, which represent it as a step taken merely in deference to his father's wishes. Yet Olivétan, or some other impelling cause, seems to have led Calvin, if one can judge from his declaration to Westphal,[1] to look into one of Luther's fiery discussions of the Lord's Supper at this time; though with the result that he was more antagonised by such Protestant polemics than attracted. He began to know something now of the questions at issue, but to hold as Doumergue does, that this initiation, slight even in that historian's opinion, deserves the name of a "sudden conversion" seems an error.

At Orléans and at Bourges Calvin undoubtedly found himself in an atmosphere favourable to the humanistic ideas of churchly reform Sympathy with the thought of a betterment of the Church by education, preaching, purer morals, and, above all, by a return from mediævalism to the sources of Christian truth, such as Erasmus had urged, was widespread in France,

[1] *Ante*, p. 76.

and nowhere more so than in the universities. It involved no intention to break with the historic Roman Church. The Cops at Paris, Daniel and Duchemin at Orléans, to speak only of Calvin's friends, were of this way of thinking. Le Fèvre, Briçonnet, Roussel, and Marguerite d'Angoulême had even made it fashionable. Calvin must have felt its influence about him, and undoubtedly sympathised with it. It is quite possible that Wolmar may have contributed to the development of these reformatory sympathies; but proof is wanting of any further service on his part to Calvin than instruction in Greek. Earnest and serious-minded always, and the holder of an ecclesiastical benefice, it is not impossible that some basis of truth may underlie the report of Beza and Colladon that he preached on occasion at Lignières, though, if so, it could not have been, as even Doumergue has pointed out, as a Protestant.[1]

But to regard Calvin as a centre of Evangelical religious activity during his stay at Orléans and Bourges, as Beza does, and as the spiritual guide of Daniel and Duchemin as Doumergue interprets Beza's statement, seems unwarranted for several reasons Calvin himself says that his activity as a religious instructor was after his "sudden conversion,"[2]—an event which, it will be seen, took place not about 1528, but subsequently to his first period of study at Orléans with which we have now to do. Moreover Beza apparently drew from Calvin's own statement just referred to his

[1] I 191, 192

[2] *Ante*, p. 72.

knowledge of the activity which he mistakenly ascribed to this period.[1] And, chief reason of all, the remains of Calvin's correspondence show him in no such light. It is not a sufficient answer to say with Doumergue[2] that the search and seizure of Calvin's letters which Beza and Colladon report as having taken place, to the peril of his friends, after Cop's Address, proves the existence of letters of a different sort and that what remain are the "non-Evangelical," and therefore harmless residuum. To say little of the fact that the existence of letters showing Evangelical activity late in 1533 would prove nothing as to such activity in 1528–31, Calvin's letters sent to his friends were not seized with his papers, since they were not in his, but in the friends' possession. It is well-nigh a moral impossibility that side by side with the cordial student-like, but religiously colourless letters which have survived of Calvin's earliest correspondence, there could have been another series in which the writer took the totally different rôle of religious adviser. Nor is Calvin's interest in religious questions any more actively

[1] Compare Calvin with Beza, *Opera*, xxxi. 22 with xxi. 122

| CALVIN | BEZA. |
|---|---|
| Itaque aliquo verae pietatis gustu imbutus tanto proficiendi studio exarsi, ut reliqua studia, quamvis non abjicerem, frigidius tamen sectarer Necdum elapsus erat annus quum omnis purioris doctrinae cupidi ad me novitium adhuc et tironem discendi causa ventitabant | Interea tamen ille sacrarum literarum studium simul diligenter excolere, in quo tantum etiam promoverat ut quicunque in ea urbe aliquo purioris religionis cognoscendae studio tangebantur ad eum etiam percontandum ventitarent |

[2] I 354, 355.

evident in his *Commentary on Seneca.* True he quotes the Bible three times—and three times only—but the passages thus relatively few in proportion to the mass of his citation are of no significance as bearing on the burning religious problems of the times.[1] In fact Lang's contention seems sustained that certainly till after the publication of the *Commentary* just cited, in April, 1532, Calvin's interest in religious questions was inconsiderable compared with his zeal for humanistic scholarship.

But between that publication and Cop's Address of November 1, 1533, a great change had taken place in Calvin, and the query naturally arises whether it is not this change that he describes as his "sudden conversion." His account of that experience shows that he regarded it as a crisis of the utmost significance, wrought by nothing less than divine power. Can that "conversion" have been only the beginning of a long period of gradual development, as Doumergue would have it,—an experience to be dated in 1528? It is Doumergue's opinion that Calvin states distinctly, in the passage already often cited,[2] that his conversion occurred while engaged in the study of law under his father's command. The phrase used does not seem to the present writer to demand that interpretation. He says that God "finally" (*finalement, tandem*) turned

[1] He cites Prov xvi 14, as illustrative of royal anger; Romans, chapter xiii, as proving that "the powers that be are ordained of God," and I Peter ii 18, as enjoining duties on masters toward their servants.

[2] *Ante*, p 72; Doumergue, i. 344.

him. It is as if Calvin anticipated the reader's question why, if he studied law, he was not a lawyer. God "at length" interfered; but he speaks as if much had happened before that interference occurred. Be this as it may, the conclusion is much more certain that is to be drawn from Calvin's statement, in the same passage, that, "before a year passed, all those who had some desire for pure doctrine betook themselves to me in order to learn, although I myself had done little more than begin. For my part, I commenced to seek some hiding-place and means of withdrawing from people." Calvin here speaks not as a student attendant on classes, but as one able to find a home for himself where he will. His search for a quiet resting-place fits in much more naturally with the months of wandering after Cop's Address than with student life at Orléans or Bourges. Furthermore, the relative indifference which Calvin declares he felt after his conversion to studies other than religious, is hard to conceive as previous to the publication of the *Commentary on Seneca*, which reveals on every page unwearied zeal in the mastery of the Greek and Latin classics. A just conclusion seems to be that Calvin's conversion must have occurred between the completion of that *Commentary* and the delivery of Cop's Address, and probably toward a year before the latter date, that is late in 1532 or early in 1533.

Calvin's conversion, moreover, does not appear to have been, as Lefranc and Lecoultre hold, one of the will only. It was, whenever it occurred, an enlightening of the understanding, no less than a determination to act. Henceforth to the eager young humanist religion became the chief concern. If we ask for the human agents in this transformation, however, the answer is difficult. The situation in Paris in the summer and autumn of 1533 was extremely favourable to the spread of Reformed opinions. Lang's suggestion of the Paris Lenten preacher of that year, Gérard Roussel, as Calvin's guide into the freer faith is not impossible. Roussel and Calvin were certainly friends in 1533, and on the strength of this friendship, Calvin upbraided Roussel, in 1537, for lack of courage to refuse a bishopric and leave the Roman communion.[1] But, if our conjecture as to the date of the conversion is at all justified, it may more probably have taken place at Orléans during Calvin's second sojourn there, when representative of the Picard "nation"; and as to its human agents, if any, it is in that case hard to say. Calvin himself referred it to the agency of God; and, if we have understood his letter to Sadoleto aright,[2] it was the conviction that God spoke directly to him through the Scriptures that formed the central element in that experience. That conviction might have come to such a man as Calvin in the quiet of his study with no less force than if impressed upon him by public discourse or friendly exhortation.

If, then, Calvin had come, by November, 1533, to doctrinal positions now universally recognised as characteristic of Protestantism, and the logical outcome of which was soon to be separation from Rome, it by no

[1] *Opera*, v 279–312; xxi 127

[2] *Ante*, p. 73.

means follows that he recognised the full consequences of his beliefs or regarded himself as a Protestant. On August 23d he was present at a meeting of the Chapter at Noyon. On October 27th, he could express himself to Daniel in a way that showed that he held himself in full sympathy with the humanistic reformers.[1] He also sent to Daniel a treatise of Roussel for confidential circulation, and he may well have shared Roussel's hope that the Church of France might be reformed from within by purer preaching and truer doctrine, without breach of its historic continuity. Nothing more radical than this is necessarily involved even in Cop's Address. Certainly it was not till the following May that Calvin resigned his benefices.

It was an ancient custom of the University that the newly elected incumbent of the annual office of rector should give an inaugural oration before the academic world and such of the general public as chose to be present in the Church of the Mathurins on All Saints'. The new rector, Nicolas Cop, Calvin's warm friend, had sufficiently followed his distinguished father's profession to have graduated as Bachelor in Medicine; but, since 1530, he had taught philosophy in the Collège Sainte-Barbe. The brief rectorate of only twenty-one days since his election had seen him actively intervening in the religious questions of the hour as a supporter of Marguerite d'Angoulême and of the freer type of preaching which she countenanced. When the conservatives of the University had desired to condemn that queen's *Le miroir de l'âme pêcheresse*, and had

[1] *Ante*, p 68.

been called to account by King Francis, as has been already narrated,[1] Cop had summoned the Faculties to consider the royal letters on October 24th, and had shown himself a determined and successful defender of the queenly author in the heated debate that followed. He had therefore already entered the lists as a champion of reform as represented by Marguerite d'Angoulême, and he now determined to make his inaugural oration tell in the same cause. He would make a declaration of significance against conservatism and in favour of reform; and so bold was the utterance, considering the time and place of its delivery, that it became at once the sensation of the hour.

Pierson has, indeed, queried whether Cop's Address is really known to us.[2] His criticism has, however, been destructively answered by Lang.[3] A letter of Bucer, probably in January 1534, to Ambrose Blaurer of Constance, speaks of the delivery of an oration by Cop, with such insistence on justifying faith as to cause his flight.[4] Consonant with this contemporary testimony as to the nature of Cop's Address are the statements of Colladon in his *Life of Calvin* of 1565.[5] That the Address which we now have is that pronounced by Cop is furthermore attested by an annotation in a sixteenth century hand on the manuscript

[1] *Ante*, p 68

[2] *Studien over Kalvijn*, pp. 72–78.

[3] *Die ältesten theologischen Arbeiten Calvin's*, in the *Neue Jahrbücher für deutsche Theologie*, ii 273–282 (1893).

[4] Herminjard, iii 129.

[5] *Opera*, xxi 56.

of a portion of it now in the Library of Geneva,[1] and is borne out by its contents. There is therefore no reasonable question that Cop's academic oration of November 1, 1533, has been preserved.

While Cop's Address is therefore well known, Calvin's authorship of it is by no means certain. In favour of that authorship may be urged the facts that Colladon evidently believed the work to be that of Calvin when, about 1570, he prepared Calvin's papers for the press;[2] but, above all, that the fragment of the Address now in the Library at Geneva is indisputably in Calvin's handwriting.[3] Against it are the considerations that the style seems hardly equal to Calvin's usual brilliant Latinity; that Colladon, in his *Life* of 1565, speaks only of Calvin's friendship with Cop, not of any authorship of Cop's Address, and that only in his final *Life*, that of 1575, does Beza declare that "Calvin furnished it."[4] These facts raise the question whether Colladon's attribution of authorship to Calvin, witnessed by his inscription on the manuscript, was not simply a deduction from a discovery, after his

[1] The hand is certainly that of Nicolas Colladon, Herminjard, iii 418, Müller, *Calvins Bekehrung*, pp 226, 228 The fragment at Geneva, containing the first sheet, is printed in Herminjard, iii 418–420, *Opera*, ix 872–876; and given in photographic facsimile by Müller, *op cit* The whole Address is printed (poorly) from a manuscript in the *Thomas-archiv* (now *Stadtarchiv*) at Strassburg, in *Opera*, xb 30–36

[2] So even Müller holds, p 231.

[3] Herminjard, iii 420, *Opera*, ix, Preface, lxxii, Lang, *op cit*, p. 274, Müller, p 224, who cites the emphatic testimony of the present director of the Geneva Library, M H V Aubert

[4] *Opera*, xxi 123

*Life* of 1565 was written, of that manuscript in Calvin's well-known handwriting. Professor Muller, to whom this striking suggestion is due, has furthermore presented evidence that the complete form of the Address preserved in Strassburg is not a perfected oration based on Calvin's manuscript as its first draft, as Lang held, but that both are copies of a now lost original.[1] Calvin may simply have desired to preserve his friend's work.

Whether Calvin actually composed any part of Cop's Address is therefore at best doubtful. The weight of evidence certainly now inclines to the negative side. But of Calvin's hearty interest in the Address there can be no question,—the existence of the manuscript in his handwriting is sufficient evidence of that, if of no more. Even though not his composition, it can hardly have been delivered without consultation between the two friends. It is impossible to suppose Calvin ignorant of it. In view of his intimacy with Cop it may therefore properly be cited as a witness to the religious development which Calvin had attained at the date of its delivery. It is no less interesting in its revelation of the books by which the spiritual life of the circle of which Cop and Calvin were members had been fostered.

Its form is that of a sermon. The Address opens with an apostrophe to "Christian Philosophy,"—that is to the Gospel, as ascertained by a study of its sources, and distinguished from current scholastic theology. As

[1] Lang, *op cit*, p 28, Müller, pp 231–237.

Lang has discovered,[1] both the phrase and the treatment are borrowed from Erasmus. The thought and not a little even of the language of this introduction rest back on Erasmus's Preface to the third edition of his Greek New Testament, published in 1524. This "Christian Philosophy," the orator declares, shows us that we are sons of God. To proclaim it, God became man. Those who have its knowledge exceed other men as men in general are superior to beasts. It is the worthiest of sciences. It reveals the remission of sins by the mere grace of God. It shows that the Holy Spirit, who sanctifies the heart and guides to life eternal, is promised to all Christians. It gives peace to distressed minds and leads to good and happy living. Having thus praised the Gospel as a whole, the speaker remarks that some selection from its wealth must be made if the limits of a discourse are to be observed, and he therefore takes as his text a verse from the Gospel read in the appointed service of the day: "Blessed are the poor in spirit." The introduction concludes with a brief invocation of the aid of Christ as "the true and only intercessor with the Father," that the discourse to follow "may praise Him, may savour of Him, may breathe Him, may call Him to mind"; and, having said this, it adds the then customary salutation to the Virgin,—a combination that illustrates the partially developed status of the reform movement at Paris.

If the writer of the discourse thus reveals the influence of Erasmus in his introduction, the first part of

[1] *Bekehrung*, pp. 44–46, *Opera*, xb. 30–31

the body of the Address which follows shows even greater use of a sermon preached by Luther, on occasion of the same church festival, probably in 1522, in which the German reformer, in treating of the Beatitudes, had discussed the relations of Law and Gospel.[1] Thanks to a Latin translation, by Martin Bucer of Strassburg, of the collection of Luther's sermons in which this has a place, it had been accessible to the learned world since 1525, and later editions had been issued in 1528 and 1530. Though not expressly mentioned, it may have been one of the volumes of the reformers, which Berthold Haller found more or less openly for sale at Paris in August, 1533.[2] In words modelled on this discourse of Luther the Parisian speaker tells his hearers: "The Law drives by commands, threatens, urges, promises no goodwill. The Gospel drives by no threats, does not force by commands, teaches God's utmost goodwill towards us." He encounters, as Luther does, the objection that Christ had said in the passage under consideration, "For great is your reward in heaven." Are not the Beatitudes then a new law, the keeping of which earns a reward? No, they set forth the Gospel, and the author explains with an illustration all his own, likening him who lives deserving of the Beatitudes to a son who has striven in a father's lifetime to do that father's pleasure, and who receives an inheritance, which may be called a reward of faithful sonship, though in no sense a debt due for filial service. The author then

[1] Lang, *Bekehrung*, pp 47–54; *Opera*, xb. 31–33.

[2] Herminjard, iii. 75

pays his respects to the "sophists"—unquestionably the conservative Roman theologians of the University of Paris—who "contend perpetually about trifles" to the neglect of "Christian Philosophy."

The speaker invokes the blessing of the peacemakers on the controversies of the time. "Would that in this our unhappy age we restore peace in the Church by the Word rather than by the sword." But the orator evidently foresees the impossibility of the fulfilment of his desire, and exclaims, "Twice blessed are they who endure persecution for righteousness' sake"; and he closes with a fervently expressed wish that God "may open our minds that we may believe the Gospel."

That this lofty and spiritually-minded Address was a carefully planned manifesto in behalf of Protestantism is an opinion that has often been expressed. Of its boldness there can be no question. But its wisdom, under the circumstances of its delivery, is not so evident. The reform movement had been growing by the tolerance of the King and the support of his gifted sister, largely because it had not, at Paris, greatly passed the bounds of orderly discussion. True, it had had its martyrs like Berquin, but the favourable situation of the movement in the year 1533 was due in no small degree to a comparative moderation which had not forfeited the goodwill of the King. Anything likely to exasperate the situation was, we can now see, certain to lead to repression of the innovating forces. But that was not then so apparent. Cop may have believed that the royal authority would support him as it had already aided Roussel through Marguerite d'Angoulême.

Much more probably there was no deep and far-sighted plan behind the Address. It grew, almost on the moment, out of the impulsive enthusiasm of a young man who, suddenly called to a great position in the University, had found himself a leader in resistance to an attempt to discipline the scholarly, reformatory, and popular Queen of Navarre, and the humanistic reformers whom she favoured. The opportunity to continue before a larger public the discussion of the principles involved in the University session of October 24th, of which their minds were full, and in which the young rector had borne a conspicuous part, is a sufficient explanation of Cop's action and of Calvin's aid if such aid was given. Protestant in doctrine as the Address is, and opposed to the "sophists" of the Sorbonne, it betrays no evidence that its author thought that he was putting himself outside the communion of the Roman Church. Ideas and expressions are borrowed from Luther; but the German reformer is not mentioned, and it is his doctrine of the way of salvation, not his breach with the Papacy, that interests him. Yet the Address clearly shows the sources from which Cop and probably Calvin were drawing their spiritual life. The New Testament, Erasmus, and Luther had already made Calvin a Protestant in most of his beliefs, and would inevitably place him on the Protestant side when lines of division should be more closely drawn.

# CHAPTER V

## FLIGHT FOR SAFETY IN CONCEALMENT AND VOLUNTARY EXILE

THE effect of Cop's bold Address was to show that the strength of the conservative party in Paris was greater than its speaker and his friends could have anticipated, if, as is unlikely, they had deliberately counted the cost before its delivery on the first of November. They doubtless expected the resentful hostility of the Theological Faculty, which he had so severely arraigned. But a more formidable adversary almost immediately appeared in the great judicial court, the Parlement of Paris, aroused not improbably by the efforts of the exasperated theologians. On complaint of two Franciscan monks, the Parlement now began proceedings against Cop for heresy. He answered at once by summoning a session of the Faculties of the University, which met on November 19th in the same Church of the Mathurins in which his discourse had been delivered. Before this academic assembly the young rector urged that the proceedings of his accusers and of Parlement were an invasion of the privileges of the University, which should have had at least primary jurisdiction in the matter of the alleged heresy of its officers. The contention would ordinarily have been effective; but, thanks probably to a vastly prevailing want of sympathy with his radical theological opinions, Cop found but a divided support. The Faculties of Medicine and of Arts took his side, those of Theology and of Law were opposed; and no action by the University as a whole could be had.[1] Cop felt the ground slipping from under his feet. On November 26th, proceedings were begun by the Faculty of Theology which resulted in the arrest of Roussel and of a preacher whom we shall meet at Geneva, Élie Coraud.[2] The same day the Parlement stated the situation to the King, and on December 10th he wrote from Lyons enjoining strict suppression of "the Lutheran sect."[3] Many of the Reform party were thrown into prison. Cop himself avoided this fate by flight, apparently before November 26th,[4] and ultimate refuge in the shelter of the Protestant city of Basel, which had, years before, been his father's home. Soon a reward of three hundred crowns was offered for his capture alive or dead.[5]

These experiences of his friend must have filled Calvin with well-grounded anxiety for his own safety. His relations to Cop had been so intimate as to involve him in suspicion. The authorities, probably late in November, therefore sent to his room in the Collège Fortet which had been his home when in Paris since 1531, hoping to effect his arrest. News of this intention

[1] Bulæus, *Hist Univ Paris*, vi 239.

[2] Herminjard, iii. 146, note

[3] *Ibid*, 114

[4] King Francis, whose information probably came from the letters of Parlement, speaks of his flight in his order of December 10th *Ibid.*, 117 He reached Basel January 25, 1534 Doumergue, i 354.

[5] Herminjard, iii 130

reached him in season to effect his escape.[1] His papers were seized, to the peril of his friends, but he himself found refuge, according to a late but not impossible report, at Noyon,[2] whither the same account says, with much greater likelihood of legendary embellishment, that he made his way disguised as a vine-dresser. Calvin cannot, however, have been as conspicuously before the public as an advocate of reform as Cop, Roussel, or Coraud; and his self-imposed exile from Paris was brief at this time. Marguerite d'Angoulême is said to have interested herself in his behalf. Proceedings against Calvin were dropped; and he returned to Paris perhaps to be received honourably by this benefactress who had a welcome for scholars of the new learning and humanistic reformatory impulse.[3] Even the friendliness of this reception, if it took place, gave Calvin no sense of security; and, partly because Paris was a place of peril, partly also to seek the peace and scholarly retirement which he loved, he soon left the city. If a conjecture may be hazarded where the chronology is so obscure, this second departure was in the opening month of 1534, or even possibly in the last days of 1533.

Fortunately an agreeable asylum opened for him at once at Angoulême, some two hundred and fifty miles southwest of Paris, in the home of a young clerical

[1] P. Masson, *Elogiorum*, p. 414, alleges that he escaped by a window, but Beza and Colladon, *Opera*, xxi 56, 123, simply say that he was not found at home Compare Doumergue, i 354

[2] Jacques Desmay, in *Archives curieuses*, v 393

[3] Beza, in *Opera*, xxi. 123. The whole matter is doubtful Compare Müller, p 214, and Wernle, p. 93

friend, Louis du Tillet, seigneur of Haultmont, canon of the cathedral of Angoulême and rector also of the village church of Claix about ten miles out of the city. The du Tillets were of a family of Angoulême which had risen into prominence in the service of the State. The father had been Vice-President of the royal Chamber of Accounts at Paris. Of Louis's three older brothers, one had held and another was now holding the office of chief Registrar of the Parlement of Paris, and a third had, like Louis, entered the Church in which he was to become, at a much later period (1562), bishop of Meaux. The family was no less conspicuous for its learning, and the home at Angoulême held a remarkable library, said to have contained three or four thousand manuscripts and printed books.[1] How Calvin's friendship with the young canon may have been begun there is no certain information; but he seems to have been about Calvin's age, and the conjecture lies close at hand that they were fellow-students. The du Tillets, like the Cops, belonged to the class that had profited by royal favour and had also welcomed the new learning, and among such people the humanistic conceptions of reform as advocated by Erasmus, Le Fèvre, and Roussel, found ready hearing. Calvin and Louis du Tillet had many studious tastes in common,[2] and a good deal of religious sympathy, but du Tillet, as compared with Calvin, was a man of weak courage,

[1] Florimond de Ræmond, *Naissance*, etc., p 885

[2] Calvin said of du Tillet to Daniel, probably in March, 1534, "the kindness of my patron . is such that I readily understand that it is shown for the sake of letters, not for myself," *Opera*, xb. 37.

and of convictions which, though inclining him to throw in his lot with the reformers for a season, led him ultimately back into the Roman communion. At this time, however, he and Calvin were undoubtedly in substantial religious agreement.

Here at Angoulême, and at the neighbouring Claix, Calvin, as he told his friend Daniel in a letter intentionally indefinite as to his whereabouts and occupations,[1] found not merely a kind "patron" in du Tillet, whose generosity he recognises in the warmest terms, but opportunity for study. The letter shows that he is valued by his host not merely as a friend, but for what he has to give; and the religious note now dominant in Calvin's life sounds clear in his expression of gratitude to God to whose wise providence he cheerfully intrusts his future. Calvin's note to his friend implies that he was aiding du Tillet in literary studies, and this intimation gives countenance to the statement of Florimond de Ræmond, published more than seventy years later, but probably written at a period considerably less remote, that Calvin instructed his friend in Greek.[2] According to the same writer, he was popularly nicknamed "the Greek of Claix," from the name of the country parish where du Tillet was beneficed, and where apparently he resided a portion of the time. At du Tillet's home, or, if Florimond de Ræmond was correctly informed, at Girac, a house belonging to the prior of Bouteville, Antoine Chaillou, outside of Angoulême, on the road to Claix, Calvin was accustomed

[1] *Opera*, xb 37.

[2] *Naissance*, etc, pp 883–885, see also Doumergue, i 370–373

to meet with the prior just named, with the abbot of Bassac, with du Tillet, and du Tillet's cousin, the seigneur de Torsac. Among Calvin's acquaintances at Angoulême was also, by his own testimony,[1] the young brother of the scholar last named, Pierre de la Place, later to be an eminent Huguenot lawyer and one of the victims of the massacre of St. Bartholomew. In this company Calvin discussed not merely congenial topics relating to classical learning, but matters of religion; and evidently with sympathetic appreciation, for Beza, as well as Colladon, report that, at du Tillet's request, he wrote Evangelical sermons for the use of certain pastors of the region who had caught something of the reformatory spirit.[2]

Of greater significance for his future was the beginning, in this period of retirement at Angoulême, of the studies which were to result in the first edition of his *Institutes*. How far they had made progress by the time he was to leave France there is no means to determine; but a careful examination of such hints as Calvin's own writings afford confirms at least enough of Florimond de Ræmond's assertion that Calvin wrote part of the *Institutes* at Angoulême to carry the conviction that Calvin must have planned and made preparation for this great service to Protestantism while du Tillet's guest, and doubtless with the aid of du Tillet's notable library.[3]

Calvin's friendship for Gérard Roussel has already been mentioned. Warmly committed to the reform

[1] *Opera*, xii 681.

[2] *Ibid*, xxi 56, 57, 123

[3] The whole subject is carefully discussed by the Strassburg editors, *Opera*, iii, Introduction, pp xi–xiv.

movement which Roussel had represented at Paris and for which that eloquent mystic had been suffering a brief imprisonment during the stormy days after the delivery of Cop's Address, it was natural that Calvin should desire to make the acquaintance of Roussel's venerable master, the leader of the humanistic reformers of France, Jacques Le Fèvre. The aged scholar was spending his last days under the protection of Marguerite d'Angoulême at Nérac, the little capital of French Navarre, and thither Calvin journeyed for a brief visit to the kindly old man.[1] The journey may be placed, with considerable probability, about the beginning of April, 1534, and, if so, is interestingly coincident with the publication, at Antwerp, early in the same month, of Le Fèvre's corrected and revised edition of his translation of the Bible into French.[2]

Calvin's work, in this period, was still that of the retiring scholar rather than of the preacher or public reformer. That he was yet to become, but not till circumstances were to force him into a rôle foreign to his natural disposition. He was already planning his great exposition of Christian doctrine, though it was but a brief handbook that he yet had in mind. He was already a leader in the little circles which he quietly influenced. His power to make friends, especially among those of good position and scholarly tastes, was remarkable. But the public Evangelical activity traditionally attributed to him before his departure

[1] Beza and Colladon, *Opera*, xxi 57, 123; Doumergue, i. 380–415.
[2] Doumergue, i 380, 401

from France, and illustrated in popular nomenclature by so-called "Calvin's pulpits," at Bourges, Nérac, Clairac,[1] —places destined later to suffer for their acceptance of the Protestant position in religion—and elsewhere, is greatly exaggerated. What he did for the Evangelical cause—and his work was not small—was still by inconspicuous and personal relations. Unjustified as was the taunt thrown at Calvin in December, 1538, by du Tillet, then returned to the Roman communion, this former intimate friend witnesses at least to the private character of Calvin's efforts in this period when he says: "It is before those to the greater part of whom you know your doctrine to be pleasing that you maintain it, not elsewhere, for you have abandoned your country because you did not dare to set it forth and maintain it publicly there."[2]

Calvin's development since the commotion aroused by Cop's Address had compelled him to leave Paris was leading him to a decision which would sever formally his connection with the Roman Church. He had held benefices at Noyon since May, 1521. He was now approaching the age of twenty-five, the normal time for ordination to the priesthood, when a decision as to his personal relations to the ecclesiastical duties thus far discharged by his deputies was to be expected.[3] These motives counselled a determination of his own future. Should he go forward, like Roussel, du Tillet, or other of his humanistic reformatory friends,

[1] Doumergue, i 416.

[2] *Opera*, xb 299.

[3] Doumergue, i 426

holding doctrines in many respects Evangelical, but refusing to break with the Church which they hoped to reform from within, and accepting promotion in its service? Or should he come out from it altogether? The decision must have been a difficult one. Honours, literary opportunity, even possibly greater usefulness, might easily seem to sway the balance in favour of a conclusion to remain. Exile, poverty, and struggle could alone, apparently, result from separation from the Roman Church. But Calvin's mind was determined. On May 4, 1534, the first certain date in Calvin's career since that of Cop's Address, his chaplaincy at the cathedral at Noyon, vacant by Calvin's resignation, was transferred to another by the Chapter;[1] and at or about the same date Calvin laid aside his rectorship at Pont-l'Évêque.[2] Probably he had taken the long journey across France from Nérac to Noyon to make the resignation in person; certainly he was in Noyon later in the same month.

The time was one of excitement and apprehension in the city. On January 19th, previous, a procession had been held in expiation of the heretical disorders of the age; on May 6th, two days after Calvin's resigned benefice had been given to his successor, an investigation based on a charge of heresy was begun, as secretly as possible, by the Chapter against his quick-tempered and contumacious older brother, Charles John Calvin himself could hardly hope to escape suspicion under such circumstances, however circumspect he had thus

[1] Records, in Lefranc, *Jeunesse*, p 201

[2] Desmay, in *Archives curieuses*, p 395; Doumergue, 1 425.

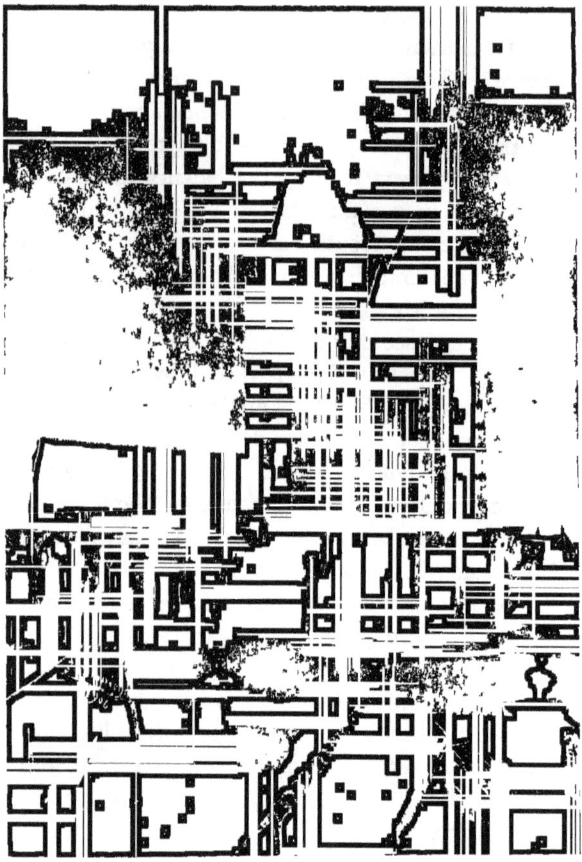

THE CATHEDRAL, NOYON.
(Reproduced by permission of Georges Compiègne, Noyon.)

far been in avoidance of publicity in the advocacy of Reformed doctrines. It is of great interest therefore to find that Calvin was imprisoned at Noyon on May 26th "for uproar made in the church on the eve of Holy Trinity," three days before.[1] The place of his confinement, the prison of the Chapter known as La Porte Corbaut is still standing, a little building, strongly barred, containing a small court-room, below which are two dungeons and above which are two cells of less forbidding aspect.[2] From this confinement Calvin was released on the eighth day of incarceration, only to be rearrested and again imprisoned on June 5th, two days later. How long this second confinement may have lasted, or under what circumstances he was finally set free, there is no means at present of forming an opinion; but in view of the very considerable activity which he was yet to show before leaving France, and the time that it must have required, his second imprisonment cannot have been more than a few weeks in duration at longest. It may, like his first, have been for a few days only.

Unfortunately little can definitely be affirmed regarding the circumstances of Calvin's arrest in his native city. Lang's view that the "uproar" in church was due to an attempt to proclaim Evangelical doctrine[3] has been effectively criticised by Doumergue, who points out that such action would have been little in consonance with Calvin's character. Nor does the

[1] Records, Lefranc, *Jeunesse*, p. 21.

[2] Doumergue, i 25, 427.

[3] *Bekehrung*, p 13, compare Doumergue, i 427.

vacillation of the Noyon authorities regarding Calvin's imprisonment indicate that they had any clearly defined charge against him, such as would have been furnished by a public attack on Roman worship or doctrine. The conjecture would seem more probable by far that popular opinion judged Calvin to be a "heretic" and found expression in an outbreak in the church. His arrest followed; but the charges against him very probably did not seem sufficiently warranted to be pressed, though suspicion availed to place him twice for a brief period in custody. Fortunately for the future reformer his arrest and imprisonment did not prove the road to the stake.

With this imprisonment two of the most careful of recent students of Calvin's history, Lefranc and Doumergue, connect whatever slight shred of fact may have served as a thread on which to hang one of the most baseless and absurd, as well as one of the most persistent of the calumnies by which Calvin's memory has been assailed. In the bitter controversies of the sixteenth and seventeenth centuries, Calvin was charged, especially after his death and that of the generation that had known him, with drunkenness, licentiousness, and, strangely enough, with ignorance.[1] These contumelies were too often in that age the weapons of all shades of theological controversialists, when vituperation was employed to an extent now almost inconceivable. The more specific charge, to which reference is now made, was formulated thirteen years after Calvin's death, by Jérôme Hermès Bolsec, a one-time Carmelite monk

[1] *E g.* Laing, *De Vita et Moribus atque Rebus gestis Haereticorum nostri Temporis*, Paris, 1581 Doumergue, i. 429

of Paris, who settled, about 1550, as a Protestant and a physician at Veigy, near Geneva Falling into a controversy with Calvin, of which an account will be given on a later page, he was banished from Geneva in December, 1551; and ultimately returned to the Roman Church. He naturally felt bitterly toward Calvin's memory; but the revenge which he now took is one which recoils on himself through the revelation of his own unscrupulous character. According to Bolsec's allegation[1] he had seen a report prepared by a "Bertelier," (probably Philibert Berthelier is meant,) and legally attested by the most prominent people of Noyon, whither he alleges Bertelier had been sent by Genevans desirous of investigating Calvin's early life, witnessing that Calvin had been convicted of heinous moral turpitude,[2] the punishment for which was then death by fire, but that the bishop of Noyon had commuted the extreme penalty into branding a fleur-de-lys with a red-hot iron, as a perpetual mark of infamy, on the future reformer's shoulder. No evidence has ever been produced of the existence of such a document as Bolsec alleges. Jacques Desmay, the earnest Catholic writer who used his stay as Advent and Lenten preacher at Noyon in 1614 and 1615 to learn all he could of Calvin's life there by records and tradition, found nothing of it.[3] An equally determined Roman historian of Noyon, Jacques Le Vasseur, in

[1] *Histoire de la vie, mœurs, actes, constance, et mort de Jean Calvin*, Lyons, 1577, chap. v , Lefranc, *Jeunesse*, p 176.

[2] Genesis xix 5.

[3] Pp 15, 16, in fac-simile in Doumergue, i. 434, 435.

his *Annales* of 1633, expressly repudiated it;[1] and careful modern Roman Catholic scholars, such as Kampschulte[2] and Paulus,[3] reject it as "unworthy of serious refutation." When repeated in the name of Cardinal Richelieu, in a volume published after the death of that statesman-prelate, it was the immediate cause of the elaborate and scholarly defence of Calvin's memory by Charles Drelincourt,[4] and its utter worthlessness has been recently exhibited in examples of historical criticism as brilliant as they are convincing by Lefranc[5] and Doumergue.[6] Whatever explication of the growth of such a fable may be found beside the malignant invention of theological controversialists, is to be discovered in the obscurity of the circumstances of Calvin's imprisonment,—the first instance of which is, however, expressly declared in the records to have been "for uproar made in the church,"—and to the remarkable coincidence of name, reported by Desmay and Le Vasseur.[7] They report that in 1550 or 1552, when Calvin had long been a well-known resident of Geneva, another John Calvin, whom they carefully distinguished from the reformer, was disciplined by the Chapter at Noyon for a breach of the law of chastity less heinous than that charged by Bolsec. The whole calumny

[1] Pp. 1172, in fac-simile in Doumergue, i 438.

[2] I 224

[3] *Luther Lebensende*, 1898, p 48, Doumergue, i 435

[4] *La défense de Calvin contre l'outrage faite à sa mémoire par le Cardinal de Richelieu*, Geneva, 1663–1667.

[5] *Jeunesse*, pp 48–52, 175–181

[6] I 428–440; iii 516

[7] *Remarques*, p 16, *Annales*, p. 1170, Doumergue, i. 435, 436.

would be unworthy of discussion had the accusation not been repeatedly renewed by a certain class of controversialists during the last century,—in one instance as recently as 1898.[1]

The same uncertainty as to the date and order of events in Calvin's life which attaches to the period from Cop's Address to the resignation of his benefices extends from the beginning of his second imprisonment at Noyon to his departure from France. How long that imprisonment lasted is unknown; but Beza and Colladon speak of a perilous visit to Paris,[2] which may most probably be placed between this imprisonment and the outbreak of persecution consequent upon the posting of Antoine Marcourt's Placards against the mass in the October following. According to the early biographers just cited, the most important incident of this brief and carefully guarded sojourn was an attempted conference with Servetus, at a house in the Rue Saint-Antoine, which failed by reason of the neglect or inability of the radical Spanish theologian to keep his appointment. At Paris Calvin not improbably found a lodging on the Rue Saint-Martin in the home of that earnest Protestant merchant, Estienne de la Forge, who was to give his life for his faith in the February following Calvin's visit; and under la Forge's roof he may have been a witness to that discussion with a member of the sect of "Libertins" of which he gave an account in his attack upon that party of extreme radicals published in 1545.[3] Of la Forge, whom Calvin

[1] Doumergue, i 432

[2] *Opera*, xxi. 57, 123.

[3] *Contre la secte phantastique des Libertins*, *Opera*, vii. 185.

knew well, the future reformer was accustomed to speak in high praise as a man of character, sincerity, and piety.[1]

If it is at least probable that Calvin's visit to Paris, which has just been described, was on his way southward from Noyon toward the friendly shelter of Angoulême immediately after his final release from imprisonment, no such comparative plausibility of conjecture applies to the course of his movements during the next few months. He probably returned, at some time in this period, to Angoulême, for when he leaves France it is in company with Louis du Tillet; he was certainly at Orléans, for he dates from there the first Preface to his *Psychopannychia;* and Florimond de Ræmond gives an account of activity at Poitiers that must have some basis in fact beneath it. As to the relations of these several sojourns one to another, or their length, there is no adequate means of forming a conclusion; and the stay at Orléans may perhaps, though less probably, have occurred before, rather than after, Calvin's imprisonment at Noyon and visit to Paris. Of these three brief halts before leaving his native land, that at Poitiers was significant as marking a new stage in Calvin's relations to Protestant worship, while that at Orléans reveals a new consciousness of his mission as a defender of Evangelical doctrine.

Florimond de Ræmond, writing indeed at a distance in point of time which causes his testimony to be received only with much uncertainty as to its value in

[1] Colladon, *Opera*, xxi. 56.

detail, represents[1] Calvin as entering, largely at first through the gateway of a common interest in letters, into more or less intimate friendship, at Poitiers, that religious city, with a little group of learned men of high station,—François Fouquet, prior of Trois Moutiers, with whom he lodged, Charles le Sage, Professor of Law, Antoine de la Duguie, afterward prominent in the Faculty of Law; Albert Babinot, Lecturer at the University, Philippe Véron and Jean Vernou, all three to be prominent teachers of the Reformed faith, and the last named to give his life in martyrdom; Jean Boisseau, sieur de la Borderie, and even the lieutenant-général, François Doyneau, seigneur de Sainte-Soline. With them Calvin is said to have held long conversations on religious as well as scholarly themes, and over a number of them he acquired much influence. The representation given by Florimond de Ræmond certainly has much verisimilitude to what we know of Calvin otherwise at this period. Not by public preaching, but by private intercourse with the friends that his high scholarship, agreeable manners, and spiritual earnestness readily secured did he now try to advance the reform which had mastered him. But, if the same historian is to be trusted, Calvin now took a step in advance of any progress he had thus far made in the direction of Protestant worship. With some of these friends, in the shelter of a cave outside the city, he observed the Lord's Supper. It was Florimond's opinion that the simple, primitive rite practised by the early Protestants of Poitiers, which he describes, had been

[1] *Naissance*, etc., pp. 891–911; Doumergue, i. 458–464, 580–583.

taught them by Calvin. In its observance the leader read a passage from the Gospels describing the institution of the Sacrament, the Roman mass was then denounced, and those present were invited to the table with the words, "Brethren, let us eat the Lord's bread in memory of His death and passion." Breaking the bread, the leader then gave a fragment to each of those seated with him, and all ate in silence; and in the same way the wine was received Then, after a prayer of thanksgiving by the leader, all repeated the Lord's Prayer and the Apostles' Creed in Latin, and with that the simple service closed.[1] In this fashion, it may be believed, Calvin ministered to the little company; and he justified his rejection of the Roman worship by an appeal to the Scriptures. To Jean Boisseau, sieur de la Borderie, who lived till 1591, Florimond de Ræmond attributed the narrative, which he may not improbably have heard from Boisseau himself, that Calvin, in a debate on the mass held with Charles le Sage during this stay at Poitiers, pointed to the Bible before him with the exclamation:[2]

> There is my mass, and throwing his cap on the table, lifting his eyes toward heaven, he cried. Lord, if on the day of judgment Thou rebukest me because I have not been at mass and have forsaken it, I shall justly say: Lord, Thou hast not commanded it; here is Thy law, here is the Scripture which is the rule that Thou hast given me, in which I could not find any other sacrifice than that which was offered on the altar of the cross.

[1] *Naissance*, p 911, Doumergue, i 460, 525.
[2] *Naissance*, p 906, Doumergue, i 460.

Certainly the story sounds very like a probable incident in the history of that Calvin whose religious development has thus far been followed. It speaks the same confidence that the Scriptures are the direct voice of God, and that they are the only law fully and implicitly to be obeyed, which had been so large factors in Calvin's conversion. But, whether Florimond de Ræmond is correct in these details or not, it is fair to conclude from his account that Calvin began the exercise of Protestant ministerial functions soon after the resignation of his benefices, though only in the comparatively secure company of his friends. Calvin had never been ordained in the Roman Church; he was never to be set apart for the ministry by the imposition of Protestant hands. He regarded his pastoral labours as a task to which he was called of God,—a call witnessed by his own clear consciousness of the divine guidance in appointing him his course in life.[1] His entrance on the pastorate was therefore gradual; but its clear manifestation may, with no little probability, be connected with his stay at Poitiers.

The chief significance of Calvin's stay at Orléans is to be seen in the completion there of his first distinctly theological treatise, the *Psychopannychia*. That Calvin's sojourn in Orléans was long enough to allow time for the composition of the whole tract[2] it is not necessary to suppose; but certainly a brief Preface to the little work was written and dated there.[3] The treatise, which

[1] The matter forms a chief part of his correspondence with du Tillet in 1538, *Opera*, xb 241, 269, 290, see also Doumergue, ii. 407–409.

[2] Doumergue, i 466, so holds.

[3] *Opera*, v. 170, 171.

was not printed till 1542, and then apparently in a revised form, is a refutation, by arguments drawn almost entirely from a careful examination of a great number of Biblical passages, of the opinion that the soul "sleeps without memory, without intelligence, without sensation, from death till the day of judgment, when it will awake from its slumber." The year in which Calvin wrote was one of widespread dread, in more conservative circles, of the rapidly growing Anabaptist movement which was just coming to its most fanatical manifestation in the establishment of what was proclaimed to be the kingdom of God on earth at Munster. The view which he combated was one to be met with among the Anabaptists, though it had neither the prominence among them, the significance in itself, nor the large number of adherents that he ascribes to it. It is difficult to see why Calvin should have selected this relatively insignificant fragment of Anabaptist speculation for refutation unless it had been more than ordinarily discussed in the little group of friends among whom he was in some sense the leader. But, though the treatise belongs distinctly to the minor writings of Calvin, its original Preface, preserved apparently in unchanged form, is of value as revealing something of his mind just before leaving France. Calvin feels that he is called to be a teacher of Christian doctrine. "If in such need I am silent or dissimulate," he says, "I do not see why I should not be called a betrayer of the truth." He must speak in its defence It may be charged, however, that by so doing he fosters schism in the Church and offends charity; but "it may be answered, that we recognise no unity, save in Christ, no charity, save that of which He is the bond; therefore the prime thing in maintaining charity is that the faith should remain inviolate and unchanged among us." The emphasis on purity of doctrine is characteristic of the reformers generally. Luther had set a similar importance upon it in his discussions with Zwingli. Nor is the feeling that by maintaining God's truth, as he saw it, he was purifying rather than dividing the Church, anything peculiar to Calvin. But it is evident that in every way the year 1534 was one of growth in Calvin's religious experience and in recognition of what he believed to be a divine call to a leadership which we may give him credence was in many ways repugnant to his shy and scholarly nature.

As the year 1534 drew toward a close, however, France became increasingly a difficult region of sojourn for a Protestant The rash and violent Placards against the mass, prepared by Antoine Marcourt, and posted on the night of October 17th or 18th, aroused a strenuous, though not long continued, policy of repression. Calvin had been careful in the public manifestation of his opinion, he was not a man to court needless risks, but he had already suffered practical banishment from Paris, and imprisonment at Noyon. His views were well known to many at Angoulême, Poitiers, and Orléans. His friend Louis du Tillet felt no more safe than he. The situation counselled flight from the kingdom if his work was to be continued or his life preserved. And, therefore, in company with du Tillet, aided by two servants, and at least two horses,—largely

it is probable at du Tillet's expense,—Calvin made ]
way through Lorraine to Strassburg and thence to Bas
where he arrived about the beginning of 1535, havi
experienced no more misadventure on the road th
the theft of most of the money of the party and of o
of the horses near Metz by an unfaithful servan
Calvin's friend Cop had found a refuge in the sar
hospitable city just about a year earlier; and his pr
ence there may have been a main reason in induci
Calvin to make it his home.

[1] Beza and Colladon, *Opera*, xxi 57, 124 Calvin was somewl
aided pecuniarily at times by du Tillet, *Ibid*, xb 272.

## CHAPTER VI

### THE "INSTITUTES," ITALY, AND ARRIVAL IN GENEVA

AT Basel Calvin found a lodging in the home of Catherine Klein, who seems for years to have received student guests, in the eastern suburb of the city,—that of St. Alban.[1] Here, as Calvin himself says, he "lived as it were concealed and known to few people,"[2] hidden under the name of Martinus Lucanius. The city afforded not merely a safe retreat, but abundant opportunities for study and publication. The reasons which had induced the now aged Erasmus to make it his home, availed to attract many a less known scholar. Under the leadership of Johann Œcolampadius, whose death had occurred more than three years before Calvin's arrival, Basel had been thoroughly committed to Protestantism; and the work thus begun was being ably continued by the chief pastor, Oswald Myconius. Here, though living very quietly, Calvin began some important friendships,—with Myconius, with Pierre Viret, to be his associate in the reformation of French-speaking Switzerland, and with Heinrich Bullinger, Zwingli's noble successor in the spiritual leadership of Zurich. Calvin was, also, in friendly relations with Farel, though this ultimately momentous

[1] Peter Ramus, in Doumergue, i 488.

[2] *Opera*, xxxi 24

acquaintance may have been earlier begun. He studied Hebrew, it is probable, under the eminent guidance of Sebastian Munster.[1] Meanwhile he stood in cordial fellowship with Pierre Robert Olivétan, whose relations to his conversion have given rise to so much discussion Olivétan had been labouring, since 1532, among the Waldenses who found protection in the valleys of the southern Alps, and he had been preparing with their approval and at their expense a translation of the Bible into French. When its printing was completed at Neuchâtel, in June, 1535, it appeared with two commendatory Prefaces from Calvin's pen.[2]

Yet the chief event of Calvin's stay at Basel was the completion and publication of the first edition of the *Institutes*, the preparation of which had been begun at Angoulême. As it was to be put forth after considerable delay at the printer's, in its original Latin dress, in March, 1536, it was not merely[3] a handbook of theology which marked its young author as the ablest interpreter of Christian doctrine that the Reformation age had produced, but it was prefaced by a bold yet dignified and respectful Letter addressed to King Francis which at once placed Calvin at the head of French reformers and revealed him in the highest degree as a man of leadership. French Protestantism had had its mystics, its fanatics, its compromisers, and its

[1] Doumergue, i 488, 489, 505, Baumgartner, *Calvin hébraïsant*, p 20

[2] *Opera* ix 787, Herminjard, ii 451–454, iii 294, 348

[3] The circumstances of its publication, etc, are best discussed by Doumergue, i 589–595, see also *Opera*, iii vii–xlvii

martyrs, but it had been lacking in men who could speak soberly, convincingly, and boldly in its name. In Calvin, such a leader made himself heard through the Letter to the King. That letter bore date of August 23, 1535, and, as it is evident that its composition was subsequent to the practical completion of the doctrinal treatise to which it was prefixed, it is plain that the manuscript of Calvin's notable volume was essentially finished when he was not yet two months entered on his twenty-seventh year.

To judge from his own statements, Calvin would have been content to have laboured peacefully at Basel on the production of the *Institutes* longer than was to be the case, and to have issued them at last as a practical, dispassionate treatise setting forth the Christian system as he saw it revealed in the Scriptures. The purpose of the *Institutes* was expository. Calvin was, above all else, in his own view, an expounder of the Word of God. Writing in 1541, he said of his treatise:[1]—

> Although the Holy Scriptures contain a perfect doctrine, to which nothing can be added, . . . still every person, not intimately acquainted with them, stands in need of some guidance and direction as to what he ought to look for in them. . . This cannot be better done in writing than by treating in succession of the principal matters which are comprised in Christian Philosophy. For he who understands these will be prepared to make more progress in the school of God in one day than any other person in three

[1] Preface to the French ed., Beveridge's translation

months. . . . With this view I have composed the present book.

As it came forth, it was not merely a calm doctrinal exposition, but, thanks to the Letter prefixed, a noble, dignified, yet none the less passionate, defence of a persecuted cause. The desire to defend that cause and its supporters by the Letter determined the author to issue his volume when he did without waiting for its further elaboration. He must vindicate the character and faith of his associates. Once more, as it seemed to Calvin, the providence of God had thrust him into a publicity which he could not avoid and still be faithful to his duty.

The severe repression with which the King followed the posting of the Placards was viewed with disfavour by the Protestants of Germany, whose goodwill Francis wished to retain as possible allies in his rivalries with Charles V. To justify his persecution of French Protestants in the eyes of their German fellow-believers, Francis issued a public letter on February 1, 1535, addressed to the estates of the Empire,[1] in which he charged the Protestants of France with anarchistic aims designing an "overthrow of all things." Any government must resist such a "contagious plague that looked toward the foulest sedition." The whole tone of the royal argument implied that there was a vast gulf between the sober, orderly German Protestants and the rabid revolutionists of France. Calvin must have had rise before his imagination, as he reflected

[1] Text in Herminjard, iii 250–254.

on this presentation, the martyred figure of his Parisian friend, that generous, peaceful, honourable merchant, Estienne de la Forge, who had suffered sixteen days after the date of the King's letter. He could not leave such calumnies unanswered. Writing twenty-two years after the event, he thus described the publication of the *Institutes:*[1]—

Leaving my native country, I removed to Germany, planning that, concealed in some obscure corner, I might enjoy long denied peace. But while I was in retirement at Basel evil and lying pamphlets were spread abroad to suppress the indignation that the fires in which many pious men had been burned in France excited here and there among the Germans, to the effect that those so cruelly treated were no other than Anabaptists and turbulent men who would overturn by their perverse insanities not religion only, but all political order. Seeing this done by the tricksters of the Court, I felt that my silence would be treachery and that I should oppose with all my might not only lest the undeserved shedding of the innocent blood of holy martyrs should be concealed by false report, but also lest they should go on in future to whatever slaughter they pleased without arousing the pity of any. These were my reasons for publishing the *Institutes*: first, that I might vindicate from unjust affront my brethren whose death was precious in the sight of the Lord, and, next, that some sorrow and anxiety should move foreign peoples, since the same sufferings threatened many. Neither was it that thick and elaborate work it now is, but only a little hand-book that then appeared, nor had it any other aim than to witness to the

[1] Preface to *Psalms, Opera*, xxxi. 23.

faith of those whom I saw evilly reviled by impious and faithless flatterers.

It was, indeed, as Calvin said, relatively a small volume as originally issued. Yet it numbered five hundred and nineteen pages. Their dimensions being however, only six and a quarter by four inches, it could be readily carried in a fair-sized pocket. In typography, it was a credit to the printers, Thomas Platter and Balthasar Lasius, and to the publisher, Johann Oporin, who stood behind them; and its sale was considerable, for in March, 1537, a year after its publication, Oporin could report to Calvin that so much was it in demand that no copies remained at Basel, and not more than fifty at Frankfort, whither a supply had been sent for sale at the great fair. A new edition was being eagerly sought.[1]

The letter to King Francis is one of the few masterpieces of apologetic literature. Courteously and respectfully, yet as one aware of his legal rights as a subject, and conscious that his sovereign has duties as a ruler which have not been fulfilled, Calvin argues the case for himself and his Protestant fellow-believers. It is no cringing seeker for toleration that here speaks, nor is it a fanatic uttering a tirade against persecutors; but the voice is of one convinced of the justice of his cause and skilled to reply to criticisms of it with carefully trained and lawyer-like acuteness and cogency of statement. It is as convincing as it is brilliant.

The Protestants, who have been so cruelly slandered,

[1] Herminjard, IV 208.

Calvin tells the King, are being condemned on mere rumour. However humble their persons, justice demands that the sovereign examine into their cause the more urgently because it involves [1]—

such mighty interests as these: how the glory of God is to be maintained on earth inviolate, how the truth of God is to preserve its dignity, how the kingdom of Christ is to continue amongst us compact and secure. The cause is worthy of your ear, worthy of your investigation, worthy of your judgment-seat. . . . Take but a cursory view, most valiant King, of all the parts of our cause, and count us of all wicked men the most iniquitous, if you do not discover plainly that "to this end we labour and suffer reproach, because we put our hope in the living God," because we believe it to be "life eternal" to "know the only true God and Jesus Christ" whom He has sent. For this hope some of us are in bonds, some beaten with rods, some made a gazing-stock, some proscribed, some most cruelly tortured, some obliged to flee; we are all pressed with poverty, loaded with dire execrations, lacerated with abuse, and treated with the greatest indignity. Look now at our adversaries. . . . The true religion which is handed down in the Scriptures, and which ought to have stood unchanged among all men, they readily permit both themselves and others to be ignorant of, to neglect and despise; and they deem it of little moment what each man may hold concerning God and Christ, or may not hold, provided he submits his opinion with implicit faith to the judgment of the Church. . . . Nevertheless, they cease not to assail our doctrine, and to accuse and defame it in what terms they may, in order to render it either hated

[1] *Opera*, i 11, 13, 14, Beveridge's translation slightly amended.

or suspected They call it new, and of recent birth; they carp at it as doubtful and uncertain, they ask by what miracles it has been confirmed, they query if it be fair to receive it against the consent of so many holy fathers and the most ancient custom; they urge us to confess either that it is schismatical in giving battle to the Church, or that the Church must have been almost dead during the many centuries in which nothing of the kind was heard. Lastly, they say there is little need of argument, for its quality may be known by its fruits, namely, the large number of sects, the many seditious disturbances, and the great licentiousness which it has produced.

Having stated his opponents' criticisms, Calvin proceeds, like an able attorney, to refute them in order. The doctrine he defends is not new, save to his enemies; it is the very Word of God. It is not doubtful, save to those that are ignorant of it. It needs no fresh miraculous confirmation, since it is the same Gospel "the truth of which is confirmed by all the miracles which Christ and the Apostles ever wrought." The Fathers, at least of a purer age, though not without much human error, are even more on the side of the reformers than those who pretend to do them special reverence; and in numerous instances, which Calvin cites, they have opposed doctrines or practices now obtaining in the Roman communion. Custom is no fitting test of truth, for "human affairs have scarcely ever been so happily constituted as that the better course pleased the greater number." Nor do Protestants hold the Church to have been dead;—those who seek reform have a truer definition of what the Church really is than their opponents:[1]—

The hinges on which our controversy turns are these first, in their contending that the form of the Church is always visible and apparent, and, secondly, in their placing that form in the see of the Church of Rome and its hierarchy. We, on the contrary, maintain that the Church may exist without any apparent form; and that the form is not ascertained by that external splendour which they foolishly admire, but by a very different mark, namely, by pure preaching of the Word of God and rightful administration of the sacraments

In so defining the "notes of the Church," Calvin stood on the general Protestant basis, expressed, for instance, six years before in the Augsburg Confession. To the allegation that the new preaching brought disorder, he replies: "The blame of these evils is wrongfully charged upon it, which ought to be ascribed to the malice of Satan"; and he concludes with the appeal.[2]—

Magnanimous King, be not moved by the absurd insinuations with which our adversaries are striving to frighten you into the belief that nothing else is wished and aimed at by this new gospel (for so they term it) than opportunity for seditions and impunity for all vices. God is not the author of division, but of peace, and the Son of God, who came to destroy the works of the devil, is not the minister

[1] *Opera*, 1 20, 21

[2] *Ibid*, 25, 26

of sin. We are undeservedly charged with desires of a kind for which we have never given even the smallest suspicion . . . [Your] good will, we are confident, we should regain, would you but once, with calmness and composure, read this our confession, which we wish to serve with your majesty instead of a defence. But if the whispers of the malevolent so possess your ears that the accused are to have no opportunity of pleading their cause, if those vindictive furies, with your connivance, are always to rage with bonds, scourgings, tortures, maimings, and burnings, we, indeed, like sheep doomed to slaughter, shall be reduced to every extremity; yet so that, in our patience, we will possess our souls, and wait for the strong hand of the Lord, which doubtless will appear in time, and show itself armed, both to rescue the poor from affliction, and to take vengeance on the despisers Most powerful and illustrious King, may the Lord, the King of kings, establish your throne in justice and your rulership in equity.

Calvin had spoken the word which French Protestantism needed to have said in its defence, and henceforth no man could doubt his leadership in its cause.

The *Institutes* themselves, to which this Letter was prefixed, were, indeed, far from the perfection of logical treatment and inclusiveness of view which were to characterise the final form attained in the edition of 1559; but they were even now sufficiently significant.[1] Calvin's work follows the ancient popular order of religious instruction which had served Luther for an

[1] Text in *Opera*, i 27–252, for comparison with later editions see *Ibid*, li–lviii, and also Köstlin, "Calvins Institutio nach Form und Inhalt," in *Theologische Studien und Kritiken*, for 1868, pp 7–62, 410–486.

outline in drafting his short *Catechism* of 1529, and was determined in its sequence by the elementary teachings which every Christian child had long been expected to learn by heart. In the first four of his six chapters he therefore treats of the Law, as set forth in the Ten Commandments; Faith, as embodied in the Apostles' Creed; Prayer, as illustrated in that of our Lord, and the Sacraments of Baptism and the Lord's Supper. To these he joins two further chapters, one treating of the "False Sacraments" which Roman teaching had added to the primal two, and the other of "Christian Liberty, Ecclesiastical Power, and Civil Administration." This order of discussion was not only historically familiar, but it gave to Calvin's legally trained mind the advantage of basing much of his exposition on definite documents generally believed to be of absolute authority. Yet Calvin's treatment is far from being confined to an exposition of these documents alone. Its range is broad, and it deserves the description which the publishers, more probably than Calvin, placed on the title-page of the first edition of the *Institutes*,—that of "containing well-nigh the whole sum of piety." Between the first three chapters and their successors a certain difference of style and atmosphere may also be noted. The earlier portion is less polemic, more simple and calm; while the closing chapters are more vivacious and controversial in tone and reflect more strongly the heat of the quarrel with the ancient Church. The supposition is natural that they were written after Calvin's rising indignation at the misrepresentation of his fellow-believers had led him to modify his earlier plan of a peacefully wrought-out work of Christian instruction. Yet the whole volume is remarkably well-poised and exhibits everywhere great self-control on the part of its author. Its denunciatory epithets are much fewer than in its later editions. As compared with them, however, it shows more of a departure from the classics-loving Calvin who had commented on Seneca. Though Ambrose, Augustine, and Plato are quoted, Calvin makes far less use of the Fathers and the great writers of Greece and Rome than in the subsequent editions of the *Institutes*.

In its doctrinal outlook, the first edition of the *Institutes* might well appear a product of the German Reformation, especially as that movement had developed in the Rhine Valley. Most of the peculiarities of Calvinism are discoverable, but they are not so prominent or so sharply put as in later editions. Yet there is already in clear evidence that profound consciousness of the reality and authority of God which marks all Calvin's thought. Next in emphasis is its doctrine of salvation through reconciliation by faith in Christ. "All the sum of the Gospel is contained in these two heads repentance and remission of sins."[1] Election is briefly set forth as a basis of confidence of salvation and as determining membership in the invisible Church; but it is not given quite the central position that seems logically to belong to the doctrine, and reprobation is simply mentioned. From election, the perseverance of those thus chosen is clearly deduced.

The treatise begins, like the later editions of the

[1] *Opera*, 1 149.

*Institutes*, with the declaration that religious truth is almost entirely comprehended in the knowledge of God and of ourselves,—of God, that He is infinite wisdom and goodness, and the source of all good everywhere, for whose glory all things are made, a just Judge and yet merciful to those that seek Him,—of ourselves, that, since the loss of that original perfection in which Adam was created, the whole human race has been totally corrupt and justly exposed to the wrath of God. Hence any effort to merit righteousness is unavailing; but God forgives sins and gives a new heart to the humbly penitent, through and for the sake of Christ, if they accept His gifts with "certain faith." The Law, therefore, is not our rule of salvation, but a "looking-glass" which shows us our condition. Calvin then explains the several commandments and concludes that the Law has three main uses,—it shows what God justly requires of us, it admonishes those whom nothing but fear of punishment will move, and it is "an exhortation to the faithful," furnishing them a rule for learning what is "the will of God" to which it is their purpose to conform. This third use of the Law as a discipline for Christian believers is a mark of Calvinism as distinguished from Lutheran interpretations. Though having no confidence in good works as of a saving value, the Christian will look for them in his life as "the fruit of the Spirit of God," done by God through him, and the evidence that he has "passed from the kingdom of sin to the kingdom of righteousness." His assurance of salvation is based on the divine election thus witnessed.

In his second chapter, "On Faith," Calvin distinguishes between an intellectual recognition of God's existence and of the historic truth of the Scripture narrative,—a possession "unworthy the name of faith,"—and a belief which places "all hope and confidence in one God and Christ," "doubting nothing of the good-will of God towards us." The basis without which this faith cannot be sustained is declared to be the Scriptures. Calvin then discusses the Trinity, and proceeds to the explanation of the Apostles' Creed. The "holy catholic Church" he defines as "the whole number of the elect"; but, since this invisible Church cannot be exactly perceived by us, we may in the judgment of charity hold to be of it "all who by confession of faith, example of life, and participation in the sacraments confess the same God and Christ as we."

Since men have nothing of good in themselves, they must look to God for all blessings, and hence Calvin devotes his third chapter to Prayer. Its first condition is humility, its next "certain faith." The merit is not in the prayer, nor in the dignity of him who offers it, but in the divine promise, which will be fulfilled to him who prays in equal faith, as truly as to Peter or to Paul. It is to be offered to God in the name of Christ only,—not to or through the saints; and public prayer should be in a tongue understood by all the congregation. Private prayer may be spoken or without words; but true prayer has always two elements,—petition and giving of thanks. Calvin then expounds the Lord's Prayer as a model of what prayer should be.

With his fourth chapter Calvin takes up the Sacraments, which he defines as "external signs by which the Lord sets forth and attests his goodwill towards us in order to sustain the weakness of our faith." No sacrament is without the preceding divine promise, to which it witnesses It is like the seal to a document, valueless in itself, but confirming that to which it is attached. Two sacraments only have been thus divinely instituted,—Baptism and the Lord's Supper. Baptism serves to strengthen our faith in God's remission of our sins, and as a confession of Him before men. It is to be administered to infants as well as to adults; and in the simple way the Scriptures indicate. Whether by immersion or sprinkling may well be left to the usages of different countries. Like Baptism, the Lord's Supper is "an exercise of faith, given to maintain, excite, and increase it." It is the attestation and witness of God's promise. It gives assurance that whatever is Christ's is ours, whatever is ours is His. "All the energy of the sacrament is in these words, 'which is given for you'" Having said this, Calvin brings to mind the "horrible dissensions" which had been manifested in the recent controversies between Lutherans and Zwinglians regarding the nature of Christ's presence in the Supper. His own view, which he argues with great acuteness, is that "the sacrament is something spiritual." It is the very condition of the existence of a physical body that it can be in but one place. Hence, in the Supper, Christ is "truly and efficaciously," but not physically, present; "not the very substance of his body nor the real and natural body of Christ is there given, but all things which Christ bestows as benefits to us by His body." Though asserting thus in the clearest terms that Christ's presence in the elements is one of spiritual power only, Calvin gives the impression of standing in closer sympathy with Luther than with Zwingli in his estimate of the nature and worth of the Supper. He then goes on to reject the Roman conception of the mass in most energetic terms, and urges that communion should be observed with simple ritual, and at least once a week,—a fact which should be weighed by those who criticise the Sunday worship of Calvinism as too bare and too purely intellectual. If a much less frequent observation became the rule in the Reformed Churches, it was not by Calvin's intention.

In his fifth chapter Calvin carries his warfare yet more vigorously against the Roman system, attacking with great vivacity of style and keenness of argument the claims of Confirmation, Penance, Extreme Unction, Orders, or Marriage to be called sacraments at all. As God alone can create a sacrament, since He alone can give the promise of which it is the witness, so His Word alone reveals the Sacraments that He has instituted; and, tried by this test, the five just enumerated are found wanting. Calvin discusses each at length, treating naturally with especial fulness that of Penance, and criticising in its connection auricular confession, satisfaction, a treasury of good works, indulgences, and purgatory. Treating of orders, Calvin holds that the Scripture "recognises no other minister of the Church than a preacher of the Word of God, called to govern the Church, whom it calls now a bishop, now a presbyter, and occasionally a pastor." Orders are simply this calling, which should be accomplished with the consent of the Church to be served, and the advice of one or two neighbouring ministers as to the fitness of the candidate. Whether this consent of the Church should be expressed by a meeting of the whole congregation, or the votes of a few elders, magistrates, princes, or a city government, Calvin leaves to be determined by circumstances. Imposition of hands may properly be used in setting the minister apart for his work, but is in no sense a sacrament.

Calvin's concluding chapter takes up the theme of Christian liberty. It consists, he holds, in a freedom which raises the Christian above the "Law" as a test of obedience, though, since we are called to sanctification, the Law remains an admonishing and stimulating influence. From this principle it follows that Christian "consciences submit to the Law not as if compelled by the force of the Law, but free from the yoke of the Law itself, they obey the will of God voluntarily." Hence, to the Christian, the Law is a rule of life. A third element in Christian liberty is freedom in the use of those gifts of God which are often called indifferent things. "Nor is it anywhere forbidden to laugh, or to enjoy food, or to add new possessions to old and ancestral property, or to be delighted with musical harmonies, or to drink wine,"—a phrase which reveals Calvin as anything but an ascetic; but he adds, "that is, indeed, true; but when the abundance of possessions leads one to be wrapped up in enjoyments and to immerse one's self in them, to intoxicate mind and soul with present pleasures and always to seek after new delights,—these things are as far as possible from a proper use of the gifts of God." "The sum is, that 'We that are strong ought to bear the infirmities of the weak and not to please ourselves.'" For his proper guidance, man is placed in this world under a double government, spiritual and temporal. That spiritual kingdom has only one King, Christ; and one law, the Word of the Gospel. Its officers are "ministers" of that Word, and have no right to add to or take from the prescriptions therein contained. "The Church is to be heard, they say. Who denies it, since she proclaims nothing save from the Word of God? If they demand anything more, they know that the words of Christ give no support to their demand." Of pastors, and all other church officers, Calvin declares, "All their function is bounded by the ministry of the Word of God, all their wisdom by the knowledge of that Word, all their eloquence by its preaching." Holding this principle, Calvin necessarily finds no authority in the decrees of councils or in the promulgations of church fathers and bishops, save as they conform to this one divine standard of faith and practice.

Calvin then proceeds to vindicate civil government from the criticisms of it as no fit employment for Christian men, often directed against it by the Anabaptists and other radical reformers of his day. It is established by divine authority "to order our life for the society of men, to conform our conduct to civil justice, to reconcile us one with another, to nourish and preserve common peace and tranquillity." The duty of the magistrate is not merely to see that "public peace be not disturbed, and each safely possess his own," but to guard lest "idolatry, sacrilege against the name of God, blasphemies against His truth, or other public offences against religion should break out or be spread among the people." Severe punishments are often necessary, but clemency is the chief ornament of a ruler. The collection of taxes and the waging of just wars are not forbidden to the Christian magistrate, any more than the establishment of such laws as equity and the teaching of God's Word counsel. The punishments by which laws are sanctioned may vary with times and places, but their purpose is always the same. They condemn what God condemns. To these laws and magistrates, even to rulers of vicious and tyrannical character, full obedience is due, save where the command contradicts the revealed will of God. Where God has spoken, no other voice deserves the slightest heed.

Such, in the barest outline, is the remarkable handbook of Christian belief with which Calvin accompanied his defence of French Protestantism. Though greatly to be enlarged and improved in the later editions on which he was unweariedly to labour till within five years of the close of his life, it stood forth, even in this early form, not merely as by far the most significant treatise that the reformers of France had yet produced, but without a superior as a clear, logical, and popularly apprehensible presentation of those principles for which all Protestantism contended. It was far more than a theoretic exposition of Christian truth. Though in form not strictly a programme for action, it could easily yield the basis of a new constitution for the Church, and of a regulation of the moral life of the community. The felicity of its style, the logical cogency of argument, the precision of statement, which marked the volume, were Calvin's own. The moral enthusiasm which shines through it was a kindling force. As a treatment of Christian doctrine, it was fresh and original. But it was even more a carefully wrought-out exposition of the Christian life, novel and inspiring in its clearness and earnestness.

Such qualities do not exclude, however, a large degree of indebtedness to those who had thought before him on these themes, and especially to his immediate predecessors in the leadership of the Reformation. Calvin's mind was formulative rather than creative. Given the fundamental principles of the Reformation, he could carry them to their logical consequences with a keenness of insight and a clearness of statement such as none of his contemporaries could equal; but it may be questioned whether in the development of Christian doctrine he could have done the path-breaking work accomplished by the first generation of the reformers.

Calvin's indebtedness to Luther was, of course, great. It is Luther's doctrines of faith alone and of the way of salvation that the *Institutes* present; and, in spite of divergencies of the highest significance from the view of Christ's presence in the Supper taught by the Saxon reformer, it is Luther's conception of the Sacraments, as attestations of the divine promise designed to strengthen our trust, that marks Calvin's definition of these Christian ordinances. Calvin's whole theological work was made possible only by the antecedent labours of Luther. But in many doctrinal details it is easy to trace an indebtedness not so much to Luther directly as to the German Reformation as it fashioned itself in the minds of the reformers of southwestern Germany. Calvin had little spiritual kinship to Zwingli. He stood nearer to Luther than to the reformer of German-speaking Switzerland. But he owed much to Martin Bucer of Strassburg[1] Such a sympathy in interpretation of the principles of the Reformation was natural to a young Frenchman by reason of the geographical proximity of the Rhineland and consequent readiness of intercourse; but in Calvin's case it seems more than a general indebtedness to influences widely prevalent in the region of which Strassburg was the centre. Views characteristic of Bucer, and which Bucer had put forth in his *Evangelienkommentar*, the first edition of which had appeared in 1527, Calvin had clearly made his own, so that there is reason to believe that Bucer's work had been used in his studies preparatory to the *Institutes*. Some colour is given by this acquaintance to the claim that a correspondence had been begun with the Strassburg reformer by Calvin before his flight

[1] See R. Seeberg, *Lehrbuch der Dogmengeschichte*, Erlangen, 1898, ii. 379–383, and, especially, August Lang, *Der Evangelienkommentar Martin Butzer's*, Leipzig, 1900, *passim*.

from France, though reasons have already been adduced showing this opinion to be improbable.[1]

Calvin's centration of his theology about the two conceptions of the universal agency of God in salvation and of the divine predestination was of the essence of Bucer's thinking; and Calvin's treatment of election, clearly apparent in the first edition of the *Institutes*, as the basis of that confidence enjoyed by those living the Christian life which distinguishes them from non-Christians, was already taught by Bucer, with whom, as with Calvin in the first edition of the *Institutes*, election was a doctrine to strengthen practical Christian living far more than an abstract explanation of the divine government of the universe. With Bucer, Calvin defined faith as "*persuasio*,"—a certainty of conviction; and as with Bucer the "glory" or "honour" of God are phrases frequently employed to denote, for example, the purpose "for which all things in heaven and in earth are created." As with Bucer, man is powerless to achieve any good thing,—all of worth is from God; but in Bucer and Calvin alike, by a kind of over-riding of logic by the demands of an ardent practical piety, the Christian life is looked upon as a strenuous, warm-hearted, self-denying effort to realise in one's self the blessings and the character which the divine election has made ours[2] The whole Reformation age made much of election, as was natural in an epoch characterised by a mighty revival of Augustinianism, but the pietistic use of the doctrine as the basis of

[1] *Ante*, p 65.

[2] Compare Lang, *op cit*, pp 194, 195

confidence and the encouragement to struggle for high attainment in the Christian life was more markedly a trait of Bucer than of any of his contemporaries among the reformers of the first generation, and was to be made by Calvin a prime characteristic of the churches which felt his moulding touch.

But besides this indebtedness to older reformers who were still living when Calvin's *Institutes* were first published, the young thinker took much, consciously or unconsciously, from the later schoolmen. Thus he owed to Scotus, doubtless without realising the obligation, the thought of God as almighty will, for motives behind whose choice it is as absurd as it is impious to inquire. To Scotus, also, was due the conception that the power of God accompanies, rather than exists in, the Sacraments. And from the general feeling of mediæval Latin Christendom that the Church is independent of the State, Calvin probably derived the conviction which was to make his theory of the relation of the Church to organised political society one involving far greater freedom than that of any other of the reformers, whatever limitations that theory was afterwards to exhibit in Calvin's Genevan practice. To point out these obligations is, however, in no way to detract from the merit of the youthful theologian. He built his edifice of Christian thought with utmost skill; but, in so doing, he did not reject the plans on which older labourers had wrought or the materials which their patient efforts had gathered

On the publication of the *Institutes*, in March, 1536, or perhaps on the completion of the revision of the proofs in the previous month,[1] Calvin set out from Basel, accompanied by his friend du Tillet, for a brief visit to Ferrara, the object of which was to meet the duchess, Renée, wife of Ercole II. He travelled under the disguised name of Charles d'Espeville, evidently reminiscent of the territory from which part of his ecclesiastical revenue at Noyon had been derived. The occasion and circumstances of this journey to Italy are obscure and have given rise to a mass of fable and conjecture; but a sufficient reason is to be seen in the existence of a state of affairs at the court of Ferrara which gave promise, for the time being, that the reform movement would there find a welcome. To aid the cause he had at heart was doubtless Calvin's purpose in crossing the Alps.

Renée, who was almost the same age as Calvin, was the daughter of King Louis XII. of France, and regarded her mission in Italy as the defence of French interests, even at the expense of long-continued disputes with her husband. Proud of her birth and nationality, she had a generous welcome for such Frenchmen as sought her aid, and was accustomed to reply to critics of her kindliness: "They are . . . of my nation, and if God had given me a beard on my chin, and I were a man, they would all be my subjects . . . if this evil salic law did not bind me too firmly."[2] In mental

[1] Beza and Colladon, *Opera*, xxi 30, 58, 125. The literature treating of this journey, which is extensive and controversial, is well considered by Doumergue, ii 3–94, see also C A Cornelius, *Historische Arbeiten*, Leipzig, 1899, pp. 105–123

[2] Brantôme, *Œuvres*, viii 111.

traits she much resembled her cousin, Marguerite d'Angoulême, possessing the same love of letters, the same desire to aid those who were advancing the cause of learning, and similar religious opinions, being probably largely an adherent of the newer views at heart all her life, as she openly became after her return to France as a widow. But, like Marguerite, she remained during her sojourn in Italy in outward conformity to the Roman Church, and was claimed by either side in the struggle. Like that of Marguerite, also, her court was a place of refuge for many whom the persecuting policy of Francis I. compelled to fly from France; and in the spring of 1536 it sheltered, among others, the Protestant poet Clément Marot, whose name had been seventh on the list of those under suspicion as having guilty knowledge of the Placards of October, 1534, which had cost French Protestantism so heavily. The suspicion with which these fugitives were regarded by the churchly authorities at Ferrara was confirmed by an act of one of Marot's companions, like him suspected of connection with the Placards, a young singer known as Jehannet. On Good Friday, April 14, 1536, he had walked out of the church, at the time of the adoration of the Cross, in evident disapproval of the service.[1] Arrested and examined by torture, he declared many of Renée's protégés adherents of the newer views. Most of those thus implicated promptly left Ferrara; but investigation continued, and, on May 4, another of the French recipients of the duchess's bounty, Jean de Bouchefort, a clergyman who had come from the

[1] *Bulletin*, x. 36, 37; xxxiv. 291, Doumergue, ii. 52.

diocese of Tournay, was arrested under a charge of "Lutheranism." The court of Ferrara might well seem to an eager French reformer a hopeful field for sowing Evangelical ideas, or even for inducing a duchess already so favourable to French refugees to take an open stand in support of the faith which many of them cherished. A young humanist, such as Calvin was, would, moreover, gladly embrace an opportunity of seeing Italy, and this desire Beza presents as one of Calvin's motives.[1]

How far Calvin's hopes may have reached or just what he attempted in Ferrara, it is impossible to say. His visit was brief. He was later wont to say that he had entered Italy only to leave it; and, though his stay has been variously estimated, it was probably at most from the middle of March to the latter part of April. The arrest of Jehannet appears to have induced him and du Tillet, as it did many other foreign visitors, to leave the dangerous city. Calvin was no rash seeker of peril. He met Renée, and made the acquaintance of others in her circle. It is inconceivable that he did not make plain his position to her, and labour to win her to a more positive Evangelicalism, so far as brief opportunity permitted, but his character and mission were not generally revealed. The learned German physician at the court of the duchess, Johann Sinapius, with whom Calvin formed an acquaintance at Ferrara, remained in ignorance;[2] and, if he did not know, it is evident that Calvin kept his dangerous secret

[1] *Opera*, xxi 125

[2] Sinapius's letter, Herminjard, vi 3, Cornelius, *Historische Arbeiten*, p. 107

from the world at large. His departure from Ferrara was unhindered. The story of a seizure by the Inquisition and an escape from its clutches, first recorded by Muratori, and since often repeated, in dramatic form for instance by Merle d'Aubigné, and with greater care of investigation by Fontana, is legendary,—the dates involved showing that, whatever the experience may have been, its hero was not Calvin.[1]

Though brief, Calvin's visit to Ferrara was not without result. His unusual power of attracting associates and rendering them friends was once more manifested. In spite of doubts cast upon the success of his intercourse with Renée,[2] it seems to have paved the way for the correspondence which, though not begun till at least a year later, was to continue till Calvin's death. But, if his success in turning the duchess to a public support of the Evangelical cause was not what he may possibly have hoped, he won the devoted friendship of a brilliant young French lady of the little court, Françoise Boussiron, daughter of the lord of Grand-Ry in Poitou, and soon to become the wife of that Johann Sinapius of whom mention has been made. To her Calvin became a spiritual adviser, and with her, and soon with her husband, he remained in correspondence. Writing to Calvin from his later home in Germany, in 1557, more than two years after her death, Sinapius could say: "She honoured you as long as she lived,

[1] Muratori, *Annali d' Italia*, 1749, x 275; Merle d'Aubigné, *La réformation en Europe au temps de Calvin*, v 567, Fontana, *Renata di Francia*, 1889, *passim*, Doumergue, ii 54–56

[2] Cornelius, p 107; compare Doumergue, ii. 57, 729–731.

and loved you, and you, in turn, regarded her as a sister."[1]

A frequent subject of Calvin's discussions with the little group into brief association with which he came at Ferrara must have been the proper attitude to assume toward the services of the ancient Church. That, he tells Renée in a letter written very possibly in 1537, had been a subject of conversation, unquestionably at Ferrara, between him and her almoner, the adroit and unstable François Richardot.[2] To Richardot he showed a "treatise," which may possibly have been the just published *Institutes*, but which was more probably one of two burning letters of entreaty and denunciation written, so Colladon recorded, on this Italian journey,[3] though not to be given to the public till they were put forth at Basel, early in 1537, by the same printers that had issued the *Institutes*.[4] The first of these letters, and probably the one shown to Richardot in manuscript, was addressed to an "excellent man and close friend" who has always been identified with Calvin's intimate associate at Orléans, Nicolas Duchemin, though it is evident that the author had in view the general body of those unwilling or afraid to carry Protestant convictions to what seemed to him their logical conclusions, rather than a single reader. He answers the question, certainly a very pressing one in those days of persecution,

[1] *Opera*, xvi 375, Doumergue, ii 66

[2] *Ibid.*, xi 326, on date, Doumergue, ii 729.

[3] *Ibid.*, xxi 60, see also Calvin's letter, Herminjard, vi 200

[4] The Preface was dated January 12, 1537 Both are given in *Opera*, v 233–278, and are respectively entitled *De fugiendis impiorum sacris* and *De sacerdotio papali abjiciendo*.

whether a man of Evangelical convictions could give the sanction of an outward conformity to much of the Roman ritual, notably to "that head of all abominations, the mass," with a decided negative. No man, he argues, can rightfully offer anything less than a conscientious obedience to God's commands as set forth in His Word. "This is specially forbidden you, that any one should see you sharing in the sacrilege of the mass, or uncovering the head before an image, or supporting any superstition whatever of a nature whereby the glory of God is dimmed, His religion profaned, His truth corrupted." Such a position was undoubtedly logical and heroic; but one cannot wonder that many could not reach it, nor can one blame these "Pseudo-Nicodemites" as much as Calvin and his age were wont to believe they deserved. The martyr spirit is not given to all; nor had Calvin been the least cautious of men in avoiding danger by overt action in Catholic lands. Calvin's other letter was addressed "to an old friend, now a prelate," who was undoubtedly that eager humanistic reformer of 1533, Gérard Roussel, to whom Calvin himself had owed much, but who had never broken with the Roman Church, and had recently received the bishopric of Oloron. Nowhere in his writings does Calvin show more passionate indignation. To him, evidently, Roussel was one who had turned from the good cause, and had made shipwreck by accepting office in a communion marked by greed and avarice. His friend had become a traitor. Calvin's indignation is easy to understand. Roussel had changed, however, far less than he supposed.

The advance toward militant Protestantism had been in Calvin himself; and Roussel carried his always incomplete yet real Evangelical ideas to his bishopric, where he continued to do much the same work as when Calvin had formed the now despised friendship with him at Paris.

The change for the worse in the situation of the French refugees at Ferrara consequent upon Jehannet's overt action induced Calvin and du Tillet to leave a city that had now become dangerous, for the safety of Switzerland. By what route they made their way over the Alps, probably early in May, 1536, we do not know; but a persistent tradition has asserted that Calvin engaged in Evangelical missionary activity in Aosta, the southern terminus of the St. Bernard pathway across the mountain barrier between Italy and the valley of the upper Rhone. Like all that relates to Calvin's Italian journey, this tradition has given rise to controversy.[1] Anything like a prolonged activity at Aosta is impossible; but the Alpine valley was the scene of much religious agitation in 1535 and 1536, and it is conceivable that Calvin may have chosen the St. Bernard route and have made a brief stay at Aosta to see with his own eyes the religious situation and the prospects of the Evangelical cause. At present it must

[1] Set forth and defended by Jules Bonnet in *Calvin au val d'Aoste*, Paris, 1861, the story was destructively and effectively criticised by Albert Rilliet, *Lettre à M. J.-H. Merle d'Aubigné*, 1864. The evidence is gone over anew by Doumergue, ii 85–94. See also Eduard Bähler, "Calvin in Aosta," in the *Jahrbuch des Schweizer Alpenclub*, xxxix. 189–195, and the *Bulletin* for March and April, 1905, pp. 177–183.

remain a matter of conjecture, though Calvin's connection with Aosta is probably purely legendary. What is certain is that Calvin and du Tillet reached Basel in safety, and there separated, du Tillet going to Neuchâtel and Geneva, and Calvin taking his journey to Paris for a brief sojourn in France, that he might put in order his few business interests in that land and bring back his brother and sister with him, to find a home in the Protestant atmosphere of Strassburg or Basel.[1]

That Calvin was thus able peacefully to return to a capital from which he had been compelled to flee less than three years before was due to the exigencies of French politics. Francis had entered but a few months on the persecutions following the Placards when he turned largely from them to begin cultivating the German Protestants as possible allies in the new war with Charles V. that was to break out early in 1536. In June, 1535, he invited Melanchthon to visit the French court. On July 16th following, he issued the Edict of Coucy, permitting those charged with heresy to return, provided they would desist from their errors and abjure them within six months. On May 31, 1536, these privileges had been confirmed.[2] Availing himself of this grace, Calvin was in Paris by June 2, 1536, for on that day he gave a power of attorney to his younger brother Antoine, who, ten days later, joined at Noyon with his elder brother, Charles, in a sale of lands which had belonged to their parents.[3] The granting of this

[1] Colladon, *Opera*, xxi. 58.

[2] *Opera*, xb. 55, 58; Doumergue, ii. 174.

[3] Documents in full in Lefranc, *Jeunesse*, pp. 205–208.

power of attorney makes it well-nigh certain that Calvin himself did not go to Noyon. From Paris, his business completed, he set forth, accompanied by Antoine and his sister Marie, for Strassburg, but knowing, as he himself later recorded, that the direct route was barred by the war, Calvin made a long detour, probably by way of Lyons, reaching Geneva in the latter half of July, and intending to pass only a single night in the city before resuming his journey to the Rhineland.[1] Recognised by an acquaintance, in all probability du Tillet, his presence was made known to Guillaume Farel, who was struggling to maintain the Evangelical cause in the recently reformed city. Farel, always fiery and eloquent, urged and adjured Calvin to stay and aid in the difficult endeavour. It was a moment of far-reaching decision, for Calvin recognised as he believed the divine call, and, if God had spoken, His voice was to be obeyed. "Farel kept me at Geneva," he said, writing of the event, "not so much by advice and entreaty as by a dreadful adjuration, as if God had stretched forth His hand upon me from on high to arrest me."[2] That the task was hard and unexpected was no reason why that divine summons should be disregarded. God, he thought, had set before him the work to be done. He would enter on it.

[1] Preface to *Psalms*, *Opera*, xxxi. 26. On time of arrival at Geneva see Herminjard, iv. 74, 75, Doumergue, ii. 7.

[2] *Ibid.*, *Opera*, xxxi. 26.

# CHAPTER VII

## GENEVA TILL CALVIN'S COMING

NO city in Christendom had had a more eventful or stormier history than Geneva [1] during the generation and especially during the decade preceding Calvin's coming. In none had more diverse forces contended for the mastery. Intermixed as political considerations were in all the religious struggles of the Reformation period, nowhere was the skein more tangled than at Geneva; and nowhere, also, did the field seem more difficult for the development of a movement predominantly religious in character.

Known certainly since the time of Julius Cæsar, Geneva had been a town of importance under Roman rule, and had become the seat of a bishopric soon after the conversion of Constantine gave peace to the Church. The downfall of the Roman empire saw Geneva the capital of the Burgundian kingdom; and, after various vicissitudes, it came, early in the twelfth century, under the overlordship of the Hohenstaufen emperors, and was known, perhaps not quite justly, as an "imperial city." The real possessors of power in the city during this

[1] By far the best sketch in English is that of Prof H. D. Foster, "Geneva before Calvin," in *The American Historical Review*, viii 217–240 (1903), where the more important sources are indicated. More extended and very valuable are Kampschulte, *Johann Calvin*, i 3–218, and Doumergue, ii 97–149

period were, however, the counts of Geneva and its bishops; and between these spiritual and lay rulers constant struggles were waged, which resulted in the decided victory of the ecclesiastical lords. With the thirteenth century, a new lay force made itself felt,—that of the rising, ambitious, and energetic house of Savoy. The Genevan bishops used its aid to rid themselves of the last remnants of the power of the Genevan counts, only to find that in the rulers of Savoy they were to meet a far abler enemy. In 1285, Amadeus V., of Savoy, entered into a compact to protect the burghers of Geneva against their bishop, and in 1290 the bishop was forced to yield as a fief to that energetic count of Savoy the appointment of the episcopal deputy for temporal administration, or *vicedominus*,—a post which its new lords retained under their control till 1528, and with it a position of influence in Genevan affairs. Meanwhile the burghers of the city, who had been of sufficient significance to be courted in the aggressions of Savoy as early as 1285, were demanding recognition of their claims, till after long struggles they forced from Bishop Adhémar Fabri, in 1387, the *Franchises*, which gave constitutional sanction to their much-prized customs. By this charter the right of the citizens to gather in a General Assembly (*Conseil général*) for the choice of administrative officers was recognised. These functionaries were four "syndics" selected annually, and a treasurer elected for a term of three years. With the addition of the syndics of the previous year and of counsellors selected by the syndics in office, there speedily developed the "Little Council,"—at first of a variable number, but ultimately of twenty-five members, which constituted the inner consultative and executive body in the administration of the interests of the burghers. A second, and larger Council, originally fifty, but speedily sixty in number, was established, in 1457, to discuss matters not conveniently debatable in the General Assembly; and the aristocratic tendencies of the Genevan citizenship are illustrated by the fact that, from 1459 onward, the members of this larger Council were designated by the "Little Council." The government of Geneva, by the end of the fourteenth century, was therefore shared by three powers, the bishop, the *vicedominus*, and the citizens, and this division of authority continued till the struggles of the third decade of the sixteenth century. The bishop, honoured with the title "Prince of Geneva" and in theory sovereign of the city under the emperor, possessed the rights of leadership in war, of coining money, of hearing appeals and of granting pardons. To the *vicedominus* fell the duties of defending the city, guarding prisoners, executing criminals and of exercising a restricted judicial function in civil and criminal cases. To the representatives of the citizens was ascribed the decision of all serious criminal charges against laymen To them belonged the maintenance of good order at night by a suitable police force throughout the city, and they were charged with a watchful supervision lest the rights guaranteed by the *Franchises* should be infringed.

The population of Geneva, which may have numbered about thirteen thousand permanent residents, was as varied as the government of the city was divided. The

11

situation of the city near the most frequented passes over the Alps made it a centre of trade where products of France, Germany, and Italy were exchanged Its merchants were prosperous, and its workmen skilled and widely famed. Its rank as a commercial city was high. As a centre of ecclesiastical foundations, it was scarcely less conspicuous. Its bishopric was accounted one of the most desirable ecclesiastical posts in Western Christendom, its cathedral chapter was largely recruited from the noble families of the region. The city was divided into seven parishes, and monasticism was represented by strong establishments of Benedictines of the Cluny congregation, of Dominicans, Franciscans, and Augustinians, and a nunnery of the Clarissines. With its three hundred clerics and nuns, its ornate churches, and its pilgrims to the ancient shrine of Saint-Victor, the ecclesiastical significance of the town was constantly in evidence, though unfortunately the character of its clergy was open to very serious reproach. A pleasant, bustling city, it was also a favourite place of residence for the lesser nobility of the neighbouring lands, not a few of whom settled permanently within its walls. With so much that was attractive was combined, also, not a little that is less pleasing in life and manners Geneva had the vices of a commercial city, situated on the highways of travel; and its population was undoubtedly more than usually pleasure-loving and luxurious. Its moral standards were low, and among those who set evil example to its dwellers were members of some of its most distinguished families, and many in priestly office or under monastic vows.

A city of contrasts and marked individuality, its inhabitants have been well characterised by a careful American student of its history [1]—

The Genevans, in fact, were not a simple, but a complex, cosmopolitan people. There was, at this crossing of the routes of trade, a mingling of French, German, and Italian stock and characteristics, a large body of clergy of very dubious morality and force, and a still larger body of burghers, rather sounder and far more energetic and extremely independent, but keenly devoted to pleasure. It had the faults and follies of a mediæval city and of a wealthy centre in all times and lands; and also the progressive power of an ambitious, self-governing, and cosmopolitan community. At their worst, the early Genevans were noisy and riotous and revolutionary; fond of processions and "mummeries" (not always respectable or safe), of gambling, immorality, and loose songs and dances; possibly not over-scrupulous at a commercial or political bargain; and very self-assertive and obstinate At their best, they were grave, shrewd, business-like statesmen, working slowly but surely, with keen knowledge of politics and human nature; with able leaders ready to devote time and money to public progress, and with a pretty intelligent, though less judicious, following. In diplomacy they were as deft, as keen at a bargain, and as quick to take advantage of the weakness of competitors, as they were shrewd and adroit in business They were thrifty, but knew how to spend well, quick-witted and gifted in the art of party-nicknames Finally, they were passionately devoted to liberty, energetic, and capable of prolonged self-sacrifice to attain and retain what they were convinced were their rights On the borders of

[1] Prof H D. Foster, *American Historical Review*, viii 239.

Switzerland, France, Germany, and Italy, they belonged in temper to none of these lands; out of their Savoyard traits, their wars, reforms, and new-comers, in time they created a distinct type, the Genevese

It is evident that the Genevan political situation contained elements of constant rivalry in the existence of divided authority. The house of Savoy sought unceasingly to increase its power over the city. Controlling the office of *vicedominus* from 1290 onward, and succeeding by purchase to the claims of the counts of Geneva in 1401 after the extinction of their direct male line in 1394, it gained the bishopric, also, when, in 1444, Amadeus VIII. of Savoy, the counter-pope of the Council of Basel, took upon himself that episcopal office. From his death in 1451 till 1490 the see was successively held by three of his grandsons, two of whom were scandalously young for entrance on their high office, and none of whom was of religious character. In the appointments of the succeeding bishops, Antoine Champion (1491–1495) and the seven-year-old Philip of Savoy (1495–1510), the influence of the rulers of Savoy was controlling, and their power was once more manifest in the establishment on the episcopal throne of John, the "Bastard of Savoy" (1513–1522), son of the third grandson of Amadeus VIII. who had held the Genevan bishopric. To him Pierre de la Baume succeeded,—a man of better personal life, but weak, luxurious, and unworthy of his office, against whom the burghers were to rise in successful rebellion.

These constant aggressions of the house of Savoy

were met with growing hostility by the burghers of Geneva. Led by two men of very unlike character but of conspicuous force, Philibert Berthelier and Bezanson Hugues, the citizens, on February 6, 1519, entered into an alliance for protection against Savoyard attack with the burghers of Freiburg,—the party favouring the league being popularly known as "Eidguenots" (*Eidgenossen*), while their opponents who supported Savoy were known as "Mamelouks." The first struggle was, however, disastrous. Duke Charles III, of Savoy, forced the abandonment of the alliance. The power of the bishop was restored. In August of the same year, Berthelier was beheaded. With the change of bishopric from John of Savoy to Pierre de la Baume in 1522, much was hoped for by the citizens; but the new prelate proved without firmness, and his own historic rights no less than those of the burghers were trampled upon by the duke, who was determined to make Geneva practically a Savoyard city. By the close of 1525, by the aid of his troops, the duke seemed to have accomplished his purpose; but his departure from the city showed the real weakness of his work and he was never again to set foot in the town. Unable to count on the bishop for help against Savoy, the citizens under the leadership of Bezanson Hugues now turned once more to Freiburg for aid, and to the most powerful of the Swiss cantons, that of Bern. By March, 1526, Geneva was in formal alliance with her two neighbours, and the weak bishop, after vain protest, became apparently and professedly a hearty supporter of the new order. It was only for a brief season, however, that Pierre de la Baume stood on the patriotic side. In 1527, he left the city, never to re-enter it, save for a few days in the summer of 1533; and, by 1528, he was fully committed to the interests of Savoy.

These successful assertions of Genevan independence led naturally to a modification of the constitution of the city, and to the growth to power of a more radical party than that of which Bezanson Hugues had been the leader. The year 1527 saw the erection of a new Council, that of the "Two Hundred," in imitation of Bern,—a body chosen, certainly from 1530 onward, by the Little Council and practically absorbing the business of the still existing Council of Sixty. Within the next two years, the authority of the *vicedominus* was abolished, and new judicial offices were established by the General Assembly of the citizens. The Savoyards pressed Geneva and made travel unsafe on the roads leading to its gates, but military aid from Bern, in 1530, relieved the situation. Thus far no serious thought of a religious revolution had entered into Genevan plans. The bishop might have kept much of his power had he sided permanently with the burghers; but he had chosen the part of their enemies, and hostility to Savoy involved more and more opposition to his authority also. In August, 1533, the syndics denied to the bishop his historic right to exercise the power of pardon; and fourteen months later his office was declared by them to be vacant.

The later developments of this struggle were complicated by the beginnings of the Reformation movement in the city,—a movement for which the attitude of the bishop more than any other single cause opened the way. From 1528 onward, Geneva was in a difficult situation in view of the religious controversies of the hour. Bern, the stronger of her two allies, accepted Protestantism that year, and thenceforward ardently furthered the Protestant cause; while Freiburg, the less powerful but the earlier and more friendly member of the league, stood staunchly by the older Church. When Bernese troops occupied the city in 1530, Protestant preaching and Protestant attack upon the symbols of Roman worship accompanied their presence; but the people as a whole had, as yet, little sympathy with religious innovation. By the ninth of June, 1532, however, there was enough Protestant feeling in Geneva to lead to the placarding of the public buildings of the city with an assertion of the Lutheran doctrine of justification by faith alone. The clerical leaders, the papal nuncio, and the Freiburg allies expressed their displeasure. The Genevan government, hard pressed between the diverse sentiments of its fellow-leaguers, disclaimed any desire to modify the faith of the fathers or to adopt Lutheranism, but at the same time requested the vicar to order preaching of "the gospel and epistle of God according to truth, without mingling with it any fables or other human inventions,"—a vote which certainly went a considerable way toward neutralising the declarations of adhesion to the Roman side, as it was doubtless intended to do. Though still relatively feeble, it is evident that enough anti-Roman feeling existed in Geneva by the summer of 1532, thanks to the attitude of Bern, popular hostility to the bishop, and, it may be, some real spiritual sympathy with the doctrines that Luther had made prominent, to insure a hearing for any bold preacher of Protestantism. In October following, such a proclaimer of reformed doctrine came in the person of Guillaume Farel

Farel's history had indeed been stormy.[1] Born in 1489 of a family of distinction near Gap, about fifty miles southward of Grenoble in southeastern France, he was Calvin's senior by twenty years. From a devoted adhesion to the Roman Church he had passed, during his student years at Paris and under the influence of Le Fèvre, through the gateway of humanistic sympathies, to a full Protestantism. Of intense nature, his development had been at the cost of much inward struggle, and he became one of the most fiery and uncompromising advocates of the Evangelical faith. After some preaching at Meaux under the countenance of Bishop Briçonnet, persecution compelled him to fly from France, and, by 1524, he was vigorously aiding the success of the party of Reform in Basel; but the opposition of Erasmus forced his withdrawal. We next find him in a strenuous and polemic ministry of two years' duration at Montbéliard, about thirty-five miles westward of the Swiss city just mentioned. Some months of sojourn in Basel and Strassburg were followed, late in 1526, by the beginning of a stormy pastorate in Aigle, a town, then under Bernese jurisdiction, situated on the Rhone a few miles above its entrance into Lake

[1] Herminjard, i 178, ii 42, 79, R. Stähelin, in Hauck's *Realencyklopädie für prot Theologie und Kirche*, v. 762–767, Doumergue, ii. 150–172.

Geneva Here he contributed not a little to the movement which won Bern for Protestantism in 1528, and he now received a roving commission to preach the Evangelical faith in all towns under Bernese authority, chiefly of course those in which his native French was spoken. He became the missionary of Protestantism to Romance Switzerland. Everywhere he went, notably at Neuchâtel, there was tumult, but his success was great. Opposition, danger, even wounds, but spurred him to more unsparing denunciation and more abundant activity. About three years of this itinerant evangelism had passed when his desire to aid the Reformed cause brought him early in October, 1532,[1] to the struggling and much-beset city of Geneva. He was a man fitted as few even of his polemic age to arouse attention and to stimulate controversy. Of stentorian voice, homely and forceful speech, and undaunted courage, men might approve or reject the messenger and his preaching, but indifference to him was scarcely possible. Accompanied by his friend Antoine Saunier, and probably also by Pierre Robert Olivétan, with both of whom he had been labouring among the Waldenses, and armed with a letter from the Bernese authorities, Farel began his work. Geneva had, as yet, scanty hearing for him. Interrogated by the civil authorities, he was cited before the bishop's vicar, and the chapter. Here he met heated attack with characteristic intrepidity; but the populace and even the cathedral canons wished to

[1] The date is given in the interesting chronicle of the nun, Jeanne de Jussie, published as *Le levain du Calvinisme*, Chambéry, 1640(?), Geneva, 1865, pp 46–51.

throw him into the Rhone, a gun burst as it was being fired at him, and he was kicked and struck in the face[1] by officers of the Church. The next day, October 4th, he and his companions had to seek safety by flight up the lake from Geneva, landing near Lausanne, and going to Orbe, not quite twenty miles northward. Here Farel found a younger fellow-believer, Antoine Froment, and persuaded him to go to Geneva to attempt the work which opposition had made impossible for Farel.

Like Farel a native of Dauphiné, Froment was now about twenty-four years of age. He had early attracted the attention not only of Le Fèvre, but of Marguerite d'Angoulême. From 1529, he had aided Farel in the spread of Reformed doctrine in Switzerland. A man of slight frame, eager spirit, and undoubted courage, this portion of his life seems to have been entirely free from the stains with which his checkered career was later to be marked. He now began his work in Geneva in the guise of a schoolmaster eager to give instruction in French, but under the protection of this occupation he propagated Evangelical doctrines to the utmost of his power. His hearers increased, till, on January 1, 1533, he ventured to preach in the square known as the "Molard."[2] The riot which followed led the Council of Two Hundred to forbid, by a vote passed the next day, any preaching without the permission of the syndics or of the bishop's vicar; but, though Geneva was still

[1] Jeanne de Jussie, p 49, Froment, *Les actes et gestes de Genève*, ed. 1854, pp 6, 7

[2] This has been called the "first public Protestant sermon in Geneva," but Megander had preached, in German, during the Bernese occupation in 1530.

almost wholly Catholic, the beginnings of a Protestant congregation had been made. Bern urged its powerful influence in favour of the reformers by a letter received on March 25, 1533;[1] and, three days later, a battle in the streets was narrowly averted by the syndics, while the Council of Two Hundred tried to keep peace by a truce which was really a partial compromise.[2] It availed little. At the Easter season the Protestants observed the Lord's supper for the first time, and on May 4th following, in a riot, Canon Werly, one of their most determined opponents, was killed. He had been a citizen of Geneva's Catholic ally, Freiburg, and the government of that canton now persuaded Bishop Pierre de la Baume to return to Geneva, as the best means of restoring ecclesiastical order, but the prelate showed himself utterly incompetent, and on July 14th left the city,—as it proved for ever. The conflict was but intensified. Guy Furbity, a Dominican preacher of denunciatory zeal, was imported, in the late autumn of 1533, to defend the Roman cause; and, in December, Farel once more ventured to come to Geneva. Freiburg and Bern now sent delegates to further their opposing religious interests; and with those of Geneva's Protestant ally came once more a pupil of Farel, who had already been for a brief time in the city ten months before, Pierre Viret, a Swiss of Orbe, of slender figure and low stature, now not quite twenty-three years of age, but already widely-known no less for his skill as a preacher than for his sweetness of temper and personal

[1] Herminjard, iii 32

[2] Foster, *Am Hist Review*, viii. 224; Doumergue, ii 118.

modesty. On March 1, 1534, Farel and his supporters seized the chapel of the Franciscan monastery known as the "Rive," and held public worship. The distracted government, drawn in both directions, was forced to side with its Protestant political ally, Bern, as the stronger; and, on May 15th, the league with Catholic Freiburg was broken under Bernese pressure. Eight days later, an iconoclastic attempt showed the growing Protestant strength, and, on the twenty-fourth of the following July, the Little Council formally voted that "the sole power is the Word of Christ and the sword which He has committed to the powers"[1]

Much of the late success of the Protestants had been due to the fatuous policy of Bishop Pierre de la Baume, who was earnestly supporting the Savoyard claims, and, by the summer of 1534, was doing all he could to raise troops against the city. Under such circumstances Geneva came increasingly under Protestant control, for its independence seemed bound up in resistance to its spiritual no less than to its ducal foes On October 1st, the Little Council, as already noted, declared the bishop's office vacant; yet Geneva was still far from Protestant by doctrinal conviction, and a Protestant observer, writing less than two weeks earlier, had affirmed that scarcely a third of its inhabitants could be counted against the bishop and the duke.[2] It was well-nigh impossible, however, to remain neutral in that strenuous age. The current now swept strongly on. An attempt, so it was widely believed, to poison the ministers,

[1] Foster, *op. cit.*, p 224

[2] Berthold Haller to Bucer, Herminjard, iii 209.

which nearly cost Viret his life on March 6, 1535, was followed by the execution of the woman who was thought its principal instrument, and being widely, though it is impossible to judge whether correctly, charged to the instigation of the Roman clergy, it greatly increased the tension between the contesting factions.[1] The government took the ministers, whom it believed imperilled, under its protection and assigned them quarters in the monastery of Rive. Farel pressed for a public debate, such as had resulted favourably for Protestantism at Zurich, Bern, and elsewhere. The bishop forbade his followers to take part. With difficulty two already wavering champions of Rome were found in the persons of Jean Chappuis, a Dominican monk, and Pierre Caroli, a doctor of the Sorbonne who had already fallen into disrepute with the Roman authorities at Paris, and was later to incur Calvin's displeasure.

The result of this one-sided discussion, which lasted from May 30th to June 24th, was of course claimed as a victory by the Protestant party, and Farel hastened to reap its fruits. On July 23d, he seized the Church of La Madeleine and preached in it The government tried to temporise. Its position was difficult, the city was still divided religiously. On July 30th, the Little Council ordered the Protestants to limit this preaching to the monastery of Rive and the Church of Saint-Germain; but Farel felt victory was with him. He had the same day declared to the Council that "he must obey God rather than men." With the support of his

[1] Kampschulte, i 159, Doumergue, ii 131

friends he now seized successively the Church of Saint-Gervais, then that of the Dominicans, and, finally, on August 8th, the Cathedral of Saint-Pierre itself. Image-breaking immediately followed. The churches were pillaged by the mob. The government bowed. On August 10th, the Council of Two Hundred, by a majority vote, while ordering image-breaking to cease, also directed that the celebration of the mass be suspended until further notice.[1] The downfall of the Roman party was evident. The revolution had taken place, and the Roman clergy, monks and nuns[2] now generally left the city. It was during these dramatic events of August, 1535, that Calvin, in his quiet retirement at Basel, was finishing the Letter to Francis I. with which his *Institutes* was to be prefaced.

Protestant conviction and aggressive zeal, and episcopal hostility to the independence of the city, were not, however, the only causes of the downfall of the Roman cause in Geneva. The clergy as a body seems to have been ignorant and inefficient. Not a few of them were unworthy. If any monastic order had deservedly a reputation in Christendom above others for learning, it was that of St. Dominic, but the Genevan Dominicans excused themselves from sharing in the debate of May, 1535, on the ground that they had no learned man among them.[3] Jeanne de Jussie makes it apparent that the moral status of many of the clergy was scandalous, and recent investigation confirms the earlier

[1] *Registres du Conseil*, quoted by Foster, *op cit*, p 225.

[2] Jeanne de Jussie gives a picturesque account.

[3] Kampschulte, i. 171

THE CATHEDRAL (SAINT PIERRE) AT GENEVA.

testimony.[1] As Kampschulte has well said: "The Catholic episcopal city fell, since it must fall, like a fortress the defence of which is intrusted to the hands of the cowardly and the unfit."[2]

While the later events just narrated were happening, Geneva was sustaining a difficult political struggle The bishop, from his castle of Peney, a few miles down the Rhone, in co-operation with the Duke of Savoy, was raising troops, pillaging the environs of Geneva, cutting off its trade, maltreating such of its citizens as were captured, and pressing it sorely. Bern would give no help, doubtless by reason of the selfish expectation that hard-beset Geneva would come under Bernese jurisdiction as the price of its deliverance. When, in the autumn of 1535, Neuchâtel marched to the aid of Geneva, Bernese agents sent these helpers homeward after an auspicious success in battle at Gingins And now, in December, 1535, King Francis of France, about to attack the Duke of Savoy who had been won by the crafty policy of Charles V., for the imperial side in the great struggle for the headship of Europe, offered French protection to Geneva on terms which seemed to promise well-nigh full local freedom Had they been accepted, Geneva would have become, ultimately, a French possession and the course of Reformation history would have been profoundly altered; but Bern was now

[1] *Le levain du Calvinisme*, p. 35. Compare Kampschulte, i 90, 169, *Mémoires et doc pub per l'Académie Salésienne*, xiv. 175 (1891), Foster remarks, *op cit*, p 223, "on this point there is substantial agreement between Catholic and Protestant historians"

[2] I. 171.

thoroughly frightened at the prospect. To have French influence established at Geneva would be to lose all Bern had hoped. On January 16, 1536, Bern, therefore, suddenly ended its halting policy and declared war against the Duke of Savoy. The Bernese army met no serious resistance It pillaged the country of Geneva's enemies almost to the gates of the city, drove out the Catholic peasants from the country roundabout, and burned hostile castles. In February, it was in Geneva. In March, it completed the conquest of the Savoyard territories bordering on the Genevan lake by the capture of Chillon and the liberation of its prisoners. All effective resistance by the Duke of Savoy was now rendered impossible, for scarcely had the Bernese army done its work when he was independently attacked in another direction by the overwhelming power of France. Geneva was suddenly freed from a peril which had been the dread of years. Yet it was in great danger of losing its newly acquired freedom by reason of the claims of its ungenerous ally. On February 5, 1536, the Bernese commanders demanded the rights over the city which had once been exercised by the bishop and the *vicedominus*. That would have made Bern the real master. The syndics and councils refused with spirit. Geneva would not forfeit its hard-won liberties; and, at last, on August 7, 1536, Bern consented to a treaty by which Geneva retained all disputed rights lately enjoyed by the bishop and duke, and held the lands once belonging to the episcopal see, its chapter, and the priory of Saint-Victor. The Genevan territories thus embraced not merely the city, but some twenty-eight adjacent villages ruled by officers appointed by the Little Council.[1]

The rejection of the authority of the bishop and the suspension of the mass left the ecclesiastical administration of Geneva completely unsettled. But the citizens of Geneva evidently regarded themselves as a Church; and the city government at once showed its determination to succeed the deposed ecclesiastical authority in the moral and religious control of the city. In large measure it stepped into the bishop's place. In September, October, and November, 1535, the Council of Two Hundred and the General Assembly used part of the monastic and ecclesiastical property to reform the older hospitals, establishing a large refuge for the sick in the former nunnery of the Clarissines, and an asylum for beggars, whose solicitation of alms was now forbidden. The prisons were unified. Early in April of the next year, under Farel's insistent urgency, preachers were sent to the outlying villages, the mass forbidden in them, and their inhabitants ordered to attend the newly established sermons.[2] The day following this vote the Little Council showed its growing sense of its own ecclesiastical authority by declaring that it held as absolved the excommunicated parishioners of the village of Thiez.[3] The government assumed no less vigorous control over the moral status of the city and its dependent territory. Even before the Reformation, when

[1] Foster, *op cit*, pp 228, 229, where the literature is given

[2] *Registres du Conseil*, *Opera*, xxi. 198, Foster, *op. cit.*, p 227.

[3] Herminjard, iv 26, Foster, p 227.

episcopal power was recognised, the councils had exercised the right to regulate games, dances, and singing;[1] and now, by a vote of February 28, 1536, the Council of Two Hundred issued a series of prohibitions, soon placarded throughout Geneva, forbidding blasphemy, oaths, card playing, and strictly regulating the sale of intoxicants and the reception of strangers into taverns. Brides were soon after ordered to cover their heads. In June, presence at the sermon was required under penalty of a fine, and the recognition of any festival save Sunday prohibited. The same month a citizen who had had his child baptized by a priest was ordered banished; and, in July, Jean Balard, once a syndic, and a man of peaceable disposition, was summoned before the Council, and, because conscientiously unwilling to listen to the new preaching, was given ten days to conform or leave the city.[2] It is evident that governmental regulation of faith and conduct at Geneva did not begin with Calvin. It was an inheritance in part from mediæval functions of the city councils, in part from the episcopal authority to which those councils regarded themselves as having succeeded.

While the government of Geneva was far from a full democracy, most of its affairs being managed by the largely aristocratic and close knit councils,[3] the full

[1] Foster, p 231, gives a series of enactments from 1481 to 1530; see also Doumergue, iii 432–436

[2] *Registres du Conseil*, xxx 32, *Opera*, xxi 203

[3] Foster, *op cit*, p 234–236, has pointed out that of the Little Council only five were elected by the General Assembly in any one year; viz the four syndics and the treasurer The syndics of the previous year remained members of the Little Council, and their sixteen associates

acceptance of Protestantism seemed a matter of so much moment as to require the General Assembly of the citizens. Urged by Farel, such a meeting gathered, on the call of the Little Council and of the Council of Two Hundred, on Sunday, May 21, 1536, at the sound of the bell and trumpet. The citizens of Geneva thus met, led by Claude Savoye, the first syndic, now voted, without expressed dissent, their "desire to live in this holy evangelical law and Word of God, as it has been announced to us, desiring to abandon all masses, images, idols, and all that which may pertain thereto." [1] Those entitled to express an opinion in the Assembly may have numbered from a thousand to fifteen hundred of the inhabitants of Geneva; and this action undoubtedly voiced the conviction which the opposition of the bishop and the long political struggle in which Bern had played so significant a rôle, as well as the labours

were chosen annually by the Council of Two Hundred The Two Hundred, composed of the Little Council and 175 others, were chosen annually after 1530, by the Little Council Elections of syndics by the General Assembly occurred usually on the first Sunday in February, on the day after, the Little Council was chosen, and on Tuesday the Two Hundred The syndics and Little Council were the legislative body and the supreme court in all ordinary cases. In serious cases of public policy the Two Hundred were called in, and they also had the right of pardon The General Assembly chose the syndics annually and treasurer triennially; and also elected, from 1529 on, five judges,—a lieutenant of justice and four *auditeurs*,—who constituted the lower civil and criminal court These judges were elected annually in November The assent of the General Assembly was also needful in very important decisions, like the one to be described, but Geneva was only remotely a democracy in all ordinary matters of civic policy, though choosing her chief officers in democratic fashion.

[1] *Registres du Conseil*, xxix 112, *Opera*, xxi. 201; English tr., Foster, *op. cit.*, p. 235.

of Farel, Froment, and Viret, had forced upon them, that the only path of municipal safety lay in adhesion to the Protestant cause.

It was not this vote alone, however, that made this meeting of the General Assembly of Genevan citizens significant. Two days before, the Two Hundred, at the advice of the Little Council, had chosen Farel's friend, Antoine Saunier, head of the "great school," at a salary of one hundred gold *écus*, and associated with him two "bachelors," as assistants in instruction. The General Assembly now voted that the education of the poor should be free, "and that every one be bound to send his children to the school and have them learn." [1] Universal popular education at Geneva was thus established, largely through Farel's influence, before Calvin's arrival, and a main feature of Genevan discipline was thus early inaugurated.

But, in spite of all that had been done, only a beginning had been made, if Geneva was to become the Protestant city that Farel wished, or even if its future Protestantism was to be secured. As matters were going, the utmost that could be expected was that Geneva would develop along the lines of state-controlled ecclesiasticism according to the pattern already established in Bern and Zürich. Though its services doubtless approximated to the form which Farel had put forth, several years before, in his *Manière et fasson quon tient en baillant le sainct Baptesme*, etc.,[2]

[1] *Registres*, *Ibid*; *Opera*, xxi 200–202; Foster, *Ibid* There had been a municipal school since February 28, 1428

[2] Printed in 1533, though written earlier, perhaps nearly a decade; see J. G Baum, *Le sommaire de Guillaume Farel*, Geneva, 1867, p. vi.

he Genevan Church lacked all organisation, save hat the city government favoured Protestantism, supported Protestant preachers, and exercised a kind of ecclesiastical control over Genevan territories. It had no creed, save the determination of the General Assembly to live according to "the Word of God," no separate discipline, no existence independent of the will of the civil rulers of the turbulent city.[1] Years later, in his farewell address, Calvin said with substantial truth regarding its state at his coming: "In this Church there was well-nigh nothing. There was preaching, and that is all. . . . All was in confusion."[2] There is no proof that Farel was not well content with the direction toward state control which the development had thus far taken, largely under his fiery discourses; but he doubtless felt that his abilities to plan were inadequate to the needs of the situation. The Papacy and the ancient worship had been rejected, but an architect was needed if a new structure of solidity and strength was to take the place of the old. It is proof of Farel's insight into character, no less than of his personal unselfishness, that he believed that the leader Geneva required was to be found in the youthful author of the *Institutes* whom the chances of war, or, as he would have more religiously declared, Divine Providence, had unexpectedly sent to the city.

[1] Compare Foster, *Ibid.*, pp. 235, 236.
[2] *Opera*, ix. 891.

## CHAPTER VIII

### CALVIN'S EARLY WORK AT GENEVA

CALVIN'S sudden determination, reached in July, 1536, under the potent exhortation of Farel, to make Geneva his home, was followed by a brief business trip to Basel. His return to Geneva, about the middle of August, saw him the victim of a sharp and painful illness,[1] so he can hardly have begun work before the end of the month. That inauguration was most informal. He did not become one of the preachers till nearly or quite a year later.[2] Under Farel's auspices, he began the exposition of the Pauline epistles in the Church of Saint-Pierre, and it was as "Professor of Sacred Letters in the Church of Geneva" that he published at Basel, in January, 1537, the two brief tracts on the proper attitude of Evangelical believers toward Roman worship and offices of which mention has already been made as having probably been written during his Italian journey.[3] Farel, anxious that his friend

[1] Calvin's letter to Daniel, Herminjard, iv. 87.

[2] Calvin said in his letter to Sadoleto (1539), "I discharged the duties first of a teacher, then of a pastor," *Opera*, v 386 Colladon stated that "a little after, he was also chosen pastor," *Ibid.*, xxi 58 But as late as August 13, 1537, the Council of Bern distinguished between Farel, "preacher," and Calvin, "reader in Holy Scripture," Herminjard, iv 276. See also C A. Cornelius, *Historische Arbeiten*, Leipzig, 1899, p. 129, of which I have made much use in this chapter.

[3] *Opera*, v 233 *Ante*, p. 154

should have an adequate livelihood, appealed in Calvin's behalf to the Little Council on September 5, 1536, but so slight an impression had the new-comer then made on the city as a whole that the Secretary, in evident ignorance of Calvin's name, recorded the request as having been made in behalf of "that Frenchman." It was not till February 13th following that a modest grant was voted [1]

From the first, however, Calvin exercised a profound influence over Farel, and his weight was soon felt in all the religious interests of Geneva. When the *Colloquia*, or meetings of the ministers of Geneva and vicinity, were established in November, 1536, Calvin became a member, and in their name he spoke the admonition to Denis Lambert, the unsatisfactory pastor at Veigy, in the opening days of the following month.[2] Even earlier, services of a more public character had brought Calvin into notice The victorious forces of Bern had entered Lausanne, the chief city of Vaud, where Viret was even then advocating the Evangelical cause, in March, 1536. In spite of the prohibition of the nominal overlord, the Emperor Charles V., that aggressively Protestant canton had determined to support the newer worship in Vaud; and, as a means to that end, appointed a public disputation at Lausanne for October first. Thither Calvin went with Farel, and, though his part was relatively modest compared with the work of his elder companion and that of Viret, in the eight days' session that ensued he gained dis-

[1] *Registres du Conseil*, xxx 51, 173, *Opera*, xxi. 204, 208.

[2] Herminjard, iv 107, 123, Cornelius, p. 129

tinction by the learning and skill with which, fortified by abundant citations from the Fathers, he attacked the doctrine of the physical presence of Christ in the Supper and thus contributed to the overthrow of the feebly championed Roman party.[1] From Lausanne Calvin went to Bern, and was present from October 16th to 18th at a synod which considered inconclusively the recently drafted Wittenberg Form of Concord, which Bucer was urging on the Swiss as a means of uniting all the forces of Protestantism. Calvin was thus rapidly making the acquaintance of the Protestant leaders of southern and central Switzerland. Those of the north and of the adjacent Rhine valley he largely knew already.

Farel's expectation was that Calvin would be a force in the organisation of the Genevan Church, and in this work the author of the *Institutes* immediately took the leadership, though popular judgment still continued to regard Farel as chief among the churchly guides of Geneva. The result of Calvin's work was the speedy preparation of Articles directive of Church government, of a Catechism for Christian instruction, and of a Confession of Faith for the whole Genevan community,—the latter possibly by Farel though expressing Calvin's thoughts. In them Calvin outlined not only the principles which had found expression in the *Institutes*, but many of the more essential features of his system of government as it was ultimately to develop.

Before Calvin's coming, on May 24, 1536, the Coun-

[1] *Opera*, ix. 877–884; Doumergue, ii. 180–218.

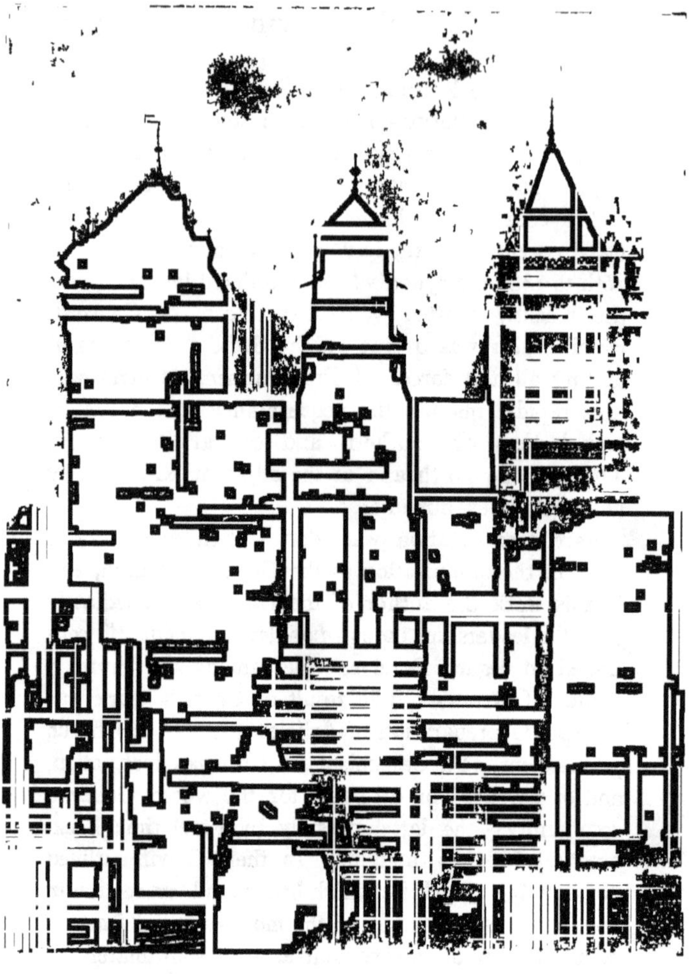

TOWERS OF THE CATHEDRAL SAINT PIERRE) AT GENEVA.

cil had ordered that Articles[1] be drafted to secure the "unity of the State." In compliance, on November 10th, following, Farel laid before the civil authorities certain propositions not now definitely known, which met with prompt approval.[2] Whether the articles then presented were those drafted by Calvin which have come down to us as of January, 1537,[3] or were, as seems more probable,[4] simply anti-Roman ordinances, is impossible absolutely to determine. If the latter be the case, however, as the writer believes, then the Articles of January, 1537, were not only entirely distinct from those of the previous November, but their presentation was an act unsolicited by the city government, and one illustrative not merely of Calvin's organising abilities, but of his prompt and conscientious determination to make Geneva what he would have it. For, though the records of the Little Council describe the Articles read before it on January 16, 1537, as "given by M$^e$G. Farel and the other preachers,"[5] the hand of Calvin and the familiar thoughts and even language of the *Institutes* are unmistakable. Calvin had won the support of his colleagues, he would win the approval of the government for this first programme for the construction of a Genevan Church as he desired that Church to be.

[1] On this general subject see A Rilliet and T Dufour, *Le catéchisme français de Calvin*, Geneva, 1878, pp. x–xxxiii; Cornelius, pp 131–137; Doumergue, ii 219–227.

[2] *Regisires du Conseil*, xxx 7, 87

[3] *E g* Rilliet, Dufour, Doumergue.

[4] Cornelius

[5] XXX 151, *Opera*, xxi 206. The full text of the Articles may be found in *Opera*, xa 5–14; and Herminjard, iv. 155–166

The Articles begin with a declaration that good churchly order demands the frequent and dignified observance of the Lord's Supper. Calvin's prime thought is evidently religious. As in the first edition of the *Institutes*, he advocates its observance at least every Sunday, yet "because the weakness of the people is such that there is danger that this holy and most excellent mystery may be despised if so often celebrated," he recommends its maintenance, for the present, once a month.[1] The dignity of this central feature of worship demands the exclusion of those of unworthy life and contemptuous conduct; and this consideration brings Calvin to the most significant element of the Articles,—their provision for church discipline. "For this reason our Lord has established in his Church the correction and discipline of excommunication."

The Articles then propose a systematic establishment of discipline, which had evidently fallen out of all use except as enforced by such sumptuary and moral enactments of the civil authorities as have already been noted:[2] —

To accomplish this we have decided to ask of you [the government] that your pleasure may be to appoint and choose certain persons of upright life and good reputation among all the faithful, likewise of firmness and not easily corruptible, who being divided and distributed in all the quarters of the city, shall have an eye to the life and conduct of each one; and if they see any notable fault to censure in any person they shall communicate with some one of the minis-

[1] *Ante*, p 142, *Opera*, xa 7, 8.

[2] *Opera*, xa 10, 11.

ters to admonish the one in fault and exhort him fraternally to reform And if it appears that such remonstrances are of no avail, he shall be informed that his obstinacy will be reported to the Church And if he confesses, there is already a great profit in this discipline But if he will not hear, it will be time for the minister, being informed by those who have this charge, to declare publicly in the assembly the effort which has been made to bring him to amendment and how all has been of no avail When it is apparent that he wishes to persevere in hardness of heart, then it will be time to excommunicate him, that is to say, he shall be held as rejected from the company of Christians. . . . Such seems to us a good way to re-establish excommunication in our Church and to maintain it in its entirety; and beyond this admonition the Church cannot go. But if there are those of such insolence and so abandoned to all wickedness that they only laugh at being excommunicated and do not concern themselves about living and dying in such exclusion, it will be for you to judge whether you will suffer such conduct long to continue and leave unpunished such contempt and such mockery of God and of His Gospel.

With this recommendation was coupled another of well-nigh equal importance:[1] —

It is certain that there is no greater division than concerning faith; and if those who agree in faith with us ought, nevertheless, to be excommunicated by reason of their ill deeds, with much more reason they ought not to be endured in the Church who are wholly contrary to us in religion. The remedy that we have thought of for this situation

[1] *Opera*, xa. p. 11.

is to ask you that all the inhabitants of your city shall make confession and give account of their faith, so that it may be understood who of them agree with the Gospel, and who love better to be of the kingdom of the Pope than of the kingdom of Jesus Christ It would therefore be an act becoming Christian magistrates if you, Gentlemen of the Council, each one for himself, would make confession in your council by which it may be understood that the doctrine of your faith is truly that whereby all the faithful are united in one Church. For by your example you would show what each one should do in imitation of you, and afterwards you should appoint certain of your body, who, being joined with some minister, should require each person to do the same This should be for this time only, since it cannot yet be seen what doctrine each person holds, which is the right beginning of a Church

Besides this sifting process by which those really in sympathy with the Evangelical cause could be distinguished among the inhabitants of Geneva, and the maintenance of the purity of the Church by discipline, Calvin and his associates proposed the training of the young in religious truth as a third important means of securing the spiritual welfare of the city:[1]—

There should be a brief and easy outline of the Christian faith, which should be taught to all children, and at certain seasons of the year they should come before the ministers to be questioned and examined, and to receive more ample explication according as there shall be need in proportion to the capacity of each, until they are approved as sufficiently instructed. But may your pleasure be to order

[1] *Opera*, xa. p. 13.

parents to exercise care and diligence that their children learn this outline and present themselves to the ministers at the time appointed

Here, then, was a programme of far-reaching significance, and of the utmost boldness as applied to a city like Geneva. All inhabitants were to be sifted by a creed test, which in the conditions of sixteenth century life meant something different from such a test to-day. It was almost impossible to be non-partisan between Protestantism and Romanism, and Calvin intended that it should be absolutely impossible. Each inhabitant must choose one side or the other with all its consequences. He must live "according to the Gospel," or according to the Papacy. But all inhabitants who accepted the Evangelical side, were, by right of their acceptance, as well as of their baptism, members of the Genevan Church. Calvin does not say what shall be done with inhabitants who refuse Protestantism. He did not need to say. The Genevan authorities had already taken the position, in the month of Calvin's arrival, and without influence from him, that they must leave the city.[1]

This Church thus established must be maintained in purity not merely by education, but by discipline; and this discipline was to be applied not, as in most American religious bodies, to that relatively small portion of the population who have made a profession of Christian experience and have "joined a church," but to all inhabitants who professed adherence to the Evan-

[1] Case of Jean Balard, July 24, 1536, *ante*, p 178.

gelical side, that is to all dwellers in Geneva after the sifting process should be completed. There was nothing novel in the idea of a strict watch by the civil government over the manners and morals of the citizens. Many regulations interfering with their conduct had been made before Calvin came, even in Roman days, nor were such supervisions peculiar in any way to Geneva.[1] Calvin's contribution was twofold, however. He would secure the appointment of lay inspectors, who should work in conjunction with the ministry,—a real Consistory, if still in undeveloped form; and, even more important, he would make the work of the inspectors a function of the Church, not of the State To the point of excommunication, which he deemed the limit of spiritual functions, these inspectors and the ministers, though appointed by the government, should act as spiritual, not as civil, officers The independent self-government of the Church was thus Calvin's aim. That self-government was far from complete as presented in these Articles; but it was real. When discipline had done its utmost, and not till then, was the State to exercise its authority over the hopelessly incorrigible. The chief peculiarity of Calvin's recommendation is not therefore its regulation of private conduct, —that existed before his work was begun,—but this provision for an independent exercise of ecclesiastical discipline in a Church which was largely the creature of the State and over which the State exercised control It was a first step toward the restoration, in a new and Protestant form, of that ancient ecclesiastical indepen-

[1] *Ante*, p 178; see also Foster, p 231, Doumergue, ii. 223, 224.

dence which the Reformation had almost universally sacrificed to its need of State support. Calvin's motive in thus asserting the principle of independent discipline was primarily pastoral, not theoretical, and grew out of his conception of the care of souls. As he declared, in 1538, in his Preface to the Genevan Catechism:[1]—

> Whatever others may think, we certainly do not regard our office as bound in so narrow limits that when the sermon is delivered we may rest as if our task were done. They whose blood will be required of us, if lost through our slothfulness, are to be cared for much more closely and vigilantly.

It was an independent discipline, aided by the civil government when discipline had done its utmost, that there might be a trained and conscientious Christian community,—the ideal of a Puritan State,—that Calvin planned, but to believe that Geneva could become such a state required high idealism, intense determination to secure the result which seemed logically desirable, and a persuasive capacity to win others to his point of view. These qualities Calvin now brought to bear on the Genevan situation.

It detracts nothing from Calvin's significance as an ecclesiastical statesman that the particular device by which he and his associates proposed to secure an independent discipline, as presented in the Articles of 1537, was not original with him. At Basel, with the affairs of which city Calvin was well acquainted, three

[1] *Opera*, v. 319, Cornelius, p 133.

men of repute had been appointed for each parish in 1530,—two from the city council and one from the general body of inhabitants,—to serve with the ministers in the supervision of the lives of their fellow-citizens. This device of Œcolampadius was not successfully carried out. It encountered opposition at once. Zwingli, and his successor, Bullinger, declared that excommunication was no function of a Church under pious civil rulers, but rather that discipline belonged to the State; yet the attempt at Basel was evidently the source of Calvin's plan.[1]

Besides these principal recommendations, the Articles advised the singing of the Psalms as a means of rendering public worship less cold; and the appointment of a civil commission which should judge matrimonial questions, with the aid of the ministers, in accordance with the "Word of God." The Little Council and that of Two Hundred promptly adopted the Articles, but with very essential reservations. The Lord's Supper was still to be celebrated but four times yearly, and marriage questions were to be determined by the Little Council, though "after conference with the preachers and ministers for guidance according to the Word of God." Discipline, the most vital part of the plan, still remained in dispute between the ministers and the magistrates. What Calvin and Farel proposed became the law of Geneva only in part.

The Articles had proposed a "brief outline of the Christian faith" as a basis of instruction for children,

[1] Doumergue, ii 224–227

and this Catechism Calvin had either prepared when the Articles were presented or brought it speedily thereafter into readiness, for he was able to exhibit it in print in discussion at Lausanne by the 17th of February.[1] Composed in Latin, it was printed in French translation as *Instruction et confession de foy dont on use en l'Église de Genève*, and was long supposed to be lost in this form, till a copy of the original edition was discovered in the Bibliothèque Nationale at Paris in 1877.[2] The Catechism itself is a nobly expressed and transparently stated presentation of the Christian system, as Calvin apprehended it, in substantially the same order and with the same emphases as in the first edition of the *Institutes*. From the point of view of its professed purpose, the instruction of children, it is far too long, elaborate, and minute. It should be remembered that catechism-making, so characteristic of the Reformation age, was still a novelty. Luther's catechisms were only seven years old Calvin, moreover, had had little experience as a teacher. He would have written far otherwise had he taught the young. It has been well described as a résumé of the *Institutes*,[3] and, as such, it is a compact and serviceable creed, presenting the system with the skill of a master-hand.

[1] Calvin to Grynæus, Herminjard, iv 240

[2] Printed with elaborate introductions by A. Rilliet and T Dufour, *Le catechisme français*, Geneva, 1878, see also Cornelius, p 137, Doumergue, ii. 230, 231 The Latin form was printed in 1538, and may be found in *Opera*, v 313–362 Some official adoption at Geneva must have taken place, for the Latin edition is described as "communibus renatæ nuper in Evangelio Genevensis Ecclesiæ suffragiis recepta"

[3] Rilliet, *Ibid*, p xlii

With this Catechism in its earliest edition, and therefore dating, at the latest, from February, 1537, was bound up the Confession of Faith, assent to which the Articles had recommended should be asked of the officers of the Genevan government and required once for all individually of the inhabitants of the city. Its title declared it to be "extracted from the Instruction [*i.e.* Catechism] of which use is made in the Church of the said city," and that "all burghers, inhabitants of Geneva, and subjects of the country, are bound to swear to guard and hold to" it. The words of this brief creed of twenty-one articles are not improbably from the pen of Farel,[1] but the order and thought is essentially that of the Catechism. Whether its actual writer or not, Calvin doubtless regarded it as expressing his convictions. Its most significant aspect, from the point of view of ecclesiastical constitution-making, is that it would base membership in the Genevan Church on an individual and personal profession of faith.[2] Looked at from the standpoint of ecclesiastical politics, its chief importance is as an endeavour to secure unity in allegiance to the new Evangelical Church and the exclusion of all who opposed. But the attempt to obtain the universal assent recommended in the Articles was one resulting in great difficulties for the reformers, and their efforts were delayed by internal and external conflicts at which it will be

[1] Rilliet, *Opera*, v pp lii–lviii, claims it for Calvin; the editors of the *Opera*, xxii 14–18, ascribe it to Farel The evidence is well summed up, with suspense of judgment, by Doumergue, ii. 237–239

[2] Doumergue, ii. 236

INTERIOR OF THE CATHEDRAL (SAINT PIERRE) WHERE CALVIN PREACHED AND TAUGHT.

well to glance before examining the fate of the Confession.

While the Articles, the Catechism, and the Confession were in preparation, Farel and Calvin were suddenly and savagely attacked by a fellow-Protestant as heretics, and heretics of what seemed to the Reformation age the blackest dye, deniers of the doctrine of the Trinity. The accusation not merely aroused in Calvin a strong sense of resentment because it was wholly undeserved, but, in so far as it was believed, it threatened not merely Farel and Calvin's whole position at Geneva, but all influence anywhere. It was peculiarly galling, moreover, to one who felt profoundly convinced, as Calvin did, that he was above all else Biblical and orthodox, — an interpreter of the very "Word of God,"— and it resulted in his first great personal antagonism.

Pierre Caroli,[1] who brought this accusation, was, like Calvin, a native of northern France, and, like him, a student at the University of Paris, where he had achieved distinction. Attracted by the semi-Protestantism of the school of Le Fèvre, he laboured under Briçonnet in his native region, expounded the Scriptures at Paris, and obtained an ecclesiastical living at Alençon. Vain, disputatious, of rather easy morals, he had no considerable fixity of belief, and was to pass

[1] The fullest treatment of this episode is that of Eduard Bähler, *Petrus Caroli und Johannes Calvin*, in the *Jahrbuch für Schweizerische Geschichte*, xxix 41–167 (1904); see also Kampschulte, i 295–298; Doumergue, ii 252–268. Calvin told his side of the story in 1545 in his *Pro G Farello et collegis ejus adversus Petri Caroli calumnias Defensio*, *Opera*, vii. 289–340.

repeatedly from one communion to the other, and to die in that of Rome. The tumult occasioned by the Placards compelled his flight to Geneva in 1535, where he fell out with Farel and Viret, and seems to have become thoroughly hostile to them. Thence he went to Basel, being there during a part of Calvin's residence and in the spring of 1536 obtained a pastorate at Neuchâtel. He therefore knew the Genevan reformers well. Through influence with the government of Bern he was appointed chief-pastor at Lausanne in November after the establishment of Protestantism in that city, and given a handsome income, to the relative discredit of Viret, to whom much of the success of the Evangelical cause in that city had been due. This discrimination in favour of one whom they deemed inferior to Viret in character and devotion to the Reformed faith aroused the protests of the Genevan ministers,[1] and their feelings were intensified, as may be imagined, when Caroli began to advocate prayers for the dead, not indeed as abridging purgatorial sufferings,—he was then too much of a Protestant for that,—but as procuring an earlier resurrection. In Caroli on the one side and Farel and Calvin on the other, the divergence clearly appears which had grown up between the semi-Protestantism of the type of Le Fèvre and of many of Calvin's early associates and the logical, convinced, thorough-going Protestantism which Calvin had attained. The same division, under very different circumstances, was soon to cost Calvin the companionship of du Tillet, whose friendship had been so valu-

[1] Herminjard, IV 107, 109.

able in his own days of spiritual struggle.[1] Yet the weakness of French Protestantism had been the large number of its adherents who had but partially broken with the ancient system. Its strength, however much our natural sympathy is drawn toward these men who did not see clearly, was unmistakably in the robuster type of which Calvin was the embodiment.

On news of this development in Caroli's teaching, Calvin went to Viret's aid at Lausanne, and the matter was brought before the commissioners of Bern, then in the city, on February 17, 1537.[2] Here Caroli turned the tables on his critics by accusing them of Arianism. Calvin presented in defence the appropriate section from the new Genevan Catechism, when, in a dramatic scene, Caroli called on his opponents to leave out of discussion the creed then hardly dry from the press, and join him in assent to the three ancient historic symbols of the Church.[3] Calvin rejected the demand, and answered: "We swear in the faith of the one God, not of Athanasius, whose creed no true Church would ever have approved." Here was, to Caroli, a seeming confirmation of his charges; and the action of Calvin in refusing to approve creeds which the Church had long reverenced, at the very moment when he was demanding that all inhabitants of Geneva assent to the Confession which he and Farel had prepared, is one

[1] Calvin to du Tillet, January 31, 1538, Herminjard, iv. 354

[2] The best account of the scene is the letter of the pastors of Geneva to those of Bern, written by Calvin within a few days of the event, *Ibid.*, iv 183–187.

[3] *I e* the Apostles', the Nicene, and the Athanasian Creeds.

the apparent inconsistency of which has often been r marked.[1] To understand his attitude we must remember the century in which he lived, and his conviction as to the final source of authority. To Calvin the ne Genevan creed was true, and therefore rightfully be pressed on others, because drawn from the "Wo of God." That ascribed to Athanasius was not so d rived, and was therefore not so binding. And a furth motive for Calvin's rejection of the ancient symb grew out of his humanistic feeling. Its want of class style, above all its repetitions, offended a scholarsh trained by the new learning and the new historic criticism.[2] To Caroli the ancient creeds seemed precious heritage from the past. To Calvin they we of value only in so far as they reproduced the "Wo of God" The humanistic reformer and the ecclesias ical revolutionist stood face to face in conflict.

Caroli's charge of Arianism was baseless, as an e amination of Calvin and Farel's writings readily show In his *Institutes* of 1536 Calvin had not hesitated to u the word "Trinity," and to describe the mode of exis ence of the Godhead in terms of historical theology But while really unsupported, Caroli's charges we given a certain plausibility by the actions and writing of the Genevan reformers and were not improbably ful

[1] Kampschulte, i 296, 297, compare Doumergue's defence, ii 26

[2] *Opera*, vii 315, 316

[3] *E g Institutes*, *Opera*, i. 71. "'I believe in the Holy Ghost,' whe we confess that we believe the Holy Spirit to be true God with the Fath and the Son, the third person of the most holy Trinity, consubstanti and coeternal with the Father and the Son, omnipotent and the Creat of all things. For there are three distinct persons, one essence."

believed by Caroli himself. With the wish to avoid technical theological terms in manuals for popular instruction, Farel had omitted the word "Trinity" from his *Sommaire*, and it, together with the word "person," for the same reason was absent from the Catechism and Confession which Calvin and Farel had just prepared for the Genevan Church. Moreover, Claude Aliodi, a wandering preacher whom the government of Bern had banished, in 1534, for opinions essentially similar to those already presented by Servetus in his *De Trinitatis Erroribus*, of 1531, had been at one time a colleague of Farel at Neuchâtel, and had affirmed to the pastors at Constance that Farel's beliefs were similar to his own.[1] He was now living at Thonon, on the southern shore of Lake Geneva. To a man of Caroli's temperament, Calvin's refusal to subscribe to the three creeds would, in any case, seem scarcely susceptible of an orthodox explanation.

From Lausanne, the matter of Caroli's prayers for the dead was carried to Bern, where, on February 28th and March 1st, Caroli renewed his charges before the ministers of the Consistory, in the presence of Calvin and Viret. Calvin defended himself and Farel in an address of great passion and extreme personal invective, but also of such convincing power that Caroli promptly withdrew the charge as far as Calvin himself was concerned.[2] Calvin refused to separate Farel's cause from his own, and with Viret asked the ministers of Bern to join in procuring from the Bernese

[1] Herminjard, iii 173, 174, Doumergue, ii 241.

[2] Calvin gives an outline of the address, *Opera*, vii. 309.

government the summons of a synod. It was obtained, though not without difficulty, for the spiritual leaders of Bern were disposed to look upon the dispute as one thrust upon them by foreigners, strangers to Switzerland, of whose orthodoxy there might be just suspicion. Before the Synod met at Lausanne on May 14th under the presidency of the pastors of Bern, and members of the Bernese government, with an attendance of more than a hundred ministers of French-speaking Switzerland, Calvin and Farel appeared, accompanied by their eloquent blind colleague, Élie Coraud. As at Bern, Calvin replied to Caroli with great heat and vehement personalities, but with such solid defence of his position that success was immediately his. The Genevan reformers were pronounced orthodox, Caroli was deprived of his ministry, and even Claude Aliodi recanted his Arianism.[1] Once more the matter came to public discussion, when a synod of German-speaking pastors from the Bernese territories met at Bern on May 31st, in connection with the civil Council of Two Hundred of that city. Here Farel brought most damaging charges against Caroli's private life, and he was forbidden to preach in Bernese territory. The Genevan reformers were declared orthodox by the government of Bern.[2] As for Caroli, he speedily returned to France and to the Roman Church, only to become a Protestant once more in 1539; but, by 1543, he was again in the older communion.

[1] Letter of Megander to Bullinger, May 22, 1537, Herminjard, iv 235; Calvin's own account is in *Opera*, vii. 310–317

[2] Herminjard, iv. 238–244; *Opera*, vii 325–337, xb. 105

Calvin and Farel had passed successfully through a great crisis; chiefly by reason of the real groundlessness of the charges against them, but in no small degree, also, because of the moral weakness of their opponent. Yet their establishment in public confidence was not easily secured. Suspicion and doubt at Bern, Basel, Zürich, and Strassburg, and even with Melanchthon, had to be overcome.[1] If Calvin displayed great asperity of temper in his treatment of his accuser, the seriousness of the situation and the baselessness of the charges are largely an explanation; and the loyal friendship with which he supported Farel and linked his own fate with that of his associate, when a separate defence would in some respects have been easier, is worthy of all praise. That he had been suspected of sympathy with Servetus by such men as Myconius, Bucer, and Melanchthon, even though but for a brief time, undoubtedly added intensity to his hostile feeling toward that speculative Spaniard when the two came in conflict at a much later period.

These weeks of struggle to vindicate himself to foreign opinion in consequence of Caroli's accusation were also a time of contest with foes in Geneva itself. In March, 1537, two Netherlandish Anabaptists appeared in the city, demanding of its authorities the right to dispute with the ministers, whose interpretation of the "Word of God" they, of course, challenged. The Little Council deemed it dangerous that they be heard in public,—the Munster catastrophe was still recent,—

[1] Letters in Herminjard, iv. *passim*. They are well summed up by Doumergue, ii 266–268.

but voted that they present their cause before the Council of Two Hundred. On Farel's insistence, however, this decision was amended and two long days of public debate—March 16th and 17th—followed, till the Council of Two Hundred, perceiving much excitement of the popular mind, ordered the dispute to cease, seized the papers prepared on either side, declared the Anabaptists defeated and banished them on pain of death.[1] In Colladon's *Life of Calvin* this repulse is attributed to Calvin's skill in debate;[2] but it may justly be questioned whether his arguments had so much force as the orders of hostile civil authority.

While these contests, within and without, were in progress, the enforcement of the acceptance of the Confession upon all the inhabitants of Geneva made slow advance. It was, at best, a dangerous experiment to undertake in a city where allegiance to the Evangelical cause was so largely the result of political conditions; but Calvin believed it to be fundamental to the erection of a proper Church, and had persuaded Farel and Coraud to a like point of view. Geneva had already seen divisions between "Eidguenots" and "Mamelouks," resulting in the victory of the former and the expulsion of the power of Savoy. Then the contest had raged between Protestants and Catholics, till the city had become, in name at least, all Protestant. But among the adherents of the Evangelical cause two points of view naturally arose. While one wing, led by such men as

[1] *Registres du Conseil*, xxx 188–193; *Opera*, xxi. 208–210, Doumergue, ii 242–243.

[2] *Opera*, xxi. 59.

the excellent Ami Porral, Michel Sept, Jean Curtet, and Jean Goulaz, supported the reformers, another considerable element valued the Protestantising of Geneva more for its political than for its religious results, wished no strenuous discipline, looked upon Calvin, Farel, and Coraud as French strangers who had crowded out old Genevan leaders, and admired the Protestantism of Bern, where the Church was controlled by the State and its pastors claimed no such disciplinary powers as were being sought by the ministry of Geneva. It was inevitable that such a party of opposition should arise, and its beginnings had appeared even before Calvin had become an effective leader of Genevan affairs or the Articles had been formulated. Of this party were such men as Jean Philippe, Claude Richardet, Ami de Chapeaurouge, and Pierre Vandel. Then, too, the aristocratic constitution of Geneva gave occasion, almost of necessity, for a party of opposition. As has been seen,[1] the Two Hundred elected sixteen of the members of the Little Council, and the Little Council chose the Two Hundred. It was almost a close corporation, but there was one very important point of popular attack. The General Assembly of citizens chose the syndics and the treasurer, who constituted the immediate executive and the most powerful element in the Little Council. A popular opposition of sufficient strength could therefore profoundly modify the government at the annual election in February, and the hope of those out of power was now set on such a reversal.

[1] *Ante*, p. 178.

In February, 1537, less than a month after the approval of the Articles, the elections had gone in favour of the party supporting the reformers, through the choice of Curtet, Goulaz, Claude Pertemps, and Pernet Desfosses as syndics. It was therefore to a friendly government that Calvin and his associates could look for the enforcement of the Confession. Requested by Farel and Calvin, the Little Council voted, on March 13th, to "cause the Articles to be observed in full." [1] But, for reasons that have been seen, the reformers were unable to press matters at the time, and it was nearly the end of April before printed copies were ordered distributed to aid in taking the assent of the citizens in groups. Opposition was evidently being encountered, however, for, on May 1st, the Little Council declared that it would do regarding the Articles "the best it could." On July 29th, urged by Farel, Calvin, and Coraud, the Council of Two Hundred ordered the local officers of the city (*dizenniers*) to bring the groups of their several districts to the Church of Saint-Pierre to assent to the Confession. This was largely done; but many refused, and, on September 19th, the Council informed such malcontents that, if persistent, "they should be told to go elsewhere to live." On November 12th, the Little Council repeated the demand for assent and threat of banishment yet more emphatically, and was reinforced three days later by the Two Hundred. Matters had,

[1] For this and the other quotations and citations in this paragraph see *Registres du Conseil*, xxx 189, 212, 219, 229, xxxi 30, 32, 45, 49, 61, 81, 90, 93, 100, *Opera*, xxi. 208–217 Compare Kampschulte, i. 298–306, Cornelius, pp 137–151; Domergue, ii 244–251.

however, reached a crisis Strengthened by an unfavourable opinion of the Confession expressed by Commissioners from Bern recently present in Geneva on quite other business, the opposition forced a meeting of the General Assembly, for which political negotiations with Bern gave more regular cause. Its session was stormy. Farel in especial was attacked, and Jean Philippe, the leader of the opposition, proposed the appointment of a commission to hear all complaints That, if carried out, would have superseded the regular officials in a fundamental part of their work. Only with great difficulty did the party in control of the government succeed in weathering the storm, and it was evident that its hold on Geneva was profoundly shaken.

Under these circumstances, had Calvin been a weaker, or possibly a more experienced man, or had his associaciates been less fiery and more worldly-wise than Farel and Coraud, he would have modified the severity of his demands and sought to lead to the results he desired by a more gradual process. He was, however, young, convinced that his way was that of obedience to God, and mastered by that Gallic logic in following a principle to its full consequences which the compromise-loving Anglo-Saxon finds hard to appreciate. Yet one can but admire his courage and his disinterested loyalty to conviction. And, at first, in spite of the unfavourable results of the General Assembly, it seemed as if Calvin were making progress. With Farel he went to Bern and secured what was practically a disavowal of the unofficial criticisms passed by the Bernese Commissioners on the Confession, the approval by the Bernese ministers of its contents, and letters from the government of that powerful canton recommending "peace, union, and tranquillity" to the inhabitants of Geneva.[1] Strengthened thus, for the moment, by evidence that Bern would not then support the opposition, Farel, Calvin, and Coraud informed the Little Council that they deemed it best to exclude from participation in the January communion "those whom they knew to be disunited,"—that is opponents of the Confession,—and asked the Council's support. It was granted, in part, for on receipt of a third letter from Bern, on January 4, 1538, the Two Hundred sent for two of the chief malcontents and induced them to swear assent to the Confession; yet, to the disappointment of the reformers, the same body voted "that the Supper should be refused to no one." Though the struggle for the Confession was substantially gained, Calvin's labours to introduce an effective, independent, ecclesiastical excommunication were thus brought to naught.[2] The opposition was evidently too threatening, though its point of attack was now shifting to the question of discipline.

With the election of February 3d following, came a complete political overturn. The leaders of the opposition, Claude Richardet, Jean Philippe, Jean Lullin, and Ami de Chapeaurouge, were chosen syndics. The next day ten new members were elected into the Little

[1] *Registres du Conseil*, xxxi 129–146, *Opera*, xxi. 217–220, Letters of December 6, 9, and 28, 1537, *Opera*, xb 130–134

[2] *Registres du Conseil*, xxxi 146, *Opera*, xxi 219, 220

Council. Even Porral was deprived of all office. Yet, though the party critical of the reformers was now in power, and Farel, Calvin, and Coraud were jeered and derided by the more disorderly of the populace, the relations of the reformers and the government were at first officially regular and undisturbed. This state of suspense could not long continue, however, without serious modifications on one side or the other, and it was speedily changed to open warfare. Certain propositions had been made in February by a Savoyard nobleman in French service, the sieur de Montchenu, to leading men in Geneva of both parties, very possibly inspired by his sovereign, Francis I., designed to further that monarch's wish to separate Geneva from the alliance with Bern and bring the city under a French protectorate. The approaches were loyally rejected; but among those addressed had been Michel Sept, a leader among the supporters of the reformers. Party hatred saw in this negotiation with the enemies of the city an opportunity to complete the discomfiture of the defeated heads of the former government, and, at a meeting of the Two Hundred, held on March 11th, six of the party which had supported the reformers, including Sept and three of the syndics of 1537, who by custom had places in the Little Council, were suspended from office. The course of these proceedings against their friends had drawn the public denunciation of Farel and Calvin, and the same session of the Two Hundred saw them forbidden "to mix in politics, but to preach the Gospel as God has commanded." This was a direct limitation on the freedom of the pulpit, and such men as the Genevan reformers were not likely willingly to submit.[1]

Strained as the relations between the reformers and the Genevan government were, a further action at this session of the Two Hundred was even more intolerable to men like Farel and Calvin than a prohibition to mix in politics. The Council voted to "live under the Word of God according to the ordinances of the lords of Bern." That is to say, the civil authorities of Geneva, without even consulting the ministers, determined the ritual of the Church. Their action swept away all partial ecclesiastical independence, such as Calvin ardently desired; and, taken as it was, it seemed well-nigh an insult to the Genevan reformers. It reveals in the clearest light the strained state of party feeling in the city.

Like most problems on which men divide, that of the Bernese "ceremonies"[2]—laying aside all question of the method of their adoption by the Genevan government—had two sides. The Reformation at Bern had not been quite so radical in its destruction of the older worship as that under the uncompromising Farel at Geneva. Bern had retained the use of the font in baptism, unleavened bread in the Supper, the festive array of brides at weddings, and the observance of Christmas, Easter, Ascension, and Pentecost.[3] At Geneva, all these had been done away. To the credit of the good

[1] See Cornelius, pp 157–159, 259, Doumergue, ii 271–272, *Registres du Conseil*, xxxi 3.

[2] See Cornelius, pp 161–169, Doumergue, ii. 273–277

[3] See Doumergue, ii 277, Herminjard gives them as Christmas, New Year's, Annunciation, and Ascension, iv 413 The contemporary documents speak of them generally as the "festivals" or "four festivals"

CALVIN'S CHAIR IN THE CATHEDRAL (SAINT PIERRE).

sense of the reformers of Bern and Geneva alike, be it said, the matter was regarded on both sides as relatively unimportant in itself.[1] But the situation was further complicated by the fact that the success of the war of 1536 against Savoy had left Lausanne, Thonon, and in fact most of the French-speaking territories about Lake Geneva—save the small tract over which that city held control—under Bernese authority. While Bern thus held most of the French-speaking Evangelical portions of Switzerland under its sway, and Bern's victories had made their Protestantism possible, it was but natural that their ministers, who were mostly Frenchmen, should look to French-speaking Geneva rather than to German-speaking Bern with sympathy, and adopt Genevan ideals of worship. In many places, as under Viret at Lausanne, the Reformation was introduced by personal friends of Farel and Calvin; and, in turn, the Genevan ministers welcomed the French-speaking pastors from Bernese territories to their "Colloquium," or ministers' meeting On the other hand, Farel and Calvin recognised the eccclesiastical supremacy of Bern in affairs concerning its own territories or ministers, as in the case of Caroli. Bern naturally wished uniform ceremonies in its territories, and, without absolutely forcing the issue, threw its influence in that direction, while the constant Bernese desire to possess as much control in the affairs of Geneva as possible, as well as the more laudable wish to have all southern Switzerland one in worship, inclined Bern to seek the establishment of its "ceremonies" in Geneva

[1] Herminjard, iv 106, 145, v 3, 4.

itself. In December, 1537, the authorities of Bern had instructed the embassy they proposed to send to Geneva to raise the question of conformity to Bernese practice.[1] On March 5, 1538,[2] they had notified the Genevan government that they had thought good to call a synod to meet at Lausanne on March 31st, "for the welfare and union of our preachers,"—that is to discuss the introduction of the ceremonies into all Bernese territories,—and asked for the presence of Farel and Calvin. It was probably the receipt of this letter that emboldened the Two Hundred to vote the introduction of the Bernese ceremonies at Geneva on March 11th.

Meanwhile the hopes of Bern rose. On March 20th, the council of that city, apparently in ignorance of what the Genevan authorities had done on March 11th, wrote again, saying that the Genevan ministers would be admitted to the synod at Lausanne only on previous acceptance of the ceremonies.[3] At this difficult juncture Farel and Calvin behaved with equal courage and wisdom. They presented themselves at the meeting at Lausanne, but attempted no part in its affairs. They would not compromise the liberty of the Genevan Church, even if the Genevan authorities had voted in favour of ceremonies to which in themselves, as practised at Bern and approved at Lausanne for the French-speaking Bernese territories, they had no se-

[1] *Opera*, xb 132.

[2] Herminjard, iv 403, gives the date as March 5th, and Cornelius and Doumergue agree The *Opera*, xb. 179, dates March 12th

[3] Herminjard, iv 403, Cornelius, pp 171–174, Doumergue, ii 278.

rious objection. On the other hand, they would not alienate Bern by open hostility. Hence, when the synod was over, and not till then, they entered into negotiation with the religious and civil leaders of Bern with a view to having the question of the ceremonies postponed till the meeting of a much larger Swiss synod at Zurich, already in prospect for April 28th. Had Kaspar Megander still been the spiritual leader at Bern, they might have succeeded even now in their request; but he had been dismissed from his post in December, 1537, and his successor, Peter Kuntz, a rough Swiss peasant by origin, was as little sympathetic with the more cultivated Frenchmen as they with him. The Bernese were too confident that the course of events was running as they wished, to desire to alter or postpone decisions already reached by the Genevan government.

On April 15th, the government of Bern wrote letters [1] to the Genevan authorities and to Calvin and Farel which were the immediate occasion of the final crisis. That to the reformers was of interest in that, for the first time in an official document, the name of Calvin was placed before that of his older associate. In these letters they reported the result of the synod at Lausanne, and asked conformity to the Bernese ceremonies. The Little Council, having received the communication, summoned Farel and Calvin and asked "whether they would observe the said ceremonies or not." The reformers urged that the matter rest till after the approaching synod at Zurich. Dismissed for the time by

[1] *Opera*, xb. 184–186

the Little Council, that body sent a messenger later in the day to Calvin and Farel, who reported that they "totally refused to preach or give the Supper in" the Bernese form. At the same session the Council forbade Coraud to preach till he had answered before judicial authority for his public criticisms of the government. The following day Coraud preached in defiance, and was promptly imprisoned. This seemed to Calvin and Farel insupportable, and accompanied by a number of the party favourable to them, including the ex-syndics Curtet and Pertemps, and also Michel Sept and Ami Perrin, they appeared before the syndics, protesting against Coraud's imprisonment and demanding a meeting of the Two Hundred. The government hesitated to proceed to final measures, and presented a compromise, offering to allow the question of the ceremonies to wait till the synod at Zurich, provided Farel and Calvin would consent to Coraud's deposition from his pastorate. The reformers declined thus to desert their colleague; and, on Calvin's repeated refusal to use the Bernese ceremonies at the approaching communion, they were forbidden to preach,—the Council declaring that it "would find others" to take their places. Its hope was in the weak-kneed Henri de la Mare, pastor of the Genevan country parish of Jussy-l'Évêque; but, by Farel and Calvin's threats of excommunication, he was induced, for the time, to agree to remain inactive.[1]

The morning following was Easter Sunday, and

[1] For these events see *Registres du Conseil*, xxxi 31–34, *Opera*, xxi. 223–226; Cornelius, pp 174–179, Doumergue, ii. 279–281

amid great excitement, in spite of the prohibition, Calvin preached at Saint-Pierre and Farel at Saint-Gervais. It was communion day; but they refused to distribute the elements, not, as they carefully explained, because they deemed the Bernese use of unleavened bread in itself wrong, but because to administer the Supper in circumstances of such popular tumult would be "to profane so holy a mystery." The breach was now complete. The Little Council met the same day, and summoned the Two Hundred for the morrow and the General Assembly for the day thereafter. By these bodies the Bernese ceremonies were once more ratified; and by a majority vote of the General Assembly, on April 23d, Farel, Calvin, and Coraud were ordered to leave Geneva within three days.

The dry pages of the official register of Geneva glow with unwonted vividness as they record Calvin's answer to the announcement of his banishment: "Well, indeed! If we had served men, we should have been ill rewarded, but we serve a great Master who will recompense us!"[1] But neither Farel nor Calvin had any thought of abandoning the struggle without effort They at once betook themselves to the authorities at Bern. The Bernese government lent them willing ears. Matters at Geneva had gone much too far to please Bern, however desirous of ceremonial uniformity. Bern began to fear for the Protestant cause in Geneva. But the controlling party at Geneva remained deaf to Bernese representations. Without waiting for the result of Bern's appeal, the reformers pushed on to

[1] *Registres du Conseil*, xxxii. 36, *Opera*, xxi 226, 227.

Zürich, where the synod representative of that canton, of Basel, Bern, Schaffhausen, St. Gall, and other Swiss Evangelical territories, of which mention has already been made, met on April 28th. Before this body they presented an elaborate statement, practically accepting the Bernese ceremonies as matters in the liberty of each church, but setting forth with unabated courage their programme of ecclesiastical reform. They urged the establishment of efficient discipline, the use of excommunication, the division of the city into parishes, more frequent observation of the Supper, singing of Psalms, and a more careful order of ministerial selection and appointment.[1] Their recent Genevan experiences had not caused them to withdraw a hair's-breadth from the strenuous ideal to which they had set themselves,—an ideal more thorough-going than anything realised in practice as yet by any of the Evangelical churches. The synod, under the persuasive influence of the reformers, approved their position, though urging them to use more Christian compliance toward an undisciplined people; and recommended the Bernese authorities to seek their restoration.[2] Thus fortified, they returned to Bern. The aid wished was granted, but again the way was barred. Though Bern despatched an embassy toward Geneva with Farel and Calvin, the Little Council forbade them to enter the city,[3]—a result to which the hostility of Peter Kuntz,

[1] Herminjard, v 3-6 The reformers would have men free to work after the sermon on the four feasts

[2] Herminjard, v 14, 17.

[3] *Registres du Conseil*, xxxii. 60, *Opera*, xxi. 229, Farel and Calvin to Bullinger, June, 1538, Herminjard, v. 21-29

the pastor at Bern, and of his correspondent, Pierre Vandel, not a little contributed.

Calvin's work at Geneva was now wholly, and, as far as could then be seen, permanently, at an end. Most various judgments have been passed upon it. It is impossible to affirm that it was always wise or skilful. A slower and more educative attempt to secure the reforms which he wished, and for which Geneva was so far from ready, would probably have been much more effective. The situation was obscured by party hatred, for the origin of which Calvin was not responsible, but in which he might have treated the opposing interests with more politic skill. He showed too much of the impetuosity of youth and inexperience. It was natural that he should. But, whatever judgment may be passed upon his methods, the ends which he had in view had never been uncertain or ignoble. He would have Geneva an orderly, disciplined, Christian city, and he would make its Church, to a degree yet unknown in Protestant circles, self-governing. Apparently he had failed; but it was a failure that carried no disgrace in the retrospect, however sharply Calvin was blamed by contemporary opponents, and criticised even by such friends of the past or present as du Tillet and Bucer.[1]

[1] Letters, Herminjard, v. 65, 103.

## CHAPTER IX

### CALVIN IN STRASSBURG

CONVINCED that their hope of restoration to the Genevan pastorate was vain for the time being, Farel and Calvin made their way to Basel, where they felt that, among friends, they might await further developments. Here they found a welcome in the home of Johann Oporin, the publisher of the *Institutes*. They watched eagerly for news from Geneva,[1] and Calvin, perhaps even more than his less sensitive companion, felt a deep sense of injury. He was profoundly wounded in spirit by the experiences through which he had passed, and his trust was still that through the aid of friends a synod of Protestant Switzerland might be called which would effect their restoration. Bernese reports spread through the Evangelical cantons that all was well under the new régime in Geneva caused these hopes to fade; but, as the days passed, Calvin began to take heart again as having received this bitter cup from an all-wise overruling Providence, which in due time would vindicate its ways[2]

Meanwhile Calvin's two Genevan associates found

[1] Their letter to Viret and Coraud, June 14, Herminjard, v 30

[2] See, for these emotions and hopes, his contemporary letters, notably to Bullinger, *Ibid*, p 21; to du Tillet, p 43, to Farel, p 70

other places of work. Coraud entered on a brief and unhappy pastorate at Orbe, which was closed in a few weeks by his death on October 4th. The call of Antoine Marcourt from Neuchatel by the Genevan authorities opened a pastorate there for Farel; and, before the end of July, he was labouring in that already familiar field. For Calvin the decision was more difficult. Farel wished him in continued association; but Calvin felt rightly that such a joint ministry so near Geneva would arouse their opponents, and Bucer urged that such companionship and location would but cause the wound which Calvin had received to rankle with fresh bitterness.[1] Bucer was, indeed, proving himself the wise and kindly friend that Calvin needed in this crisis. The letter that brought this advice, repeated to the chagrined young scholar at Basel a warm invitation, already urged upon him, to make Strassburg his home,—in which Capito and Johann Sturm also joined.[2] The body of French refugees which he might serve in that German city, Bucer told him, was indeed small, but it needed his aid; and a ministry at Strassburg might be of some service even to the cause which he had at heart at Geneva. Calvin hesitated. To take up a new work filled him with distrust. But now Bucer, as Farel had done at Geneva, urged the call as of God and cited the example of Jonah as parallel to his own.[3] Thus adjured, Calvin decided; and, probably on September 8th, he preached his first sermon to

[1] Herminjard, v. 65, 77, 87, 88, Cornelius, pp 197–200.

[2] Letter about August 1st, Herminjard, v. 64.

[3] Preface to the Psalms, *Opera*, xxxi. 28.

the French congregation in the Church of St. Nicolas at Strassburg.[1]

Strassburg, where Martin Bucer, Wolfgang Capito, and Kaspar Hedio had laboured since 1523, was the bulwark of the Reformation in southwestern Germany. In Bucer the city enjoyed a spiritual leader second only to Luther and Melanchthon. In Johann Sturm it possessed an educational reformer who was making its school, at the time of Calvin's arrival, a model of pedagogical method. In Jakob Sturm Strassburg had the guidance of a statesman of remarkable talents and breadth of view; and all had worked in harmony to promote a sane, moderate, and co-operant type of Evangelical Reformation. The city had been noted for its friendliness in receiving those who sought refuge within its walls when persecuted for their allegiance to the Protestant cause. No greater good fortune could have come to Calvin, in his depressed and wounded frame of mind, nor, indeed, under any circumstances, in view of his later usefulness, than to be given three years of activity in such associations as Strassburg offered. He was to be relieved, in large part, of the conflicts which he had been called upon to sustain at Geneva. He was to be treated with full respect. Time was to be his for study and for the perfection of his theological system. He was to make the acquaintance of many of the leaders of the German Reformation. He was to marry. He was to ripen and deepen by experience, thought, and contact with

[1] Herminjard, v iii., Doumergue, ii. 358.

DR. MARTIN BUCER.

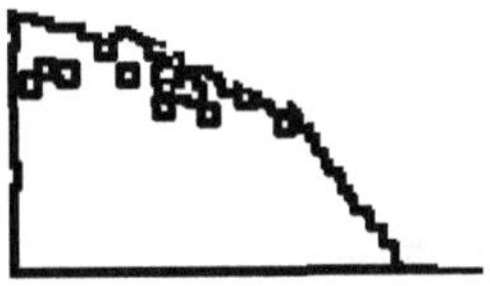

men, so that the years of sojourn at Strassburg must be reckoned among the most valuable, and in some aspects the most agreeable, in his experience.[1]

At Strassburg, in spite of the fact that he spoke no German, Calvin speedily felt at home. The spiritual and civil leaders of the city were cordial; and, so far did he respond to the attractions of his new environment—doubly grateful after the storms of Geneva—that, in July, 1539, he became a citizen of Strassburg, being enrolled in the guild of tailors.[2] This association implied no necessary working connection with the trade. Calvin's act shows his confidence in the Strassburg situation, for it was not till more than eighteen years after his return to Geneva that he was to enter the citizenship of that community.[3] But, though in friendly associations, Calvin had never been so pressed by poverty as he was to be during these months at Strassburg. His pay at Geneva had, of course, ceased. Du Tillet's aid had helped him before, and the prompt offer was not wanting now; but his old friend was now on his way back to the Roman Church, and coupled his offer with the request—under the circumstances almost the condition—that Calvin refrain from public activity. A man of Calvin's conscientious and sensitive spirit could not but refuse; and he declined the offer in words full of gratitude for the past, but positive as to the pres-

[1] Compare the remarks of Kampschulte, i 321 By far the best account of Calvin's stay in Strassburg is that of Doumergue, ii. 293–649.

[2] *Ibid*, ii 350.

[3] December 25, 1559, *Registres du Conseil*, lv 163; *Opera*, xxi 725. The delay was for prudential reasons.

ent.[1] At first he had no salary, and the recompense of fifty-two florins annually allowed him by the school board from May 1, 1539, was merely a nominal honorarium. A larger benefice Calvin seems never to have received at Strassburg.[2] Calvin's financial position was, therefore, oftentimes one of distress. It is not probable that he sold his personal library, as has often been said; though something came to him from the sale of books belonging to Olivétan's estate.[3] As a means of easing his fortunes, and doubtless, also, of extending his influence as a teacher, he took young French boarders, for the most part students, into his house.[4]

As a pastor of the French refugees gathered in Strassburg, Calvin soon found opportunity to put into practice much that he had attempted in vain at Geneva. The French exiles in Strassburg, who may have numbered from four to six hundred, cannot be said to have become a completely organised religious body before Calvin's coming. Under the supervision of the Strassburg authorities, to whom they, like all other worshippers, were responsible, they had had occasional preaching in their own language. But with Calvin's arrival they had a leader acceptable to the Strassburg

[1] Du Tillet's letter of September 7, 1538, Calvin's reply of October 20th, Herminjard, v. 107, 165, see also 292.

[2] See Doumergue, ii. 454–458, where the matter is fully discussed. The florin was worth about a dollar, though its purchasing power was of course greater than now

[3] *Ibid.*, Herminjard, vi. 13–26.

[4] Doumergue, ii. 458–462, has collected some facts regarding those thus received.

pastors, and permission was now given them to celebrate the Supper. Calvin's organising genius showed its power at once. To the "little Church," as he describes it, he preached four times a week. The communion he administered monthly,[1]—a frequency that he had vainly recommended to Geneva. In spite of criticism and opposition, he established a vigorous ecclesiastical discipline; and, though the congregation was under the control of the civil and religious authorities of Strassburg, he succeeded, thanks doubtless to the foreign character of its membership, in rendering the exercise of that discipline an independent ecclesiastical act. So far did he carry it that he not only forbade the communion to the unworthy, but he required all who would partake of the Supper to present themselves to him for a previous spiritual interrogation. Such an examination Calvin thought the only proper substitute for the Roman confessional.[2] He built up an orderly, disciplined congregation. Under his ministry it grew in influence, and his work was distinguished, also, by its success in winning Anabaptists not only of the city, but of the region about, to his way of thinking. Among the trophies of this zeal were one of the Netherlandish propagators of this faith with whom he had vainly debated at Geneva, and Jean Stordeur, then husband of the woman whom Calvin was later to marry.

Probably Calvin's most interesting, though not his

[1] Herminjard, v 111, 112, 145. It was celebrated "according to the rite of the city"

[2] *Ibid*, v. 291, vi 200, 223, compare Doumergue, ii 412, 413

most original, labour in behalf of the "little Church" was the development of its liturgy,—a form which, established with considerable modifications in Geneva on his return, became the general model of Reformed, as distinguished from Lutheran and Anglican worship, and is the primary source from which the type of service familiar in the churches of England, Scotland, and America that trace their spiritual ancestry in large part to Calvin is derived. Here, as in much else that Calvin did, he drew from the best that was at hand rather than created outright; but the result bore the stamp of his impressive spiritual personality.[1] Recent investigation has shown that the form of public worship at Strassburg had been gradually modified, largely under the influence of Bucer, from the revised translation of the Roman mass introduced by Diebold Schwarz, in 1524, till it had acquired probably by 1537, and certainly by 1539, the form of which Calvin made use. Calvin's work in preparing this first draft of his liturgy was essentially that of a translator. The order is identical with that of Bucer, and the form of words is largely the same. But Calvin added not a little in brief phrases and modifications of expression which gave to the original German service a happy adaptation to the use of French-speaking worshippers.

As employed at Strassburg, in 1539, Calvin's service,

[1] The subject has been opened as never before by Alfred Erichson, *Die Calvinische und die Altstrassburgische Gottesdienstordnung*, Strassburg, 1894, who perhaps allows too little to Calvin though clearly making out his main contention It is largely treated by Doumergue, ii 488–504

like that of Bucer from which it was taken, began with the Invocation and the famous Confession still in use in many of the Reformed Churches of the continent, corresponding to, though far from identical with, that of the Anglican worship. Next followed the announcement of absolution to all who repent and "seek Jesus Christ for their salvation." Then the first table of the Decalogue—that is the first four Commandments—was sung by the congregation.[1] Upon this followed a brief form of prayer for forgiveness and for strength to keep the divine law, succeeded by the singing of the remaining Commandments. A short form of prayer for spiritual illumination was then followed by the central feature of the service, the reading of the "Word of God" and its exposition in the sermon. That completed, there followed the long, liturgical petition of general supplication, ending in the Lord's Prayer. This was succeeded by the singing of the Apostles' Creed or of a Psalm, and the service concluded with the Aaronic benediction.[2]

It may be well to note the principal changes made in this service by Calvin when introduced into Genevan use on his return to that city,[3]—the more that they illustrate a principal characteristic of his thought on liturgical usages. Most of these modifications were in the direction of approximation to the relatively undeveloped, yet more radically non-Roman, service which Farel had established in Geneva when the Reformation gained

[1] Doubtless in the rhymed form to be found in *Opera*, vi 221.

[2] Numbers vi 24–26 Text in part in *Opera*, vi. 174, 175; Erichson and Doumergue, *op cit*

[3] Full text, *Opera*, vi 161–224.

control in 1536, and that doubtless continued in use till Calvin's return. With this end in view, against his own preference,[1] he omitted the promise of absolution, as offensive by its apparent Romanism to some more strict than he. He substituted the singing of a Psalm for the twofold chanting of the Commandments and the intermediate prayer. As Farel had done, he now gave room for extempore prayer, saying of the petition before the sermon, "The form is at the discretion of the minister." At first he substituted an enlarged paraphrase of the Lord's Prayer in the body of the general petition following the sermon for its literal repetition at its conclusion, but later restored it. For the chanting of the Apostles' Creed he substituted that of a Psalm.[2] These modifications are not inconsiderable, though they do not affect the general order, dignity, and simplicity of the service, or its resemblance to the Strassburg original to which Calvin was indebted, but they show that, within the limits imposed by the rejection of what he deemed unscriptural or superstitious, Calvin felt that public worship might be modified and adjusted to meet local needs and even prejudices. As between a fixed liturgy and free prayer he evidently had none of the scruples which later controversy was to develop among his spiritual disciples in England, Scotland, and

[1] *Opera*, xa 213, Doumergue, ii 502 Doumergue remarks "it was accommodated to the worship of Geneva to such a degree that the liturgy deserves the title of Genevese much more than of Calvinist"

[2] Doumergue, ii. 746, shows that the Apostles' Creed was recited at Geneva at the close of Lord's Prayer, ending the general petition

America; and his Genevan form of worship, at least, was a happy combination of both.

A service of a yet more wide-reaching character done by Calvin for the Strassburg congregation of which he was pastor, and through it to the Reformed churches generally, was the establishment of the singing of Psalms in French. The part that the hymns of Luther played in the German Reformation is well known. But not all reformers had so recognised the value of song. Zwingli had wholly done away with it at Zürich, and the earliest French Protestants made no use of hymns.[1] Farel's circle felt the value of songs, at least as a means of attacking Roman beliefs, if not of public worship, and a little volume of such popular compositions was printed at Neuchâtel in 1533.[2] But the most positive step toward the introduction of the hymn into French-speaking Protestant worship was that taken by Farel and Calvin in the Articles of January, 1537.[3] Not till he came to Strassburg was Calvin able to carry the intentions therein expressed into practice. He acted with his accustomed vigor, aided doubtless by the example of the German-speaking churches of the city, in which singing was the rule. Within two months of the beginning of his pastorate, the "little Church" was singing Psalms; and, in 1539, he published a brief collection, containing eighteen Psalms and three other compo-

[1] Doumergue has an admirable discussion of Calvin's relation to music in worship, ii 505–524.

[2] *Ibid*, p 506, Rilliet and Dufour, *Le catéchisme françats de Calvin*, p cc

[3] *Ante*, p. 192.

sitions in French verse,—eight of them by Clémei Marot, whose poetic gifts were to make him the Psaln translator above all others of French Protestantisn but seven of the pieces from the pen of Calvin himself Calvin's own composition, if not of high poetic orde was dignified, clear, and far removed from doggere Indeed, in his own estimate, he had something of th poetic spirit, and in youth, like many another youn man, tried his hand at verse.[2] But, as later editions c the Psalter were issued, Calvin's critical taste led him t substitute increasingly Marot's more inspired compo sitions, as they were put forth, for his own. Thougl chiefly drawn from the Psalms, Calvin would not con fine the service of song to the rhymed words of Scripture The Genevan liturgy of 1545 contains, besides nin Psalms, the *Nunc Dimittis* of Simeon, the Ten Com mandments versified, and a free hymn of "salutation tc Christ."[3] The later Puritan restriction to the words o the Bible was evidently not of Calvin's making. On the other hand, whatever may have been Calvin's feeling toward the organ as an instrument of music, he did not regard its use as appropriate in public worship because of its tendency to take the thought of the congregation from the words of the hymn.[4] Far from being an enemy of song in Christian worship, Calvin was the great supporter and advocate of the use of the Psalm in the Reformed churches.

[1] Doumergue, ii 511

[2] *Ibid*, p 510, quoting *Opera*, xvi 488

[3] *Opera*, vi 211–224

[4] Doumergue, ii 521, quoting *Opera*, xxx 259.

While Calvin was thus busily engaged in Strassburg as a pastor, he was developing a like activity as a teacher, so that, with the additional burden of a large correspondence and his constant struggle with poverty, his days must have been full indeed. Theological lectures had been given at Strassburg[1] since the introduction of the Reformation, and since 1532, in formal fashion, by Bucer, Capito, and Hedio in the choir of the cathedral As systematised by Johann Sturm, in the month of Calvin's arrival, the school curriculum of Strassburg included not merely elementary teaching, and advanced courses in Greek, Latin, Hebrew, Mathematics, and Law, but was crowned by instruction in theology given by the Strassburg ministers of whom mention has been made. The orderly, thorough, and progressive educational constitution of Strassburg must have impressed Calvin profoundly and have influenced his later action at Geneva. Naturally the Strassburg pastors, to whom theological instruction was committed, wished the aid of the author of the *Institutes*, and, in January, 1539, Calvin began his work,[2] at first without compensation, and from May onward with the modest honorarium of which mention has been made. The form of instruction in theology was by Biblical exposition, and the natural supposition would be that the first theme of Calvin's public interpretation was the Epistle to the Romans. His *Commentary* on this letter of the Apostle to the

[1] Here again the sources and literature have been well summarised by Doumergue, ii. 428–440.

[2] Letter to Farel, Herminjard, v. 230, Doumergue, ii. 434. He was invited by Capito

Gentiles, the preface of which is dated October 18, 1539, was published at Strassburg by Wendelin Rihel in March, 1540,[1] and inaugurated the long series of Biblical expositions which were to give to Calvin the first rank as an exegete among the leaders of the Reformation age. But adequate testimony seems to make it evident that Calvin's first work as a public instructor was the interpretation of the Gospel according to Saint John, and that this teaching was followed by the exposition of Corinthians.[2]

The lectures attracted wide attention, and drew Calvin's fellow-countrymen of Evangelical sentiments in considerable numbers from the home-land to Strassburg, as well as added to his rising fame in the city of his residence. And to all who came, he was able to show an example, in miniature it is true, but of striking clearness, of a Christian community as he believed such a community should be,—his Church of earnest-minded exiles for their faith, well disciplined, clearly taught, and knit together in common worship, while their pastor bore his share in the larger religious interests of Strassburg and extended his influence far beyond the city's walls.

This multiform activity as pastor and teacher was accompanied by a productivity in authorship that reveals the strength and concentration with which Calvin was able to work, in spite of frequent physical disability, chiefly manifested in attacks of headache,

1 *Opera*, xlix 1–296; Herminjard, vi 74–78, compare *Ibid*, v 230

2 Johann Sturm, *Quarti Antipappi*, p 20, as cited by Doumergue, ii 434.

indigestion, and nervous irritability,[1]—a condition of health largely due, doubtless, to his overstrain as a student in Paris and Orléans, and the anxieties and burdens borne at Geneva. In August, 1539, he brought out a carefully revised and much enlarged edition of the *Institutes.*[2] Though still lacking much of the logical perfection of arrangement which this treatise was to acquire in the final edition of 1559, it may be said that, with the edition of 1539, the *Institutes* attained their doctrinal completeness. The treatment was everywhere more ample; and the second edition now published immediately superseded the relatively brief handbook of 1536. In particular, the opening sections, on the knowledge of God and of ourselves, were greatly enlarged. The distinctions between natural and revealed theology were clearly set forth. The final authority of Scripture was firmly based on the inward testimony of the Holy Spirit witnessing to the reader that it is God who speaks through the words. The original state of man and the consequences of the fall were discussed with much greater amplitude. Election and reprobation were now much more fully and sharply set forth, and were elaborately defended as taught in the divine revelation. In a word, without essentially departing in any fundamental respect from the theological system set forth in the edition of the *Institutes* published in 1536, this Strassburg revision of three years later reveals a mind of greater maturity, more elaborated

[1] Letters to Farel, Herminjard, v. 88, 270, vi. 312, 313.

[2] Text, *Opera*, i 253–1152.

thought and sharper definition of the doctrines commonly called Calvinistic. The theologian had come to his full stature.

In the *Institutes* of 1539, the doctrine of the Lord's Supper, that burning point of contention between the Lutherans and the older reformers of Switzerland, is so treated that, without alteration of his fundamental view, Calvin's language is less opposed to the conception of Luther than in the earlier edition. This irenic spirit, anxious to present a basis of mutual agreement between the contending factions, is well illustrated in the *Petit Traicté de la saincte Cene*,[1]—an exposition designed especially for those without technical theological training. Written in Strassburg, it was published at Geneva in 1541, and was doubtless designed for circulation in France quite as much as in Switzerland. Even more than thus far at Geneva, Calvin's work in Strassburg was revealing to him the possibility of exercising a moulding influence on the course of the Evangelical movement in his home-land such as he had always desired.

As compared with his life at Geneva, Calvin's sojourn at Strassburg was free from personal controversies; but an exception is worthy of mention. Caroli, whose accusations against Farel and Calvin have already been described, had returned to the Roman Church after his failure to make good his charges at the synods of Lausanne and Bern in 1537. His restless spirit, and

[1] Text, *Opera*, v 429–460 See especially his remarks about Luther, Zwingli, and Œcolampadius, *Ibid.*, 457–460 Compare Henry, i 261–285

we may believe his semi-Protestantism, was not satisfied, however; and, in July, 1539, he sought Farel and Viret, by whom he was once more received into friendship.[1] Armed with a letter of commendation from Simon Grynæus, professor at Basel, to Calvin, he came to Strassburg, about the beginning of October, and set about to win the approval of its ministers and professors. At Bucer's request, as having been already in controversy with Caroli, Calvin did not meet him face to face;[2] and Caroli, anxious to excuse his recent reconciliation with Rome, brought up in discussion with the Strassburg divines Farel and Calvin's refusal to sign the three ancient creeds. On Caroli's retirement from the conference-room, Calvin told his side of the late controversy to the Strassburg ministers and teachers. They regarded Calvin as innocent of any wrong to Caroli, though his refusal to subscribe the creeds met their disapproval. A long Act of Reconciliation was drawn up for signature by Caroli and the Strassburg divines, in which he assented to the Augsburg Confession, but specified many peculiarities of his, at best, fluctuating beliefs. This document was not sent to Calvin for signature till late at night; and, before being seen by him, it had received the approval of his colleagues. As he read it, he saw that it permitted Caroli to say that he left to God's judgment "the offences by

[1] The letters regarding this incident may be found in Herminjard, v 352, 355, 370, vi 35, 40, 52 It is suggestively treated by Doumergue, ii 397–405.

[2] Calvin's letter of October 8th to Farel, Herminjard, vi 52–58, is our source.

which he had been forced to desertion" of the Evangelical cause. That implied that Farel and Calvin were blameworthy for his lapse. It was an aggravating and unjust accusation. Calvin had a right to resent it But he did much more. He lost all control of himself He sought Sturm, and his colleagues, Bucer and Matthias Zell. In words of the utmost excitement and bitterness he declared that he would die before he would sign. He rushed, so he tells Farel, from the room; but Bucer followed and in a measure calmed him, though his return home was succeeded by what must be called an attack of hysterics. In the letter which recounts these events, he blames himself severely for his ungoverned conduct; but he blames his friend Farel no less as the cause of his woes. Farel's acceptance of the apparently repentant Caroli should not have been so hasty. Indeed, in the mood in which he wrote, the fault seemed to him more that of Farel than of Caroli, who having been received into favour must now be treated with kindness. Calvin succeeded in having the objectionable clause erased, and signed the Reconciliation; but the incident is one to be borne in mind in a consideration of his later controversies. He was liable to violent anger, and was easily aroused to high nervous excitement, and in this state was unguarded in the extreme in what he said, or to whom he expressed his wrath. He clearly recognised his own fault;[1] but it was one which many times overcame him, and obscured

[1] Doumergue, ii, 401–405, makes this incident the text of a discussion, with other examples, of this side of Calvin's nature.

too much in his own lifetime and in later recollection other, and much more attractive, qualities of mind and heart.

It is pleasant to turn from this incident of Calvin's life in Strassburg to one of a more intimate and personal nature,—his marriage. His life of study and of exile, followed by the stormy months at Geneva, had not been such hitherto as to turn his thoughts toward the establishment of a home. He had not been without companionship. His younger brother, Antoine, and his half-sister, Marie, had accompanied him to Geneva; and the former, after a few months' delay, followed him to Strassburg, arriving in December, 1539, and continuing thenceforth, as had probably been the case at Geneva, a member of Calvin's household as long as he remained in the city.[1] In the comparative quiet of Strassburg, notwithstanding his poverty,—and perhaps in the eyes of some of his friends, though not of Calvin himself, by reason of that poverty,—the question of marriage soon began to assume importance. His former associate Viret had married in October, 1538. That example, and that of the Strassburg ministry, together with the advice of Bucer, may have had weight. At all events, it was the desirability of marriage in itself considered rather than affection for any one person that awoke the thought of his own union in Calvin's mind. He apparently first presented the matter to his bachelor friend, Farel, in a letter now lost; and writing, a little

[1] Marie seems not to have gone to Strassburg. She ultimately married Charles Costan, probably of Geneva (*Opera*, xx. 300), and may have been married before Calvin left Geneva.

later, to that intimate correspondent in May, 1539, he thus described the wife that he desired:[1]—

> I am not of that insane class of lovers who, once captivated by beauty, kiss even its faults The only comeliness that attracts me is this —that she be modest, complaisant, unostentatious, thrifty, patient, and likely to be careful of my health.

To appreciate the unromantic and rather self-centred ideal here set forth by a man who had not reached thirty years of age, we must remember the century in which he lived, with its low estimate of the position of women as compared with their place in our own, and the absorption which Calvin felt in the reformatory task that was before him. Such as it was, his ideal was to be realised, but not immediately.[2] Nine months later, in February, 1540, Calvin informed Farel[3] that marriage had been proposed to him in behalf of a well-to-do and nobly born young woman,—the agents being apparently the girl's brother and brother's wife, who were devotedly attached to him and wished their sister married to one they so much admired. Calvin

[1] Herminjard, v 314, Doumergue, ii 448 Doumergue, *Ibid*, pp 441–478, has treated Calvin's marriage with characteristic thoroughness See also Henry, i 407–423, Bonnet, *Idelette de Bure*, in *Bulletin de la Soc de l'hist du Prot français*, iv 636–646 (1856), A Lang, *Das häusliche Leben Johannes Calvins*, in the *Allgemeine Zeitung*, June 16–22, and separately, Munich, 1893

[2] Apparently Farel came to Strassburg in June, 1539, for some marriage project of Calvin of which we have no definite knowledge Herminjard, vi. 168

[3] *Ibid.*, vi. 167

insisted that she learn his native French. She asked time to think it over; a request which he seems to have looked upon as a divinely appointed way of deliverance from a marriage in which inequality of birth and education might have clouded the prospect of happiness. Calvin took a prompt way to break off further negotiations. He sent his brother, Antoine, to ask in his behalf the hand of another and much poorer young woman, "who, if she answers to her reputation, would bring dowry enough without any money." So hopeful was he that this vicarious wooing would prosper that he wished Farel to plan to perform the ceremony not later than the tenth of the next month. Such confidence was, as may readily be imagined, unwarranted. The young woman delayed; and when at last, in the following June, she consented to an engagement, Calvin heard such reports of her that he speedily released her.[1] In all this there seems little sentiment save an honest fear lest he marry above his station in life and with one unsympathetic with his aims. But the search was evidently continued, for on August 17, 1540, Christopher Fabri wrote Calvin from Thonon, bidding him salute the wife whom they had heard he had recently married.[2] The wife to whom he was at last joined, "with the aid and advice of Bucer," was "a grave and honourable

[1] Herminjard, vi 191, 199, 238 It is possible that the person to whom he became engaged in June is not identical with the poor girl sought in February, but I have followed what seems the more probable interpretation of Calvin's letters

[2] *Ibid.*, vi. 275. Herminjard and Doumergue seem justified in regarding this letter as fixing the month of the marriage, though many earlier scholars placed it a month or more later.

woman," Idelette de Bure, widow of Calvin's Anabaptist convert, Jean Stordeur of Liège, who had died some time before of the plague[1] The ceremony was probably simple, and Farel himself, there is reason to suppose, officiated[2]

Calvin's married life has left fewer traces than could be wished in his correspondence, but enough remains to show that husband and wife lived on terms of cordial affection and of mutual trust. In character and devotion she was to him all that his ideal of a wife had pictured. To Viret he wrote of her immediately after her death.[3]—

> I have been bereaved of the best companion of my life, who, if our lot had been harsher, would have been not only the willing sharer of exile and poverty, but even of death. While she lived, she was the faithful helper of my ministry. From her I never experienced the slightest hindrance.

That she was a woman of unusual Christian faith, and not without force and some degree of individuality, the story of her death-bed bears witness.[4] But we know far less of her and of her influence on her husband than we desire. At best, she stands in the shadow of his much clearer seen personality.

[1] Colladon, *Life*, *Opera*, xxi 62 Lefranc conjectures that she may have been of the family of de Bures of Noyon, and hence that the marriage may not have been "the result of a meeting wholly due to chance" *Jeunesse*, p 191 There were Bures, however, at Liège, Doumergue, ii 463 Idelette had a son and a daughter by her first husband

[2] Doumergue, ii 463

[3] *Opera*, xiii 230; compare *Ibid*, viii 73, "*singularis exempli femina*"

[4] Calvin to Farel, *Ibid*, p 228

Calvin's married life, though happy in mutual companionship, was one of sorrow through the trials incident to human experience. His only child,[1] Jacques, born July 28, 1542, lived but a few days, and his wife's health was always feeble after the birth of their son. On March 29, 1549, she, too, was taken from him. In spite of the severe repression of Calvin's references to his affliction,—a fortitude of mind worthy of admiration in the judgment of his intimate friends at the time,[2] —it would be an injustice to regard his sense of bereavement as other than profound and lasting. His marriage, though having little of romance in its beginnings, had in it much of the satisfaction that comes from mutual trust, and of loving absorption, at least on the part of the wife, in the other's interests and work.

The years at Strassburg, so fruitful in the development of Calvin's intellectual life, his religious programme and his personal experience, were no less significant in their enlargement of his acquaintance with the men and affairs of the Reformation in its broader aspects. He was now reckoned as one of the leaders in an influential German Protestant city, trusted by its authorities, and accredited as its representative in discussions of the highest importance. As such he now came into intimate contact with the problems which pressed for solution in the land of the Reformation's birth, and

[1] Many writers, among them Bonnet and Lang, have thought that Calvin had three children, but Doumergue, ii. 470–473, shows conclusively that there was but one

[2] *E g.* Viret to Calvin, April 10, 1549, *Opera*, xiii. 233

gained the lasting friendship of one of its earliest champions,—Philip Melanchthon.[1]

Calvin's stay at Strassburg coincided with the period when the Emperor Charles V., long hindered from crushing Protestantism by the wars with France and with the Turks, as well as by the strength of the Schmalkaldic league, and not yet ready for the open attack which was to bring him seeming victory in 1547, was attempting to secure a basis of compromise between the divided wings of Christendom. Preliminary to the Frankfort Reichstag of April, 1539, an imperial conference was held in the same city in February. At the Reichstag it was agreed that a friendly discussion looking toward "Christian union" should be held between the representatives of both types of faith. In compliance, after a futile meeting at Hagenau, in June, 1540, eleven champions from each side debated at Worms in November, and, after adjournment in January, 1541, the discussion was continued, in April, under the presidency of the Emperor himself at Regensburg. The outcome was a failure. No agreement was reached; but the attempt is one of the reckoning points of the German Reformation, and at all these meetings, except that of the Reichstag, Calvin was present. In the two last mentioned he bore a prominent part.

Calvin's visit to the Frankfort conference, for which

[1] The chief source for this episode are Calvin's letters to Farel A brief sketch is that of Kampschulte, i 327–342 Doumergue, ii 525–649, in a much ampler treatment sharply criticises Kampschulte, and points out errors into which he fell. For Calvin's tracts growing out of these experiences, see *Opera*, v 461–684

he left Strassburg in company with Johann Sturm and other friends on February 21, 1539, was undertaken partly to secure aid for his persecuted French fellow-believers, in whose behalf Bucer was already labouring at Frankfort, and partly to make the acquaintance of Melanchthon.[1] He went in no official capacity. In the endeavour in behalf of French Protestants he had little, if any, success; but he began a friendship with Melanchthon which was to be one of the most winsome of his relationships. Unlike in so many characteristics, and differing more and more on the theological doctrine of predestination, the severely logical, courageous, firm young Frenchman, and the more timid, cautious, and compromising elder German scholar, found much in common. Their correspondence, though not frequent and not without expressions of disagreement, shows, especially on Calvin's part, great consideration, affection, and respect, and this continued Calvin's feeling always. Calvin's patience and confidence in his friend are exhibited in a most attractive light. To Melanchthon he dedicated his reply to Pighius in 1543, and, three years later, he published and commended a French translation of Melanchthon's *Loci Communes*.[2] In any judgment of Calvin's character, his friendships not only with such intimates as Farel, or with such fellow-workers as Bucer and Sturm, but with a man with

[1] He described his experiences and observations in a long letter to Farel, March 16, 1539, Herminjard, v 247–260

[2] *Opera*, vi 229, ix 847 Their relations are interestingly discussed by Philip Schaff, *History of the Christian Church*, vii. 385–398; Doumergue, ii. 545–561, and Lang, *Melanchthon und Calvin*, in the *Reformirte Kirchen-Zeitung*, February 21–March 28, 1897.

whom possible points of disagreement were as numerous as with Melanchthon, must be no less regarded than such scenes as have been narrated in connection with Caroli.

Calvin's letters describing his observations and experiences at Frankfort and Hagenau[1] reveal him as a keen observer and a penetrating critic of persons and parties in Germany, and, indeed, of the whole European religious situation. He was evidently using his opportunities for acquaintance to the full; and a man of such statesmanlike grasp of conditions as Calvin shows himself could not long remain without fitting employment for his abilities in a representative capacity. At the Colloquy in Worms, Calvin appeared, therefore, not as a spectator, but as a delegate of Strassburg, and a representative, also, of Duke Ernst of Lüneburg. Here he did much to prepare the Protestant case in preliminary discussion.[2] In the brief public debate permitted before adjournment to Regensburg he bore no part, the chief disputants being Melanchthon and Luther's old enemy, Eck, of whom the cultivated Frenchman formed a most unfavourable opinion.[3]

To the final Colloquy, that at Regensburg, Calvin went with Bucer and the others of the Strassburg

[1] Notably those in Herminjard, v 247–260, vi 234–241, 256–261 Compare the remarks of Kampschulte, i 329

[2] *Opera*, xxi. 269–271

[3] "Picture to yourself the figure of a barbarous sophist, vaunting himself stupidly among the unlearned, and you will have half of Eck," letter to Farel, Herminjard, vii 10 For Calvin's account of his experiences at Worms see *Ibid*, vi. 405–415, vii 8–12

party, arriving on March 10, 1541. Melanchthon had urged the willing Strassburg authorities to send him, as having "a great reputation among learned men,"[1] but he went with reluctance. He felt himself unfitted for the task,[2] and he probably had become convinced, also, that little good was to be expected from the discussions. His stay was a time of grievous anxiety. The news from home distressed him. That scourge of the age, the plague, devastated Strassburg, and, in March, cost the lives of two of the young members of his household to whom he was greatly attached, Claude Féray, a promising Greek scholar, and Féray's pupil, a Norman nobleman, Louis de Richebourg. No one can read the touching and Christian letter which Calvin wrote to the father of the boy without being impressed with Calvin's warmth of feeling and genuine affection for those who stood in intimate relations with him.[3] His grief was profound, and his distress was increased by anxiety for his wife and brother yet in peril. Yet through these weeks of sadness and anxiety, Calvin's keenness of observation of men and things continued unabated. He was somewhat in the background of the more public discussions. Anxious to secure conciliation, if possible, the Emperor had obtained the appointment

[1] *Opera*, v lvi, Doumergue, ii 626.

[2] To Farel, Herminjard, vii 41. Calvin's letters continue of great interest. See *Ibid*, pp 48–51, 55–64, 87–90, 105–107, 111–116, 150–152; also Bucer's, p 157 On the course of the Colloquy see Paul Vetter, *Die Religionsverhandlungen auf dem Reichstage zu Regensburg*, Jena, 1889.

[3] Herminjard, vii 66–73 (to Richebourg); see also *Ibid*, pp. 55, 63 (to Farel).

of the moderate Cardinal Gasparo Contarini as papal nuncio, and, as negotiators for the Protestant side, Melanchthon, Bucer, and Johann Pistorius,—all conciliatory men. Opposed to them were Eck, Johann Gropper, and Julius Pflug. The Protestant representatives were ready to concede much,—too much to suit Calvin's strenuous Evangelicalism,—but, though their plans displeased him, for Melanchthon and Bucer as men of good intention he had the highest regard.[1] But the Colloquy failed of its purpose. Agreement could not be reached, and Calvin gladly obtained permission to leave before its close. On June 25, 1541, he was once more in his home in Strassburg.

Throughout the discussions at Regensburg, which he followed so eagerly, Calvin was engaged in an effort to obtain some relief for the persecuted Protestants of France. Just what this involved has been debated by historians with a good deal of diversity of opinion. But there seems no reason to doubt that he regarded the cultivation of cordial relations between the German Protestants and Francis I. as one of the most promising means of aid to his French fellow-believers[2] Such relations almost of necessity implied an alliance with France as against the Emperor, and it was because of efforts to this end that Calvin was thanked in the name of the King as well as in her own, in July, 1541, by no less a personage than Marguerite d'Angoulême.[3] His endeavors,

[1] Herminjard, vii p 115 Contrast Kampschulte's interpretation, i. 337, with that of Doumergue, ii 637

[2] *Ibid*, p 151.

[3] *Ibid.*, pp 198–202.

joined with those of the magistrates of Strassburg, and of the Swiss Protestants, secured from the Evangelical leaders and forces of Germany gathered at Regensburg a letter to the French King,—Calvin had wished an embassy,—protesting against the persecution of the Waldenses and of others of the Reformed faith.[1] While not so conspicuous at Regensburg and the other Colloquies as Melanchthon and Bucer, no French Protestant had so fully become a figure of European significance as had this exile for his religious convictions. Though his real stature had not yet been reached, the events from the publication of the first edition of the *Institutes* to the Colloquy at Regensburg had made Calvin beyond comparison the most conspicuous representative of the Evangelical interests of his native land.

Calvin's labour at the Colloquies brought him into intimate acquaintance with the conditions and with many of the chief men of German Protestantism. Luther, indeed, he never met, and that greatest of the German reformers seems to have known comparatively little about him. Calvin treasured highly, however, a word of greeting and of approval of his letter to Sadoleto,—of which mention will be made in the next chapter,—which came to him through Bucer in October, 1539;[2] and there were a few other evidences of goodwill on the part of the elder reformer. His own high estimate of Luther, Calvin often expressed, even

[1] Herminjard, vii pp 126–128

[2] *Opera*, xb 402 The whole subject is discussed by Doumergue, ii. 562–587

when making evident the differences between his point of view and that of the Saxon reformer.[1]

Yet Calvin's acquaintance with Germany probably confirmed, rather than weakened, his confidence in his own programme for a proper regeneration of the Church. He admired many of the leaders of the German Reformation, but he disapproved of its want of ecclesiastical discipline, the low estimate in which the ministry was held, and the extent to which the churches were dependent on civil authority.[2] He had learned much during his years in Strassburg, but his fundamental principles had remained unaltered.

[1] *E g* Calvin to Bullinger, November 25, 1544, "I have frequently said, even if he should call me a devil, I should, nevertheless, render him the honour of recognising him as an eminent servant of God." Herminjard, ix 374. See also *Opera*, vi 250; xii. 7.

[2] Compare Kampschulte, i 339

# CHAPTER X

## CALVIN RETURNS TO GENEVA.—ITS ECCLESIASTICAL CONSTITUTION

CALVIN left Geneva in the spring of 1538, burning with a sense of personal wrongs.[1] He felt that he had been cruelly thrust out of a position in which he had stood by divine appointment; and that his place, and those of Farel and Coraud, were being occupied by "traitors under the mask of pastors." Of these ministers, Henri de la Marc and Jacques Bernard, though to serve the Church of Geneva after Calvin's return, were weak and inferior men; and while Antoine Marcourt and Jean Morand, whom the city authorities associated with them, were men of greater abilities, and Marcourt certainly of superior if not always judicious character, all were to show themselves inadequate to the task before them. From the first, their difficulties were many. They had been put in office by a reaction

[1] His letters, Herminjard, v.–vii., or *Opera*, xb, xi, with the extracts from the *Registres du Conseil*, of Geneva, *Opera*, xxi 227–282 The most recent thorough discussions are those of Cornelius, pp 192–353, and of Doumergue, ii 653–713 See also J. A Gautier, *Histoire de Genève*, completed in 1713, but published vol ii in 1896, and vol. iii. in 1898, J. B. G. Galiffe, in *Mémoires et Documents publiés par la Soc. de l'Hist. de Genève*, xix. 262–283; Kampschulte, i. 342–412; A. Roget, *Histoire du peuple de Genève*, 1870–1883, i. 113–315, ii 1–84. A good brief sketch is that of Eugène Choisy, *La théocratie à Genève au temps de Calvin*, pp. 36–62,

against the strictness and independence of their pr decessors; and such a reaction was, in the nature things, followed by greater license of conduct on t part of the populace. In spite of stringent gover mental enactments and good advice given by the ne preachers, there can be no question that the mor condition of Geneva was decidedly lower—at least outward manifestation—than under Farel and Calvi The government, moreover, treated the ministers its creatures; and they in turn looked up to it, as the other Swiss cantons, as the authority regulati of Church practice.[1] The ecclesiastical independen which Calvin had sought was gone.

To render a difficult situation more trying, the par differences which had been so evident before Farel an Calvin's banishment still persisted with unabated i tensity. That of Michel Sept, which had supporte the old ecclesiastical régime, was now nicknamed th "Guillermins,"—a title borrowed from Farel's Christia name; and it included, undoubtedly, the more religio elements of the Genevan population.[2] That such a part was arrayed against the new preachers made their pos tion doubly difficult, and the more determined "Gui lermins" proposed, by absenting themselves from th Christmas communion, to disown the existing Geneva ministry. Though Farel would express no opinion, h evidently thought well of the plan; but at this junctur Calvin showed his superiority to mere party leadershi

[1] *E g* regarding Christmas and feasts, *Opera*, xxi. 239. Compar Doumergue, ii. 661

[2] Cornelius, p 203.

He urged that schism be avoided, "and the ministry and sacraments be held in such reverence that wherever they [*i e.* Christians] perceive them to exist, they should judge the Church to be."[1] It was most Christian advice; and not without cost to himself, for it was anything but popular with many of his personal friends, as well as with a large part of the "Guillermins." For the time being, however, the party in power in Geneva showed itself master of the situation. The chief intellectual centre of the "Guillermin" faction was the Collège, taught by Antoine Saunier, by Calvin's old instructor, Mathurin Cordier, and others friendly to the banished pastors. Two of its younger teachers, having shown themselves hostile to the preachers and the new ecclesiastical administration, were exiled on September 26, 1538; and a similar fate overtook their older colleagues, for the same reason, on December 26th.[2] By this drastic action and other banishments the "Guillermin" cause was greatly lamed, and the position of the party in power and of its preachers much strengthened—though the effect on the school was most damaging. Yet their hold on the Genevan community was unsatisfactory from a religious point of view; and, on December 31st, the four preachers offered their resignations to the Little Council, "since we can no longer have fruit such as we desire in this place, matters being in such disorder." The Council refused their dismission and

[1] Herminjard, v 168, 169 Letter to Farel of October 24, 1538. See *Ibid.*, p 449.

[2] *Registres du Conseil*, xxxii 144, 248, 251; *Opera*, xxi. 236, 240.

took measures for active support by further punishing their critics [1]

The policy of refusal to accept the Supper at the hands of the new preachers, which was the immediate occasion of the "Guillermin" defeat, had met with Calvin's disapproval, and time was overcoming his sense of personal injury. Bad as the Genevan situation seemed to him, it seemed worse to him and to Farel that a serious division in the ecclesiastical forces of Switzerland should continue. The vindicatory council for which both reformers had hoped was evidently unattainable without the aid of Bern. Farel accordingly, at considerable sacrifice of personal feeling, approached the Bernese pastor, Peter Kuntz Kuntz's views had altered Farel, settled at Neuchâtel, and no longer merely a Genevan exile, was a power in the French-speaking churches of the Bernese territories, and his friendship was now worth much to Bern. And so, under Bernese auspices, there came about, on March 12, 1539, not the desired council, but a meeting at Morges between the Genevan pastors, ministers from French Switzerland, and Farel, under the presidency of two ministers of Bern, by which a reconciliation of the French-speaking Protestant pastors was effected.[2] The Genevan ministers acknowledged that they should have consulted Farel, Calvin, and Coraud before taking their places. The exiles were declared

[1] *Opera*, xb 304–306, xxi 243.
[2] Herminjard, v 243–246

to have been faithful pastors, and their successors promised to do their best to strengthen discipline, care for the poor and aid the school. Not all that the exiles wished had been secured; but Calvin from his Strassburg home wrote to Farel [1]—

> We have in part obtained that which we have chiefly sought,—that those evil dissensions between brethren which were wholly devastating the Church should be adjusted We can never sufficiently render thanks to the Lord who by His goodness so surpasses our hope.

To show this re-established goodwill, Viret and Fabri now preached in Geneva; Farel, whom banishment still held away, declared his readiness to help in any manner in his power; and, on June 25th, Calvin wrote to the Genevan Church a calm yet most earnest letter, without a trace of personal resentment, but breathing the utmost goodwill and pastoral solicitude. He deplores their divisions, urges the sacredness of the pastoral office; declares that the trying circumstances of his own departure were due to the work of Satan, but that the appointment of their new pastors was "not without the will of God," who has preserved the Reformation and not left them to the Papacy; and urges the cordial support of their ministers as the only course pleasing to God.[2] If Calvin in the heat of sudden temper or of personal resentment would often speak with

[1] April, 1539, Herminjard, v. p 290.

[2] *Ibid.*, pp 336–341

regrettable rashness, none have been able to express themselves, in the quietness of sober judgment, more nobly or unselfishly.

Calvin followed this service to the cause of religion in Geneva by one of even greater conspicuity not merely to the Genevan Church, but to the whole Protestant cause. The revolution of 1538, which had driven Farel and Calvin from the city, had been in no sense a Romanising movement, the new ministers and the government were thoroughly Protestant; but the very fact of religious division in Geneva was enough to arouse the hopes of its discarded bishop and the friends of the older Church. Something might come to their advantage out of the troubled situation. Whether meetings of bishops were held at Lyons to discuss measures for Catholic restoration is doubtful;[1] but, at the request of such a gathering, if held, or on his own initiative, the learned, moderate, and humanistic bishop of Carpentras, Cardinal Jacopo Sadoleto (1477–1547), sent an appeal to Geneva to return to the ancient faith, which was delivered, with a letter, to the Little Council on March 26, 1539.[2] Courteous, rhetorical, but superficial in its appreciation of the questions involved, it attacked the Reformation as without justification, urged the charge that the reformers were actuated by disappointed

[1] Herminjard (v 266) regards it as historically unsupported, Cornelius (p 247) believes the report, Doumergue (ii 678) holds his judgment in suspense It was believed in Geneva in December, 1538, *Registres du Conseil*, xxxii 252.

[2] *Registres du Conseil*, xxxiii 57, *Opera*, xxi 245 The text of Sadoleto's appeal is given in *Opera*, v 369–384

personal ambition, commended humble obedience to the Church as a prime Christian duty, and asked:[1]—

> Whether is it more expedient for your salvation, and whether you think you will do what is more pleasing to God, by believing and following what the Catholic Church throughout the whole world, now for more than fifteen hundred years, approves with general consent; or innovations introduced within these twenty-five years, by crafty, or, as they think themselves, acute men

Written in Latin, and without attempt to make it popularly available by translation into French, it had no apparent effect, save possibly to encourage Roman sympathisers by its existence. The Genevan government was little disturbed by it. It sent the appeal to Bern; and, in July, apparently after having thought of committing the task to Viret, the Bernese authorities, at the suggestion of Peter Kuntz, asked Calvin to reply. The request was itself evidence of the better state of feeling that had come to exist between the ministry and government at Bern and the exiled pastors of Geneva.

Calvin received the request in August, and, urged by his Strassburg friends, he undertook the answer. If, as he regarded it while at work upon it, it really proved a task of six days only, it is certainly a marvellous evidence of Calvin's mental alertness and readiness with

[1] *Opera*, v. 378; Henry Beveridge's translation, *Tracts*, i 13 Sadoleto's letter and Calvin's reply are admirably characterised by Cornelius, pp 249–252.

the pen.[1] In any case, it was quickly done. Printed copies were in Geneva on September 5th. But Calvin's Answer to Sadoleto had much more than a local significance. As in his letter to Francis I., he now spoke for the whole movement in which he was a leader. It was the most brilliant popular defence of the Protestant cause that had yet appeared or that the Reformation was to produce. With great courtesy for a writer of the sixteenth century, yet with profound depth of feeling, with thorough grasp of the doctrinal questions involved, Calvin first defends his ministry and that of Farel from the charge of self-seeking. He then invokes the authority of the Word of God against that of a Church which Christian antiquity shows has not been always one and the same. With immense effectiveness he presents, following the example of Sadoleto, two confessions, one of a layman and the other of a minister, before the judgment-seat of God, which were doubtless drawn from Calvin's personal experience, and as such have been largely quoted in these pages in describing his conversion.[2] Obedience to God, and to God's revelation of Himself and of His truth rather than to the teaching of men, Calvin presents with tremendous power as the Protestant justification. Undoubtedly the Reply made friends for him at Geneva among those who had been his opponents, but it voiced the feelings of Protestantism everywhere.[3]

[1] Letter to Farel, Herminjard, v 373 Text of reply, *Opera*, v 385–416

[2] *Ante*, pp 73–75.

[3] Its translation into French was immediately begun Pignet to Calvin, October 4, 1539, Herminjard, vi 37. Luther's opinion has already been noted, *ante*, p. 243.

While these friendly acts unquestionably greatly increased the prestige of Calvin at Geneva, they were not, in themselves, sufficient to bring about efforts to secure his return to the pastorate from which he had been expelled. For that result a new revolution was responsible that was to thrust from power the party that had won the election of 1538, and put the leaders then defeated once more in control. The immediate causes of that revolution grew out of the involved political relations of Geneva with Bern. The war of 1536, which had secured Geneva's release from danger of control by Savoy, had been won by Bern, and left Geneva in a difficult position in relation to its aggressive protector. Bern, in the flush of triumph over Savoy, had asserted possession of the political rights over Geneva once held by its bishop and by the Duke of Savoy; but the determined resistance of the little city had brought about the treaty of August 7, 1536, by which Bern abandoned these pretensions and turned over to Geneva not merely the churches, monasteries, possessions of the *vicedominus*, and estates of the bishop and chapter, but also the property and temporal powers of the prior of Saint-Victor, reserving only an ill-defined right of appeal in the administration of justice. It is evident that in the provision last named there was fuel for constant disputes, especially regarding those properties of the chapter and of Saint-Victor which lay at a distance from Geneva and were adjacent to or surrounded by territories in which Bern held undisputed sway. Quarrels were constant, and the question was one involving interests which a large portion of the inhabitants of Geneva deemed vital to the independence of the city.

The election of February, 1539, but strengthened the hold upon the government of Geneva of the party victorious in 1538, by which the reformers had been exiled. In March, that government sent three of its own members—Jean Lullin, Ami de Chapeaurouge and Jean Monathon—to Bern to attempt a new treaty. In three days their task was done They had signed the agreement, and Bern had approved the result. The reason of this prompt acquiescence by Geneva's powerful neighbour in a treaty which was designed to settle questions so vexed as those in dispute was that the three Genevan representatives had abandoned a large share of the Genevan claims. They had transgressed their instructions,[1] and no adequate explanation of their conduct is apparent. Nor is the attitude of the Little Council easier to understand. Though signed March 30th, the agreement was not laid before that body till June 27th, and then, though contrary to the instructions of the Little Council itself, simply "not accepted."[2] No vigorous denunciation of the treaty and prosecution of its authors immediately followed. Though Bern was asked to explain certain sections, and negotiations were carried on, it was not till November that the Bernese government was officially informed that Geneva rejected it. Certainly great incompetency,

[1] The latest discussion is a careful note by Alfred Cartier, Doumergue, ii 766–768.

[2] *Registres du Conseil*, xxxiii 186 See Cornelius, pp 268, 273, Doumergue, ii. 684.

if nothing worse, was exhibited in this transaction, and an amazing blindness to the probable effects on the party in power. From the articles into which the treaty was divided, its framers were nicknamed "Articulants," a title which the populace transformed into "Artichauds" and attached not merely to the negotiators, but to the whole party of which they were members.

These events gave the "Guillermins" their opportunity. Under the lead of Sept, Perrin, and Pertemps they attacked the party in power, and, on August 25, 1539, the two last named secured a vote from the Two Hundred that the hated treaty should never be sealed. A General Assembly, on November 16th, ordered Bern informed that Geneva refused the treaty. Bern insisted on its maintenance. Party division in Geneva, in spite of the fact that both sides were now arrayed against the treaty, grew worse, though, in January and February, 1540, it seemed for a little as if a compromise could be effected between the "Guillermins" and "Artichauds." By popular demand in a General Assembly, the rivals, Sept and Philippe, shook hands in token of reconciliation on January 27th; and at the election of February 8th two syndics were chosen from either party. Though the majority in the Little Council remained to the "Artichauds," Sept and Pertemps were given seats in it. But Bern's action made any adjustment difficult. On April 18th, a Bernese embassy declared, in the General Assembly at Geneva, that that city had no right to repudiate a treaty made by its duly appointed negotiators. Geneva once more refused;

and, four days later, a new General Assembly broke forth in stormy wrath against the three to whom the treaty was due,—or "three traitors," as they were now styled, and demanded their punishment. A wave of popular feeling was now in control of the city; the government was nearly powerless. The negotiators fled; and, on May 20th, their places in the Little Council were taken by three "Guillermins," giving to that party for the first time in more than two years a majority in that body. Under the impulse of popular passion, on June 5th, in spite of Bern's efforts in their behalf,—or perhaps the more because of those efforts,—the three negotiators were condemned to death,—fortunately for them in their absence from Geneva. But worse followed. A street fight took place on the evening of the day following between members of the rival factions. It would appear that the "Artichauds" were the aggressors; and, at all events, the quick-tempered and impetuous Jean Philippe, leader of that party, and captain-general of the city, was drawn into the riot, which resulted in two deaths. In its heat he and Michel Sept, his opponent, who was looking on the scene from a window, exchanged recriminations. Popular fury turned against Philippe, and the next day his trial began, if such it can be called. Under threat of torture he confessed himself the cause of the death of one of the rioters,—an allegation which he had previously denied. In spite of the efforts of the representatives of Bern in his behalf, popular excitement overcame all governmental scruples, and, on June 10th, he was beheaded, dying, whatever may have been his faults, a victim of judicial murder, forced by the will of the multitude.[1]

With the death of Jean Philippe the leaders of the "Artichauds" were broken, his associate, Claude Richardet, fled the city the night following the execution. Two of the four syndics under whom Calvin had been banished had been condemned to death as traitors for negotiating the unhappy treaty; the third had been beheaded (Philippe), and the fourth, as has just been mentioned, was in flight. This result had come about, however, not so much through the skill of the "Guillermin" leaders as through the excitement of the populace. In spite of their majority in the government, the "Guillermins" were unable to exercise efficient control of the turbulent city. But, during the summer of 1540, Bern and Geneva stood on the brink of war. By August and September, Geneva was making preparations for defence; and the danger, together with the efforts to meet it, gradually brought about order and governmental control. Fortunately the war cloud passed. During this period of anarchy, however, two of the pastors, Jean Morand and Antoine Marcourt, dropped their work and left the city without seeking dismission. The religious situation of Geneva was, therefore, one imperatively demanding a much stronger leadership than Henri de la Mare or Jacques Bernard

[1] The death of Philippe is naturally one of the most debated points in Genevan history, and its motives and merits have been judged with much divergence by Galiffe, Kampschulte, Roget, Cornelius, and Doumergue Of the main facts and of its consequences there can be no question. The chief points of divergence are as to his deserts, and as to the seriousness of the riot.

could exercise. The government was in the hands of the party that had supported Farel and Calvin; and, on news of Marcourt's demission of his pastoral office, the Little Council, by vote on September 21, 1540, instructed Ami Perrin "to find means, if possible, to make Master Caulvin come"[1] back to Geneva. It would be an error to ascribe this action to a popular demand. Even as long after it was taken as October 17th, Jacques Bernard had no knowledge of an attempt to secure Calvin's return.[2] It was rather the plan of the "Guillermin" leaders, who thus sought to strengthen the fallen religious state of the city and establish their own position.

Calvin's return to Geneva had long been wished by Farel and Farel's friends. Indeed, mention had been made of it as possible in the correspondence of the reformers as early as April, 1539, and again in March, 1540; but Calvin had declared to Farel that he would rather endure "a hundred other deaths than that cross."[3] It must have been clear to those who knew him that Calvin could not easily be persuaded to leave the quiet, the usefulness, and the growing honours of Strassburg for the inevitable struggles of Geneva. In order to ascertain his probable action before making the matter more public, and to bring as much pressure to bear on Calvin as possible, the desire of the Little

[1] *Registres du Conseil*, xxxiv 452, *Opera*, xxi. 265

[2] His letter to Calvin, Herminjard, vii 23

[3] Herminjard, v 290, vi. 199, 217 The letters of the reformers and the *Registres du Conseil* continue the chief source Recent discussions are those of Cornelius, pp 316–353, and of Doumergue, ii. 694–710

Council was made known to some of Calvin's friends in the ministry of French-speaking Switzerland. Christopher Fabri, of Thonon, discussed the matter at Geneva and wrote to Farel of what had been done;[1] and the warm-hearted Farel, in spite of his natural chagrin that no mention of his own possible restoration to Geneva had been made, became at once the most indefatigable of workers in the cause.[2] To him, more than to any other, Calvin's return, like that reformer's original settlement in Geneva, was to be due. Farel himself journeyed at once to Strassburg, and with him went urgent letters from Antoine Marcourt, Mathurin Cordier; and André Zébédée, pastor at Orbe. Soon Viret's appeal followed.[3]

To Calvin the call, pressed by Farel, caused great mental perturbation, but he gave answer that his immediate duty was attendance on the Colloquy at Worms, of which some account has already been given. As for his work at Geneva, he shuddered when he thought of a return, nor would "any bond have held [him] there so long, save that [he] did not dare throw off the yoke of the calling which [he] knew had been laid upon [him] by God."[4] Still, he did not absolutely refuse, for a reason that throws much light on his own view of duty. As he said to Farel: "If I were given the choice, I would do anything rather than yield to you

[1] Herminjard, vi 309

[2] *Ibid*, pp 311, 388 Compare Cornelius, p 326

[3] *Ibid*, pp 317–324, 329

[4] Letter to Farel of October 21, 1540, *Ibid*, pp. 325, 326; see also Calvin's letter to the Little Council, *Ibid*, p 334

in this matter; but since I remember that I am not my own, I offer my heart as if slain in sacrifice to the Lord."[1]

There is no reason to doubt the thorough honesty of Calvin's expression of his inmost feeling to his intimate correspondent; nor to question that obedience to the will of God was his highest motive in this decision. Equally plain is it, here and earlier, that, strong-willed as he was himself, he was highly susceptible to representations as to his duty by those he loved and trusted. The decision was, indeed, a hard one. Strassburg offered peace; the agreeable companionship of Bucer, Capito, and Hedio, with whom, especially with Bucer, he had much in common; a pastorate from which he could influence France; a professorship which touched students from many lands; acquaintance with the leaders of Germany; and a growing fame and influence. Geneva meant the renewal of weary struggles and, at best, doubtful success; but it meant, too, greater influence on the Evangelical cause in France than Strassburg afforded, and, above all, an opportunity to put in practice his programme for the organisation of a well disciplined Church, and therefore an ideal commonwealth, which he had, indeed, realised in his congregation at Strassburg, but which he could never hope to apply to that city as a whole. He might well doubt which was the path of duty; if he looked for comfort and repute,—save from a pecuniary standpoint, and there is no evidence that this consideration weighed with him in the matter,—his prospects at Strassburg were the brighter.

[1] Letter of October 24, 1540, Herminjard, vi. p. 339.

The Genevan leaders hoped, however, for a favourable decision, and now took more public action. On October 19th and 20th, the Two Hundred and the General Assembly formally invited Calvin to return; and, the next day, the Little Council appointed Ami Perrin, "with a herald" to seek him with the message.[1] The formal notice of his honourable recall reached Calvin at Worms. It must have been a moment of high satisfaction. The disgrace of 1538, if such it can be called, had been thoroughly removed. But it was a day of great perplexity, also, for the Strassburg authorities, and the ministers of that city made evident to him, as never before, how great was their desire that he should continue the work there begun. Calvin could only reply undecidedly to the Genevan request.[2] As time went on, in spite of constant urgency from Farel and all whom Farel could influence, Calvin's inclination seemed to turn increasingly toward Strassburg; till late in February, 1541, he received from his fiery friend a "thundering" letter which, according to the testimony of Claude Féray,—the young member of Calvin's household who was to die a few days later of the plague,—turned Calvin's wavering mind Geneva-ward.[3]

[1] *Registres du Conseil*, xxxiv 483–487, *Opera*, xxi 267 The letter is in Herminjard, vi 331

[2] See the letter of (1) Calvin to Geneva, (2) the ministers of Strassburg and Basel in attendance at Worms to Geneva, and (3) Calvin to Farel, from Worms November 12 and 13, 1540, Herminjard, vi 352–367

[3] Farel's letter to Calvin is not known to exist. Calvin replied from Ulm on his way to Regensburg, Herminjard, vii. 40–42. Féray's letter of March 8th is given *Ibid*, p 46. He died about the middle of the same month, see *ante*, p. 241.

Though almost certainly decided in Calvin's own thought at this juncture that he would return to Geneva, at least for a time, he was long detained at the Colloquy in Regensburg. Farel knew no rest. He stirred up the pastors of Zurich to urge on Calvin the importance of Geneva for the Evangelical cause in France and Italy. Geneva asked the aid of Zurich and Basel, and pleaded its cause with the authorities of Strassburg. And, at last, Calvin fully resolved, that whether his stay should be brief or permanent, he would go to Geneva, and attempt the restoration of church-order as he understood it. He hoped to go with Bucer's companionship; failing that, he desired aid from Basel and Bern; but, in the end, he had to enter on his work alone.[1] On September 13, 1541, apparently, he re-entered the city which was thenceforth to be his residence, simply and unostentatiously.[2] With business-like directness, and perfect clearness of vision he entered on his task. On the day of his arrival, he presented himself before the Little Council, explained his long indecision, asked that the Council choose a committee to aid in preparing a written constitution for the Genevan Church, and declared his wish to serve the city.[3] The Strassburg episode was past. Calvin's Genevan work had once more begun.

[1] Cornelius, pp 350, 351.

[2] In spite of Beza's statement (*Opera*, xxi 131) that he was received with the greatest congratulations of all the people and of the Council, Fabri's letter to Farel of September 18th (Herminjard, vii 260) gives no impression of a popular demonstration Doumergue (ii 710) shows reasons for believing there was none Beza gives the date.

[3] *Registres du Conseil*, xxxv. 324; *Opera*, xxi. 282.

It was undoubtedly Calvin's feeling that he had been restored to Geneva by the hand of God. He treated his banishment as a mere interruption; and, therefore, when he resumed his preaching, apparently on the Sunday following his return, instead of the sensational discourse which his hearers eagerly expected, he spoke not a word about the recent past; but, after a brief definition of his office and of his motives in undertaking its duties, began his exposition of the Scriptures at the passage with which he had closed when banished.[1] He made no effort, at the time, to have his fellow-ministers removed, though they were thoroughly unsatisfactory to him, and he expressed his dislike of them freely in letters to confidential correspondents. He was conciliatory toward former opponents. He acted with wisdom and prudence; and for one of so impulsive a temperament, with great self-restraint. This attitude was made all the easier by the honourable treatment that he received from the government. He was provided with a house and garden that had once belonged to one of the canons of the Cathedral;[2]

[1] Calvin's letter of January, 1542, is full of interesting details, Herminjard, vii 408–413; see also *Ibid.*, pp 249, 350, 438

[2] *Registres du Conseil*, xxxv 297, 327, 352, 368, *Opera*, xxi 281–284 The house had been purchased of the government by de Fresneville, Sieur de Sansoex, in 1539, and was bought back by the Genevan authorities in 1543 It stood on the site of the present No 11 Rue de Calvin Calvin's house has disappeared, the site having been built upon anew early in the 18th century Not being ready at once, Calvin occupied for a few months the house adjoining (on the site of No 9). From 1543 to his death, No 11 was his home The facts are fully presented by Doumergue, iii 491–508 It was very meagrely furnished, in part at governmental expense

his wife and household goods were brought from Strassburg at the expense of the city, a salary of five hundred florins was voted him, the sum being considered large partly because of his necessary entertainment of passing visitors, and allowances were made him of wheat, wine and clothing. His income was probably equivalent to the present purchasing power of eight hundred to a thousand dollars, aside from the worth of his house.[1] At best it was a frugal living for one in his position; though he was henceforth relieved from such poverty as he had borne in Strassburg.

Calvin's return to Geneva had for its object, from his point of view, the establishment of an ecclesiastical constitution which should make of the city a model Christian community The party now in power in Geneva was weary of civil disorders, convinced of the ill-estate of the Church, and of the insufficiency of its ministers. The moment was therefore ripe for the

[1] The purchasing power of Calvin's salary has been most variously estimated, from the computation of Jules Bonnet, who valued the 500 florins at $50, to that of Galiffe, $1200, and of Marcel Suès-Ducommun, $1500 Doumergue (iii 449-477) discusses it amply, and while admitting that the subject is one on which an exact decision is impossible, he values Calvin's 500 florins at 3000 to 3500 francs, and his total compensation, aside from his house, at 4000 francs It was double that of an ordinary minister If these payments seem small, it must be remembered that Geneva was a little, and not very wealthy, city, and that ministerial compensation in all non-prelatical Protestant lands was then meagre, partly because pre-Reformation incomes had been gauged to the needs of a celibate clergy, but even more because governmental confiscation of Church properties, abolition of fees, etc, had operated universally to the financial disadvantage of the Church. Calvin was, of course, paid from the city treasury

work. Yet very little evidence appears of anything that can be called a popular religious awakening, such as is witnessed in the story of English Puritanism.

In accordance with Calvin's request, on the day of his arrival, the Little Council appointed a committee of six to co-operate with Calvin and the other ministers of the city, among whom was Viret, then on leave of absence from Lausanne. Four of this committee, Claude Pertemps, Ami Perrin, Claude Roset, and Jean Lambert, were from the Little Council itself; two, Ami Porral and Jean Balard, were from the Two Hundred. All, save Balard, had been determined "Guillermins." Of Balard's reluctant acceptance of Protestantism, in 1536, mention has already been made;[1] and his Evangelicalism was afterwards in doubt. Three days later the Little Council voted that the *Ordonnances*, when drafted, should be submitted successively to itself, the Two Hundred, and the General Assembly. The work moved rapidly. On September 26th, it was laid before the Little Council, which proceeded, three days later, to examine it article by article,—a process which was completed at the cost of much discussion and of strenuous labour on Calvin's part, on November 3d Six days later, the draft as modified by the Little Council was laid before the Two Hundred, and slightly altered

[1] *Ante*, p 178 The text of the first draft of the *Ordonnances*, and its various modifications till adopted, is given in *Opera*, xa 16–30 Much of the pertinent government action is recorded in the *Registres du Conseil*, xxxv 324–410, is printed in *Opera*, xxi 282–287. The fullest discussion is that of Cornelius, pp 353–387

by its action. On November 20th, the General Assembly approved the ecclesiastical constitution without dissent. The tenacity with which the Genevan government held to its right to initiate and establish an ecclesiastical constitution, even in the days of first enthusiasm over Calvin's return, is shown, however, in the refusal of the Little Council to let the ministers see the changes which it had made in their draft before transmitting it to the Two Hundred.[1] It would have Calvin as an adviser, but not intentionally as a ruler.

The *Ordonnances* of 1541 show great advance over the Articles of 1537, in elaboration and preciseness, yet there is no essential alteration of the thoughts that underlay the less mature and definite document of nearly five years earlier. That of 1541 was much more minute and circumstantial, but its prime purposes, like those of the earlier Articles, are to give a measure of self-government elsewhere unknown in Protestant lands to the Church, while maintaining helpful relations with the State, and to put into operation an effective discipline whereby the Church might fulfil that which Calvin regarded as its most urgent duty, the initiation of its members into, and their maintenance in, right doctrine and right living. They gave to the Church no control over the State in political concerns or in the infliction of civil punishments.

As finally passed, the *Ordonnances* were not, indeed, in all respects what Calvin desired.[2] Some of the

[1] *Registres du Conseil*, xxxv 384, *Opera*, xxi 286

[2] "Not indeed quite perfect, but passable considering the difficulty of the times," Calvin said of them, Herminjard, vii 409.

regulations that he wished were rejected on grounds of religious conviction or even of prejudice. More were modified lest the control exercised by the government be too much diminished. The principal illustrations will be mentioned in giving an outline of the document.

The *Ordonnances* begin with the declaration that Christ has instituted in His Church the four offices of pastor, teacher, elder, and deacon. The pastors of the Genevan city Church are designated as five, with three assistants,—a number afterwards increased. For the dependent villages pastors are also to be appointed. Their office is to preach, admonish, and reprove in public and in private, to administer the Sacraments, and, in conjunction with the elders, to make "fraternal corrections." They enter office by election by their fellow-ministers; and approval by the government. This provision was modified from Calvin's draft by the reservation that the Little Council should be made cognisant of the election at the time of its occurrence, and should accept the one chosen to office only "if it seems to be expedient," thus strengthening governmental control. To the people was assigned only a right of "common consent," which amounted to little in Genevan practice.[1] Election was to be preceded by the examination of the candidate by the ministers as to doctrine and life. Calvin would have preferred induction into office by laying on of hands, but this ancient ceremony was omitted as tending to foster superstition. As

[1] In the revision of 1561, this was defined as a right to enter protest between election and installation. *Opera*, xa. 94

provided in the *Ordonnances*, entrance upon the pastoral office was, therefore, by ministerial initiative and magisterial approval; and its twofold relation of fidelity to God in all spiritual matters and obedience to the government in all temporal concerns is indicated in the oath required of each minister.[1]

As Calvin had vainly sought during his earlier Genevan ministry, the city was now divided into three parishes,—those of Saint-Pierre, Saint-Gervais, and La Madeleine,—the first-named being the ancient cathedral and Calvin's regular place of preaching. Sermons, to modern thinking in excessive abundance, were prescribed; for Calvin, like the leaders of the Reformation generally, had a hunger for the exposition of the "Word of God" Sundays saw discourses at daybreak in two churches, at nine in all three; at noon, there was instruction in the Catechism, on which Calvin laid great weight, in all the churches, and, at three, sermons in each church once more. On Monday, Wednesday, and Friday there was further preaching; and, before Calvin's death, a daily sermon had been instituted in each church of the city. Calvin wished a monthly celebration of the Supper; but, as in 1537, he was now unable to carry public opinion with him, and the communion continued to be observed four times a year. No child was to partake till he was familiar with and had made profession of the faith set forth in the Catechism. Baptisms and marriages had place only in the public congregation. Calvin would have admitted the Bernese custom of the font,—a fresh evidence that

[1] Oath of 1542, *Opera*, xa p 31.

his opposition, in 1538, was not so much to the Bernese ceremonies, as to their imposition by governmental authority,—but here "Guillermin" prejudice would have none of it. Visitation of the sick was an important ministerial duty, and no inhabitant was to be bedridden for more than three days without information being given to one of the pastors.

A most important provision of the *Ordonnances* was that requiring all the ministers of the city and as many as possible of those in its dependent villages to meet weekly for discussion of the Scriptures. These assemblies were the natural successors to the informal *Colloquia* inaugurated in 1536; they took place on Fridays and were soon popularly known as the *Congrégation.* The exegetical exercises were open to the public. But, beside these learned deliberations, the ministers collectively, or *Vénérable Compagnie,* as they were soon called, were charged with the examination and election of ministerial candidates, and with mutual supervision. Every three months they were required by the *Ordonnances* to meet for criticism one of another. A list of offences discreditable to or intolerable in a holder of the ministerial office was enumerated, and the *Ordonnances* provided that if the ministers themselves proved unable to end a contention in their ranks, recourse should be had to the aid of the elders, and then to the magistrates. This left the city government the court of final resort in questions of doctrine as well as of conduct. The object of Calvin's provisions regarding the ministry was evidently to secure a body of pastors of learning, character, and mutual helpfulness. A purely ministerial body, the *Vénérable Compagnie* soon had an influence in Genevan affairs much greater than that indicated by its constitutional rights, though impossible of exact definition, for it had the force that comes from frequent discussion and consequent united opinion.

Calvin viewed the office of teacher as of divine appointment,[1] having as its highest duty that of educating "the faithful in sound doctrine" from the Old and New Testaments. But he felt no less strongly that before the learner "can profit by such lessons he must first be instructed in the languages and worldly sciences."[2] Calvin therefore sought to develop the Genevan school system under this ecclesiastical conception of the teachership. A "learned and expert man" was to be appointed as head of the school, and teacher-in-chief, with "readers" to give secondary instruction, and "bachelors" to teach the "little children" under his control. The teacher was reckoned in the ministry, put under its disciplinary regulations; and, in Calvin's intention, was to be installed on ministerial approval,—an exercise of ministerial authority which the jealous Little Council modified by the provision that he first be "presented" to the government and examined in the presence of two of its members. In Calvin's judgment, the school was an integral factor in the religious training of the community.

No section of the *Ordonnances* was more important than that having to do with the third order of church-officers,—that of elders. Here Calvin made a great

[1] Ephesians, iv 11

[2] *Ordonnances*, *Opera*, xa 21, "sciences humaines."

advance upon the undeveloped recommendation of the Articles of 1537. The office of the eldership is defined as involving the duty "to watch over the life of each individual, to admonish affectionately those who are seen to err and to lead a disorderly life, and, where there shall be need, to make report to the body which shall be appointed to make fraternal corrections." It was, therefore, the chief disciplining office,—and was lay, not ministerial. The *Ordonnances* provided that the Little Council should choose twelve elders, subject to consultation with the ministers, and final approval by the Two Hundred. Of these officers, two were to be taken from the Little Council itself, four from the Council of Sixty, and six from that of Two Hundred. There was no popular share in their appointment; and governmental jealousy of possible growth of ecclesiastical power is here illustrated by the addition to the simple designation "elders," given them by Calvin, of their further definition as "commissioned or deputed by the *seigneurie* to the consistory."

In the *Consistoire*, just mentioned, composed of the twelve elders, and members of the regular ministry of Geneva, four to twelve in number, is to be seen the heart of Calvin's disciplinary system. As provided in the *Ordonnances*, it met every Thursday, under the presidency of one of the syndics. Calvin was not its president,—though he presided a few times, and may possibly have been regarded as an informal, non-elected vice-president.[1] Of the preponderance of his influence

[1] *E g* he presided three times in 1547, though Hudriot du Molard was president for the year Editorial note to *Opera*, xxi. 396

in this body, the first session of which was held, apparently, on December 15, 1541, there can be no question. As defined in the *Ordonnances,* the Consistory could summon for examination, censure, and ultimate excommunication any who opposed "received doctrine," neglected Church attendance, rebelled against ecclesiastical good order, or were of evil life; but all was so to be done "that the corrections should be naught but medicines to bring back sinners to our Lord." This ecclesiastical power of admonition and excommunication had its background of civil authority, however. Perverse and contumacious offenders were to be reported, as less definitely recommended in the Articles of 1537, to the Little Council, which should deal with them as it deemed best. It was in regard to this question of the relation of the power of the Consistory to that of the civil government that Calvin had his severest struggle in connection with the adoption of the *Ordonnances* and won his most decided victory. He had no wish to take from the Little Council any of its civil police power, or its rights as the final punisher of contumacious ecclesiastical offenders; but he desired to give the Consistory independent authority in its own ecclesiastical field. In the debate on the *Ordonnances,* the Little Council secured the insertion of the declaration:—

> We have ordered that the said ministers shall have no jurisdiction in this province, but simply should hear the parties and make the aforesaid remonstrances. And on their report we [magistrates] can deliberate and render judgment according to the merits of the case.

That would have been greatly to lame Calvin's cherished ecclesiastical independence; and, before the adoption of the *Ordonnances*, he procured a final modification, which may be regarded as expressing in classic form not merely Calvin's conception, but the whole sixteenth and seventeenth century Puritan thought, of the relations of Church discipline to the co-operant authority of a friendly government:—

> That all this [*i.e* discipline] shall be done in such fashion that the ministers shall have no civil jurisdiction and shall use none but the spiritual sword of the Word of God as Saint Paul directs them; and that the authority of the government and of ordinary justice shall in no way be diminished by the Consistory, but that civil authority shall remain unimpaired. And, in particular, where it shall be necessary to make some punishment or constrain the parties, the ministers with the Consistory, having heard the parties and made remonstrances and admonitions as shall be fitting, shall report all to the Council, which shall deliberate on their report and order and render judgment according to the merits of the case

Calvin's establishment provided, therefore, for an independent ecclesiastical exercise of discipline up to the point of excommunication; with the further punishment of refractory or gross offenders by the friendly magistrates as beyond the scope of churchly remedy As the members of the Church included all baptised inhabitants of a given territory, discipline was for all. The Christian life, in Calvin's conception far more than in Luther's, is one of dependence on the training and repressing power of the Church; and, in so viewing it, Calvin carried over to the Reformed congregations, in highly modified form, a principle characteristic of the Roman Church. Yet the basis of that discipline and the rule of its application, was not to be the wisdom of the Church, but the "Word of God." God has revealed the proper ordering of all right human life. It is the duty of the Church and of the State alike, each in its separate but mutually helpful sphere, to make men conform to His law. The transgression of one part of that divine rule, by error in faith, for example, is no less and no more heinous than the breach of another part, by sin in conduct. Each is to be corrected, if possible, by the Church, and where the Church has done its utmost without avail, is to be remedied or punished by the State.

The fourth, and final, class of church-officers named by the *Ordonnances* was that of deacons. These included not merely those specially charged with poor-relief, but the four trustees of the city hospital, and they were to be chosen in the same way as the elders. The hospital provided care not merely for the sick, for whose relief a physician and a surgeon were ordered; but a refuge for the superannuated, for indigent widows, and orphans. Begging was to be strenuously repressed.

Side by side with the preparation and discussion of the *Ordonnances*, and his ministerial activities, Calvin found himself impelled to other labours for the Genevan Church, the sum total of which rendered the closing months of 1541 so busy that one may readily credit his statement that he had worked unsparingly and had not since his return enjoyed two hours without interruption.[1] He prepared a revised liturgy, based on that of which he had made use at Strassburg, but conformed in many important respects, as has already been pointed out, to the existing Genevan usages.[2] He drafted a *Catechism* to take the place of that of 1537, and to serve as the basis of the Sunday noon instruction of children on which he laid great stress. Calvin had learned much as to the teaching of young people during his Strassburg sojourn, and, instead of the pedagogically ill-adapted form of his earlier Genevan ministry, the new *Catechism* presented a series of brief and simple questions and answers. From a modern standpoint, it is far too long and minute and demands for its thorough comprehension a theologic insight beyond childish years; but it shows great improvement in teachable qualities, and its length and elaboration is largely to be accounted for by the fact that it was designed not merely for learning, but for pulpit explication.[3]

Two other services rendered by Calvin to Geneva in the months immediately following his return are worthy of mention not merely as significant in themselves, but as showing his relations to the civil administration. The first had to do with a recodification of the Genevan laws and constitution. Fifteen days after Calvin's return, but, as far as the evidence goes,

[1] Letter of January, 1542, Herminjard, vii 410

[2] *Ante*, p. 223. Text, *Opera*, vi 161–210.

[3] Text, *Opera*, vi. 1–134. On its date see Calvin's letter just cited, Herminjard, vi. 410.

without impulse from him, the Little Council appointed a commission of laymen for this task.[1] In May, 1542, the work thus begun was intrusted to the syndic, Claude Roset, to Dr. Jean Fabri, a lawyer of Evian, and to Calvin. In September following, Fabri being apparently unavailable, Calvin and Roset were directed to take up the work, and, to afford leisure, Calvin was released by the government from some of his duties as a preacher. Like all that Calvin undertook, the work was promptly done; and on January 28, 1543, the results were essentially approved by the General Assembly. An examination of the work shows that the intention of giving to Geneva a new political constitution was entirely foreign to Calvin's mind. Practically nothing of importance was changed. Calvin's aristocratic and anti-demagogic feeling doubtless appears in the recommendation in which he and Roset joined, that only two of the four syndics should be elected in any one year, the other two holding over. The intention was evidently to prevent such an overturn of the government as had taken place in 1538; but the General Assembly, jealous of its privileges, rejected it. Doubtless the Genevan government was glad to avail itself then and often of the legal training of its chief minister; but the observation is essentially correct,

[1] The passages from the *Registres du Conseil* are given by Cornelius, pp 394, 395 The resultant revision by H Fazy, *Constitutions de la République de Genève*, pp 289 *et seq*; further see Roget, *Hist. du Peuple de Genève*, ii. 62–70; F. Tissot, *Les relations entre l'église et l'état à Genève au temps du Calvin*, Lausanne, 1875, pp 73–75.

"that it was in the capacity of a draughtsman and not of a legislator" [1] that Calvin did this work.

The second service related to the long and complicated disputes with Bern which had nearly resulted in war during the summer of 1540. As a means of escaping that calamity, the points of difference had been laid before arbitrators from Basel, and the report of those investigators, on reaching Geneva, was referred on January 19, 1542, by the Little Council to a committee of which Calvin was appointed by it a member.[2] Thanks to his conciliatory spirit, the Little Council, the Sixty, and the Two Hundred were brought, after long negotiation, to an agreement; only to have the whole prospect of a settlement frustrated for the time being by the opposition and threats of the popular leader, François Paguet. Negotiations were carried on afresh for a year, till, in September, 1543, chiefly through Calvin's efforts in favour of moderation,[3] all the Genevan councils were won, in spite of the hostility of Paguet, who escaped punishment for his violent opposition only by flight. Even now the task was not done. It needed all Calvin's influence at Basel, as well as in Geneva, to bring the matter to a successful issue, but, at last, on February 3, 1544, the treaty was achieved, and good relations re-established between

[1] Roget, *Histoire du peuple de Geneve*, ii 68.

[2] See E. Dunant, *Les relations politiques de Genève avec Berne et les Suisses*, Geneva, 1894, pp. 15–184, for Calvin's relations to the foreign politics of the city, also Roget, ii 85–109, Cornelius, pp. 398–414.

[3] See Calvin's letter to Viret of September 16 to 20, 1543, Herminjard, ix. 34.

Geneva and her powerful neighbour. By the leaders of Geneva and of Bern alike, this agreement, only a few of the steps preliminary to which have been indicated, was looked upon as due in high degree to the patience, skill, and moderation of Calvin.

Enough has been said, however, to make evident Calvin's position in Geneva in the period immediately following his return. He was its most influential resident. He was everywhere recognised as its chief religious leader. He was regarded as the foremost interpreter of the "Word of God" in a community which professedly made the Scriptures its guide. As such, and by reason of his learning, legal training, and the high esteem in which he was held by the other leaders of Protestantism, his opinions commanded great respect, while his singleness of purpose, iron will, and definiteness of aim made opposition difficult. But he was in no official position of rulership, he held no civil office, he usurped none of the powers of government, however strongly he influenced their exercise. In the adoption of the *Ordonnances* he could by no means have all to his liking. In civil concerns he took part as an adviser, and not as a magistrate. What was true of these opening years continued to be characteristic of his whole Genevan work But while Calvin had thus no civil office, and did not interfere with the ordinary machinery of government, it would be absurd to deny that he was really a ruler. His power was that of the spirit It was the force of intellect, of persuasion, and of will, but it was none the less compelling.

It has often been affirmed and denied that the

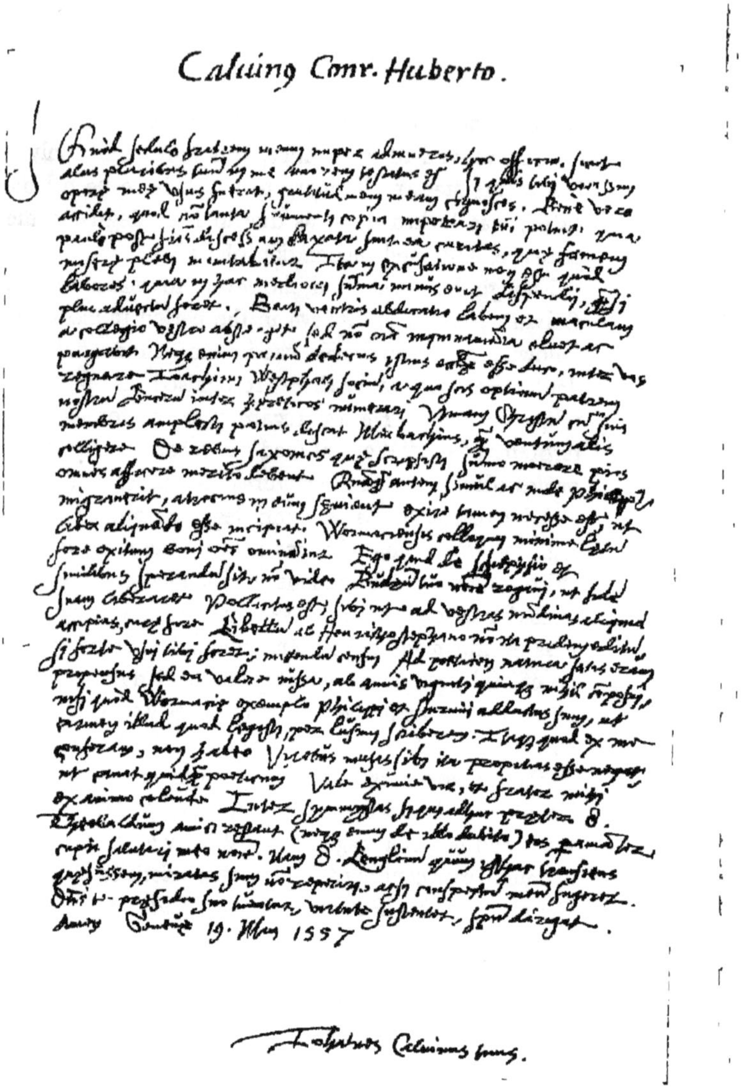


AUTOGRAPH OF CALVIN.

system established by the *Ordonnances* deserves the name of a theocracy. If by this term is meant that Calvin intended to submit all Genevan life to clerical rule, and make the minister dominant over the State, that designation is incorrect.[1] Calvin would abridge none of the civil powers of government, and he left to it, partly because he must, large influence in churchly affairs. But if by theocracy is meant that all government, whether in Church or State, should be but the expression, as nearly as human imperfection will admit, of the will of the divine Law-giver, then Calvin's ideal for Geneva was a theocracy. His system implied that there is a definitely ascertainable rule of faith and practice in the Scriptures.[2] His sole authority was as interpreter of that rule. The dangers of his position were that not all would accept his cardinal principle of Scriptural authority, or, accepting it, would agree with his interpretation; and that, while Church and State had theoretically their separate spheres, in the exigencies of contest appeal would be made to the stronger,—and that was usually the State,—to enforce his interpretation by its characteristic weapons. These perils were to have their abundant illustration in the story of

[1] Roget, *Histoire du peuple de Genève*, ii 18; compare Choisy, *La théocratie à Genève*, p. 51.

[2] Choisy well says, p 55 "The calvinistic theocracy established the rule of the Bible, the statute book of divine law Religion is thus conceived ecclesiastically, not as a principle of life, but as a government, and man becomes the subject of an absolute sovereign whose will is expressed by ordinances That these be observed there is need of a body to keep watch, as a police force, regarding the divine law."

Geneva under Calvin's rule; but none can deny the simplicity and grandeur of his conception, though its truth as an interpretation of the Gospel is more than doubtful, and its extensive application to complex, individualistic modern life is utterly impossible.

## CHAPTER XI

### STRUGGLES AND CONFLICTS

UNDOUBTEDLY a considerable part of the relative ease with which Calvin established his ecclesiastical constitution in Geneva, in spite of difficulties which have been mentioned, was due to the loss of several conspicuous leaders of the city-life just before or soon after his return Not to speak of the death of Jean Philippe and the collapse of the "Artichauds," which alone made that return possible, the chief "Guillermin" leader, Michel Sept, died in the autumn of 1540, while Calvin was still at Strassburg, the religious-minded Ami Porral followed him two years later, and, in 1544, the end came to the vigorous Claude Pertemps. Ami Perrin, upon whom the "Guillermin" leadership may be said to have devolved, was by no means their equal. The time of Calvin's opening work was one of relative weakness among the older leaders of both parties in Genevan affairs.

Under these circumstances, the introduction of the new ecclesiastical discipline was easier than it might otherwise have been. The Consistory began its work promptly. No age or distinction exempted one from its censures. Men and women were examined as to their religious knowledge, their criticisms of ministers, their absences from sermons, their use of charms, their family quarrels, as well as to more serious offences.[1] Other examples, from the later activity of the Consistory in Calvin's time, show disciplinary procedure against a widow who prayed a "*requiescat in pace*" on her husband's grave; for having fortunes told by gypsies;[2] against a goldsmith for making a chalice, for saying that the incoming of French refugees had raised the cost of living and that a minister had declared that all those who had died earlier (*i.e* before the Reformation) were damned; for dancing;[3] for possessing a copy of the *Golden Legend;* against a woman of seventy who was about to marry a man of twenty-five, against a barber for tonsuring a priest, for declaring the pope to be a good man; making a noise during the sermon;[4] laughing during preaching, criticising Geneva for putting men to death on account of differences in religion; having a copy of *Amadis des Gaules;* or singing a song defamatory of Calvin[5] Of course these instances are illustrative of only the more curious part of its work. It had to do, much of the time, with offences which any age would deem serious, but they exhibit its minute and inquisitorial interference with the lives of the people of Geneva.

The more flagrant faults detected by the Consistory were called by it to the attention of the magistrates;

[1] Excerpts from the *Registres du Consistoire*, 1542, in *Opera*, xxi, 292–305

[2] 1548, *Ibid*, pp 422, 428

[3] 1550–51, *Ibid*, pp. 466, 489, 506

[4] 1556, 1557, *Ibid*, 653, 657, 664, 669.

[5] 1558, 1559, *Ibid*, pp 700, 701, 712, 723

while really serious cases of crime and of error in doctrine appear to have received direct judicial cognisance without consistorial intervention. In their dealings with the accused, whether brought to them from the Consistory, or in the ordinary course of justice, the magistrates acted with great severity. Torture was freely used, as in most European states of that day. There seems to be no adequate ground to hold that Calvin's influence increased the rigours with which occasional penal cases had previously been handled,—one remembers the proposed torture of Jean Philippe,—and it is to his credit that he made a successful protest against the cruelty with which death sentences were executed,[1] but when this has been said, it must be equally recognized that Calvin's spirit favoured the full and stringent execution of the laws, and the increase of penalties for offences having to do with breaches of chastity and similar infringements of moral order. The sum total of persons punished and the breadth of the incidence of punishment, were doubtless very considerably augmented under his influence. Between 1542 and 1546, fifty-eight persons were condemned to death and seventy-six to banishment, but it must be remembered that the frightful panic of 1545 which alleged the plague to have been spread by witchcraft and conspiracy, and led to thirty-four executions, falls in this period.[2]

[1] March 9, 1545, *Registres du Conseil*, xl 42; *Opera*, xxi 348.

[2] These figures are from the investigations of J. G B Galiffe-*Mémoires de l'Inst nat genevois*, for 1863, pp 1–116; and Kampschulte, i 422–428 The conclusions drawn by these authors do not, however, do full justice to Calvin.

Undoubtedly the Consistory, as new and as limiting the authority of the magistrates, was the least popular, as it was in Calvin's judgment the most essential, of his reformatory measures. By March, 1543, public hostility made itself manifest. The Council of Sixty voted "that the Consistory has no jurisdiction or power to refuse [the Supper] but only to admonish and then report to the Council so that the government may judge the delinquents according to their demerits."[1] This would have been to take from the Consistory its power of excommunication, and to have broken down Calvin's system at a vital point. Calvin's energetic protest that he would taste exile or death rather than yield, won the day, for the time being; but the action of the Sixty was ominous of contests to come.

Next to the difficulties involved in the adoption of the *Ordonnances* in the form in which Calvin wished, his first trials were from want of sympathy on the part of his ministerial associates. Henri de la Mare and Jacques Bernard could not be expected to give him more than a grudging support. The same was true of Aimé Champereaux, whom the Genevan magistrates had called before Calvin's coming. He would gladly have secured Farel and Viret, but though Viret obtained permission from the Bernese authorities to come to Geneva for a few months, and greatly aided Calvin at the time of his return, it was impossible to secure Calvin's two friends for a permanent ministry at Geneva. The claims upon them of Neuchâtel and

[1] *Registres du Conseil*, xxxvii 37, *Opera*, xxi 309; Calvin to Viret, Herminjard, viii 298.

Lausanne, and the importance of holding those posts for the general cause, proved insurmountable obstacles. Gradually, however, Calvin effected a change in the complexion of the Genevan ministry; but worthy and effective ministers were rare, still rarer were those who sympathised with his strenuous zeal. It was not till he had done his training work that his spiritual disciples were to become abundant. Bernard was glad to exchange his city pastorate for a similar post in one of Geneva's country dependences early in 1542. In April, 1543, a like transfer removed Henri de la Mare. Meanwhile, in July, 1542, four Frenchmen, of varying degrees of satisfactoriness to Calvin, and of differing merits, Philippe de l'Église, Pierre Blanchet, Matthieu de Geneston, and Louis Treppereau, were added to the Genevan ministry[1] Blanchet soon died under circumstances which, as will be seen, bore witness to his courage and pastoral fidelity, de l'Église and Treppereau were removed to the country in 1544, while Geneston proved acceptable to Calvin. Two other pastors, both Frenchmen of opinions sympathetic with those of Calvin, were next added to the Genevan ministry, Abel Poupin in April, 1543, and Jean Ferron in March, 1544. By the time of Ferron's accession, therefore, thanks to these rapid changes, Calvin was surrounded by a fairly congenial group of fellow-workers, but the older inhabitants of the city may be pardoned for looking upon this foreign-born and rapidly shifting ministry as something imposed on Genevan life, even

[1] *Registres du Conseil*, xxxvi 65, *Opera*, xxi. 298 Calvin to Farel and Viret, Herminjard, viii 79, 105

if established in each instance by the Genevan government. The most permanent and the most powerful factor was Calvin himself.

Nor did this ministry, strenuous in its demands as far as Calvin could make it, command the full respect of the community. The plague, the ravages of which at Strassburg have already been noted, reached Geneva in the autumn of 1542. Blanchet courageously offered his services at the hospital, where the magistrates required a minister; but such was the reluctance of his colleagues, that Calvin felt, not without apprehension, that should Blanchet die, he must step into the breach lest the members of his flock be left unconsoled in their extremity.[1] The test soon came. In April, 1543, the plague broke out again, and before the month was over the Little Council ordered the ministers to send one of their number to the hospital. They shrank back. It was reported to the Council that some declared they "would rather be with the devil." Sébastien Castellio, the head of the school, of whom more will be said later, offered himself, but for some reason, perhaps because the government did not wish to leave the school without his oversight,[2] was not finally sent; and Blanchet once more took the task, only to fall a victim to the pestilence less than three weeks later. The Little Council ordered the ministers to choose his

[1] *Registres du Conseil*, xxxvi 151, 153, *Opera*, xxi 304, Calvin's letter to Viret, Herminjard, viii 163 See also, Kampschulte, i 484, F Buisson, *Sébastien Castellion, sa vie et son œuvre*, Paris, 1892, i 184, Cornelius, p 436

[2] So Cornelius suggests, p 437

successor, excepting Calvin as "necessary for the Church"; but five days later the pastors presented themselves before the government and declared that while they recognised the task as a duty, "God had not yet given them grace to have force and constancy to go to the hospital." They presented, instead, a French lay refugee, Simon Moreau, who took the burden, but who, in discharging it, laid himself open to grave charges of wrong-doing.[1] Calvin's action, at least, can hardly be charged to cowardice. When in Basel, just after his banishment from Geneva, in 1538, he had visited Farel's nephew then dying of the same dread disease.[2] He had lofty ideas of pastoral duty;[3] and it may be that Beza was correct in affirming that Calvin reluctantly received exemption now from this service;[4] though nothing in the contemporary records supports his statement. The more natural interpretation is that Calvin shared the feeling of the Little Council that his life was too valuable for the larger service of the city to be risked. Such a cool judgment, however unattractive, probably bore the stamp of wisdom. Granted that the organisation and discipline of the Genevan Church was a work of God,—and Calvin firmly believed it so to be,—it was well that the leader on whom all depended should not be exposed to danger. But the incident shows in how great a degree

[1] *Registres du Conseil*, xxxvii 80, 82, 89, 110, 113, 117, xl. 72, 79; *Opera*, xxi 312–314, 350, 351

[2] Calvin to Farel, August 20, 1538, Herminjard, v. 88. See also Doumergue, ii 294, 295; iii. 147–150.

[3] Herminjard, viii 164

[4] Life of 1575, *Opera*, xxi. 134.

the larger aspects of his work outweighed the sense of responsibility for the individual souls committed to his charge. Calvin's feeling was that of a general in battle, rather than of a pastor toward a suffering flock.

The pest had its melancholy sequel in 1545, when popular rumour, charging its spread to conspiracy and witchcraft, resulted in a series of cruel tortures and executions. Calvin was not in advance of his age. He believed the allegations to be facts,[1] but his plea for more merciful executions has already been noted.

Unfortunately a conscientious difference of opinion led Calvin, while these untoward events were happening, into a dispute that cost Geneva the services of one who had showed himself courageous when most displayed cowardice, Sébastien Castellio. Castellio (1515–63), who was six years younger than Calvin, was a Savoyard by birth, had risen from very humble origins to distinction in humanistic learning at Lyons, had fled to Strassburg by reason of his Protestant sympathies, and, while there, had for a brief time been a member of Calvin's household.[2] Impetuous and rather arrogant of his scholarship, he was courageous and kind-hearted. At Farel's recommendation he had become a teacher of the Genevan school on June 20, 1541, nearly three months before Calvin's return. It was natural that Calvin should prefer the restoration

[1] *Registres du Conseil*, xl. 42, 60, *Opera*, xxi 348, 349; Calvin to Myconius, *Ibid*, xii 55.

[2] The best account of Castellio is that of Buisson, already cited, p 286 See also R Stähelin, in Hauck's *Realencyklopadie fur prot Theol u. Kirche*, iii 750, Cornelius, pp 438–445, Choisy, pp. 63–76.

of his old friend Mathurin Cordier to the rectorship in the school which that teacher had occupied before Calvin's banishment; but when it proved impossible to draw Cordier from his new home in Neuchâtel, Castellio was given the place in permanency, in April, 1542, with the understanding that he should maintain two sub-teachers and preach at the village of Vendovre.[1] The time was one of great scarcity in Geneva, and his salary proved all too small for his needs. This, and possibly other considerations, added to a real desire for the pastorate, led him to propose to exchange his teachership for the active ministry. The Little Council favoured the plan on December 17, 1543; but Calvin opposed, since on his examination by the *Vénérable Compagnie* Castellio had criticised the inspiration of Solomon's Song, holding it to be illustrative of that monarch's less reputable characteristics, and also the current Genevan interpretation of the clause in the Apostles' Creed, "He descended into hell," which taught that it means that Christ on the cross suffered vicariously the pains of hell. For these reasons, Calvin declared to the Little Council that Castellio ought not to enter the pastorate.[2]

In Calvin's judgment, the chief point at issue was Castellio's rejection of an accepted book of the Old Testament. It is easy to see why he so felt. The Scriptures were to him the corner-stone of faith and

[1] *Registres du Conseil*, xxxv 543; *Opera*, xxi. 294

[2] *Registres du Conseil*, xxxviii. 10, 30, 45, *Opera*, xxi. 326–329, Calvin to Viret, February 11, 1544, Herminjard, ix. 156; the certificate given by the Genevan ministers to Castellio, *Ibid.*, pp 157–160.

practice. In them the Holy Spirit spake with unquestionable authority. From the vantage ground of an absolute acceptance of them, whole, and entire, as the "Word of God" and from that only, in his judgment, could the Papacy be resisted and a Christian community be built up. In an age when no doctrine of progress in revelation or of the colouration of divine truth through its human interpreters had yet commanded assent, Castellio's position seemed extremely dangerous. The attack thus begun might end in destroying the authority of all Scripture, and what Evangelical foundation would then be left? Yet the Genevan ministers, led by Calvin, treated Castellio with what, for the time, was moderation. On his expressed intention to remove to Basel they gave him a certificate over Calvin's signature, stating frankly the points at issue, but testifying also:[1]—

He resigned the headship of the school voluntarily. In that office he so bore himself that we judged him worthy of the sacred ministry, but that he was not admitted was not on account of any faults of life, nor any impious dogma regarding the chief points of our faith, but this one reason prevented which we have set forth.

Castellio felt, naturally enough, that Calvin had stood the one barrier to the realisation of his hopes. He complained to Viret that Calvin "had never admonished him save with temper and reproaches",[2]

[1] Herminjard, ix 159, 160

[2] So Viret told Calvin in a letter of February 16, 1544, in which he urged considerate treatment of Castellio, *Ibid*, p 164.

and, doubtless, as he brooded over the matter, his sense of antagonism grew to hostility toward the whole Genevan ministry. At its regular meeting on May 30, 1544, he drew an unflattering comparison between the conduct of the Genevan pastors and that of Paul as set forth in the sixth chapter of II. Corinthians. The whole bitterness of a disappointed man spoke in his words. Calvin reported his conduct to the Little Council, which heard all parties at length, and, on June 12th, dismissed Castellio from his small charge at Vendovre "during the good pleasure of the government."[1] He left Geneva at once to begin a career harassed by distressing poverty at Basel; and these Genevan experiences led to a lifelong hostility between Calvin and Castellio. In Castellio the use of compulsion in matters of religion in general, and its employment in the case of Servetus in particular, was to find a manly and able opponent, who stood in advance of the spirit of his age.

On the whole, however, Calvin was strengthening his position in Geneva. By the autumn of 1545, he had succeeded substantially in completing the transformation of the city ministry. Nicolas des Gallars and Michel Cop, the latter a brother of the one-time Parisian rector and both hearty supporters of Calvin, were added to the Genevan pastorate in 1544 and 1545. The place of the deceased Geneston was filled, in the last named year, by Raimond Chauvet. Champereaux, the only remaining representative of those in

[1] *Registres du Conseil*, xxxviii 231, 237, 246, *Opera*, xxi 336–338, Calvin's letter of May 31, 1544, to Farel, Herminjard, ix. 264.

office at Calvin's return, was removed to the country in July, 1545. The Genevan ministry thus became a fairly homogeneous body, of which Calvin was the ruling spirit. Thus strengthened, Calvin turned his attention, in 1545, to a more strenuous administration of discipline, especially in breaches of chastity. The supervision of the Consistory was intensified in regard to such offences, and the zeal of the magistrates stimulated. It was ordered that, after having received punishment from the civil authorities, those guilty of such wrong-doing should be required to appear before the Consistory for proper ecclesiastical admonition,[1]—a proceeding which appeared to many an added and unnecessary disgrace. To Calvin, it was an assertion of the just disciplinary powers of the Church.

Though Calvin had been thus far, on the whole, successful in his work, it is evident that elements in abundance existed for the growth of an opposition party in Geneva, and the forces unfriendly to him had been strengthened by the results of the peace made with Bern in February, 1544, in obtaining which he bore so honourable a part. As one of its consequences, the survivors of the "Artichauds" and their sympathisers had returned to swell the ranks of those hostile to Calvin's ecclesiastical constitution. This opposition was made up of most various forces. Some were simply representatives of old Genevan families, not opposed to the Reformation, but disinclined to view with favour the strict rule which Calvin had imposed, and disposed to look

[1] *Registres du Conseil*, of October 13, 1545, quoted by Cornelius, p 456

upon him, the other ministers, and the French refugees whom he attracted to Geneva, as so many intruders into a city which had won liberty for itself only to come under the spiritual bondage of foreigners. Others were hostile to any kind of ecclesiastical or governmental discipline that would limit the free life and abundant amusements for which Geneva was noted. To be forced to hear sermons and to be reprimanded by the Consistory was not that for which they had thrown off the power of Savoy and withstood Bern at such cost. But neither element produced a really worthy and efficient leader, and to the incompetence of the opposition, in the face of Calvin's iron determination, rather than to its want of numbers, his success in the conflicts from 1546 to 1555 was to be due

Many writers have deduced the chief features of this opposition, the principal causes of which have just been noted, from the alleged prevalence in Geneva of religious Libertinism The ascription of hostility to this source has, indeed, become almost a Calvinistic tradition.[1] The Libertins or, as they preferred to call themselves, the "Spirituels," were a pantheistic antinomian sect which had its origin in the preaching of a certain Coppin, at Lille, about 1529, and, by 1545, was considerably widespread in France, where its supporters obtained protection for a time from Marguerite d'Angoulême, though there is no evidence that she shared their views. Calvin had encountered two of its

[1] *E g* Henry, ii 398–446, E Stahelin, *Johannes Calvin: Leben und ausgewahlte Schriften*, 1863, i 383, Schaff, vii. 498–501; R. Stähelin, in Hauck's *Realencyklopadie*, iii 669.

principal representatives, an enthusiast named Quintin soon after his acceptance of the Reformed faith at Paris, and an ex-priest, Antoine Pocquet, in Geneva itself, probably in 1542. To their thinking, all is but a manifestation of the one Spirit—all is God. Nothing can be really bad, and the common distinction between good and evil acts is baseless, since all are alike the work of God. Anything more repugnant to Calvin's strenuous morality it would be hard to imagine. And, early in 1545, Calvin wrote against the holders of these views one of his most vigorous and effective tracts, that *Contre la Secte phantastique et furieuse des Libertins qui se nomment Spirituels*;[1] which caused displeasure to Marguerite,[2] but seems to have done much to check the spread of these opinions in France. Yet neither in this tract nor in his letters of this and the immediately subsequent time does Calvin seem to feel that the Spirituels were a Genevan peril. He tells Marguerite d'Angoulême that it was the ill wrought in the Netherlands, Artois, and Hainault that induced him to enter the lists against them. Though he speaks of Pocquet's sojourn at Geneva and attempt to win approval from him, the characteristic incidents of Spirituel teaching which he relates in the tract have to do with Quintin and his stay in Paris[3] True some incidents of the time show sporadic examples of opinions and practices

[1] *Opera*, vii 145–248

[2] See Calvin's letter to her of April 28, 1545, *Opera*, xii 65.

[3] *Opera*, vii 160, 163, 185 He says of Pocquet's stay at Geneva that he had "*dissimulé sa meschante doctrine*," and gives no impression of effective labours there done by this Spirituel

at Geneva which were essentially those of the Spirituels.[1] There were doubtless occasional spiritual Libertines in the city; but to ascribe any considerable weight to them in the opposition to Calvin is to give them an importance not their due. They did not constitute a party.[2]

Calvin's first conspicuous conflict with the elements in opposition came early in 1546. Pierre Ameaux[3] was a member of the Little Council, though not sprung from any Genevan family of prominence. His ancestral business of manufacturing playing-cards had been broken up by the new discipline, he seems to have been imbittered by the protracted litigation necessary before he could secure a divorce from his unworthy wife, and he had been on cordial terms with the ministers, de la Mare and de l'Église, whose feeling towards Calvin was now far from one of friendliness. On January 26, 1645, at a supper-party in his own house, after the wine

[1] Notably in the case of Benoîte Ameaux, wife of Pierre Ameaux, whose trial for divorce, sought by her husband, between January, 1544, and June, 1545, falls just in this period. See Henry, ii 412, J G. B Galiffe, *Mém de l'Inst nat genevois*, 1863, p 14, Kampschulte, ii 19 The opinions of Gruet do not seem to have been specially those of the Spirituels on important points, *e g* God and Christ Compare Calvin's report on his book, Henry, ii, appendix, pp. 120–122, and Calvin's account of the Spirituels, *Opera*, vii. 178–181, 198–200

[2] The subject is well discussed by Kampschulte, ii 13–19 (published in 1899) He shows, furthermore, that the application of the nickname "Libertin" to the party in political opposition to Calvin is not contemporary with the reformer.

[3] J G. B Galiffe, *Nouvelles pages d'histoire exacte* in *Mémoires de l'Inst nat genevois* for 1863, pp 1–16, Kampschulte, ii. 20–27, Cornelius, pp. 462–471, Choisy, pp 77–80.

had circulated freely, Ameaux expressed his dislike of Calvin, declaring him to be only a Picard, a preacher of false doctrine, and an evil man.[1] He also accused his fellow-counsellors of undue dependence on the reformer, and affirmed that foreign residents would soon be masters of the city. It was the utterance of an imbittered man to a supposedly confidential audience; but one of his hearers reported the speech at once to the Little Council and Ameaux was imprisoned. To Calvin the attack seemed more than a personal affront, it was a denial of his authority as an interpreter of the Word of God, and therefore an insult to "the honour of Christ," whose servant Calvin felt himself to be.[2] We have here an illustration of that identification of his own cause with that of God, which was the source of much of Calvin's strength, and also of much of his severity. The trial dragged. The Little Council was divided, and a considerable portion would have exacted slight punishment of the offender. The Two Hundred were called in; and, after a stormy discussion, it was ordered, on March 2d, that Ameaux appear before it, Calvin also being present, and ask pardon on his knees, "of God, the government, and Calvin." To Calvin's thinking this was not enough. He declared that he would neither accept the Council's invitation to be present at its session nor enter the pulpit, till the "name of God" had been vindicated. At the head of the

[1] *Registres du Conseil*, xl 359, *Opera*, xxi 368. Many excerpts from the *Registres* relating to this matter may be found, *Ibid*, pp 368–377, Cornelius also gives the chief passages

[2] Calvin to Farel, February 13, 1546, *Opera*, xi 284 See Choisy, p. 80.

Consistory, he now appeared before the Little Council, the Sixty, and the Two Hundred, and demanded adequate punishment. Thus admonished, the Two Hundred retracted its mild sentence and ordered the Little Council to take up the case anew. In spite of popular restiveness in the Saint-Gervais district in which Ameaux lived, he was sentenced, on April 8th, to make the tour of the city, clad in a shirt, bareheaded, torch in hand, and on his knees to beg mercy of God and the government.

Calvin had won a notable triumph, as he believed, for the cause of Gospel order. A member of the inner circle of government had criticised him in his office and had paid the penalty by a humiliating penance. Nor was this all. Henry de la Mare ventured to express his dissent from Calvin's methods. He was imprisoned by order of the Little Council on March 17th, and ultimately deprived of the rural pastorate that still remained to him. Yet the situation was ominous as to the future.

It has already been pointed out that the completion of the process by which the Genevan city ministry became a body in sympathy with Calvin was followed, in 1545, by a marked increase in the activity of the Consistory. Evidences of multiplied exercise of discipline continued, and, in the main, had the support of the city government. To ministerial initiative, though enacted of course by the civil authorities, must be credited the curious laws regarding taverns, of April and May, 1546.[1]

[1] Roget, ii 232, 234, Cornelius, p 474, Doumergue, iii. 70–73 Many features were borrowed from earlier regulations

In their place, five "abbeys" were established, as religiously conducted houses of entertainment. No food or drink was to be served to any guest who refused to say grace, the Bible was to be at hand; all oaths and unseemly conversation were to be severely repressed. Worthy as was the object sought, the attempt, of course, failed, and before the end of June the impracticable new regulations were abandoned.

But some of Calvin's ministerial colleagues surpassed him in intensity of disciplinary zeal. In his own work there was not infrequently a moderation wanting in theirs. Such an instance occurred in the spring and summer of 1546. The day of morality plays, so beloved in the middle ages, had not yet passed. At the request of some of his flock Abel Poupin, one of the ministers, had drawn a drama from the Acts of the Apostles; but though Calvin did not disapprove, the fiery Michel Cop opposed that theatrical representation in the *Vénérable Compagnie*, and forced a protest from that body in the name of all the ministers to the Little Council.[1] That board of magistrates ordered Poupin to continue his work and told the ministers "not to mix in politics." Cop, not to be restrained, carried his denunciation into the pulpit. Almost a riot occurred. Calvin did his utmost to calm it; but on Cop's being brought before the Little Council, Calvin defended the rights of the ministry to freedom of expression; yet with such moderation and skill that the matter was adjusted, so that, after the disputed play had

[1] *Registres du Conseil*, xli 114, 142, *Opera*, xxi 382, 385, Calvin to Farel, *Ibid*, xii 347, 355, Cornelius, p 475

been held, further theatrical representations were suspended by the civil authorities "till the times should be more fitting." Undoubtedly Calvin found his situation in the face of the public made more trying by an over-zeal in an associate which he did not share, but could not wholly repudiate.

Not so moderate was Calvin's attitude on the dispute regarding baptismal names which arose in the month following the settlement of the controversy regarding theatrical representations. Moved undoubtedly by ministerial impulse, the Little Council, on August 27, 1546, forbade the imposition of the favourite name "Claude," as showing an idolatrous reverence to a saint once revered in the Genevan territory. The order grew out of the refusal of Ami Chappius to permit the minister to substitute in the baptism of his son the name "Abraham" for that now condemned. About two months later, a similar refusal of the preacher at Saint-Gervais to give the names Aimé or Martin resulted in a riotous protest from a part of the congregation. At the suggestion of Calvin and the other ministers, the Little Council ordered Calvin "to make a list" of objectionable names. The result was the edict on baptismal names which became a law on November 22d of the same year.[1] Undoubtedly much could be said in favour of its prohibition of such names as Sepulcre, Cross, Pentecost, Sunday, and that of Jesus; but by no means all were in these categories. To modern thinking, it was an unwarranted invasion of personal freedom.

[1] Text, *Opera*, xa 49 For action of the Council see *Ibid*, xxi 386–391.

On the whole, the year 1546 was one of decided success for Calvin in his task of imposing what he believed to be Gospel discipline on Geneva, and it must have been with satisfaction that he saw citizenship given to his brother Antoine by the Little Council on August 3d, "in view of the great pains which his brother [*i.e.* Calvin] had taken for the advancement of the Word of God and to maintain the honour of the city."[1] Yet he did not deceive himself as to the growth of opposition or the extent to which his work lacked permanency and completion. His strength was also in a measure his weakness. From the time of his return, in spite of temporary diminution of their numbers during the ravages of the plague, refugees from lands where the Evangelical cause was persecuted had been flocking to Geneva. The vast majority of these new residents were French. Most of them were men of character and industry, many were men of property. From them the whole ministry of the city had been recruited. They filled the houses which the banishments and voluntary exiles due to the long party struggles had made vacant, they built up the trade of the city. They were a most valuable addition to the population—but they were foreigners.[2] The older Genevans resented their prominence, and this resentment directed itself especially against the ecclesiastical constitution and above all against the disciplinary activity of the Consistory, which seemed to these

[1] *Opera*, XXI. 385

[2] Compare Kampschulte, II 37-47

opponents the chief yoke that the new-comers, led by Calvin, had laid on the city.

Most conspicuous at this time as a critic of the Consistory was a Genevan of wealth, and of influence by reason of his family connections, François Favre, whose ungovernable daughter, Franchequine, was the wife of Ami Perrin,—the latter a man prominently identified, as will be recalled, with the "Guillermins," and instrumental in Calvin's return. Both François and his son Gaspard were of easy morals; and, with the strengthening of the discipline of the Consistory which was begun in 1545, their words and actions, prominent as they themselves were, were speedily brought under its cognisance. In February and March, 1546, they appeared indeed before the Consistory, but criticised and as far as possible repudiated its authority "as that of another jurisdiction above the courts of Geneva."[1] Yet if church-government was to be effective it must apply to small and great alike. A fresh problem soon occurred. On March 21, 1546, Antoine Lect celebrated the betrothal of his daughter to Claude Philippe, son of the executed "Artichaud" leader. Among the guests, who included Ami Perrin and his wife, and the syndic Amblard Corne, then president of the Consistory itself, dancing was indulged, in contravention of the city ordinances. The Consistory proceeded to discipline, the offence was reported to the Little Council, and the dancers imprisoned. On the expiration of their brief sentence they were ordered before the Consistory for admonition. Corne, who had

[1] Consistory records, quoted by Cornelius, p. 483.

the religious interest of the city at heart, readily obeyed; but Perrin held out for nearly a month before yielding compliance, while his wife took a defiant attitude throughout the whole proceeding.[1] For the time being Perrin yielded; but in heart he had become Calvin's opponent, and from now on he, even more than the Favres, was the real strength of the opposition. Vain and self-seeking, he had not in him the stuff to make a rallying centre of moral force, but he was strong enough to cause Calvin abundant difficulties, and had he been a man of more character might have won the struggle. Calvin's success in the condemnation of Ameaux, while these events were taking place, rendered opposition for the time being unpromising, and during the summer of 1546, his control seemed fairly secure. Gaspard Favre, having shown his contempt by playing bowls in a garden during service, was made to appear before the Consistory on June 27th; and so heatedly replied to Calvin, that the latter, quick-tempered as has already been seen, abruptly left the meeting. The Consistory secured his imprisonment by the Little Council for his various offences.[2]

With the opening month of 1547, however, came a change unfavourable to Calvin. The February election was largely won by Calvin's opponents. Just before they had taken place, François Favre had at last

[1] *Opera*, xxi 376-381, Calvin to Viret and Farel, *Ibid*, xii 334; Cornelius, p 473 On the first hearing, the sharp-tongued Franchequine cried out against Calvin "Wicked man, you wish to drink the blood of our [Favre] family; but you will leave Geneva before we do"

[2] *Opera*, xxi 382, 383.

been punished, on January 24, 1547, by the civil authorities for his offences against the seventh commandment; and, on the expiration of his sentence, was ordered to appear before the Consistory for admonition. The war between Charles V. and the German Protestants was in progress, and Calvin had been sent to northern Switzerland to ascertain its threatening course, so the admonition was spoken in the name of the Consistory by one of the most strenuous of the pastors, Abel Poupin. Favre defiantly declared that he "did not recognise" the ministers; they rejoined that they "did not recognise him as a sheep of the flock of Jesus Christ, but as a dog and excommunicate." The scene was one of recrimination. On Calvin's return, this "rebellion" was reported to the civil authorities, by whom, in spite of the results of the recent election, Favre was ordered to pay due reverence to the Consistory.[1] He failed to appear, but his daughter, who was Perrin's wife, and his son, Gaspard, presented themselves in his behalf with loud protests against the treatment he had experienced from the ministers, insisting that the matter be carried to the Little Council. On March 7th, accompanied by her husband, Favre's daughter repeated the demand before the civil authorities. Perrin was thus publicly ranged with the opposition. The question at issue was as to whether offenders punished by the government must endure further discipline by the Consistory. None disputed judicial control; but to add ecclesiastical censure to civil imprisonment was what Favre, and now Perrin

[1] *Ibid.*, pp 395, 396, Cornelius, p 493

also, resented. Their hostility is readily comprehensible. It was in a certain sense double punishment that was imposed. Yet to Calvin the whole maintenance of the ecclesiastical constitution seemed bound up in the preservation of this consistorial power.[1] The Little Council was divided. It inclined to the position that reference to the Consistory was only at the good pleasure of the civil authorities; but the firm attitude of the ministers, led by Calvin, worked a compromise. On March 29th, the Council voted that the rebellious and obstinate should be sent to the Consistory after punishment by the civil courts; but not the repentant. On the whole, Calvin had held his own in a difficult struggle. The power of the Consistory was practically intact, though Calvin could count on no hearty support from the Little Council.

But a new peril threatened him,—that of a popular demonstration. Perrin, conscious that Calvin had substantially held his own with the Little Council, determined to make use of the relations which his position as General-captain of the city might establish between him and the Arquebusiers, whose target-practice was regarded as a popular festival. Just how far he planned to go is uncertain; but he evidently purposed a demonstration which should modify the disciplinary policy which Calvin upheld in Church and State. The issue took a curious turn. Slashed hose were much admired by the youth of Geneva, but had been forbidden by the government as a sign of sinful

[1] Calvin to Viret, March 27, 1547, *Opera*, xii. 505; Cornelius, pp. 494, 495

luxury. Perrin, on May 9, 1547, asked the Little Council to permit the target festival. The authorities promptly consented; but renewed therewith the prohibition of the desired garments. Here then was a lever to arouse popular feeling against the supporters of discipline in the Little Council. The Arquebusiers asked that their use be allowed at the festival. The issue was so threatening that the Little Council called the Two Hundred for the 25th,—the day before the appointed parade and festival. Could Perrin succeed, he intended doubtless to push the matter much further, but before the Two Hundred Calvin's persuasive skill proved an insurmountable barrier. In an appeal of great force, Calvin urged that of itself the question of slashed hose was of small consequence, but to open the door to excess was very serious. Such would be the effect of the repeal of the recently re-enacted prohibition. It would lead to contempt of God and of the government. The Two Hundred supported Calvin's contention; and Perrin showed his feeling of defeat by a sudden journey to Bern. As Calvin wrote to Viret, Perrin had found that the people were with the reformers far more than he had imagined.[1]

Calvin had escaped, for the time being, the imminent peril of the overthrow of his system by governmental action or popular tumult; but he was far from secure. Perrin, though defeated, had influence enough to be sent, in June, on a highly honourable embassy to the court of France to greet the new king, Henry II. His

[1] *Opera*, xii. 531, 532 On the whole transaction, see Roget, ii. 275–284, and Cornelius, pp. 497–501

friend, Pierre Vandel, still carried on a work of opposition in the city. Though François Favre deemed it best to retire to his estates, his daughter, Perrin's wife, once more defied the ecclesiastical discipline by dancing, and after a heated interview with the Consistory, in which she insulted Abel Poupin who had once called her father a dog, she was ordered imprisoned on June 24th, by the Little Council,—a punishment which she avoided by flight. Three days later, a threatening placard, aimed primarily at Poupin, but including the whole body of ministers in its declaration, "When too much has been endured revenge is taken," was affixed to the pulpit at Saint-Pierre. Suspicion fell at once on Jacques Gruet, who had breakfasted that morning with François Favre.[1] A man of some education, inclined to the use of his pen for his private amusement, though not thus far for public influence, he was at heart a "free-thinker" in the modern sense, and also a man of sensual standards of morality. Arrested at once, he admitted the authorship of the placard under threat of torture. But a search of his house yielded documents, to the thinking of the time of even more incriminating nature. Among his papers were drafts of an appeal to the people against the moral discipline of the community, and of a letter proposing that the King of France be induced to attempt the removal of Calvin from Geneva by diplomatic threats. On a scrap of paper were traced the words, "All laws, divine and human, are

[1] For Gruet see H Fazy, *Procès de J Gruet*, in *Mémoire de l'Inst. nat genevois*, for 1886, i. 5–141, Roget, ii 289–312, Kampschulte, ii 59–67, Cornelius, pp 501–505, also, *Opera*, xii 563–568

made by the caprice of men." On the margin of a passage in which Calvin had argued the truth of human immortality he had written, "All nonsense." These were private papers. No consequent act, save the placard, could be traced to him, but to the judges they seemed an attack on the majesty of God no less than of the State. The severest of tortures, however, failed to wring from Gruet any satisfactory evidences of a conspiracy or of accomplices. But the sixteenth century had only one opinion of the deserts of such an offender[1] On July 26th, he was beheaded.

Gruet was a worthless fellow. The real danger from him was slight to modern thinking, if not to the judgment of that age. But to Calvin, in the heat of a difficult struggle, Gruet's discovery and condemnation was a great advantage. He felt that the trial moved too slowly and rejoiced in its result.[2] Gruet, though denying that he had had accomplices, and himself so abhorrent to the conception of the time that none of Calvin's enemies would say a word in his defence, nevertheless seemed by his own wickedness to prove the fundamental viciousness of the opposition which the reformer had encountered and to justify the severity of Genevan discipline.

Strong as Calvin appeared after the collapse of

[1] Some time after Gruet's death, a draft of a volume was found hidden in his former home showing his hostility to the Christian religion and attacking the characters of Christ, His mother, and the Apostles Made a subject of judicial inquiry in which Calvin bore a part, it was publicly burned on May 23, 1550. Henry, ii., Appendix, pp. 120–124, *Opera*, xiii 566–572

[2] Calvin's letters, *Opera*, xi. 559, 576

Perrin's plans and the death of Gruet, before the end of the year he was to reach almost his lowest point of power. Perrin, as has been noted, had gone in June to the French court as an ambassador of Geneva. The time was one of distress for the Protestant cause brought low in Germany by the successes of Charles V. Switzerland feared his victorious arms. Under these circumstances of danger from Germany, Perrin made or listened to a suggestion that a small force in French pay, but under his command, be sent to Geneva to strengthen the city against the Emperor.[1] The arrangement was not concluded, but the advantages of such a force to an ambitious party leader are evident. Before Perrin's return the plan was made known, however, through the correspondence of a brilliant, rather spendthrift, but able French refugee resident of Geneva, Laurent Maigret, nicknamed *Magnifique* from his style of living, who had always maintained close relations with the French court, and with whom partly as an admiring fellow-countryman and partly as a possible agent for advancing the Evangelical cause in France, Calvin stood in friendly relations. Perrin's home-coming, in September, 1547, was, therefore, sure to lead to questioning; but it was aggravated by the return to the city of his father-in-law and his wife, François and Franchequine Favre, both of whom had avoided governmental punishment by flight. They were now arrested, and Perrin having denounced their seizure in bitter words, was joined with them. At the request of Bern, with which canton they

[1] For this whole controversy see Roget, iii 1–39, Kampschulte, ii 70–100, Cornelius, pp 505–537

stood on good terms, the Favres were soon released from confinement, and, on October 6th, at last made their peace with the Consistory. Not so Perrin. Though aided by Bern, his trial continued.

Thus far all had gone well for Calvin, but a change now came. The Bernese ambassador denounced Maigret as much worse than Perrin, as a constant correspondent with the French authorities, a dangerous intriguant with France and the real traitor. The result was that two trials went on side by side, that of Calvin's opponent, Perrin, and that of his friend, Maigret. Factional feeling was excited in high degree; but its most interesting exhibition for Calvin's story is that it gave him an opportunity to display a physical courage which shows how completely his strength of spirit could triumph over his natural timidity. On December 16th, the Two Hundred met. The scene within was one of violence, and the crowd in the street outside seemed on the point of battle. Bern and France had their friends and foes in the throng. At imminent peril of his life, and against protest, warning, and threat, Calvin went to the hall, at the head of the *Vénérable Compagnie*, and by the courage of his personal appearance and the skill of his words of exhortation brought at least external good order. It was a triumph of pluck and persuasive force.[1] But Calvin had little hope either of Maigret's acquittal or of his own continuance in the city. "I am

[1] Even Audin, *Histoire de la vie, des ouvrages et des doctrines de Calvin*, I 394, praises his courage. For contemporary accounts see *Opera*, XII 632, XXI 418, Cornelius, p. 550; see also Calvin's Farewell Address, *Opera*, IX 892.

broken," he wrote to Viret, "unless God stretches forth his hand."[1] Yet so evenly balanced were the two parties in Geneva that the result was compromise and partial reconciliation. Perrin and Maigret both went free. But Perrin gained most. He was restored to all his rights and honours, while Maigret remained out of office. This balance of parties was also evident in the choice of syndics at the election of February, 1548. By the Perrinists and the friends of Calvin the board was evenly divided; and in this equality of power lay Calvin's danger and his hope alike.

Calvin's story during the next two or three years is one of effort to hold what had been gained, involving many petty, but none the less harassing struggles to maintain Church-discipline. By the lighter-minded of his opponents Calvin was nicknamed Cain, dogs were named in derision for him, placards were posted criticising him, ballads ridiculing him were sung; he was exposed to all the annoyances of petty attack. When discovered, the authors of these insults were disciplined by the Consistory, and reported to the magistrates; but they rendered his life uncomfortable, and increased the sense of danger which was his constant companion.

The ablest leader among Calvin's opponents was undoubtedly Ami Perrin, of whom frequent mention has been made. Self-centred, ambitious, without deep principles of any sort, he was yet an effective party leader, and proved himself, when in office, possessed of considerable gifts as a magistrate. His chief supporter was Pierre Vandel, forward in the original establishment

[1] *Opera*, xii 633.

of the Reformation in Geneva, but hostile to Calvin, as has been seen, even before the close of his stormy first ministry in the city. Vandel represented well the old Genevan spirit of independence; but his own disposition was such as to make any discipline irksome. Much inferior in intellectual gifts and in political talents, but popular, bold, eager for conflict with foreign influences, as well as hostile to any form of restraint, were the two sons of the Genevan patriot-martyr of 1519, Philibert and François Daniel Berthelier, of whom the first-named, in spite of his weaknesses, deserves to rank with Perrin and Vandel as a leader of the forces of opposition to Calvin. Among the common people Philibert Berthelier enjoyed the largest popularity. To him, chiefly, appears to have been due the renewal in 1546 or 1547, of the "Enfants de Genève,"—an ancient association of young men professedly for the military defence of Geneva, the title of which recalled the patriots of his father's time. Berthelier's own character was weak, immoral, and ungoverned, and his temper and excesses rendered him an ally of doubtful permanent value to any cause. That it was compelled to use such instruments as the best available reveals the fundamental inefficiency of the opposition to Calvin. It could in no way equal his determination, his intellectual strength, and least of all his character.

Yet this opposition was formidable enough, in spite of its weaknesses In January, 1548, Berthelier began a defiance of the Consistory, which was to continue, in varying forms, for years. It was to bring before the Little Council, in 1551, the much vexed question of consistorial right to pronounce excommunication;[1] and to lead, in 1553, as there will be occasion to point out, to a most serious effort to do away with consistorial independence. Calvin's situation was continually harassed. In May, 1548, he was admonished by the Little Council for criticisms passed upon the magistrates, in a sermon.[2] The following September one of his free-written letters to his friend Viret fell into governmental hands, and caused him much difficult explanation by reason of its criticisms of the Genevan situation.[3] The elections of February, 1549, saw Ami Perrin made first syndic, and were immediately followed by a struggle for the removal of de l'Église and Ferron from the pastoral offices of which Calvin and the majority of their associates deemed them on good grounds unworthy. In spite of Calvin's conviction that de l'Église should be dismissed, he remained in office under the protection of the Little Council. While these events were in progress, Calvin passed through the bitter personal affliction caused by the death, on March 29th, of his wife.[4] His own health was precarious. His old enemy, the severe nervous headaches from which he had long suffered, distressed him. The outbreak of persecutions in France and the apparent collapse of the defeated Protestant cause in Germany, crushed by the victories of Charles V., wore upon him.[5] His situation was painful in almost every aspect.

[1] *Opera*, xxi 419, 473–479, Roget, iii 44, 145–148.
[2] *Registres du Conseil*, xliii. 94, *Opera*, xxi 426
[3] *Ibid*, xliii 194, xxi 434, Roget, iii 63–67.
[4] See *ante*, p 237
[5] Compare Kampschulte, ii. 114, 115.

One feature of the situation was, however, full of promise and of menace alike. From the beginning of Calvin's ministry he had welcomed refugees for their faith. He had encouraged them to come by exhortation and by letter. His ideal, as he assured the Genevan authorities a little later, was "that your city may be a firm sanctuary for God amid these horrible commotions, and a faithful asylum for the members of Christ."[1] It was far more than local policy that dictated this resolution Calvin would make, and in the end did make, of Geneva the bulwark of the Protestant cause in his native France, and in less degree in Italy, the Netherlands, Scotland, and England, by the cordial reception and generous aid there afforded to exiles from those lands. It was this that was to make of Geneva a training school for the reformation of western Europe. But while the purpose of Calvin was thus far-reaching, the effect of this welcome extended to refugees was in the highest degree beneficial to his ultimate position in Geneva, since they were prevailingly men of religious principle, and very generally filled with admiration for his theology and discipline. The menace of the situation was, however, that the coming of these exiles aroused the natural jealousy of the older inhabitants, and more than any other single cause fed the fires of opposition to Calvin's rule. It was to this feeling, more than to any other, that Perrin, Vandel, and Berthelier could make successful appeal. Calvin's time of chief peril was that between the realisation that

[1] Prefatory letter of 1552 to Calvin's *De aeterna Dei Praedestinatione*, *Opera*, viii 256

the refugees were a serious menace to the older forces of Geneva and their attainment of such strength as to constitute an efficient basis of his control of the city.

The accession of Henry II. to the French throne was soon followed by severe persecution. By 1549, French refugees, in numbers and rank such as had not previously made their way to Switzerland, were streaming to Geneva. Besides the many whose sojourn was temporary, seventy-two received permission to become inhabitants of the city in 1549, and one hundred and twenty-two in 1550. By 1554, no less than 1376 had obtained the right of residence. Among those who came to Geneva between 1548 and 1550, were such men as Laurent de Normandie, a royal officer of Noyon; Theodore Beza, to be Calvin's successor; Guillaume Trie, a wealthy merchant of Lyons; the Colladon family, eminent in Berry, and Robert Estienne, the celebrated Parisian printer. Not only did they encounter much popular ill-will; but the Little Council, though granting rights of residence, was very chary in admissions to the *bourgeoisie* with its privilege of a vote in municipal affairs. This feeling resulted, in January, 1551, in a proposal by the Little Council that the newcomers should not be eligible to vote in any Council till after a residence of twenty-five years.[1] No law to that effect was enacted; but the attempt reveals the fear with which these new inhabitants were viewed by the party which had Perrin, Vandel, and Berthelier as its chief representatives.

Yet it was from one of these refugees that a greater

[1] Roget, iii. 136.

danger was to come to Calvin, in 1551, than the Genevan opponents, just mentioned, could alone have aroused. Jérôme Hermès Bolsec,[1] the source of this attack, was a former Carmelite monk of Paris, who, fleeing from the repressive action of the French government, had found a brief refuge at the court of Renée in Ferrara, and then, in 1550, a home at Veigy, a village near Geneva but under Bernese jurisdiction, where he served as physician to a refugee Protestant nobleman, Jacques de Bourgogne, Sieur of Falais, with whom Calvin had long been on terms of intimacy. A man of education, eminence in his new profession, and, as far as had yet appeared, of character, he soon won much respect in the Genevan community. Interested in theological questions, he frequently attended the *Congrégation*, or public discussion, which the *Vénérable Compagnie* held each Friday. In the main he found himself in hearty accord with Calvin's theology; but on the doctrine of predestination he was in sharp disagreement. To his thinking, absolute predestination made God a tyrant, and was contrary to the Scripture representation that man's acceptance or rejection with God depends on the presence or absence of faith. These criticisms he had expressed in the *Congrégation*, in one instance on May 15, 1551; and before the ministers gathered in

[1] The documents in the Bolsec affair may be found in the *Opera*, viii 141–248, contemporary letters and extracts from registers in *Ibid.*, xiv 191–291, xv 252, 320, 362, xxi 481, 489–505, see also H. Fazy, *Procès de Bolsec*, in *Mémoires de l'Inst nat genevois*, x 1–74 (1866), Kampschulte, ii. 125–150, Roget, iii 156–206; Choisy, pp. 113–120, and in Hauck's *Realencyklopädie*, iii. 281.

Calvin's house. On October 16th, of the same year, he proceeded to a much more violent attack on the Genevan reformer, declaring to the *Congrégation* that Calvin's views were not merely erroneous and absurd, but that Calvin was not a true interpreter of Scripture or of the historic teaching of the Church.

Here was a criticism that struck at the basis of Calvin's whole Genevan position. As has been pointed out in speaking of Castellio, Calvin had no other post in the city than that of an interpreter of the Word of God, as pastor and teacher, and if he was, as Bolsec asserted, a false interpreter, all real claim to authority was swept away. Calvin had left no room for the admission of possible mistake on important doctrines. He must be right in all that was vital, or he must stand thoroughly discredited,—a false teacher. And Bolsec's attack involved much more than a deadly thrust at his Genevan position, to Calvin's thinking. It was the rejection not merely of what seemed to Calvin, however it may appear to the modern world, a plain teaching of Scripture, but of a doctrine of special comfort to the Christian life. In that light Calvin always viewed the dogma of predestination. Granted, as he held, that human nature is wholly bad, and of itself incapable of goodness, what assurance has any man of salvation save in the Divine purpose to rescue him by all-powerful, transforming might from his sins? Nothing but the will of God, Calvin thought, gave any man rational ground for hope of salvation; but if one had reason to feel that God's will was manifested in grace, one had a confidence of Divine favour and ultimate complete redemption such as nothing else could bestow. An attack upon a doctrine so important in itself, and so bound up with Calvin's own credit as a religious teacher, demanded his most strenuous resistance. While Bolsec might be the agent, the real author of the criticism, in Calvin's judgment, was Satan himself.[1]

Holding such views, Calvin not merely replied to Bolsec at length and with vehemence in the *Congrégation;* aided by his clerical associates, he caused the matter to be laid at once before the civil authorities of Geneva. It became immediately a legal trial involving the truth or falsity of his own doctrinal teaching. Bolsec was promptly arrested, and defended himself with no little skill, but he was a foreigner and as such had slight support even among Calvin's opponents.[2] Repeated hearings failed to shake his constancy, and a two days' discussion before the authorities in the City Hall being equally fruitless, the Little Council so far complied with Bolsec's requests as to agree that the opinion of neighbouring churches should be sought on the question at issue. This was, indeed, something of a defeat for Calvin, implying, as it did, that his views on predestination were debatable; and the ministers under his lead met it by laying further accusations against Bolsec In spite of his protests, and those of the Sieur de Falais, he was still kept in prison, and

[1] *Opera*, viii 254

[2] Roget, iii 158, and Choisy, p 113, regard Bolsec as acting at the instance of Calvin's adversaries Kampschulte, ii 129, views his attack, probably rightly, as due simply to Bolsec's own liking for theologic discussion

began to be seriously distressed as to the probable outcome of his trial. The Genevan ministers, with Calvin at their head, now anticipated the action of the government by sending letters strongly denunciatory of Bolsec, on November 14th, to their colleagues of Basel, Bern, and Zurich The official letter of the syndics and Little Council went out a week later. Before the answers could be received, a piece of verse written by Bolsec in his prison fell into the hands of the authorities, and led to a painful examination as to the criticisms of his treatment that might be drawn from its several couplets. The whole course of the trial, both on the part of the ministers and of the magistrates, gives an impression of pressure and unseemly severity.

To Calvin, the letters which at length came from the friendly Swiss churches were exceedingly disappointing.[1] That of Basel viewed Bolsec as heretical, but its writers affirmed that they treated this "most intricate question" of predestination with "simplicity," laying stress neither on foreknowledge nor on election, but on faith. It was evident that predestination held no such place in the teachings at Basel as it did at Geneva. That of Zurich regretted the strife, but thought both sides too bitter in controversy It treated the question at issue only in the most untechnical and general fashion. That of Bern went further, its writers declaring that they had heard that Bolsec was "not a very bad man," that his principles, even on the point in debate, had in them much that might serve as a basis of reconciliation, that

[1] See his letter of December, 1551, to the ministers of Neuchâtel, *Opera*, xiv 213, 218.

the question of predestination was one of difficulty for many excellent men, and that moderation in such disputes was desirable. On the other hand, the pastors of Neuchâtel, led by Farel, though not asked, volunteered an opinion in which Bolsec was denounced as wholly profane, an instrument of Satan, and in no way to be endured.[1] The effect of the letters from Basel, Zurich, and Bern was not what Calvin wished. He protested to the Little Council, on December 14th, against showing them to Bolsec; but in vain. It was evident that the Genevan ministry must fight its own battle unaided, and in the *Congrégation* of December 18th, led by Calvin, the pastors proceeded to a long declaration setting forth the fundamental importance of right views on predestination.[2] This determined action on the part of the ministers evidently decided the magistrates to end the already long trial. On December 23, 1551, Bolsec was for ever banished for "false opinions, contrary to the holy Scriptures, and pure Evangelical religion."

Calvin had won a victory. His critic had been exiled. His doctrine had been declared, by implication, "pure" by the Genevan government, then largely in the hands of his opponents; but the cost was great. The struggle had been won at the expense of an insistence on predestination as a fundamental Christian doctrine with which, it was evident, German-speaking Switzerland was far from sympathising. His position as an unassailable interpreter of the Word of God was really

[1] Roget, iii 193–195

[2] In full in *Opera*, viii 93–138, see Colladon's *Life*, *Ibid.*, xxi. 75.

more vulnerable than it had been before,—though for the time being apparently strengthened. The controversy had undoubtedly been carried on with unnecessary bitterness. The gain that it had brought was temporary, rather than decisive.

As for Bolsec himself, his later conduct was such as to deprive him of much claim to sympathy. Protected for a while in Bernese territory, whence he continued to attack Calvin, he was driven thence, in 1555, chiefly through Calvin's efforts. Returning to France, he recanted what he then styled his errors at the National Synod at Orléans in 1562. A year later he was deposed from the French Protestant ministry as an "apostate." Ultimately he returned to the Roman communion, and in 1577, when Calvin had been thirteen years dead, revenged himself on Calvin's memory by a biography of the Genevan reformer filled with the grossest calumnies and with ascriptions of moral turpitude, a peculiarly atrocious instance of which has already been discussed.[1]

With the exile of Bolsec the troubles aroused by the debate regarding predestination were by no means ended. The controversy, which at first excited little interest among Calvin's native Genevan opponents, was gradually seen by them to afford a new ground of attack,—not now upon his discipline but upon his orthodoxy. Such a charge was pressed in June, 1552, by Jean Trolliet, a former monk, whose reception as pastor had been much desired, in 1545, by many of his fellow-Genevans; but whose ambitions, being then

[1] *Ante*, p. 117.

defeated by Calvin, had led him to cherish a grudge against the reformer. Trolliet had become a lawyer, and had attached himself to the Perrinist party. He now affirmed that Calvin's *Institutes* were heretical, since the logical consequence of their teaching regarding predestination must be that God is the author of sin. Calvin complained to the Little Council, and both sides were heard.[1] Trolliet had many friends, and the result was undecided. On August 29th, Calvin, therefore, appeared before the Little Council once more and demanded that justice be done him under threat of resigning his ministry. At the hearing which followed Trolliet defended himself by an appeal to the well-known views of Melanchthon. Finally, on November 9th, the Little Council voted that the *Institutes* present "the holy doctrine of God" and that "in future no one should dare to speak against that book or that doctrine," a judgment in which Trolliet thought it prudent to acquiesce; but all satisfaction which Calvin may have felt in this decision was dampened by the further vote of the same body, on the 15th, assenting to Trolliet's request that it declare him, officially, to be "a good man and a good citizen." The balance of forces in the government was undoubtedly the cause of this indecisive result.

Such a state of affairs could not continue indefinitely, and the situation was constantly complicated and imbittered by hostility aroused by the growing numbers and influence of the refugees. The inefficiency of the

[1] *Opera*, xxi 510–527, Roget, iii 235–248, Kampschulte, ii. 155–157, Choisy, pp 121–126

government, in 1552, was pleasing to neither party. But the situation, as far as Calvin was concerned, grew rapidly worse with the opening of 1553. The February elections resulted in a sweeping Perrinist victory. Not only did Perrin himself once more become a syndic, but he could now count on fourteen votes in the Little Council. The balance of parties, which had continued since 1547, was now broken in favour of Calvin's opponents. The consequences were speedily apparent. On March 16th, those ministers who, as burghers, had voted in the General Assembly were deprived of this small share in city politics while in office, in spite of Calvin's protest. The Little Council asserted increased authority in the examination of ministerial candidates. The right of the Consistory to excommunicate was once more brought into dispute. It was a time of annoyance and of petty attack not merely for Calvin, but for the whole ministerial body. Yet more positive were the measures taken by the Perrinist government against Calvin's friends, the refugees. Moved in part by fears of French plots suggested by Bern, but largely by their own hostility, the authorities ordered in April that all not burghers be deprived of arms, save swords only, and that these were not to be carried in the streets. None of the non-citizen refugees should share in the city [illegible].[1] These regulations increased in marked degree [illegible] between the older and the newer inhabitants of Geneva which so largely underlay the divisions of its parties, and they made Calvin's position yet more difficult. By the summer of 1553, it seemed as if his

[1] Roget, iii. 287–[illegible]

fall and the collapse of his Genevan system could be but little delayed.

Through these years of struggle and anxiety Calvin had been busy with his preaching, his teaching, and his pen. A succession of writings, large and small, in addition to an enormous correspondence, flowed from his study. Beside careful revision of the *Institutes* in 1543 and 1550, the more important writings of Calvin during this period include his *Traicté des Reliques* of 1543, perhaps the keenest and most bitingly satirical criticism on this feature of the older worship that the Reformation age produced.[1] His treatise against the *Libertins* of 1545 has already been noted.[2] The Roman Council of Trent drew from him a vigorous *Antidote* in 1547;[3] and the Interim, by which the victorious Charles V. sought to regulate the Protestant churches of Germany pending their expected reconciliation with the papacy, encountered his earnest protest in 1549.[4] The next year came Calvin's treatise on those offences due to quarrels among Protestants, the unworthy lives of some who professed the Evangelical faith, and other hindrances by which many were turned away from the Reformed cause.[5] The doctrine of predestination drew from him elaborate arguments in 1543, 1550, and 1552.[6]

[1] *Opera*, vi 405–452 Eng tr by Beveridge, in *Calvin's Tracts*, i 255–302.

[2] *Ante*, p 294.

[3] *Acta Synodi Tridentinae cum Antidoto*, *Opera*, vii 365–506

[4] *Interim adultero-germanum*, *Ibid*, vii 545–674

[5] *De Scandalis*, *Ibid*, viii 1–84

[6] *Defensio doctrinae de servitute arbitrii contra Pighium*, *Ibid.*, vi. 225–404; *De praedestinatione et providentia Dei*, *Ibid.*, i. 861–902; *De aeterna Dei praedestinatione*, *Ibid*, viii. 249–366.

A series of significant commentaries on the Scripture, of the general character of which there will be something said on a later page, opened with his exposition of Romans, in 1540, while at Strassburg, and was rapidly continued at Geneva. In 1546 and 1547, he discussed I. and II. Corinthians; Galatians, Ephesians, Philippians, Colossians, I. and II. Timothy, were explained in 1548, the next year Titus and Hebrews were added to the list; in 1550 came his commentaries on the epistles to the Thessalonians, and James; I. and II. Peter, and Jude followed in 1551; then Acts and Isaiah were expounded; and the Gospel according to John was discussed in 1553. In these tracts and commentaries, Calvin made firmer and broader his claim, already established by the *Institutes*, to a position in the first rank of theologians not merely of his own age, but of the universal Church.

# CHAPTER XII

## THE TRAGEDY OF SERVETUS.—CALVIN'S VICTORY OVER HIS OPPONENTS, 1553–1557

CALVIN'S position in the summer of 1553 was, as has been seen, almost desperate in its prospects. Famed as a theologian, revered as the real head of French Protestantism, his hold on Geneva seemed slipping. His disciplinary system met with constant, though often petty, resistance. His friends, the refugees, aroused jealousy. It seemed probable that the next election, at the latest, might secure such a combination of the elements of opposition as would drive him from the city, as in 1538. From this situation he was saved, and was placed on the sure path to ultimate victory, by the unexpected coming to Geneva of one who was deemed an arch-heretic, Michael Servetus, whose martyrdom constitutes the most discussed episode of the Reformation age. As in the case of Ameaux, the identification of Calvin's opponents, in part, with the interests of one whom public sentiment condemned, gave renewed strength to his position, and seemed to the common man a proof of the identity of his cause with that of righteousness. To understand the case of Servetus and its effects on Calvin's fortunes, as well as Calvin's attitude toward it, one must so far as possible divest one's self of the prejudgments which three centuries and a half of progress in religious freedom since that time have engendered and try to look upon it from the common view-point of the sixteenth century. The gravest injustice to Calvin's memory would be to minimise his share in a tragedy, which, however repugnant to modern thinking, was to him the exercise of a conscientious duty to the Church, and a means of triumph, at the same time, over his enemies.

Miguel Serveto[1] was almost certainly born in Villaneuva in the old Spanish kingdom of Aragon in 1509 or 1511. He was, therefore, about the same age as Calvin. He may have studied law at Toulouse, but his early life is very uncertain.[2] In 1530, however, he was in Basel, and there met Œcolampadius, thence he went to Strassburg, where he was kindly received by Capito This favour was abruptly ended when he published, at Hagenau in 1531, his *De Trinitatis Erroribus*. This radical work, of a man but little, if at all, over twenty years of age, anticipated much not only of what

[1] The documents relating to his trials are given in *Opera*, viii 721–856, his letters to Calvin, *Ibid*, 645–720, Calvin's critical account of him and his "errors," the *Defensio Orthodoxae Fidei*, of 1554, is in *Ibid*, 453–644 The contemporary letters of Calvin and his friends may be found in *Opera*, viii 857–872, xii 283, xiv 480, 510, 589–709 For Colladon and Beza's accounts see *Ibid*, xxi 57, 76, 146 The literature is voluminous To be mentioned are, L. Mosheim, *Geschichte des beruhmten spanischen Arztes Michael Serveto*, 1748, F Treschel, *Michael Servet*, 1839, H Tollin, *Characterbild Michael Servets, u das Lehrsystem Michael Servets*, 1876–78, R Willis, *Servetus and Calvin*, 1877; see also Henry, iii 95–223, T. H Dyer, *Life of John Calvin*, pp 296–367, Schaff, *Hist of the Christian Church*, vii 681–798, Roget, iv 1–131, Kampschulte, ii 167–203, Harnack, *Dogmengeschichte*, iii 661–698, Choisy, pp. 130–151, *The Cambridge Modern History*, ii 411

[2] Servetus's own statements were conflicting.

Socinianism afterwards asserted, but some Christological views which now have wide currency. To Protestants and Catholics alike, in that day, however, he seemed an extreme heretic, and he was, indeed, a radical of radicals. Of great speculative gifts, and high talents, he was undoubtedly a man of genius. His judgment was erratic, however; and his controversial manner was notoriously overbearing and contemptuous of opponents, even in that age of scanty regard for the courtesies of debate; but there can be no question that he sincerely believed that he had a mission of the highest importance as a reformer of historic theology.

Compelled to conceal his identity, he became a student of medicine and natural sciences in Paris under the name of Villeneuve. Here he met Calvin, who strongly disapproved his views, and, it is said, sought an opportunity to refute them in a discussion before witnesses which Servetus doubtless deemed too perilous.[1] He next appears as a corrector of proofs in the publishing office of Melchior and Gaspard Trechsel at Lyons, where he edited, in 1535, a most creditable edition of Ptolemy's *Geography*. But he was soon back in Paris, and threw himself with passionate zeal into the medical controversies of the day, winning many enemies thereby. His own keenly observant mind is revealed, however, in his discovery, three-quarters of a century before William Harvey, of the pulmonary circulation of the blood.[2]

[1] Colladon, in *Opera*, xxi 57

[2] *Christianismi Restitutio*, p 169; it is translated and criticised by Willis, himself a physician, pp 205–213.

After brief sojourns in Avignon, Lyons, and Charlie
Servetus settled, about 1540, as a physician
Vienne, still under the name of Villeneuve, and the
won the goodwill of men of learning, especially of th
clergy, and developed a large practice. Here he la
boured in secret on a new volume which he was to pul
lish, early in 1553, as the *Restitution of Christianity*
probably completing the manuscript in 1546. Servetu
believed that he was bringing Christianity back to i
pristine simplicity. On the basis of an essentially pan
theistic view of God, he taught that Christ was trul
the Son of God, that all the Godhead was corporeall
manifested in Him, but that His personality was no
pre-existent, save in the mind of God, and really bega
with His earthly conception and birth To Servetus
thinking, the Nicene doctrine of the Trinity,—"a so
of three-headed Cerberus,"—the Chalcedonian Chris
tology, and infant baptism were the three chief source
of churchly corruption.[2] He recognised, far more tha
his opponents, a progress in revelation from the Ol
Testament to the New; he rejected predestination an
attached merit to good works; and believed the en
of the present age with the millennial reign of Christ t
be just at hand. For that reign his *Restitution* was t
be a preparation.

It was while working on this volume, in 1545, tha
Servetus entered into correspondence with Calvin

[1] *Christianismi Restitutio* Two copies of this edition exist, or
at Paris, the other at Vienna.

[2] The writer has taken a few sentences from his volume on *Th
Reformation.*

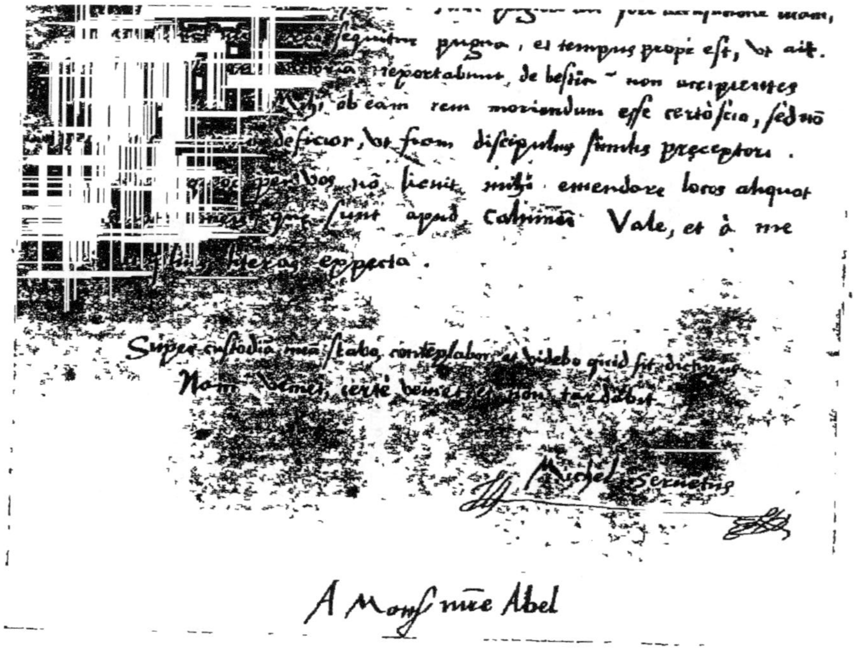

AUTOGRAPH OF SERVETUS.

Begun with courtesy, though with great self-assertion on Servetus's part, it speedily degenerated into an exasperating controversy. Calvin sent to Servetus a copy of his *Institutes*, which the Spanish thinker returned filled with critical, dissenting, and contemptuous annotations. On the other hand, Servetus transmitted to Calvin a portion of the manuscript of his volume which Calvin retained He appealed, also, to Poupin and Viret, evidently hoping to win some one of the leaders of French-speaking Switzerland for his opinions. Calvin, however, wearied speedily of so fruitless a correspondence with one whom he deemed a heretic, and, writing to Farel, on February 13, 1546, he declared that, should Servetus come to Geneva, as the over-sanguine Spaniard proposed, he would never suffer Servetus to go forth alive, if his authority had weight.[1]

Many causes conspired to induce such sanguinary feelings in Calvin toward Servetus. The tone in which the Spaniard framed his criticisms, not merely of Genevan, but of all generally accepted thinking on the Trinity, was exasperating; Calvin's own orthodoxy on the doctrine had been a tender point ever since the controversy raised by Caroli in 1537, the honour of God seemed to him even more grievously attacked than in the case of Ameaux; but deepest of all was Calvin's profound conviction that only the historic doctrine of the Trinity, taught, he believed, throughout the Scriptures, maintained the full divinity of Christ, and only as that divinity was perfect was there adequate

[1] *Opera*, xi 283. The letter was written in the midst of the trial of Ameaux.

atonement for human sin, availing intercession with the Father, or true sonship for the redeemed.[1] Servetus, to Calvin's thinking, destroyed the Christian hope; and, repulsive as it seems to the modern man, he deemed it his duty to rid the world of such "impiety," should the opportunity be his, and Servetus still be unrepentant of his "errors."

Early in 1553, a copy of the *Restitution*, then just secretly printed by Balthasar Arnoullet and his head-manager Guillaume Geroult, at Vienne, reached Geneva, possibly sent by Servetus to Calvin.[2] It happened that, at the time, Calvin's friend, Guillaume Trie, once a merchant at Lyons, but now a fugitive for his faith at Geneva, was in correspondence with a cousin, Antoine Arneys, who still resided at Lyons, was an ardent adherent of the Roman communion, and was disposed to rally Trie on the alleged license in belief prevalent in Geneva. To him Trie replied on February 26, 1553, declaring that it was in Catholic France, rather than in Geneva, that blasphemies were tolerated, and giving as his proof the *Restitution*, whose author and publisher he named. As evidence of his charges he enclosed the first few pages of the volume, and declared of Servetus, that he "ought to be burned alive, wherever he might be found." This letter was no official denunciation. It was from one cousin to another. But, in spite of the fact that, writing just a month later, Trie tells Arneys that the letter was meant for himself alone,

[1] Compare G Kawerau, in Moeller's *Lehrbuch der Kirchengeschichte*, iii. 432

[2] This is the opinion of Willis, pp 231–234.

its writer can have had no great unwillingness that it be laid before the ecclesiastical authorities at Lyons,—as it was. Process was at once opened against Servetus, but he denied his identity, alleging that he was simply the physician, Villeneuve; and neither with him nor with the printers were incriminating papers found. Recourse was had to Trie for further proof, who now, on March 26th, forwarded to Lyons the annotated copy of Calvin's *Institutes*, and a number of Servetus's letters to Calvin. These documents he declared had been procured from Calvin with great difficulty. Under date of March 31st, further information was furnished by Trie.

The transaction just narrated raises a difficult question. Was Calvin the instigator, and Trie simply the tool in this denunciation of Servetus to the French authorities? The affirmative opinion is that of many recent scholars.[1] It was that of Servetus himself.[2] On the other hand, it has been vigorously denied,[3] and Trie's own statements already cited, are confirmed by Calvin's rejection of the imputation that he had himself delivered Servetus to the Roman ecclesiastics.[4] To the writer the simplest explanation seems to be that Trie, as a friend of Calvin, knew in general of Servetus's identity and book; that he wrote the first letter of his own motion to Arneys, thinking the opportunity of a reply to his cousin's criticisms of Geneva too good to miss; but that from the time of his second

[1] *E g* Roget, iv 25–27, Willis, pp 235–251, R. Stähelin, p 675

[2] *Opera*, viii 732, 789, 805

[3] *E g.* Henry, iii 140; Choisy, p 131.

[4] *Opera*, viii 479

letter, and with no great difficulty in spite of his allegation, he procured from Calvin all the aid and documents that the Genevan reformer was able to furnish, so that, from the date of that letter, at least, Calvin must be deemed the chief, though indirect, agent in the denunciation of Servetus to the Catholic court.[1]

The case at Vienne moved slowly. Servetus had personal friends, though no sympathisers in his beliefs By their connivance, it would seem, he escaped from prison, on April 7th; on June 17th, his trial was ended by a sentence to death by slow fire, which was executed in effigy,[2] Servetus himself having fled more than two months earlier. After wandering for a number of weeks in Southern France, Servetus came, for no reason that seems conclusive, to Geneva itself, intending to make it a stopping-place on his way to Naples. Though it has often been asserted that he spent a month unrecognised in the city, there is no real reason to believe his sojourn was more than a few days in length.[3] He had negotiated for a boat through his landlord of the "Rose" tavern to continue his journey, when, on August 13th, while listening to a sermon by Calvin, it is said,[4] he was recognised, and soon after arrested, undoubtedly at Calvin's instigation.[5] Had Calvin been

[1] I owe to Rev Nathanaël Weiss the probable suggestion that Calvin may have hoped to aid the "five scholars of Lausanne," (p 382) by unmasking Servetus and thus doing a favour to their captors in Lyons.

[2] *Opera*, VIII 784–787.

[3] Compare Servetus's own statement, *Opera*, VIII 770, the notes of the Strassburg editors, *Ibid*, XIV. 590, and Roget, IV. 41–43.

[4] Notes to *Opera*, VIII. 725

[5] Calvin's letters, *Opera*, XIV 589, 615

indisposed to severity, he might have prevented Servetus's incarceration till it was evident that the Spaniard intended to remain in Geneva, but he felt that Servetus had been delivered into his hands, and that he ought to prevent further "contagion." From the first, Calvin hoped that Servetus would forfeit his life, though not by a painful death [1]

The trial opened quite as Calvin wished. A refugee in his employ, Nicolas de la Fontaine, made the complaint, and took upon himself the liabilities of a false accuser, should it not be proved. Thirty-eight counts were alleged against Servetus before the civil court, mostly of a theological character, though embracing also his attacks on Calvin To these Servetus replied with skill, and now a new force made itself apparent. Servetus won no converts, his theological speculations in themselves were not approved, but he was Calvin's opponent. His conviction would be a triumph for Calvin's waning authority in the city. These considerations, rather than any doctrinal sympathy, explain the support which Servetus now received from Calvin's Genevan foes. At the hearing on August 16th, hot words were exchanged between Philibert Berthelier representing the lieutenant of justice, and the learned refugee lawyer, Calvin's friend, Germain Colladon, who now appeared as counsel for the prosecution. It was evident that the case was to involve much more than Servetus's heresies. It was to test the relative strength

[1] "I hope the judgment will be capital in any event, but I desire cruelty of punishment withheld" Letter to Farel, August 20th, above cited.

of the rival parties in Geneva, and the permanence of Calvin's control. For this new struggle, in spite of a personally hostile majority in the Little Council, Calvin had the great advantage of demanding justice on one who seemed to most religious men an intolerable heretic. Berthelier, blind with party hatred, had put himself in the precarious position of staking his success on the defence of a discredited cause, and that not because he believed in the accused, but because he disliked the accuser. The condemnation of Servetus now became vital to Calvin's whole Genevan status.

Calvin felt the gravity of the situation. On August 17th, he appeared in person before the Little Council against Servetus. The examination took a technical character. Not only were the Trinitarian attacks in the *Restitution* debated, but a criticism of the fertility of Palestine implying that it was not a land "flowing with milk and honey," which Servetus had copied into his edition of Ptolemy, was made the basis by Calvin of accusation that Servetus had brought charges of falsity against Moses, and therefore of blasphemy against the Holy Spirit by whose inspiration Moses, Calvin believed, had spoken. Calvin also pushed Servetus to the declaration consonant with his pantheistic principles, that the very floor and benches of the court-room were "the substance of God," upon which Calvin declared, "Then the devil is God in substance," to which Servetus replied, with a laugh that must have prejudiced his case with the judges, "Do you doubt it?"[1]

---

[1] This is Calvin's account of the point last discussed, *Opera*, viii. 496 Perhaps it is to be taken with some reserve, Roget, iv. 52.

The Little Council, however averse to Calvin some of its members were, could not doubt that the case was one of great seriousness. On August 17th, it freed de la Fontaine from further responsibility, and the prosecution now fell into the charge of the states-attorney of the city, Claude Rigot, a friend of Calvin. Four days later, the Little Council determined to ask the advice of Bern, Basel, Zurich, and Schaffhausen, and also to obtain from Vienne the action of its court against the prisoner. There is no reason to see any plan to aid Servetus in this determination to ask outside opinion. The condemnation of one accused of heresy was a formidable step, and the Council, doubtless, desired to act with care. But this consultation undoubtedly encouraged the hopes of Servetus and of Calvin's opponents. It must have been remembered that in the recent case of Bolsec the advice of the Swiss cantons, and their ministers, had been in favour of leniency. To that extent it was a rebuff to Calvin, who preferred that the court should convict the prisoner without delay On August 23d, Servetus had to answer to a new series of charges prepared by the states-attorney and of such a character that, while the trial did not cease to be for heresy, Servetus's life and the general evil influences of his teachings, rather than theological minutiæ, were emphasised. The attempt to prove Servetus of unworthy life failed completely; nor could it be shown that he was an intentional turmoiler of public peace He asserted with sincerity that his advocacy of his views had been under the impulse of a sense of duty. Undoubtedly Servetus, thus interrogated, made a much better impression on the court than earlier, and this slight success was strengthened by his plea that his discussions had always been with learned men on abstruse questions of theology, and involved no seditious actions whatever. Rigot's efforts had injured, rather than aided, the prosecution. To the demand of the authorities of Vienne that Servetus be extradited to them for execution, the Little Council, on August 31st, sent a politely phrased refusal.

On August 17th, the Little Council had directed that an attempt be made to show Servetus his "errors." That indicated a discussion, for which Calvin was nothing loath; and on September 1st, such a colloquy was begun between the two contestants, before the judges, including Ami Perrin and Philibert Berthelier. The debate was confused and unsatisfactory. Servetus objected that the prison was no fit place; to which Calvin agreed and expressed a wish for a public disputation; but the authorities cut short all debate, ordering Calvin to present Servetus's errors in writing and the latter to reply, both using Latin. Two reasons seem to have induced this action. Perrin and Berthelier undoubtedly feared that a public disputation with so able a debater as Calvin would mean a popular victory for the reformer,—a result highly displeasing to them; and the preparation of such documents would afford material, in which Servetus could make the best statement of his case possible, for presentation to the Swiss cantons, the advice of which it had been decided to ask. Calvin's opponents, though not daring to back

Servetus openly, were causing all the delay they could, and making the outcome of the trial as dubious as possible, and Servetus himself took great encouragement from their support. The accusations of heresy drawn from Servetus's writings were quickly formulated by Calvin; and the prisoner was prompt with his reply,—his confidence in the support of Calvin's enemies appearing in the contemptuous tone of the answer. Servetus declares Calvin to be a disciple of Simon Magus, of confused mind, who hopes by barking like a dog to overwhelm the judges. To this reply a rejoinder, couched in severe terms, was made and signed by all the Genevan ministers. Delivered to Servetus on September 15th, in the course of the next two or three days he annotated the paper with replies that are marvellous in their exasperating character considering the circumstances under which they were written.[1] "You lie," "you play the fool," "you rave," "cheat," "vile scoundrel" are among the accusations and epithets which he employed. On the 22d, Servetus sent a remarkable appeal to the Genevan government, demanding the arrest of Calvin under the *lex talionis*, as a false accuser and a heretic, and "that the case be settled by his or my death or other penalty." He asked that Calvin "be not merely condemned but driven out" and his goods adjudged to himself. Meanwhile, on September 22d, the letters of inquiry, voted on August 17th, were despatched by the Little Council to the ministers and magistrates of Bern, Basel, Zurich,

[1] All these documents are given in *Opera*, viii. 501–553.

and Schaffhausen. The progress of events now awaited their answer.

The reasons of Servetus's defiant attitude and expectations of acquittal were largely temperamental, but they were undoubtedly greatly strengthened by a new struggle in which Calvin found himself engaged and that promised indirect advantage to the prisoner. There has been frequent occasion to note the aversion of Calvin's opponents, both of those of undisciplined life and the more worthy representatives of old Genevan independence, towards the central element of his ecclesiastical government, the Consistory, and especially towards the power of excommunication exercised by it. That power, though regularly employed, had long been in dispute, and had several times seemed on the point of being taken away by the Little Council. To Perrin, Vandel, and Berthelier the present juncture seemed a fitting time to assert the superiority of the Little Council over the Consistory. Calvin was busied with the case of Servetus, the issue of the trial depended on the Little Council and was of utmost consequence to him. Should the Little Council, in which the Perrinists had a decided majority, now withdraw the right of independent excommunication from the Consistory, Calvin might acquiesce, however reluctantly, lest his opposition should cost him the support of the Little Council in the conviction of Servetus. Berthelier seemed the fitting agent for the attack. He was courageous, fond of fighting, popular, and under excommunication by the Consistory; unfortunately for his party, however, his life was notoriously blameworthy, and his discipline not undeserved. On September 1st, he now appeared before the Little Council, and demanded that it supersede the excommunication of the Consistory, and admit him to the communion to be held on Sunday, September 3d. Calvin was called to express his opinion. It was a crisis as vital for his church-government as it was unexpected; but he protested against the proposed action to the utmost of his power. In vain, however, for the Little Council granted Berthelier's request.[1] That result called for Calvin's utmost energy of protest. He demanded, and obtained, a meeting of the Little Council on Saturday, and declared that he would die before he would administer the Sacrament to Berthelier. To all outward appearance he failed once more. The Little Council held to its decision. But really his iron firmness of will snatched success from defeat, for while reaffirming its release of Berthelier from excommunication, the Little Council advised him, secretly it would appear, not to present himself at the Lord's Table. It was a thoroughly weak compromise. Whether Calvin was aware of it is uncertain, but he was determined that there should be no popular doubt as to his position. Before the crowded congregation, gathered the next day for the Lord's Supper in Saint-Pierre, and eagerly anticipating a scene, he forbade anyone under bann of the Consistory to commune, and declared that none should do so while he had strength to oppose.

[1] *Registres*, and Calvin's letters, *Opera*, xiv 605, 654; xxi 551; Roget, iv. 61–73; Kampschulte, ii 203–223.

Fortunately for Calvin, Berthelier had heeded the advice and was absent. The situation was in the highest degree critical. Calvin had defied the Little Council. He was so convinced that his action would be resented that he preached, that afternoon, what was well-nigh a farewell sermon. His courage had, however, but increased the indecision of the Council. On September 7th, he and his fellow-ministers made formal protest to that body; again on the 15th; and on the 18th, the Little Council voted to "hold to the *Ordonnances* as before." That left the question of excommunication where it had been previous to Berthelier's attack. It was still one in dispute, but the real victory was Calvin's. Berthelier's attempt had been frustrated by Calvin's force of character.

It is not surprising, however, that Servetus took courage and gained hope of release from this struggle. Calvin's defeat would have been his advantage; but the result left him in worse case than ever. And, on October 18th, the replies of the Swiss ministers and governments arrived. In marked contrast to the answers in the case of Bolsec, all now condemned the teachings of the prisoner, and approved the attitude of Calvin and his associates. While no direct recommendations as to punishment were made, all, and notably Bern, made it evident that it should be such as would "remove this pest" from the churches.[1] It was evident to all that Calvin had the support of Protestant Switzerland. His opponents were beaten. Perrin

[1] *Opera*, viii 819 For these letters, see *Ibid*, pp. 555–558, 808–823

tried to delay the conclusion by absenting himself from the Little Council and by proposing an appeal to the Two Hundred,[1] but to no purpose. On October 26th, the Council ordered that Servetus be burned alive the day following. Calvin sought a milder form of death,—his disinclination toward cruel executions has already been noted,[2]—but in this the court gave him no heed.

To Servetus the sentence seems to have been wholly unexpected, and its first effect was crushing. His courage came again, however, and he never appeared to better advantage than in his last hours. He sent for Calvin, and begged pardon for any wrong he might have done the Genevan reformer; he asked an easier death, not because he retracted any of his opinions, but lest in the agony of fire he should deny the truths which he championed. He went in simple dignity to the place of execution on the hill of Champel, lectured and urged to repent by Farel, who had come to Geneva for the final scene. At the sight of the flaming torch, Servetus could not repress a cry of horror; but his courage was adequate to his extremity. The unskilfulness of the executioner,—not any intention as has been sometimes charged,—prolonged his agony; but the last utterance that escaped his blistering lips, as the flames tortured his body, was a prayer expressive at once of his Christian hope, and of the peculiar interpretation of the mysterious doctrine of the Trinity which he had championed, and for which he died:

[1] Calvin to Farel, October 26th, *Opera*, xiv 657

[2] *Ibid*; see *ante*, p 283 The sentence is given in *Opera*, viii, 827–830.

"Jesus, thou Son of the eternal God, have pity on me!"[1]

To one whose fortune it is to live under the greater freedom of the twentieth century, such a scene, and the bitter prosecution of which it was the crown, is utterly repulsive. His sympathies, whatever his estimate of the theological questions involved, or however keenly he may recognise the many weaknesses of the sufferer, go out toward the victim of the tragedy. Calvin's eagerness to secure his conviction and the co-operation with the authorities at Vienne, however explainable, are not pleasant to contemplate. Those who erected a monument to Servetus, near the place of his martyrdom, on its three hundred and fiftieth anniversary in 1903, did well.[2] That faggot-heap was a mile-stone from which the world's progress along the pathway toward freedom of utterance may be reckoned.

The burning of Servetus did not, indeed, pass altogether uncondemned in its own time. At Basel, especially, where greater freedom existed than elsewhere in Switzerland, and where Castellio had some slight influence, voices were raised in criticism. Many of the Italian Protestant refugees, themselves for the most part radicals, dissented. Calvin felt the criticism, and, in February, 1554, he published, with the approving

[1] It is perhaps unnecessary to point out, even in an untheological age, that the difference between the phrases "Son of the eternal God" and "eternal Son of God," with their implications, epitomises the dispute

[2] See the *Monument expiatoire du supplice de M Servet*, Geneva, 1903.

EXPIATORY MONUMENT TO SERVETUS. (ERECTED IN 1903.)

signatures of his colleagues in the Genevan ministry, his *Refutation of the Errors of Servetus*,[1] in which he gave not merely his own version of the tragedy, but a defence of the employment of capital punishment for the repression of heretics in general.[2] To Calvin's anger, this narrative drew from his old opponent Castellio, and some associates, a volume sharply criticising the use of force in religion, and containing a widely selected collection of opinions in favour of toleration. "Christ would be a Moloch," it urged, "if He required that men should be offered and burned alive."[3]

These voices were, however, relatively few and uninfluential. The general opinion in Protestant circles was that the world was happily rid of Servetus and that Calvin had done well. His Genevan associates approved; the Swiss churches favoured him, even so mild a man as Melanchthon declared that it was "justly done."[4] Nor can there be any question as to its effect upon his own position and the Evangelical cause. He had freed the Swiss churches from imputation of heresy; he had prevented any toleration of anti-Trinitarian opinions in the religious circles that looked to him for guidance. Above all, his Genevan opponents had compromised themselves irretrievably by countenancing,

[1] *Defensio Orthodoxae Fidei de Sacra Trinitate*, etc., *Opera*, viii. 453–644

[2] *Ibid*, pp 461–479.

[3] It was published in March, 1554, under the pseudonym of Martinus Bellius, and ostensibly at Magdeburg, as *De Haereticis, an sint persequendi?* In Calvin's opinion, Castellio was a "beast, no less virulent, than untamed and obstinate" *Opera*, xv. 209

[4] Letter of October 14, 1554, to Calvin, *Opera*, xv. 268.

not out of theologic sympathy, but out of hatred to him, a man whom most of the world looked upon as a justly punished heretic.

Yet this enfeeblement of Calvin's opponents was not immediately evident. Scarcely had Servetus been executed when Berthelier renewed the long struggle with the Consistory. On November 7th, the Little Council referred the thorny problem to the Two Hundred, which decreed that the Consistory had no power to excommunicate without orders from the Council. So energetic was the protest of the ministers, led by Calvin, however, that the Little Council and the Two Hundred weakened its position, so far as to decide to ask the opinions of the churches of Bern, Zurich, Basel, and Schaffhausen.[1] As might have been expected, from the customs of other Swiss churches, the replies were far from a complete support of Calvin's discipline. Thanks to his efforts, aided by Bullinger, those of Zurich and Schaffhausen were favourable; but Bern was distinctly hostile. Yet it shows the weakening of the opposition, that, instead of asserting their claims, the Little Council and the Two Hundred now patched up a truce that, while nominally leaving the question where it was before, was really a victory for Calvin's discipline. Even Perrin saw that his attack had failed. The events of the year 1553 had changed the balance of power in Geneva, and further evidence of the decline of the opposition was manifest in the choice, at the February election of 1554, of three of the four syndics from among Calvin's supporters. In October following,

[1] *Registres du Conseil*, xlvii 175–177, *Opera*, xxi 559–561.

Berthelier still continuing his refusal of obedience to the Consistory, a commission was appointed to consider the problem of the right of excommunication; and finally, in January, 1555, to Calvin's great satisfaction, the question which had been agitated for years was settled by the successive votes of the Little Council, the Sixty, and the Two Hundred, that they abide by the *Ordonnances*.[1] In form this was, indeed, inconclusive. The interpretation of the *Ordonnances* had been in dispute. But, in reality, the decision finally confirmed the existing usage, which Calvin had so long struggled to maintain. He could now rest satisfied that the power of excommunication without interference from the civil authorities was secure. The cornerstone of his Genevan ecclesiastical edifice was at last firmly laid

While Calvin's position was rapidly strengthening in Geneva, he was subject, to a degree never before experienced, to attack from outside Genevan territories. Some of this hostility which centred in Castellio at Basel, but was by no means confined to him there, has already been noted. In that city, to be called a disciple of Calvin passed with many for a term of reproach,[2]—the reason being far more Calvin's strenuous insistence on the doctrine of predestination, than his action in the case of Servetus. That doctrine, as was noted in connection with the trial of Bolsec, won no hearty ap-

[1] *Registres du Conseil*, xlviii 138, 176–182, *Opera*, xxi 588, 593, 594, Roget, iv 186–192, Kampschulte, ii 254–256. See Calvin's letter to Bullinger, *Opera*, xv 449

[2] Hotman to Bullinger, quoted by Kampschulte, ii 225

proval, in its strenuous Genevan form, from the otl Swiss churches.[1] Bern, in particular, had dissente and from Bern Calvin's chief troubles now can There were many causes for Bernese hostility. Be and Geneva had long-standing sources of quarrel their political relations. Bern was suspicious of t growing influence of the French refugees on who Calvin so largely depended. It preferred and support the old Genevan element represented by Perrin ar Vandel, as more pliable toward its own interests ar hostile to any possible French alliances. The Berne ministry viewed with distrust the Genevan disciplin so different from their own; and the internation fame of the head of the Genevan church was regarde with some natural jealousy. Chief of all sources friction was, however, the state of the French-speakir territories under Bernese jurisdiction. They extende almost to the walls of Geneva, their ministry was i general sympathy with Calvin and his methods,— notable example is that of Viret, at Lausanne,- yet their churches were under the Bernese goverı ment.

Since Bolsec's banishment from Geneva in 1551, l had been permitted the range of its territories by Berı and had laboured in French-speaking Switzerland a the determined enemy of Calvin. Bolsec's attacks c Calvin's strict doctrine of predestination found hearin André Zébédée and Jean Lange, pastors at Nyon an Bursin, sympathised with him, and Calvin was soo

[1] *Ante*, p. 318 Except, of course, those, like Neuchâtel, in whi Calvin's friends were in control.

denounced as "a heretic and antichrist."[1] The Genevan ministers complained to the Bernese authorities, but received little satisfaction In January, 1555, the Bernese Council ordered attacks, indeed, to cease; but at the same time declared the disputed doctrine to be more fitted to awaken strife, hatred, and immorality than edification. This was painful enough for Calvin, but worse was to follow. In March, an embassy from the Genevan Little Council, in which Calvin's friends now had a majority, appeared in his behalf before the Bernese government, accompanied by Calvin himself. Bolsec's ejection from Bernese territory, as a disturber of the peace, was obtained.[2] But the Council of Bern affirmed that both Calvin and his opponents had been too contentious and too eager to pry into the hidden mysteries of the Divine counsels; and they added the insulting declaration that if any books by him or others contrary to the Bernese reformation were found in their jurisdiction they should be burned.[3] Calvin was not, indeed, expressly declared a heretic on the question of predestination by Geneva's chief Protestant neighbour; but that was the interpretation naturally put upon this action by a large part of the public, and in Bernese territories heated attacks upon his orthodoxy were widely made.

Had these events occurred two years earlier, there

[1] Complaint to the Bernese government of the Genevan pastors, October 4, 1554, *Opera*, xv 252 For the whole case see the letters in *Opera*, xv., also Roget, iv 171–183, 202–224; Kampschulte, ii. 232–243.

[2] Farel to Haller, March 29, *Opera*, xv. 533.

[3] *Opera*, xv. 543–549.

can be little doubt that, combined with the hostility of Perrin, Vandel, and Berthelier, they would have sufficed to end his Genevan ministry. But in Geneva itself, Calvin's situation had been growing steadily stronger since the close of 1553. The errors of his opponents had aided him. A body of young citizens was being trained year by year under his ministry, and was increasingly influenced by his ideals. But, above all, the refugees were a steadily augmenting force in the community and their weight was almost wholly on Calvin's side. As compared with the ordinary Genevan artisan-citizen they were men of character, learning, often of wealth and high social standing. They had had the courage to leave home and country for conscience's sake. They were a picked body of men, chiefly from France, and in much fewer numbers from Italy, but also from England and Scotland, especially after Catholic Mary had succeeded Edward VI. on the English throne. Such men as the Neapolitan nobleman Galeazzo Caraccioli, marquis of Vico, the Colladons and the Budés, or Laurent de Normandie, would have been eminent anywhere,—in little Geneva they were imposing. As has been well said: "There was perhaps in the Protestant world no other community that could show so many noble, distinguished, and aristocratic names." [1] And their presence in Geneva was Calvin's work. Such refugees could not but gradually win favour with the ordinary Genevan citizen, however heartily Perrin, Vandel, Berthelier, and their followers might hate them; and in so far as they com-

[1] Kampschulte, II 247.

mended themselves they increased Calvin's credit and influence in the Genevan community. The common Genevan was pleased alike with the distinction they gave the city, and with the added trade which they brought.

Though many of these immigrants had received the right of habitation, relatively few had been admitted burghers and become possessed in consequence of a voice in city politics. Twenty-six had been so received in 1553, and seven in 1554. But the elections, which had been favourable to Calvin in the latter year, resulted yet more satisfactorily for the reformer in February, 1555, partly on account of Calvin's growing strength and partly by reason of popular weariness because of the degree to which Perrin had used his position in the government to exalt himself, his relatives, and friends. Not merely were all four syndics now decided Calvinists, but the Calvinist vote in the Little Council and the Two Hundred was greatly increased. The party favourable to the reformer now determined to make its position permanently secure by admitting a sufficient number of refugees as burghers,[1] thus rendering forever idle such opposition as the old Genevan party had hitherto made Beginning on April 16th, by May 9th, sixty new burghers had thus been created, among them such men as Guillaume Trie, Laurent de Normandie, Germain Colladon, Jean and François Budé, and Jean Crespin, devoted supporters of Calvin. Perrin, Vandel, and Berthelier, at first scarcely suspicious, soon saw all

[1] Calvin to Bullinger, July 15, 1555, *Opera*, xv 678, 679 He states the purpose distinctly.

too clearly what the consequences of this drastic action would be. They sought in vain to keep the new citizens unarmed, and to deprive them of the right of voting for ten years. The fears of Calvin's opponents rapidly increased. On May 13th, the old-Genevan Lieutenant of Justice, Hudriot du Molard, made formal protest to the Little Council and demanded the summons of the Two Hundred. The Little Council replied by voting to continue to receive new citizens. The next day he renewed his protest, accompanied by a crowd of sympathisers, only to receive the same answer[1]

The evident defeat of the lately powerful Perrinist party, and their inability to accomplish anything to avert the catastrophe by legal means, now led to a step which proved their ruin, the exact nature of which has been much controverted, though its results are evident.[2] On the evening of May 16, 1555, a number of the Perrinist party, including Perrin and Vandel, supped at two taverns and denounced with much heat the Genevan situation. They probably intended some further and more energetic demonstration against the policy of the government than that of May 14th, but no carefully

[1] *Registres du Conseil*, xlix. 70–76; *Opera*, xxi. 604, 605

[2] Calvin gave his version in a long letter to Bullinger, *Opera*, xv 676–685, see also his letters to Farel, *Ibid*, 617, 686, 693. Colladon and Beza treat it from a strongly Calvinistic standpoint, *Lives*, *Ibid*, xxi 79, 150 The defeated party's account may be found in E Dunant, *Les relations politiques de Genève avec Berne*, pp 142–146 Among modern discussions may be mentioned, Henry, iii 374–378, J B G Galiffe, *Quelques pages d'histoire exacte*, Roget, iv 245–336, Kampschulte, ii 258–278, Choisy, pp 174–186. Roget in particular gives an epitome of much of the testimony at the trials

thought-out course of action seems to have been decided upon. The supper parties broke up early. Perrin and Vandel had gone home by nine; but the main body of the guests proceeded through the city streets in more or less menacing and disorderly fashion. Arrived opposite the house of Jean Baudichon de la Maisonneuve, one of the partisans of Calvin recently elected to the Little Council, they cried out against the French refugees, and Claude Dumont, servant of Jean Pernet, like Baudichon one of the new Calvinist members of the Little Council, was hit by a stone thrown by the younger of the Comparet brothers, boatmen who had been of the party at the taverns. Dumont was not dangerously wounded, and his injury was the sole physical harm done in the whole affair. His cries attracted a watchman, and also brought Henri Aubert, one of the syndics, from his adjacent drug shop Aubert attempted to arrest the stone-thrower. The Comparet brothers resisted. A crowd soon gathered. Hot words were exchanged between the two factions. Cries of "traitors," "kill, kill," "beat down the French," and the like resounded. Perrin appeared on the scene and attempted to take from Aubert his bâton, significant of his authority as a syndic, and repeated his effort a little later with the syndic, Pierre Bonna.

The original quarrel spent its force in a few minutes; but sinister rumours ran through the city. It was declared that the refugees had been collecting arms, and that they were assembling in numbers. A crowd of Perrinists gathered in the Bourg-de-Four quarter, of which Vandel was captain, and refused to disperse when ordered by a syndic, only yielding when Vandel joined his entreaties. Many threats were uttered against the refugees; but all ended before midnight. The Comparets were arrested, and the city was once more in peaceful charge of its sixteen watchmen.

Considered in itself this event of the evening of May 16th was a very trifling affair; but it might easily have led to a bloody riot.[1] It showed a disposition, also, to go beyond legal means in expression of opposition toward further admissions of refugees to the franchise. But the facts speak too clearly against the existence of any well-planned conspiracy to overturn the Genevan government to make that interpretation tenable. Perrin and Vandel had gone home quietly and early from the supper. Vandel helped to disperse the crowd. Of any attempt to master the city by attack on the Little Council, then in evening session, there is no evidence. No barricades were raised, no organisation from a military point of view was apparent. But to Calvin and his friends the affair took the proportions of a formidable attempt upon the freedom of the government. It was, they declared, a revolutionary conspiracy aimed at the slaughter of the French refugees and the overthrow of the four syndics and their obnoxious associates in the Little Council.[2] There is no reason to doubt that Calvin and most of his sympathisers sincerely

[1] To the writer the interpretation of Choisy seems better justified than the too minimising judgment of Roget

[2] Calvin to Bullinger, June 5, 1555, *Opera*, xv 681.

believed that the affair was a deep-laid plot. He thought no good of Perrin, and Vandel.[1] Their work was, and had long been, in his judgment one hostile to God. But it was a very convenient belief, also, in the existing political situation. If the Perrinists were guilty of high treason, their party could be forever swept from power. Contentions in a small city-republic like Geneva have always been bitter. The victorious side had pushed its triumph far against the "Mamelouks" and "Artichauds," in the past. It was to show itself yet more unsparing now to the Perrinists.

The brothers Comparet had been arrested at the time of the disturbance, and a general investigation of the whole affair was begun by the Little Council the next day,—Perrin and Vandel taking their accustomed place among its membership. Many witnesses were heard, and the case was prolonged. On the 23d, the Council ordered further arrests. The day following the Two Hundred met, and strengthened by its action, the Little Council now decreed the arrest of Perrin and others of his party. Fortunately for them, they perceived their danger, and escaped by timely flight. The Bernese authorities made representations in their behalf, but neither Calvin nor his friends were likely to give a welcome to anything that Bern had to say. On June 3d, Perrin and four associates were formally sentenced to be beheaded and quartered,—though happily for them not in Geneva's power. The Comparets, who were in the city prison, were now

[1] See his description of them to Bullinger, July 15, 1555, *Ibid.*, 677, 678.

examined with cruel torture to force from them the acknowledgment of a conspiracy. The efforts were successful while the pain endured, but before their execution, on June 27th, they denied that the riot had been a premeditated act. On August 27th, and September 11th, Claude Genève, and François Daniel Berthelier, Philibert's younger brother, followed them in death by the same bloody path. Meanwhile, on August 6th, Piérre Vandel and Philibert Berthelier had been sentenced in their absence to the same fate, and others involved to punishments of varying severity. Even the wives of the condemned were banished from the city; and at a meeting of the General Assembly on September 6th, not only was what had been done approved, but all effort to aid the return of the fugitives to the city was forbidden under pain of death.[1] The Perrinist party, as a political force in Geneva, had been totally destroyed.

Calvin's share in these events was not official. The trials and condemnations were the work of the civil authorities. His participation in the struggle was none the less real. He visited the condemned in prison and sought to secure from them an acknowledgment of the alleged conspiracy.[2] He wrote full accounts of his version of the event to Bullinger for influence on the governments of Zurich and Schaffhausen.[3] He expressed satisfaction that torture would probably wring

[1] *Opera*, xv 752

[2] Letter to Bullinger, *Opera*, xv. 831.

[3] *Ibid.*, p 677.

from two of the prisoners the information desired.[1] In spite of his aversion to cruel deaths, which has already been noted, he saw a special act of God's judgment in the prolongation of the sufferings of the Comparets through an unskilfulness on the part of the executioner which the Genevan government rebuked by the banishment of that official.[2] He felt that the authorities had been, if anything, too moderate in their action.[3] It is Calvin in his hardest and most unsympathetic mood that here expresses himself; but it should be remembered in explanation that he had suffered for years almost to the shipwreck of a work which he believed to be even more that of God than his own at the hands of the party the destruction of which he now witnessed with such satisfaction.

To Calvin the fall of the Perrinists brought the cessation of serious opposition in Geneva. Refugees were freely admitted to citizenship. Before February 1, 1556,[4] one hundred and seventy had become burghers, and eighty-four more received the same right in the next twelve months.[5] The Consistory acted with a freedom and an undisputed authority that it had not

[1] To Farel, *Opera*, xv 693 Eng. trans. *Letters of John Calvin*, (Phila ) Vol. iii. 206. "Before ten days we shall see, I hope, what the rack will wring from them"

[2] *Ibid*; *Opera*, xxi 610.

[3] To Bullinger, *Ibid*, xv 684

[4] *I e* between February 1, 1555, and February 1, 1556 These are Roget's figures, iv. 327, v 48, Kampschulte, ii. 285, gives somewhat different figures.

[5] In 1559 alone 1708 received the right of habitation, between 1549 and 1559 the number of inhabitants received was 5017 Doumergue, iii 11, 74

yet enjoyed. Geneva had become, not the city of Calvin's ideal,—that it was never to be,—but a Puritan town, religious, conscientious, strict in supervision of conduct, and efficient in ecclesiastical censures. The work to which he had set his hand on his return in 1541, had been largely accomplished.

Yet Calvin's hard-won success might even now have been largely frustrated had it not been for unanticipated political good-fortune. Though united at home to a degree never heretofore realised, Geneva's external relations, notably with Bern, had never been worse than at the fall of the Perrinists. To Bern's shelter of Calvin's critics already noted was now added its protection of the banished Perrinist leaders. The alliance between Geneva and this powerful and politically valuable neighbour was to expire by limitation in March, 1556. Geneva wished it renewed; but Bern refused consent, save on terms humiliating to the Calvinist government. Geneva therefore dropped the alliance. Yet the situation of the little city, without the political aid of Bern, was precarious in the extreme, and negotiations, in which Calvin bore his full share, were carried on at great length with other cantons and with Bern for a restoration of the confederacy. Bern's terms were too exacting and asked too much in favour of the Perrinists for Geneva to accept. A change came unexpectedly, however, in 1557, when the great victory of the Spaniards over the French at Saint-Quentin on August 10th, of that year, won under the generalship of Emmanuel Philibert, duke of Savoy, made him the most famous commander in Europe, lamed the power of

France, and rendered it possible for him to lay claim to the ancient Savoyard lands. The danger both to Bern and Geneva was real, and under a common sense of peril, what negotiations had thus far failed to achieve was now quickly attained. A "perpetual alliance" in which Geneva was for the first time placed on a full equality with Bern was effected in January, 1558; the Perrinists found the hopes that they had built on Bernese aid utterly frustrated, and the results of 1555 were made permanent. The party of Calvin had not merely won victory at home, but had secured that victory by the abatement of the most dangerous external perils to which Geneva was exposed, and the attainment of a political independence greater than that which their city had ever before enjoyed.

These months of anxious negotiation with Bern were a time of severe domestic trial for Calvin. The wife of his beloved brother, Antoine, long suspected of unworthy conduct, was charged with adultery committed with Calvin's hunchbacked secretary-servant, Pierre Dagnet, while all were inhabiting Calvin's house. On January 7, 1557, Calvin and his brother laid the case before the Consistory, by which it was referred to the Little Council. On February 16th, the crime having been proved, the Little Council gave Antoine a divorce and ordered his former wife to leave the city. The scandal and the chagrin of the reformer were great; but the case seems to have been aggravated. It gave to his enemies, however, an annoying point of attack, especially when Antoine Calvin shocked Roman

Catholic feeling by marrying again in 1560.[1] Nor was this the only trial occasioned by those of his own household and circle that Calvin was to experience In 1562, his step-daughter, Judith, fell into similar disgrace,—a matter which Calvin felt so keenly that he left the city to seek the solitude of the country for a few days after the misdeed became public knowledge.[2]

[1] Calvin to Viret, *Opera*, xvi 379, *Registres du Consistoire* and *du Conseil*, *Ibid*, xxi 658–661, Doumergue, iii 572

[2] Calvin to Bullinger, *Opera*, xix 327

## CHAPTER XIII

### CALVIN CROWNS HIS GENEVAN WORK, 1559

CALVIN'S interest in Geneva was primarily religious. He would make the city an example of a Christian community, a refuge for oppressed Protestants, and a centre of influence for the spread of the Evangelical cause. His own interpretation of his duties was broad, and he was keen to see that material well-being and education were essential to the realisation of his ideal. A well-ordered population should be no less industrious than religious. With this aim in view, as early as December 29, 1544, he urged the Little Council to develop the weaving industry as an aid to the prosperity of the city. His efforts in this direction had very considerable success and were efficiently aided by the character and thrift of many of the refugees. Geneva prospered in a material way under his influence.[1] For his time, Calvin held liberal views on questions of trade. Though he did not approve money-lending as an exclusive profession, he believed the receipt of a fair interest on the use of

[1] See H Wiskemann, *Darstellung der in Deutschland zur Zeit der Reformation herreschenden national-ökonomischen Ansichten*, in the *Schriften der Jablonowskischen Gesellschaft*, for 1861, pp 79–87. Less value, but still a decided significance, is attached to this work by Kampschulte, i. 429, 430. See Schaff, vii. 516.

money not only unforbidden by Scripture, but wise and just.[1] This growth in popular well-being is a factor to be taken into account in explaining the increasing favour with which his system was regarded by the inhabitants of the city.

Calvin's concern for Geneva was, however, far more spiritual and intellectual than material. In his estimate, religion and education were closely associated. A true faith must be intelligent. The School and the Church are necessary and mutually supplementary agencies, or rather the School is an essential part of any effective Church organisation. Intelligence, not ignorance, was to Calvin the mother of piety; and no other conception characteristic of him was more fully impressed on the churches which came under his spiritual influence. France, Holland, Scotland, Puritan England, and New England were all to feel its power and to draw from it lasting benefit

Calvin had long desired the establishment of a really efficient school at Geneva, effective in its methods, especially in instilling a fundamental basis of philological learning, and having as its crown instruction in theology, by which pastors could be trained for the service of the Church His ideal was undoubtedly the school system of Strassburg, made familiar to him by participation in its instruction during his sojourn in that city. But circumstances had long been unfavourable to its

[1] *Opera*, xx. 245–249.

realisation.[1] Given a prominent place in the *Ordonnances* of 1541, the school was, nevertheless, long the weak point of Calvin's structure. Mention has already been made of the vain efforts to secure Mathurin Cordier for its service, and of the unhappy breach with its head-master, Castellio.[2] The school continued; but so inefficient was its instruction, that Genevan parents who desired a thorough education for their sons, had to send them to other cities.[3] Theology was, indeed, vigorously taught by Calvin himself throughout his Genevan ministry.

On the fall of the Perrinists, and especially after Calvin had renewed old associations by a brief visit to Strassburg in 1556, he set his hand earnestly to the regeneration of the Genevan school system. The conflict with Bern delayed the action then begun, but on its successful conclusion, in January, 1558, the Little Council, at Calvin's instigation, ordered the selection of a site for a "College".[4] The buildings, which have survived in large part to the present day, were begun in the following April, and Calvin undertook to enlist competent teachers. Geneva was poor, and Calvin asked for gifts and legacies, with such success

[1] An admirable account of Calvin's work for Genevan education is that of Charles Borgeaud, *Histoire de l'Université de Genève*, Geneva, 1900, i. 1–83. Roget, v. 225–248, and Kampschulte, ii. 310–342, have much of value. See, also, Doumergue, iii. 372–392.

[2] *Ante*, p. 289.

[3] Beza's introduction to the *Laws of the Genevan Academy*, 1559, *Opera*, xa. 66; Borgeaud, i. 1.

[4] *Registres du Conseil*, quoted by Roget, v. 227; see, also, Borgeaud, i. 34, 35.

that the current of beneficence thus started brought more than five hundred gifts to the new foundation in the course of the next sixty years.[1] Yet it was impossible, at first, to offer an adequate compensation to the instructors invited, and Calvin's efforts were hampered by this and other difficulties, till an unexpected controversy at Lausanne led to the immediate realisation of his purpose.

A school at Lausanne, begun by the theological lectures of Viret in 1537, had been developed into a regular foundation by the Bernese authorities in 1540.[2] There Mathurin Cordier had taught since 1545, but was now supplemented by reason of old age, by François Bérauld, a native of Orléans. With them Calvin's friend and disciple, Theodore Beza, had been associated as professor of Greek since 1549, and Jean Tagaut, like Beza a French refugee, as professor of "arts," his specialty being mathematics, since 1557. The school was flourishing and highly respected; and for some years it constituted the only seat of advanced instruction for French-speaking Protestants. The ministers and teachers at Lausanne, notably Viret and Beza, fully sympathised with Calvin's ecclesiastical discipline, and, in March, 1558, they tried to introduce there his independent right of excommunication. The consequences were disastrous.[3] The Bernese government,

[1] Borgeaud, i. 35, 36 1074 florins were received in legacies in 1559, certain fines were also so disposed, Roget, v 232, 233, 10,024 florins are said to have been collected in six months, Kampschulte, ii 314.

[2] Borgeaud, i 38–42

[3] Roget, v 207–224

THE COLLEGE OF GENEVA, BEFORE ITS RESTORATION

under which Lausanne stood, would have none of it. Beza foresaw the result of the storm, and betook himself to Geneva in September of the same year. Here he was warmly welcomed, nominated to the Genevan ministry by the *Vénérable Compagnie*, and designated by it and the Little Council as professor of Greek in the College to be. Thenceforth Beza was to be Calvin's right-hand man. In mental equipment very like Calvin, though without his originality, Beza was devoted to Calvin's theology, discipline, and ideals, and bound to him by ties of intimate friendship. No master ever had a more apt or admiring disciple, and it was Beza who for more than forty years after Calvin's death was to carry on Calvin's work in the path and with much of the success of the older Genevan reformer. Viret, aided by his pastoral associates, maintained the struggle at Lausanne a few months longer; but, in January, 1559, he was deposed from his long pastorate, and now came with many of his companions in the ministry and the school to the welcome shelter of Geneva. For the next three years, Viret was a Genevan minister.

By this exodus from Lausanne Calvin was provided with instructors for his Academy. On nomination of the *Vénérable Compagnie*, for, in accordance with the principles enunciated in the *Ordonnances* of 1542, Calvin would have the school under ecclesiastical control, he presented to the Little Council, on May 22, 1559, the names of François Bérauld as professor of Greek, and of Jean Tagaut as professor of philosophy.[1]

[1] *Registres du Conseil*, lv. 48, *Opera*, xxi. 716

With them was joined a brilliant teacher, once the tutor in French of the Princess Elizabeth, now Queen of England, Antoine Chevalier, as professor of Hebrew. To Beza was given the rectorship of the school instead of the chair of Greek as originally intended. These teachers were, like Calvin, all Frenchmen, and all had been at Lausanne, though Chevalier only for a brief time, and unlike the others not as an instructor in its school. Below them, as teachers in the secondary department, seven *régents* of classes were appointed, of whom Jean Randon, the head-master, had been of the school at Lausanne. Thus equipped, the Academy was formally inaugurated under the guidance of Calvin, and with an address by Beza, in the presence of the syndics, counsellors, ministers, and other dignitaries of the little city, gathered in Saint-Pierre on June 5, 1559.

On May 22d, Calvin had presented, and the Little Council had approved, the translation into French of the constitution of the Academy,—the *Leges Academiae Genevensis*.[1] In all probability it was his work.[2] Built in large part on what had been achieved at Strass-

[1] *Opera*, xxi 716, text in *Opera*, xa. 65–90.

[2] Always ascribed to him by tradition, his authorship was denied by Berthault in his *Mathurin Cordier*, Paris, 1876; and Bourchenin in his *Étude sur les académies protestantes*, Paris, 1882, p 62, in favour of Beza and Cordier Borgeaud has replied with effect, even if unable to furnish an absolute demonstration of Calvin's authorship, i 5–47. Cordier, then in his eightieth year, came with the exodus from Lausanne to Geneva, and was given a lodging in one of the college buildings in recognition of his deserts He was apparently in feeble health.

burg by Johann Sturm, and by Claude Baduel at Nîmes,[1] the Genevan academical constitution gave Greek an equal place with Latin in the curriculum, and emphasised even more than the earlier educational reformers the value of thorough preparatory linguistic studies. The institution was divided into what would now be described as a department of primary and secondary education, and a course of higher studies of university grade. The former, the *schola privata* or gymnasium, was strictly graded into seven classes, each under a *régent*. In each class the scholars were grouped in tens according to progress and abilities. The seventh or lowest class was taught to read in French and Latin Grammar and exercises filled the next two years. With the fourth class Greek was begun; and with the second the elements of dialectics. The scholar finished his preliminary course in the first class, with a considerable command of Latin and Greek, some knowledge of their literatures, and a moderate acquaintance with logic. The higher instruction was given in the *schola publica* by "public professors" of Hebrew, Greek, and Philosophy, or "Arts," and by Calvin and Beza as instructors in theology though without professorial title. Here there were no classes, the students being received by inscription and signature of a confession of faith. They were allowed comparative freedom, as in a modern German university Instruction was free. While an annual public promotion was appointed for the *schola privata*, the celebration of which on May 1st became an important festival, Calvin made no provision for

[1] See Borgeaud, i 42–45

the bestowment of degrees, nor did the magistrates feel such powers to be within their competence. The scholar of the *schola publica* had to content himself with a certificate of attendance and character, to which the reputation of the Academy soon gave widely recognised value.[1]

Calvin's object in founding the Academy of Geneva was twofold. He would give opportunity for instruction to the children of the city, and provide training in theology for students from abroad. He would make Geneva the theological seminary of Reformed Protestantism. From the first, the addition of courses in law and medicine were contemplated, but this enlargement was not effected till after Calvin's death. Its success, in point of attendance, was immediately assured. At Calvin's death, twelve hundred scholars were enrolled in the *schola privata*, and three hundred in the *schola publica*.[2] The vast majority of those in the higher studies were foreigners, attracted to Geneva by the fame of the school as a fountain of Protestant theology. Within three years of its opening, it numbered among its scholars such names as those of Kaspar Olevianus, to be one of the two authors of the Heidelberg Catechism, of Philippe de Marnix de Saint-Aldegonde, of Netherlandish memory; of Florent Chrestien, tutor of Henry IV. of France; of Thomas Bodley, the founder of the library known by his name at the English Oxford; of Francis Junius, later to be the ornament of the University of Leyden. France, England, Scotland, the

[1] Borgeaud, i 160–165.

[2] *Ibid*, p 63

Netherlands, Germany, Italy, and Switzerland had their representatives, but France most of all.[1]

The Academy was the crown of Calvin's Genevan work. It was a final step toward the realisation of his ideal of a Christian commonwealth. To pure preaching and thorough discipline he now added religious education. His disciples should not merely have the Evangelical faith, they should be able to give a reason worthy of the respect of every man of learning for the faith that was in them. Powerful as was the moulding force of the Academy upon Geneva, its influence was even greater outside the city's walls, for the students that it trained and inspired with the ideal that it championed, and the example that it presented, spread its spirit to France, the Netherlands, Scotland, and England. It sent out scores of earnest disciples, convinced that Calvin's message was that of God, and eager to fight and to suffer for the faith that it taught. It was the mother of the Huguenot seminaries. No other force was so powerful in disseminating Calvin's ideals, save his *Institutes*, and no school in all Protestantism ranked higher in public repute for a century after his death. Its honourable history has continued to the present day, when it has long since become in name, as it was always, one may say, in fact, the University of Geneva.

While these negotiations which resulted in the foundation of the Academy were in progress, Calvin was suffering from serious ill-health. His constitution, long racked by over-work, anxiety, and excessive hours of

[1] Borgeaud, i. pp. 55–63. Compare Kampschulte's interesting discussion, ii. 333–342

study, was breaking, and he languished from September, 1558, till the spring following, under attacks of the intermittent disease then known as quartan fever. The symptoms would point to severe nervous dyspepsia. From this illness his health was never fully restored. Always extremely temperate in food and drink, from now onward he took regularly but one meal a day, and frequently in the distress of his attacks would pass forty-eight hours without food.[1] Much of his time from this illness onward he was compelled to spend in bed, going out to preach or lecture, and returning to his couch to study, to dictate his letters, and to compose his books.

It is illustrative at once of Calvin's facility in the accomplishment of scholarly work, and of his firmness of will, that during this illness of the autumn and winter of 1558–59, besides maintaining his enormous correspondence, and revising his commentary on Isaiah, he brought to its classic completion the perfected edition of the *Institutes*. This, in itself, was a scholarly task of great labour; and its accomplishment under circumstances of illness is doubly remarkable. The *Institutes* had now attained their growth. Issued in 1536, as has been seen, in six considerable chapters, they revealed Calvin's full theological development in the edition of 1539; but in that of 1559, under consideration, they exhibited the experienced teacher and the developed master of logical order. It was, as the title-page declared "almost a new work" As now presented, the *Institutes* followed the sequence of the Apostles' Creed, and had grown to a compass of four books, in eighty

[1] Colladon, *Life*, *Opera*, xxi 87–89, 109

chapters, though these chapters average much less in length than those of the original edition.[1] Designed for popular reading, as well as for scholars, the qualities of vivacity and clearness conspicuously mark this masterpiece of Reformation theology. From its publication, this edition of the *Institutes* became the standard presentation of the Calvinistic system Its circulation was European. Before the definitive Latin edition of 1559, the *Institutes* had been repeatedly published in French, beginning in 1541, and once, in 1557, in Italian. In its final form, it appeared in French in 1560, in Dutch, during the same year; in English, in 1561; in German, in 1572; and in Spanish, in 1597. Before the close of the sixteenth century, to speak of no other versions, eight editions of the entire work had been issued in English, and abridgments in that tongue had been four times published.

Mention was made, in speaking of Calvin's labours during this illness, of his commentary on Isaiah, and earlier exegetical publications have been enumerated.[2] These series of Bible expositions grew out of Calvin's theological lectures, which took largely the form of Scriptural interpretation, and their publication continued as long as he lived. His commentary on Genesis and on the Canonical Epistles appeared in 1554, his Harmony of the Gospels in 1555, the year 1557 saw his exposition of the Psalms and of Isaiah; the Minor Prophets were explained in 1559, Daniel in 1561, the

[1] Text in *Opera*, ii That of the French edition, published in 1560, is in vols. iii. and iv The best English edition is that translated by Beveridge, 3 vols, Edinburgh, 1845–46.

[2] *Ante*, p. 324.

whole Pentateuch, Jeremiah, and Lamentations in 1563, and Joshua in 1564. It was not merely very extensive and rapid work that Calvin accomplished as a commentator.[1] It was the best work of Biblical interpretation that the Reformation age produced. Brief, clear, of great spiritual insight, and resting on the basis of ample philological knowledge and of a sound and practical judgment, he held that each Scripture passage must be understood as containing a definite message, and not a threefold or fourfold meaning as the early Church and the Middle Ages had believed. That meaning was to be ascertained by natural grammatical and historical interpretation The modern conceptions of a progressive revelation, and of human admixture of error, to say nothing of such views as regard the Bible as a literature embodying the religious conceptions of many ages and of a variety of writers, were of course unknown to him. The language might be the humble speech of a Paul, but the thoughts were those of the Holy Spirit. Yet, for his time, Calvin was remarkably fresh, translucent, and sensible in his comments, and the series of expositions from his Romans of 1540, to his Joshua of 1564, were second only to his *Institutes* and the Academy in the propagation of his theology.[2]

The time of the foundation of the Academy was not only one of physical distress to Calvin, it was a period of anxiety to the entire Genevan community, in which the

[1] These commentaries fill nearly all of vols xxiii–lv of the *Opera*

[2] Calvin's services as a commentator are well treated by Schaff, vii. 524–538, where references to the further literature of the subject are given.

whole existence of the Reform movement there and the independence of the city seemed at stake. On April 3, 1559, the struggle between Henry II. of France and Philip II. of Spain was brought to a close by the peace of Câteau Cambrésis. As had been foreshadowed by the Spanish victory at Saint-Quentin, the results of the struggle had been decidedly favourable to Spain; and its ruler regarded the suppression of Protestantism as his God-appointed task. It was evident to all that the close of the armed contests between the two great Catholic powers would endanger the status of Protestantism; and the thirty years from 1559 to 1589 were to be the darkest period of the Evangelical cause. For Geneva the situation brought about by the peace was alarming. Not only was the city justly regarded as the stronghold of French-speaking Protestantism, Calvin was, as there will be occasion to see in the next chapter, the real, though unofficial, head of the French Evangelical party. His pupils were its ministers, his advice and exhortation had for years encouraged its struggles, his labours had made Geneva an asylum for its refugees. To crush Geneva would be to deal a blow to all French Protestantism, and as the event proved, though it was not then so evident, to that of the Netherlands also. The instrument seemed at hand. The victor of Saint-Quentin, Emmanuel Philibert, the young and able duke of Savoy, was restored by the peace to the territories which France had taken from his house.[1] It would be

[1] To save French pride, this restoration was nominally subject to legal adjudication within three years. E. Armstrong, in *The Cambridge Modern History*, iii. 400.

natural that he should seek also to gain what Bern had seized, and Geneva itself, in which his ancestors had had so large a stake; and it was to be anticipated, too, that in this, or in some other, effort against its freedom Geneva would find itself confronted by the power of Spain and of France, eager to end an independence so obnoxious to the Roman cause.

Geneva was in anxiety, but not in panic.[1] On news of the peace, fortification was begun at once, and the month of the opening of the Academy saw, as Haller wrote from Bern to Bullinger, on June 22d, all the inhabitants, "magistrates, ministers, nobles, artisans," working feverishly on its defences.[2] It was an exhibition of courage and firmness worthy of the little city which Calvin led. Yet, fortunately for Geneva, its guns and its earthworks were not to be put to the test. Though Pope Paul IV. urged the Kings of Spain and France "to smother the snake in its nest," political and military jealousies prevented action lest one or the other sovereign gain the profit.[3] Geneva's chief deliverance came, however, through the unexpected death of Henry II., on July 10, 1559, from wounds received in a tournament. Though not immediately relieved from its fears, the turmoils and party divisions in France, begun with the brief reign of Francis II., and to lead, in 1562, to the Huguenot wars, rendered Geneva comparatively secure from any attack in which France or

[1] Roget, v. 249–266.

[2] Quoted, *Ibid*, p. 254.

[3] Roget, *Ibid*, pp 255, 256, ascribes the unwillingness to Spain; Armstrong, *op cit.*, p. 405, to France.

Spain should have a part. Though a fresh danger, that was long to continue, was created when Emmanuel Philibert, after long negotiations, secured for the Savoyard House the restoration in 1564, the year of Calvin's death, of the territories on the south shore of Lake Geneva which Bern had conquered in 1536,[1] Geneva's political situation was never again so perilous during Calvin's life, as in 1559,—while the intellectual influence of the city was vastly augmented from that date. It was indeed an advance-post of Protestantism, thrust into the midst of perils; but the foundation of the Academy was its noblest answer to its enemies.

The relations of the civil authorities of Geneva, now composed almost exclusively of Calvin's friends and admirers, took on increasingly an aspect of respectful reverence; but Calvin was indisposed to profit personally by their bounty. At the meeting of the Little Council, on May 22, 1559, at which he presented the statutes of the Academy about to be, he thanked the magistrates most heartily for their "great benefits" during his recent illness, but begged them not to carry out their purpose of paying the apothecary for the medicines prescribed. The Council voted "to remonstrate with him," requesting him to take it in good part, because it "wished to do that and more, if there was need."[2] Again, in June, 1563, the Little Council made a donation of twenty-five *écus* to Calvin, through his brother, Antoine, to defray the cost of medicines and other incidents of illness. Calvin promptly returned

[1] Armstrong, p 405

[2] *Registres du Conseil*, lv. 49; *Opera*, xxi 716

the gift with an expression of his grateful appreciation; and once more the Council asked him "to keep it and to spare nothing."[1] In his last illness, in March, 1564, the Council repeated the gift, only to have Calvin again decline it, this time with the message "that he felt scruples about receiving his ordinary salary when he could not serve."[2] Calvin was no self-seeker in financial relations, or exploiter of the bounty of others, even when freely offered; and his reserve in these cases is the more creditable since the gifts proposed were from the public treasury of a city which he had reason to feel that he had greatly served.

These endeavours to ease Calvin's increasing physical disabilities by pecuniary assistance were only a part of the expressions of governmental goodwill. On December 25, 1559, the Little Council requested him to become a burgher, an honourable invitation which he gratefully accepted[3] In May following, it voted him a cask of the best white wine to be found, "because indebted by reason of the great labours which he undertakes for the government",[4] and in his last illness, besides the money gift already mentioned, it ordered prayers in his behalf, directed the syndics to "visit him often"; and, finally, went in a body to his sick-room, on April 27, 1564, "to hear what he should wish to say, and afterwards to express to him all warm affection and friendship, even to his relatives after his decease, by

[1] *Registres du Conseil*, lviii 67, 68; *Opera*, xxi. 804.
[2] *Ibid*, lix 18, 20, xxi 813
[3] *Ibid*, lv 163; xxi 725
[4] *Ibid*, lvi 38, xxi 731.

reason of the acceptable services which he has performed for the government, and because he has acquitted himself faithfully in his office."[1] The message thus tersely indicated in the arid pages of the public records must have been grateful to Calvin's heart, and must have sweetened with a sense of public recognition achieved the recollection of many a bitter struggle and many a rebuff from the government which then did him affectionate reverence.

[1] *Registres du Conseil*, lix 38, *Opera*, xxi. 815.

# CHAPTER XIV

## CALVIN'S INFLUENCE OUTSIDE OF GENEVA

UNREMITTING as was Calvin's struggle to make of Geneva a city answering to his religious ideal, he had always more than the reformation of that city in view. He would transform it into a model Christian community, he would render it an asylum for all who were oppressed in the profession of their Evangelical faith; and, above all, by example, by hospitality, by training, by the sending forth of pastors, and by the influence of its ministers and magistrates he would make Geneva a power for the spread of the Reformation. In all this effort he largely succeeded. Geneva was never to Calvin an end in itself. It was a means by which the conception he held of the Protestant faith should be advanced far beyond even the bounds of a single nation throughout western Europe. That non-German Protestantism, in spite of diversities of races, of governments, and of intellectual developments, attained essential doctrinal unity, and so largely exhibited a common type of religious life, was primarily due to Calvin's forceful impress. Where, as in a certain section of the English Reformed party, other influences prevented the full dominance of Calvin's ideals, a divergent type of Protestantism was manifest, yet even Anglicanism felt the moulding touch of Calvin's doctrinal system for half a century after his death; and struggled long for the mastery of England with a Puritanism that was almost wholly his own. Elsewhere in western Europe no influence was to be compared, during the latter half of the sixteenth century with that of Calvin.[1]

The prime reason for this influence was Calvin's transcendent ability as a theologian. The propagating and unifying power of the *Institutes* was due to the fact that in them the Reformation epoch received its clearest, most logical, and most characteristic presentation of Christian truth. However inadequate it may appear to our own age, there can be no question that, more than any other work, it seemed to the sixteenth century the ablest answer to Roman claims, and the most complete presentation of the Gospel. Second only to the impressive power of the *Institutes* was the influence of the apparent realisation of a reformed Christian community in Geneva. Though to us Calvin's system gives the conviction of unendurable spiritual tyranny, there were thousands of his religious and earnest contemporaries to whom it seemed, as it did to John Knox, "the most perfect school of Christ that ever was on the earth since the days of the Apostles."[2] But, beside these gifts, as a theologian and an organiser, Calvin had a statesmanlike breadth of view which enabled him better than any other reformer to grasp

[1] A valuable account of Calvin's influence is that of E. Stähelin, *Johannes Calvin*, i 505, ii 244

[2] In letter to Mrs. Anne Locke, December 9, 1556. In *Works*, ed. Laing, iv. 240

the whole European religious situation. The only Protestant divine at all comparable to him in this quality of mind was Zwingli, and the field in which the Zurich pastor laboured was relatively circumscribed.

As a preparation for Calvin's far-reaching acquaintance with the position and the possibilities of the Evangelical cause the circumstances of Calvin's life previous to his return to Geneva in 1541, were most fortunate. Acquainted as a student of law and of the humanities with a considerable circle in France outside of that moved by the religious impulse which became dominant in him by 1533, he rose to recognised leadership as the spokesman of French Protestantism by his letter to Francis I., in 1536. His life at Basel brought him familiarity with Northern Switzerland, his journeyings to Ferrara showed him a little of Italy, his stay at Strassburg strengthened his hold upon the Protestantism of his native France, while bringing to him ample knowledge of the parties and leaders of Germany. By the time of his return to Geneva, he had become the most widely travelled and the most variously engaged of the reformers. Thenceforth his journeys were few; but Geneva became at once a city of refuge, and the future religious leaders of France, the Netherlands, England, and Scotland, in no small numbers came thither to him

Calvin's personal acquaintance was maintained and supplemented by a correspondence of remarkable extent. Even aided as he was by the constant employment of amanuenses, the number and importance of the epistolatory demands upon his strength, especially during the later years of his life, are such as to make evident the value which he attached to this means of serving the Evangelical cause and its time-consuming burden.[1] The variety and significance of his correspondents are equally impressive. Besides his familiar and frequent letters to Farel, Viret, Bucer, Bullinger, and Beza, the roll of his correspondents contains such names of reformers as those of Melanchthon, Hedio, Brentz, Sturm, Jonas, Olevianus, and Sleidan of Germany,[2] Cranmer, Grindal, Hooper, Coverdale, Norton, Cox, and Whittingham of England; Knox of Scotland; Blaurer, Grynæus, Haller, Musculus, Myconius, and Sulzer of Switzerland, à Lasco of Poland, Friesland, and England; the Italian refugees, Peter Martyr, Ochino, and Zanchi; the radicals Lælius Socinus and Servetus; besides many in France, including Admiral Coligny, Condé, and Anthony of Navarre. Many of his correspondents were of great social and political distinction. He wrote to Marguerite d'Angoulême, Renée of Ferrara; Somerset, the Lord Protector of England, and Edward VI. of that realm; Frederick III., the elector Palatine; Philip of Hesse, and Sigismund August, king of Poland. They are letters of a writer

[1] The surviving letters to, from, and about Calvin fill volumes xb–xx of the *Opera*, and number 4271 pieces Calvin's own letters, beside a number the address of which is uncertain, were directed to no less than 307 persons and bodies, and this collection must contain only a portion of those actually written

[2] Luther should perhaps be mentioned, though Calvin's acquaintance with him was slight and they never met. *Ante*, p 243

fully acquainted with the usages of the cultivated world, clear, tactful, energetic, seldom of much personal emotion, but penetrated by a profound conviction of the truth of his cause, a marvellous grasp of the situation, and a transparent appeal to the reason and will. He warns, he comforts, he intercedes, he gives the news of the hour, he endeavors to foster the Evangelical cause, and to bring victory in the contests in which he was engaged in Geneva and beyond the borders of the city.

Calvin's thoughts turned first of all to his native France. For him Geneva was always a vantage-point for French evangelisation. Situated on the borders of France, and speaking the language of that land, Geneva was naturally the city toward which French refugees turned. Calvin welcomed them; and, in turn he made Geneva a power for the propagation of Reformed ideas in the home-land.[1] French Protestantism had always had its large proportion of unacknowledged adherents, and toward them, in spite of their danger from persecution, Calvin directed his utmost urgency. In his *Petit traicté monstrant que c'est que doit faire un homme fidèle congnoissant la verité de l'Evangile quand il est entre les Papistes*,[2] published as a reply to many individual in-

[1] On Calvin's relations to French Protestantism, see Karl Müller, *Calvin und die Anfänge der französischen Hugonottenkirche*, in the *Preussische Jahrbücher*, cxiv 371–389 (December, 1903), A. A. Tilley, in *The Cambridge Modern History*, ii 287–296. Of less value is H Diener-Wyss, *Calvin: ein aktengetreues Lebensbild*, Zurich, 1904, pp 80–97

[2] *Opera*, vi 537–588.

quiries in 1543, he urged the duty of complete conformity to the Gospel:[1]—

> I am asked what advice I would give to a believer who is thus dwelling in some Egypt or some Babylon where he is not allowed to worship God purely, but is constrained, according to the common fashion to accommodate himself to evil things. First, that he go forth, if he is able. . . . If any one has not the means of going away, I would counsel him to consider whether it is not possible for him to abstain from all idolatry, . . furthermore that he make it his duty to instruct and edify the poor ignorant people as far as he is able. If he answers that he cannot do this without danger of death, I acknowledge it But the glory of God, which is here in question, ought to be much more precious to us than this fading and transitory life.

To many French Protestants this seemed hard doctrine, and to these accommodating and halting souls Calvin replied in 1544, in his *Excuse . . . à Messieurs les Nicodemites*,[2]—a nickname which he coined for them. But to many, also, Calvin's insistence on the maintenance of "the glory of God," was a trumpet-call to utmost self-sacrifice.

Calvin was in no way indifferent to the course of governmental repression to which he urged such manful though wholly spiritual resistance. His efforts while at Regensburg to secure German action aimed at a mitigation of persecution in France have already been noted.[3] On his return to Geneva they were continued,

[1] *Opera*, vi. 576

[2] *Ibid*, pp. 559–644.

[3] *Ante*, p. 242.

when occasion demanded, though with little success. On the outbreak of the savage attack upon the Waldenses of Provence, in 1545, he aroused the Genevan government to assist the fugitives, and, with its countenance, journeyed to Bern, Basel, Zürich, Schaffhausen, and Strassburg to secure action by the several Protestant governments in their behalf.[1] Each case of persecution for the Evangelical faith was to Calvin a matter of profound interest, and, as far as possible, of effort in behalf of the victim, either by exciting Protestant attempts at intervention or by letters of encouragement to those under suffering,—though of course the fate of the majority of martyrs was too speedily determined to permit of either form of attempted assistance.

One of the most notable instances of Calvin's masterly relation to the cause of the persecuted in France occurred in 1552 in connection with the "five scholars of Lausanne." Severe as was the persecution under Francis I., after the Placards, its intensity was increased after the accession of Henry II. in 1547. Five young Frenchmen, who had studied under Beza and Viret at Lausanne, now on their way home to preach the Evangelical faith, were arrested, in May, 1552, at Lyons, and sentenced by the ecclesiastical court. By an appeal to the Parlement of Paris their death by fire was delayed till May 16, 1553. The government of Bern, and of other cantons, protested to the King in vain in their behalf; and Calvin sent to them encouragement, without a trace of sentimentality, but breathing a spirit

[1] Letters in *Opera*, xii 75–84, see also xxi 352–354 See Baird, *Rise of the Huguenots*, i 244–251, *The Camb Mod Hist*, ii 289

like that of a commander in battle.[1] A single quotation may exhibit this quality:[2]—

It is needful that you sustain hard conflicts, that that which was said to Peter be accomplished in you "You shall be carried whither ye would not" But you know in what strength you have to fight, upon which all who rely shall never be surprised and still less confounded Therefore, my brothers, be confident that you will be strengthened according to your need by the spirit of our Lord Jesus that you fail not under the burden of temptations, however pressing they may be, any more than He who had so glorious a victory that it is an infallible pledge to us of our triumph in the midst of our miseries If He pleases to make use of you even to death in His battle, He will uphold you by His mighty hand to fight firmly, and will not suffer a single drop of your blood to remain useless

The whole Evangelical cause in France drew strength from the contagious example set by Calvin at Geneva, from the courage of the preachers that he trained and the firmness of his system of churchly organisation In some respects that system was at its best outside of Geneva; for in a degree unmatched by that of any other of the reformers it suited the needs of an oppressed cause which had to rely on its own inherent strength. In Geneva the principles enunciated in the *Institutes* were limited by dependence on a civil government theoretically friendly and co-operant, but often

[1] *Opera*, XIV 331, 423, 469, 491, 544; Baird, i. 283–285; *The Camb Mod Hist*, II 293

[2] *Opera*, XIV 413

jealous of ecclesiastical independence. In lands where the authorities were hostile, or of another race as at Strassburg, Calvin's church government showed its full power. Lutheranism, Zwinglianism, and Anglicanism were dependent on the State; Calvinistic Presbyterianism secured a self-governing, intelligently served, and strictly disciplined Church,—an ecclesiastical *imperium in imperio.*

Calvin discouraged the formation of churches, with the administration of the Sacraments, until the close-knit congregation after the Genevan model could be had.[1] Informal assemblies of Evangelical believers had existed, more or less continuously in Paris, Meaux, Nîmes, and elsewhere in France; but, in 1555, the considerable organisation of Protestant churches, equipped on the Genevan pattern with pastors, elders, and deacons began. In that year, the Paris congregation was definitely organised, and others were constituted in Angers, Poitiers, Loudon, and Arvert. Churches in Blois, Montoire, Bourges, Issoudun, Aubigny, and Tours followed in 1556, Orléans and Rouen were thus supplied in 1557; and, in 1558, no less than twenty came into being. By the beginning of 1559, there were seventy-two in France.[2] Under Calvin's leadership, Geneva set itself to supply them with pastors, and these churches in turn looked to Calvin for their ministry. In 1559, nineteen ministers were either asked of

[1] Müller, *op. cit*, p 384.

[2] *The Camb Mod Hist*, ii 293, 294, Müller, *op cit*, p 385 The number of Protestant gatherings, of incomplete organisation, was much greater.

or sent from Geneva; in 1560, twelve; while in 1561 the number of demands for such assistance rose to ninety.[1] It was, of course, impossible for Geneva to supply all this need, but between 1555 and 1566, one hundred and twenty pastors were sent by the *Vénérable Compagnie* to French churches.[2] No wonder French Protestantism was moulded by Calvin's spirit.

In spite of relentless persecution, the French Church went forward with its organisation. From May 26 to 28, 1559, the first Protestant General Synod met at Paris. A firm constitution, on Calvin's principles, was adopted, by which adjacent churches were grouped in a "colloquy," and the neighbouring "colloquies" in a "provincial synod," while all were represented in a national synod. A confession of faith was issued, often, though apparently erroneously, attributed to Calvin; but epitomising with great clearness his theological system, and largely the work of his devoted pupil, Antoine de la Roche Chandieu.[3] A great national Church, for the first time in Reformation history, was created independent of a hostile State; and the work was one for which Calvin had given the model, the inspiration, and the training, even though its actual accomplishment aroused, at the moment, his anxiety

[1] *Opera*, xxi 710–771

[2] *The Camb. Mod. Hist.*, ii 294; the same work, p. 373, gives the number as 161

[3] Text, *Opera*, ix 731–752, Schaff, *Creeds of Christendom*, iii 356–382 See also *Opera, Ibid*, p lvii, Schaff, *Ibid*, i 493; *The Camb Mod Hist*, ii 295; Stähelin, in *Realencyklopädie*, iii 677, Müller, *op. cit.*, p. 388.

rather than won his approval.[1] With its churches he continued in constant correspondence. They sought his advice in difficulties and his comfort in trial In a real sense, Calvin was a bishop to the Huguenot congregations of France and took upon himself, so long as he lived, the "care of all the churches."

As the Protestant cause developed in France, it began to attract converts from the higher classes, and by the time of the first meeting of the General Synod it was becoming a political party as well as a religious propaganda. Calvin promptly put himself in communication with these more distinguished converts. By 1558, he was writing to François d'Andelot, whose conversion to Protestantism had been wrought by Calvin's publications, to Anthony of Navarre and to Admiral Coligny. He followed with painful interest the course of persecution that marked the last days of Henry II., and the accession of the Guises to power when Francis II. came to the throne in July, 1559. He disapproved of the plot to break the control of that intensely Catholic family in March, 1560, known as the "Tumult of Amboise."[2] He had no confidence in such illegitimate intrigues, and distrusted the use of force Yet he was glad to have Beza do what he could to arouse the King of Navarre to put himself at the head of a proposed demonstration of a more legitimate character in the South of France, which, had Anthony of Bourbon been a man of vigour, might easily have led to civil war in the summer of the same year.

[1] See Calvin's letter of May 17, 1559, *Opera*, xvii 525

[2] Letters to Bullinger, Blaurer, and Coligny, *Opera*, xviii. 84, 95, 425.

With the death of Francis II. on December 5, 1560, the power of the Guises was broken, and the position of French Protestantism immediately improved. Its adherents were growing rapidly in numbers; and in July, 1561, the Evangelicals were summoned to present their case before the new king, Charles IX. At the Colloquy held in consequence at Poissy in September following, the Protestants were represented by twelve ministers, headed by Beza. They would gladly have had Calvin as their spokesman; but even his most ardent friends did not dare advise so hated a foe of the older communion to expose himself to the dangers of a journey to France, nor was the Genevan Little Council willing that he should thus imperil his life.[1] With the following March, and the massacre at Vassy, the great Huguenot wars began; but Calvin could well hope that the peace of Amboise, of March 18, 1563, by which the first of the long series of struggles was ended, was but the dawn of the triumph of Protestantism in his native land, though he disapproved its relatively slight advantages to the cause he had at heart and felt much anxiety for the future.[2] To his thinking war was a poor means of advancing the Gospel. "I would always counsel," he wrote on news of the peace, "that arms be laid aside, and that we all perish rather than enter again on the confusions that have been witnessed."[3] Calvin did not live to see the renewal of the conflict.

In the neighbouring Netherlands Calvin's theologic

[1] *Opera*, xviii. 555, xxi 755, Baird, *Theodore Beza*, p. 136.
[2] *Opera*, xix 687–693.
[3] *Ibid*, p. 688.

and organising influence proved as determinative as in France, though he exercised no such superintendence as there over the churches,—few of which, indeed, were founded till near the close of his life. Under the influx of preachers from France into the French-speaking southern provinces, the movement in the Netherlands in favour of Protestantism, which in its beginnings had been Lutheran and Anabaptist, became prevailingly Calvinistic. Most extensive at first among the Walloons, it won its strongest support, though not till after Calvin's death, in the northern territories which were ultimately to gain their independence of Spain. Guy de Bray, the Netherlandish martyr, to whom, whatever may have been the aid received from others, the preparation of the Belgic Confession of 1561 was due, had almost unquestionably come into personal relations with Calvin at Frankfort in 1556.[1] This Confession, which was to become a doctrinal basis of the Reformed Church of Holland and of its spiritual offspring in America, was modelled in large part on that adopted by the Huguenot synod at Paris in 1559,[2] and shows its author to have been a convinced disciple of Calvin. As in France, and amid even severer struggles, the Calvinistic system proved itself a discipline for battle. The State Church of the victorious northern provinces was to be one of the most eminent members of the Calvinistic family.

Calvin's relations to the leaders of the Reformation

[1] L. A. van Langeraad, in Hauck's *Realencyklopädie*, iii 364 For the Confession and its history see Schaff, *Creeds of Christendom*, i 502–508; iii. 383–436.

[2] *Ante*, p. 385

in England and Scotland were even more direct and personal. He wrote to the Lord Protector, the Duke of Somerset, in the early months of the reign of Edward VI., urging strenuous preaching of pure doctrine, extirpation of Roman abuses and vigorous discipline. "You have," said Calvin, "two sorts of headstrong fellows who raise themselves against the King and the state of the kingdom. The one is of fantastic folk who would put all in confusion under pretence of the Gospel. The other is of persons obstinate in the superstitions of the Roman antichrist. Both will deserve to be repressed by the sword which is intrusted to you."[1] He corresponded with Cranmer. He exhorted the young King to support the Reformation cause with zeal. As Edward's brief reign advanced, his influence and the acceptance of his doctrines in England increased. But it was by reason of the cordial welcome that Calvin gave to the exiles whom the policy of Mary drove to seek shelter on the Continent, and their acquaintance with his system, at its Genevan fountain-head, that his following in England was chiefly developed. Those refugees, rejected by the Protestant cities of Northern Germany on account of their non-conformity to Luther's views of the Lord's Supper, found in Calvin a warm friend. He endeavoured, though without success, to heal the breach between the adherents of the English Prayer-Book and their more radical opponents in the exiled congregation at Frankfort. Though his sympathies were with its critics, the English service seemed to him, at worst, to be chargeable only with "many en-

[1] October 22, 1548, *Opera*, xiii 65–90.

durable trifles."[1] When the Frankfort refugees divided on the issue, he welcomed to Geneva the critical wing, led by John Knox, and secured for their use, and that of the Italian Protestant exiles, the Church of Mary the New, (the "Auditoire") with careful definition of their rights of worship in their own languages.[2] On one day in October, 1557, no less than fifty English refugees were admitted inhabitants of the city, and, on May 30, 1560, when the favourable reign of Elizabeth permitted their return to England, these sojourners for their faith formally thanked the Genevan government for the hospitality they had enjoyed.[3]

The return of the Marian exiles to England was followed by a greatly increased acquaintance with, and acceptance of, Calvin's system in that land. The more eager Protestants looked upon the reform of the Church largely from his point of view. They desired its further purification from Roman observances, the establishment of an earnest, preaching ministry, and of a thorough parochial discipline. The result was the growth of the Puritan party,—a movement which was only in its beginnings at the time of Calvin's death, but which was to grow all through the reigns of Elizabeth and James, to lead to the settlement of New England, and to wrest the sceptre for a time from the House of Stuart. In the Confession and Catechisms of the Westminster Assembly, called in 1643, in the midst of the great civil war, Calvinism was to be given a symbolic

[1] January 18, 1555, *Opera*, xv 394 See also 337, 554, 776.

[2] *Ibid.*, xxi 619, 620 (November, 1555).

[3] *Ibid*, pp. 676, 732

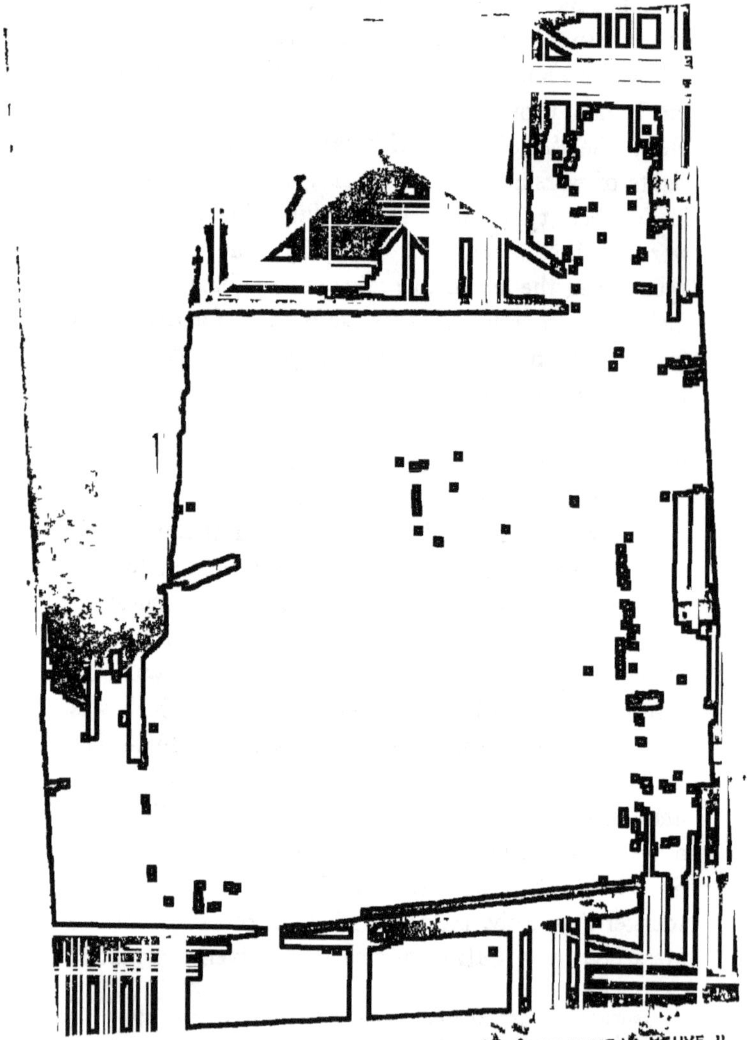

EXTERIOR OF THE "AUDITOIRE," ORIGINALLY "NOTRE DAME-LA-NEUVE," IN GENEVA.

expression that is still in its essential features the recognised creed of thousands of Christians in Scotland and America. And even where Calvin's theories of church organisation and discipline were rejected, there was in England for years after his death a general use of his *Institutes* and Catechism in the theological instruction in the universities, and a wide sympathy with his theology, of which that arch-enemy of the Puritans, Archbishop John Whitgift, may be cited as an illustration.

Calvin's connection with the Reformation in Scotland was closely bound up with his association with the chief Scottish reformer, John Knox The beginnings of Knox's Evangelical activity in Scotland, and his imprisonment by the French captors of St. Andrews, were followed by ministerial labours in England under the reign of Edward VI. Soon after the accession of Mary he had to fly to the Continent, and in 1554 was in Geneva, an eager student of theology and of Hebrew, and an enthusiastic admirer and disciple of Calvin. From Geneva he went, in the same year, to become a preacher to the mixed congregation of English and French refugees at Frankfort, only to involve that body in controversies over the use of the Edwardine liturgy, and to be forced to leave the city in March, 1555. With his fellow-believers he now made his way once more to Geneva. Thence, in the autumn of the same year, Knox returned to Scotland to spend a few stormy months in premature efforts to establish the Reformation. The close of the summer of 1556, saw him once more in Geneva where he now became the pastor of the English fugitive congregation,—an office which he held till his final and successful return to Scotland in M 1559. The estimate in which he was held by Ca and his Genevan friends is shown by his gratui admission, on June 24, 1558, as a burgher of town,—the records curiously describing him as Scotland in England, English minister in this cit

Knox's return to Scotland was followed by the sl battle for the establishment of Protestantism anc victorious outcome in the summer of 1560. The Kirk of Scotland, erected with such violent overtl of older institutions, and as a consequence of what no less a civil than a religious revolution, was fashi on the model created by Calvin. Its Confes drafted by Knox and his associates in four stren days of August, 1560,[2] was essentially Calvinistic emphasised true preaching, the right administratic the Sacraments, and the characteristic Calvi trait of discipline, as the notes of the Church; it vi the "conservation and purgation" of religion prime duty of civil rulers. The worship of the Sc Church Knox attempted to regulate after the moc the English refugee services in Geneva. Its Presbyt constitution, with the session of minister, elders deacons in each normal congregation, the stated ings which soon developed into "presbyteries,' district "synods," and the "General Assembly

[1] *Opera*, xxi 697.

[2] Schaff, *Creeds of Christendom*, i 680–685, iii 437–479 E and reprobation, though taught, are not made so prominent would probably have been by Calvin. Presbyterianism is *jure divino* polity.

ministers and delegated elders over all, was the application to the whole kingdom of the principles of the *Institutes* as already embodied in the practice of Geneva and of the Huguenot churches of France. If Knox in his "superintendents" retained a prelatical element in his constitution, it was destined to be short-lived. In Scotland, Calvinism was to bear some of its noblest fruits. It proved marvellously adapted to the training of the nation, from the semi-barbarism of pre-Reformation days into the forceful, intelligent, able Scotland of modern history. If the great Reformation upheaval was given its form by the genius of Knox, his work was moulded and made possible by the training and inspiration that flowed from Calvin.

The Genevan reformer followed the course of Knox's work in Scotland with affection for a disciple, as well as with interest in the cause. Knox presented inquiries, signing himself *vobis addictissimus*. In replying, Calvin addressed him as *eximie vir et frater nobis carissime.* He had a word of moderation for Knox's rough-shod impetuosity, but the work as a whole must have been one of thorough satisfaction to Calvin.[1]

Calvin's influence penetrated even earlier to eastern Europe, with much apparent prospect of large results, though with far less permanency and ultimate success than in the countries just considered. In Poland, Calvin's teaching found a prompt hearing, not only as offering the most effective weapon against the strong Roman party, but as more acceptable than anything which savoured of German origin,—a source which the

[1] See letters in *Opera*, xvii. 619, 665; xviii. 434, xix. 74.

Polish leaders viewed with no little jealousy. By 1545, Calvinism was spreading rapidly among the nobles and educated classes of "Little Poland" about Cracow. Calvin's *Institutes* were widely read. In 1549, Calvin dedicated his Commentary on Hebrews to the young king, Sigismund Augustus.[1] The King, who was at heart a very tolerant Catholic, married a sister of Nicolas Radziwill, the leading Calvinist among the nobility. Calvin wrote to Sigismund and to Radziwill in 1554 and 1555, earnestly commending activity in the Reformation cause, and favouring, at least by implication, the retention of an episcopal order in Poland.[2] The next year he was invited to Poland by the Calvinistic ministers and nobles assembled in a synod at Pinczow,—a request to which he returned a regretful refusal in March, 1557.[3] His interest and participation by letter in Polish affairs continued unabated; but the work of organisation which Calvin might have undertaken was carried on from the close of 1556 till ended by death in 1560, by John à Lasco, already distinguished in Friesland and England. It promised much. But, though Calvin did not live to witness its decline, the Protestant cause was soon weakened in Poland by internal quarrels between Lutherans, Calvinists, and Anti-Trinitarians. It never took strong hold upon the lower classes; and, with the exception of à Lasco, never developed a champion of commanding abilities.

---

[1] *Opera*, xiii. 281. See R. N. Bain, in *The Camb. Mod. Hist.*, iii. 74–86, Dalton, in Hauck's *Realencyklopädie*, xv. 514–525.

[2] *Opera*, xv. 329, 428, especially, 333.

[3] *Ibid.*, xvi. 128, 420.

[n yet another region of eastern Europe, Calvinism
:ame a power, though at a somewhat later period
ın in Poland. In Hungary, its appeal was especially
the Magyar element in the population. At a Cal-
ıistic synod held at Czenger in 1557 or 1558, the
ıngarian Confession was drafted; and by 1563, Cal-
ıism was widespread and its characteristic discipline
d organisation introduced.[1] Calvinism in Hungary
s survived the vicissitudes of fierce persecution, and
: adherents of churches Calvinistic in origin and
ɔfession even now number two thirds of the Evan-
lical population of the land, or not far from one
'enth of its inhabitants.

Calvin's most difficult relations were with the churches
German-speaking Switzerland which were his nearest
ighbours. Already established before he began his
ırk, and not in the making, as were those of which
:ntion has been made, they were not easily to be
ɔulded to his ideas. Their constitutions all gave an
:lesiastical authority to the civil magistrates which he
ected in theory, and in practice so far as he was able
Geneva. Bern stood in constant hostility to his
stem of discipline, and never became wholly recon-
ed to his teaching in his lifetime. The freer thought
Basel looked with grave suspicion on his emphasis on
:destination. In Zurich he was long regarded as too
ıch of a Lutheran on the doctrine of the Lord's
pper. Yet he obtained an agreement, in 1549, with
: Zürich divines, led by the peace-loving Bullinger,
this burning question of the Reformation age, that

[1] Schaff, *Creeds of Christendom*, i. 589–592.

paved the way to more friendly relations which resulted ultimately in the general acceptance of Calvin's doctrinal system in essential, if moderate form, though not of his disciplinary peculiarities, by all the Protestant churches of Switzerland. The work of Zwingli was absorbed in the larger and abler development due to Calvin, very much as was the theological system of Bucer.

The agreement between the spiritual leaders of Geneva and of Zurich shows to much advantage the skill and good-feeling of both. Calvin, as has already been pointed out,[1] was far more in sympathy with Luther than with Zwingli in the conception of Christ's presence in the Supper set forth in the first edition of the *Institutes*, though denying to that presence the physical quality which Luther had made so essential. Bullinger, who had succeeded at Zwingli's premature death to the leadership of the Zurich ministry, had departed from Zwingli so far as to lay much greater emphasis than he on the work wrought by Christ through the Sacrament in the believing recipient, and was consequently approaching Calvin's intermediate position between the interpretations of founders of German and Swiss Protestantism. Agreement on this much disputed question was therefore relatively easy; and, after considerable correspondence in 1548 and 1549, supplemented by personal conference, Calvin and Bullinger united, in the year last named, in the Consensus of Zurich.[2]

[1] *Ante*, p 142.

[2] Text, *Opera*, vii 659–748, see also *Ibid.*, xi 480, 590, 705, 727; xiii. 110, 164, 221, 223, 259, 278, Schaff, *Creeds*, i 471–473.

Undoubtedly in this agreement, and in his desire for union, Calvin went as far as he could in the Zwinglian direction. Bullinger's decidedly modified Zwinglianism was substantially unaltered.[1] Any form of physical presence was rejected. But an emphasis wholly agreeable to Calvin, and not objectionable to Bullinger, was laid on the true spiritual union wrought between Christ and the believer by the Sacrament, while a characteristically Calvinistic note was struck in the restriction of the reception of its benefits to the elect. Not printed till 1551, this Consensus was soon accepted not merely by the churches of Geneva and Zurich, but by those of Schaffhausen, St. Gall, Neuchâtel, and Basel, and constituted a bond of theologic union between German and French speaking Switzerland.

Calvin had less success, as has already been noted in speaking of the controversy with Bolsec, in securing prompt acceptance for his uncompromising presentation of the doctrine of a twofold predestination. The Genevan Consensus of 1552 on this matter failed to secure a symbolic authority outside that city.[2] But the doctrine, in Calvin's interpretation of it, even if with some caution in expression, won its way in the Reformed churches; and here, as elsewhere, the master mind of the Genevan reformer tended to bring all non-Lutheran and non-Anglican Protestantism under its sway.[3]

[1] Egli and Heer, in Hauck's *Realencyklopädie*, iii 543, 545

[2] Text, *Opera*, viii 249–366

[3] A discussion of much value is that of Prof B B Warfield, "Predestination in the Reformed Confessions," in the *Presbyterian and Reformed Review*, January, 1901, pp 49–128

The agreement of the Swiss churches on the nature and effects of Christ's presence in the Supper, brought about by the Consensus of Zurich, became the occasion of the bitterest doctrinal controversy of Calvin's later life,—that with the extreme Lutheran, Joachim Westphal of Hamburg, who regarded its denial of Christ's physical presence not merely as a restatement of the hated Zwinglian heresy, but believed that by attacking it he was defending original and pure Lutheranism against secret Melanchthonian modifications. In the bitter exchange of controversial pamphlets that ensued from 1552 to 1557; and again in the dispute on the same thorny doctrine with Tilemann Hesshusen of Heidelberg and Magdeburg in 1560 and 1561,[1] Calvin claimed Melanchthon for his doctrine; and with no little justification, though the cautious German reformer held himself as far as possible from the battle. The struggle gave to Calvin, however, a painful feeling of estrangement from the German Protestants, whose leaders he had earlier known and admired and whose interests he had defended with his pen against the emperor, Charles V.

Though Calvin's relations to the German divines of the stricter Lutheran school thus became increasingly strained during the later years of his life, he had the satisfaction of seeing his theology, though only in a very moderate degree his system of church discipline, begin a career of conquest on German soil that was to be continued long after his death.[2] The bitterness of

[1] *Opera*, ix 1–120, 137–252, 457–524.

[2] An excellent epitome of this theme, with references to its literature, is that of Gustav Kawerau, in the 2nd ed. of Moeller, *Lehrbuch der Kirchengeschichte*, iii 276–292

the attack made by the strict Lutherans upon the Philippists, as the followers of the moderate Melanchthon were styled, drew these milder Lutherans into increasing sympathy with the Genevan reformer. Agreeing at first with Calvin principally in the essential features of his theory of Christ's presence in the Supper, and little inclined to accept his strenuous views of predestination, the exigencies of conflict with their ultra-Lutheran opponents, the force of the *Institutes*, and to some extent the influence of the Genevan Academy in attracting and impressing its students, inclined the Philippist party, especially in south-western Germany, to a growing appreciation of Calvinism. It was in the Palatinate that these results were most evident in Calvin's lifetime.

Frederick III., of the Palatinate, long of earnestly religious temper, was led by the controversies between the extreme Lutheran Tilemann Hesshusen, already mentioned, and the latter's deacon, Wilhelm Klebitz of Heidelberg, to a careful study of theology which left him a convinced Calvinist. He now summoned to his aid two young divines, both personally acquainted with Calvin and Bullinger, Kaspar Olevianus in January, 1560, and Zacharias Ursinus in September of the year following. Olevianus had studied in the Genevan Academy, while Ursinus had been a pupil of Melanchthon at Wittenberg. Both were earnest Calvinists. By these theologians, one twenty-six and the other twenty-eight years of age, with the help of other churchly leaders of the Palatinate, the famous Heidelberg Catechism was prepared in 1562, and set forth by order of the Elector in 1563.[1] Sweet-spirited, experiential, clear, moderate, and happily-phrased, the Heidelberg Catechism has always been regarded as one of the noblest presentations of the Calvinistic system in its least controversial aspects. As such, it is the most widely accepted symbol of the Calvinistic faith. Calvin himself could not possibly have written it; but Olevianus, gratefully recognisant of student days at Geneva and anxious for Calvin's help in the establishment of church-discipline, sent Calvin an early copy, with an affectionate letter in which he addresses the Genevan reformer as "*carissime pater*."[2] Calvin, in turn dedicated his Lectures on Jeremiah, of 1563, to the Elector.[3] The discipline regarding which Olevianus wished Calvin's aid was introduced, though imperfectly in 1570, when elders were ordered in every parish. With greater success public worship was reduced to Genevan simplicity.

Though the Palatinate was carried back to strict Lutheranism under Frederick's son, Lewis IV. (1576–83) and more than five hundred Calvinistic ministers and teachers deprived of office, the tables were turned, and Calvinism restored under Lewis's brother, John Casimir. Calvinism continued to win recognition in Germany long after Calvin's death, gaining Nassau in 1577, a strong footing in Bremen, Anhalt, Baden, and Hesse before the close of the sixteenth century, and in

[1] Text, Schaff, *Creeds*, iii 307–355 See M Lauterburg, in Hauck's *Realencyklopädie*, x 164–173; Schaff, i 529–554.

[2] *Opera*, xix 683, see *Ibid*, 538

[3] *Ibid*, xx. 72

Brandenburg, its most important conquest after that of the Palatinate, in 1613. Yet it was Calvin's theology rather than his discipline that thus won assent, and the observation of a modern German historian that the Calvinistic churches of Germany constituted "an intermediate stage between pure Calvinism and pure Lutheranism"[1] is amply justified.

Calvin for one brief period looked beyond the bounds even of Europe, and shared in an attempt to plant the Evangelical faith in the New World. Like the reformers generally, he was strangely insensitive—so it seems to the modern Christian world—to the claims of missions.[2] But when the treacherous Villegagnon sought to strengthen his ill-fated and mismanaged colony in Brazil, in 1556, by securing Protestant recruits and Protestant preachers, Calvin provided two ministers from Geneva with letters to him and encouraged them on their enterprise, which, though having the spiritual welfare of the settlers primarily in view, did not wholly forget the needs of the natives.[3] The colony was soon ruined by Villegagnon's own duplicity and cruelty, and with it ended Calvin's only direct connection with efforts to establish Protestantism beyond the Atlantic. Calvin's system was to be a powerful influence in moulding the religious history of America. The English Puritans, the Scotch and Irish Presbyterians,

[1] Kawerau, *op cit*, p 277.

[2] *Ibid.*, p 409; G Warneck, in Hauck's *Realencyklopädie*, xiii 127–130; *Ibid.*, *History of Protestant Missions*, Eng. tr, pp 19, 20

[3] See letters of Villegagnon and of the ministers from Brazil to Calvin, March, 1557, *Opera*, xvi 433–443. On the colony, see Parkman, *Pioneers of France in the New World*, pp. 16–27.

the Hollanders, and the Huguenot exiles of France were to establish his faith, and to a large extent his polity, wide over the North American continent; but this work was yet far in the future when he died.

Calvin would gladly have secured a more visible and effective evidence of the spiritual union of Protestantism, and its fellowship in doctrine and in opposition to Rome than proved feasible under the conditions of the sixteenth century. When the English archbishop, Thomas Cranmer, proposed to him, in March, 1552, that a council of learned Protestants should be gathered, to promote the unity of the Evangelical churches, and to offset the Roman council then meeting at Trent, Calvin welcomed the plan with enthusiasm, and declared his readiness to support it to his utmost,[1] but it remained only a pious wish.

In this wide extended influence is to be seen one of Calvin's largest claims to permanent remembrance. He knit the forces of non-Lutheran Protestantism into a real spiritual communion animated by similar ideals and dominated by one view of the Christian life. The ill-related Reformation movements of France, of the Netherlands, of Scotland, to a less degree of Poland and Hungary, found in him their unifying force. He gave them creed, discipline, and organisation. He formulated their theology. He inspired their martyr-courage. He taught them how best to oppose Rome. He trained many of their leaders, provided them a city of refuge in persecution, and an example of a disciplined Christian community which attracted their ad-

[1] Letters in *Opera*, xiv 306, 312.

miration and imitation. Over all this vast region he exercised an unofficial but far-reaching episcopate. By constant correspondence, by personal acquaintance and appeal to those whom he never met face to face, by the labours of those who had been his pupils and reproduced his spirit, he moulded the growth and determined the form of the Reformation movement to a degree comparable with the work of no other among the reformers save Luther. But for him the story of the Reformation outside of the land of its birth would have been vastly different. He has been called a "pope,"[1] but the designation is apt only in its indication of the geographical extent of his authority. That authority was not due to office or peculiar advantage of station. It was purely one of mind over mind. But it was all the more real and long enduring. Calvin so impressed his interpretation of Christian truth and of the Christian life upon men that they thought his thoughts after him, and his ideas became part of the mental fabric of a large portion of the inhabitants of central and western Europe, and ultimately of North America.

The influence of Calvinism, for more than a century after the death of the Genevan reformer, was the most potent force in western Europe in the development of civil liberty. What the modern world owes to it is almost incalculable. Yet Calvin was never by intention a political reformer. His interests were always overwhelmingly religious; and the results of Calvinism in the cause of religious freedom were the indirect and

[1] *E g.* W. H Frere, *The English Church in the Reigns of Elizabeth and James I.*, p. 78.

unexpected, rather than the anticipated consequences of his work. They were the effect of the logic of Calvin's principles, rather than any conscious part of his reformatory aim.

Calvin's views on civil government are succinctly stated in the *Institutes* and come to their fullest expression in the final form of that work issued in 1559. Its object is,[1]—

> that no idolatry, no blasphemy against the name of God, no calumnies against His truth, nor other offences to religion, break out and be disseminated among the people, that the public quiet be not disturbed, that every man's property be kept secure, that men may carry on innocent commerce with each other, that honesty and modesty be cultivated; in short, that a public form of religion may exist among Christians, and humanity among men.

In Calvin's opinion and practice the preservation of religion is an even more important function of the State than the maintenance of order. As to the various types of government, each has its characteristic dangers. No one is absolutely best:[2]—

> Monarchy is prone to tyranny In an aristocracy, again, the tendency is not less to the faction of a few, while in popular ascendancy there is the strongest tendency to sedition

[1] *Inst*, IV xx 3, Beveridge's translation, Edinburgh, 1846 See also W A Dunning, *A History of Political Theories from Luther to Montesquieu*, pp 26–33

[2] *Ibid*, IV. xx 8.

His own preference, characteristic alike of his temperament and of his Genevan environment is for "aristocracy, either pure or modified by popular government"; but no one form is adapted to all times and places, nor ought changes to be agitated, for,[1]—

if it has pleased Him [God] to appoint kings over kingdoms, and senates or burgomasters over free states, whatever be the form which He has appointed in the places in which we live, our duty is to obey and submit

To Calvin's mind the obligation of obedience even to bad rulers is no less complete [2]—

If we have respect to the Word of God, it will lead us farther, and make us subject not only to the authority of those princes who honestly and faithfully perform their duty toward us, but all princes, by whatever means they have so become, although there is nothing they less perform than the duty of princes

Diets and parliaments, indeed, have the duty of restraining the tyranny of unworthy rulers; but the private citizen must submit, save with one fundamentally important exception·[3]—

We are subject to the men who rule over us, but subject only in the Lord. If they command anything

[1] *Inst.*, IV xx. 8.
[2] *Ibid.*, IV. xx. 25
[3] *Ibid*, IV. xx. 32.

against Him, let us not pay the least regard to it, nor be moved by all the dignity which they possess as magistrates

There is little in these utterances of Calvin's mature judgment, except in that last quoted, to stimulate civil freedom, but the principle that when God commands, all obedience to human rulers ceases is of far-reaching influence. It struck a note already sounded by Zwingli, that, more than any other, served to interpret the intellectual individualism of the Renaissance and the religious individualism of the Reformation in terms of political freedom. Who shall decide whether a command of a ruler is contrary to the will of God, if not each thinking man, weighing it by the tests of his own divinely implanted judgment? Calvin formulated no such conclusion; but his principle inevitably tended to make men question the rightfulness of human statutes and institutions, and to demand some other justification for obnoxious laws than the mere fact of their enactment by those in authority.

Calvin's ecclesiastical constitution, moreover, made for civil freedom, especially in the conditions of his age. His insistence that the Church, though served by the State, was yet independent of it, gave a place, as in Scotland and in France, if not so fully in his own Genevan practice, for the development of a system of representative ecclesiastical institutions largely free from State control. In the Scottish General Assembly, for instance, rather than in the Scottish Parliament, was to be found throughout the latter portion of the sixteenth and the whole of the seventeenth centuries the truer embodiment of the wishes and hopes of the people of Scotland. French Protestantism, from 1559 onward, found expression in a series of national synods held in the face of a hostile government.

The system of Church-discipline characteristic of Calvin, executed in the congregation, or in Geneva as the work of the united Church of the city, by an aristocracy of the minister or ministers and his associated lay elders, made every Calvinistic parish a school of government in a sense true of no other communion of the Reformation age; while his principle that officers should serve only with the consent of the congregation over which they were placed, however imperfectly worked out under Genevan conditions, had in it the germ of a real responsibility of ecclesiastical governors to those whom they ruled. Calvin did not carry the principle to its logical consequences; but it is impossible for men long to hold one theory in ecclesiastical and another in civil government. If church-officers are responsible to the people they serve, why not kings and magistrates? Scotland and Puritan England asked the question and wrote the answer large in the history of the seventeenth century. King James I., of England, voiced the results of this aspect of Calvinism, and its effects on such theories of the absolute monarchy as he entertained, when he declared at the Hampton Court Conference in 1604:[1]—

> A Scottish Presbytery as well agreth with a Monarchy, as God and the Devill Then *Jacke*, and *Tom*, and *Will*,

[1] W. Barlow, *The Summe and Substance of the Conference*, London, 1638, p. 81.

and *Dick* shall meet, and at their pleasures censure me and my Councell, and all our proceedings.

Calvin's aristocratic soul might have revolted as much as the Stuart King's from the democratic freedom thus satirised; but it was none the less a natural fruit of his system.

The Calvinistic theory of the Church furnished, moreover, the only effective system in the Reformation age for the organisation of an oppressed Protestant party. Lutheranism, Anglicanism, and Zwinglianism were all dependent upon the State. Calvinism could be effective without state-support, as France, Holland, Scotland, and England were to bear abundant witness. But it was only where Calvinism did its work as a discipline as well as a theology that its services to civil liberty were considerable. Where, as in Germany, its position was that of a representative of a certain type of doctrine, and not also of a peculiar conception of the Christian life, its effect on political thought was inconspicuous.

INTERIOR OF THE "AUDITOIRE."

(Here Calvin taught, the "Congregation" met, and English and Italian refugees worshipped.)

these can no more be disconnected from each other than rays of light from the sun."[1] "The full authority which [the Scriptures] ought to possess with the faithful is not recognised, unless they are believed to have come from heaven, as directly as if God had been heard giving utterance to them."[2] This conviction can, indeed, be fortified by arguments drawn from their arrangement, dignity, truth, simplicity, and efficacy; "still it is preposterous to attempt, by discussion, to rear up a full faith in Scripture." Our confidence "must be derived from a higher source than human conjectures, judgments, or reasons, namely, the secret testimony of the Spirit."[3] The Bible is therefore no arbitrary body of truth to be accepted on the authority of the Church or of external miracles. It approves itself to men by its own clear illumination; by the response of the soul enlightened by the Spirit of God to the voice of the same Spirit speaking through its pages. That testimony carries with it acceptance of all that the Scriptures contain. "Those who are inwardly taught by the Holy Spirit acquiesce implicitly in Scripture."[4] It is no mere Christian consciousness selecting and appropriating truth wherever truth can be found; it is Truth itself awakening recognition of its clear, ample, and final authority in the divinely enlightened soul. In this doctrine of the absolute and unique authority of the Word of God, Calvin stood on ground

[1] III. ii. 6.
[2] I vii 1
[3] I vii. 4.
[4] I. vii. 5.

common to all the reformers; and his teaching as to the immediate witness of the Holy Spirit had been anticipated, though less clearly by Luther;[1] but his presentation of this cardinal principle of the Reformation is the amplest that it had yet received, and may be said to be its classic expression. Far more than Luther, however, Calvin treated the Scriptures as a new law regulative of the Christian life. som.

While God is thus the source of all that is good,[2]
in his present fallen state is in himself wholly ba avail
created in Adam—and Adam with Calvin So long
Augustine is a personage of great signifi Him, noth-
was made in the image of God the salvation of the
endowments and qualities benefit to us." "He must
by "infidelity," dwell in us." He is "our Head."[3]
"ingratitude ng is effected by faith on man's part; but
original, which, as with Paul and Luther, is no mere
ourptance of historic facts or of a system of belief, but
a vital union in a new life between the believer and Christ, is due to nothing in man, but has its origin in "the secret efficacy of the Spirit."[4] Its consequence and inseparable accompaniment is repentance. While genuine disciples may at times be assailed by doubts, "full assurance" is a proper attribute of this faith, doubts must be temporary, and "he only is a true believer who, firmly persuaded that God is reconciled and is a kind Father to him, hopes every thing from

[1] II xvii 1

[2] II xvii 2 Compare G B Stevens, *The Christian Doctrine of Salvation*, pp 153, 154.

[3] III i 1

[4] *Ibid*

His kindness, who, trusting to the promises of the divine favour, with undoubting confidence anticipates salvation."[1]

The consequence of this faith is the Christian life. "Christ cannot be known without the sanctification of His Spirit, therefore faith cannot possibly be disjoined from pious affection."[2] That life, far more than in Luther's conception of it, is one of struggle and effort in which the Law, though no longer the test of acceptance with God, is the stimulus to endeavour. "The whole lives of Christians ought to be a kind of aspiration after piety, seeing they are called unto holiness The office of the Law is to excite them to the study of purity and holiness by reminding them of their duty."[3] Calvin thus saves himself, in spite of his doctrines of election, irresistible grace, and perseverance, from any possible antinomianism. He leaves room for a conception of "works" as strenuous and as effort-demanding as any claimed by the Roman communion, though very different in relation to the accomplishment of salvation. "We are justified not without, and yet not by works, since in the participation of Christ, by which we are justified, is contained not less sanctification than justification."[4] "If the end of election is holiness of life, it ought to arouse and stimulate us strenuously to aspire to it, instead of serving as a pretext for sloth."[5]

Calvin is next confronted by the evident fact that

[1] III ii 15, 16

[2] III ii 8.

[3] III xix. 2.

[4] III xvi. 1.

[5] III. xxiii 12.

men are very unlike in their reception of the Gospe "Among a hundred to whom the same discourse is de livered, twenty, perhaps, receive it with the promp obedience of faith; the others set no value upon it, o deride, or spurn, or abominate it."[1] Holding, as Cal vin does, that all good is from God, and viewing mai as helpless to initiate or resist his conversion, Calvii can but ascribe this dissimilarity to "the mere pleasure of God." He was not peculiar in this view. The Reformation age was markedly one of revived Augus tinianism. In its essential features the doctrine of election had been equally the property of Luther and Zwingli. Melanchthon, under the influence of his belief in the power of the human will to co-operate with or resist the divine leadings, was swinging away from it, and was ultimately to lead the Lutheran churches in the direction that he pointed out; but an acceptance of predestination was widely characteristic of the theology of the age. Yet the use which Calvin made of the doctrine is far more vital than that of Luther, for example. To Luther the prime question was always, how are men saved? When he asked why, and he did not often ask the question, he gave the Augustinian answer. To Calvin, as to Bucer before him, the problem of the origin of salvation was of much more fundamental importance, and this significance was strengthened by his controversies with Bolsec. Yet it is an error to describe predestination as the "central doctrine" of Calvinism,[2]

[1] III xxiv 12

[2] A Schweizer, *Die protestantischen Centraldogmen*, i 57; see R. Seeberg, *Lehrbuch der Dogmengeschichte*, ii 397.

though it became so under his successors and interpreters. Its prime value for him was always its comfort as giving assurance of salvation to the Christian believer.

Calvin advanced beyond Augustine in two ways. The great African theologian had represented God as active in election to life only. The lost were simply passed by and left to the deserved consequences of sin. To Calvin's thinking, election and reprobation are both alike manifestations of the divine activity. In Augustine's estimate, not all believers even are given the grace of perseverance. With Calvin all in whom God has begun the work of salvation would have it brought to complete fruition. Calvin's severe logic, insistent that all salvation is independent of merit, led him to assert that damnation is equally antecedent to and independent of demerit. The lost do indeed deserve their fate; but "if we cannot assign any reason for His bestowing mercy on His people, but just that it so pleases Him, neither can we have any reason for His reprobating others but His will." The sole cause of salvation or of loss is the divine choice.[1]—

> The will of God is the supreme rule of righteousness, so that everything which He wills must be held to be righteous by the mere fact of His willing it. Therefore, when it is asked why the Lord did so, we must answer, Because He pleased. But if you proceed further to ask why He pleased, you ask for something greater and more sublime than the will of God, and nothing such can be found

[1] III. xxii. 11; xxiii. 2.

Whether this Scotist doctrine of the rightfulness of all that God wills by the mere fact of His willing it leaves God a moral character it is perhaps useless to inquire. The thesis here advocated has always had its earnest supporters and its determined critics. But of the comfort which Calvin and his disciples drew from the doctrine of election there can be no question. To a persecuted Protestant of Paris it must have been an unspeakable consolation to feel that God had a plan of salvation for him, individually, from all eternity, and that nothing that priest or king could do could frustrate the divine purpose in his behalf. Nor was it less a source of strength to one profoundly conscious of his own sinfulness to feel that his salvation was based on the unshakable rock of the decree of God Himself. Reprobation, too, gave an explanation for the hostility of rulers to the Evangelical cause, and for the great number of those who, in that age, as in any epoch, were notoriously irreligious of life. Calvin was far too politic a man to suggest that a Henry II. or a Catherine de' Medici were of the reprobate; but it must have been a grim satisfaction for those under their persecuting sway to believe that they and others like them "were raised up by the just but inscrutable judgment of God, to show forth His glory by their condemnation."[1]

Calvin's doctrine of the Church has often come under our notice in this volume. It is the means by which we are nourished in the Christian life. "To those to whom [God] is a Father, the Church must also be a

[1] III. xxiv. 14.

mother."[1] Following the line already marked out by Wyclif, Huss, and Zwingli, Calvin defines the Church in the last analysis as "all the elect of God, including in the number even those who have departed this life."[2] But, besides its application to this invisible fellowship, the name "Church" is properly used of "the whole body of mankind scattered throughout the world who profess to worship one God and Christ, who by baptism are initiated into the faith, by partaking of the Lord's Supper profess unity in true doctrine and charity, agree in holding the Word of the Lord, and observe the ministry which Christ has appointed for the preaching of it."[3] Whoever alienates himself from it is a "deserter of religion." Yet to leave the Papacy is in no sense to leave the Church, for "it is certain that there is no Church where lying and falsehood have usurped the ascendency."[4] Calvin admits, however, that even in the Roman communion some vestiges of the Church exist, though in ruins.

This visible Church is properly governed only by officers of divine appointment made known in the New Testament. These are pastors, teachers, elders, and deacons,—partly clerical and partly lay office-bearers, for in Calvin's system the recognition of the rights of the layman, characteristic of the whole Reformation movement, comes to its completest development. This recognition receives further illustration in that the offi-

[1] IV. i. 1.
[2] IV. i. 2.
[3] IV. i. 7.
[4] IV. ii. 1.

cers of the Calvinistic churches, unlike those of the Roman, Anglican, Lutheran, and Zwinglian communions, properly enter on their charges only with the assent of the congregation that they serve. Their "call" is twofold,—the secret inclination which has God as its author, and their election "on the consent and approbation of the people."[1] Peculiar circumstances at Geneva disposed Calvin to regard that "consent of the people" as there expressed by the city government; but elsewhere, especially where Calvinism was face to face with hostile civil authority, the system developed its more normal form.

One main object of the establishment of church-officers is discipline, the importance of which in the Calvinistic system, as contrasted with other theories of the Church current in the Reformation age, there has been frequent occasion to point out. "As the saving doctrine of Christ is the life of the Church, so discipline is, as it were, its sinews." It "is altogether distinct from civil government"; and belongs "to the consistory of elders, which [is] in the Church what a council is in a city." "The legitimate course to be taken in excommunication . . . is not for the elders alone to act apart from others, but with the knowledge and approbation of the Church, so that the body of the people, without regulating the procedure, may, as witnesses and guardians, observe it, and prevent the few from doing anything capriciously."[2]

This ecclesiastical independence which Calvin em-

[1] IV iii. 15

[2] IV. xi. 1, 6, xii. 1, 7.

phasised more than any other of the reformers and for which he fought with such intensity and persistence at Geneva, was very far, however, from implying that civil government had no duties toward the Church. Minister and magistrate were alike charged with the administration of government in the name of God. Further than excommunication the Church could not go. When that failed or was insufficient for the enormity of the offence, as in case of flagrant heresy or crime, the magistrate, as equally charged with maintaining the honour of God, must apply his civil penalties. His duty it was to defend, support, and care for the Church, though in its proper sphere the Church was to be independent of his control. Calvin thus took up into his system the characteristic theory of the middle ages regarding this matter, carefully guarding it, however, from becoming, as the mediæval contention too often was, an assertion of the supremacy of the Church over the State. It was to become the view of Puritanism and to have ample illustration, for instance, in the early history of New England.

Characteristic of Calvin is his doctrine of the Sacraments, and of the Lord's Supper in particular. Nowhere was his desire for the union of divided Protestantism more evident than in the treatment of these vexed questions, in spite of the heat of his later polemic with Westphal and Hesshusen.[1] He stood, as has already been pointed out, in an intermediate position between Luther and Zwingli. To Calvin the value of a sacrament is that of a seal attesting God's grace. "It

[1] *Ante*, p. 398.

is an external sign, by which the Lord seals on our consciences His promises of goodwill toward us, in order to sustain the weakness of our faith, and we in turn testify our piety towards Him."[1] Baptism "is a kind of sealed instrument by which He assures us that all our sins are so deleted, covered, and effaced that they will never come into His sight."[2] The benefit is not wrought by the sacrament itself, it accompanies it, and is received only by the predestinate. "From this sacrament, as from all others, we gain nothing, unless in so far as we receive in faith." To them it is a perpetual witness to forgiveness, so that there is no room for the Roman doctrine of penance. "The godly may, ... whenever they are vexed by a consciousness of their sins, recall the remembrance of their baptism, that they may thereby assure themselves of that sole and perpetual ablution which we have in the blood of Christ."[3] The rite, Calvin argues at great length, and with much use of the analogy of circumcision, is to be administered to infants as well as to those of years of intelligence.

In Calvin's conception, as in that of the Roman and Lutheran communions, whatever else the Lord's Supper may signify, it is "a spiritual feast, at which Christ testifies that He Himself is living bread on which our souls feed for a true and blessed immortality."[4] The

[1] IV xiv 1 See a most valuable brief treatment of Calvin's views in Seeberg, *Lehrbuch der Dogmengeschichte*, ii 401–409.

[2] IV xv 1

[3] IV xv 4, 15

[4] IV. xvii. 1.

heart of the discussion in the Reformation age was, however, as to the nature of Christ's presence in this sacrament. Luther had insistently asserted, in substantial agreement with the older Church, that that presence is physical. Zwingli rejected all physical presence, made the chief value of the Supper its memorial character, and reduced the nourishment of the participating soul to a stimulation of faith in His death for us. To Calvin's thinking, as to Zwingli's, it seemed impossible that Christ's physical body could be at the same time in heaven and in many places on earth. "Let no property be assigned to His body inconsistent with His human nature."[1] But Calvin's religious feeling revolted, no less than Luther's, from any representation that did not imply a true presence of Christ in the Supper and that "only makes us partakers of the spirit, omitting all mention of flesh and blood." "By the symbols of bread and wine, Christ, His body and His blood, are truly exhibited to us."[2] Yet this participation is spiritual and by faith. "It is enough for us, that Christ, out of the substance of His flesh, breathes life into our souls, nay, diffuses His own life into us, though the real flesh of Christ does not enter us."[3] Christ "breathes" into the disciple "power"; He "feeds" him. But only the disciple receives. "I deny," said Calvin, "that it can be eaten without the taste of faith, or, (if it is more agreeable to speak with Augustine,) I deny that men carry away

[1] IV. xvii 19

[2] IV. xvii 7, 11.

[3] IV. xvii. 32.

more from the sacrament than they collect in the vessel of faith."[1] Calvin's relations to Luther and Zwingli have been well defined by a recent writer:[2]—

> If one asks whether Calvin's doctrine approaches nearer to Luther or to Zwingli, the decision is usually rendered, through credal interests, in favour of the latter. But if one observes that, in contrast to the purely subjective commemorative interpretation of Zwingli, Calvin accepts a special presence of the living Christ, together with the religious inworking thereby caused, in the manner of Luther, we may, nevertheless, conclude,—while recognising the permanent dissimilarity,—that in religious comprehension of the sacrament Calvin stands nearer to Luther than to Zwingli.

The doctrinal positions just enumerated contain the main emphases and chief peculiarities of Calvin's theology, though they by no means exhaust the round of his teaching. On such themes as the judgment, the resurrection, or future rewards and punishments, he stood on the common basis of the religious thought of his age, and had little, if anything, novel to offer for their elucidation.

In Calvin's exposition the theology of the Reformation age rose to a clearness and dignity of statement and a logical precision of definition that have never been surpassed. A logician of critical acumen, a lawyer by training, a master of Latin and of French expression, a

[1] IV xvii 33

[2] Seeberg, *op cit*, ii 404.

humanist, a student of history and of Christian antiquity, Calvin brought to the service of Christian theology gifts which must always make the *Institutes* a classic presentation of doctrine. But to recognise the transcendent qualities of his work is by no means to assert its perpetuity. His system has been no exception to the general rule of modification and supersession which seems essential to all progress even in the apprehension of the deepest of Christian verities. Calvin's system has stood the test of time better than most expositions of religious truth, but it has suffered a general attrition, and though the degrees in which its various aspects are now rejected are very unequal, it is nowhere held in its pristine integrity; while the larger part of the Protestant world, even in the churches which most honour his memory, has turned far aside from it.

Most universally abandoned is Calvin's conception of the duty of civil rulers to guard the purity of the Church. A trial like that of Servetus has happily long been impossible; and the first name on the list of subscribers to Servetus's monument at Geneva is that of the Consistory of the present Genevan Church which traces its historic continuity from his foundation. His doctrines of election and reprobation aroused profound dissent in the early seventeenth century, and Arminianism preserves the memory and the results of the protest then initiated; and even where these explanations of God's ways with men are nominally maintained they are held in reality with far less than his rigour and with little of his sense of satisfaction. His valuation of discipline has been wholly rejected. No modern Christian community would tolerate the iron inquisitorial rule which he laid on Geneva; and discipline, even in its milder forms, instead of being thought of as a prime duty of the ministerial office is now regarded as one of the most difficult and seldom-to-be-employed means of Christian edification.

More widely accepted in theory, perhaps, but none the less generally abandoned by modern Christian thinking, is his view of human nature as utterly depraved. The appeal of evangelists and the training of the Sunday School and of the catechetical class alike now addresses itself to those whom they regard as indeed enfeebled by sin and in grievous need of divine aid, but not hopelessly incapable of turning to or of accepting the light. Much modern thinking, in churches which still regard Calvin as their spiritual ancestor, denies that men are, even in their worst state, other than wandering children of God, needing to be made conscious of their sonship, but in no sense useful in their destruction only. Nor has the modern Christian world followed Calvin in confining all revelation to the Scriptures. The protest begun by the Quakers in the seventeenth century has become common property. The thought of the Reformation age that a God who rules the world by the constant activity of His providence, and whose Spirit works how and when and where He will, has yet confined all revelation to long closed Scriptures is recognised as inconsistent. The light is seen to have been and to be much more widely diffused than Calvin imagined, and to have shone not merely in ages but among peoples who, to his thinking, had been consigned by God's decree to utter darkness.

Nor is Calvin's estimate of the Scriptures themselves that of the modern Christian world. Their writers are almost nowhere now viewed as "amanuenses" of the Holy Spirit. The human element in them, though in very varying degrees of apportionment, is everywhere recognised as real. A degree of progress in revelation, of which he never dreamed, is universally admitted. With many even their inspiration, in the sense in which he understood it, is denied. His interpretation of patriarch, psalmist, and prophet is inconsistent with that evolutionary philosophy under the light of which the present age believes that it has come to truer and worthier views of man's religious development. His ideal Adam, so marvellous in endowments, and so fateful in relation to the race, has been very generally relegated to the legendary explanations of the origin of evil; his restriction of salvation to those under the light of the Gospel little accords with the modern sense of the extent of the divine compassion. His theory of the Atonement gives to it a significance as a penal satisfaction now widely abandoned. His emphasis on the sovereignty of God has been increasingly displaced by a clearer conception of the divine Fatherhood.

To the present Christian world Calvin's representations of the divine dealings with men seem not without considerable elements of hardness and even of cruelty. That they so appear, is, it may be hoped, to be ascribed to clearer apprehensions of the Gospel and of the message, life, and significance of Christ.

But while Calvin's system as a whole can no longer command the allegiance it once claimed, its value in the progress of Christian thought is not to be minimised or forgotten. It laid a profound emphasis on Christian intelligence. Its appeal was primarily to the intellect, and it has trained a sturdy race of thinkers on the problems of the faith wherever it has gone. It has been the foe of popular ignorance, and of shallow, emotional, or sentimental views of Christian truth. Equally significant as an educative force has been its insistence on the individual nature of salvation. A personal relation of each man to God, a definite divine plan for each life, a value for the humblest individual in the God-appointed ordering of the universe, are thoughts which, however justly the social rather than the individual aspects of Christianity are now being emphasised, have demonstrated their worth in Christian history. Yet perhaps the crowning historic significance of Calvinism is to be seen in its valuation of character. Its conception of the duty to know and do the will of God, not, indeed, as a means of salvation, but as that for which we are elected to life, and as the only fitting tribute to the "honour of God" which we are bound to maintain, has made of the Calvinist always a representative of a strenuous morality. In this respect Calvin's system has been like a tonic in the blood, and its educative effects are to be traced in the lands in which it has held sway even among those who have departed widely from his habit of thought. The spiritual indebtedness of western Europe and of North America to the educative influence of Calvin's theology is well-night measureless.

# CHAPTER XVI

## CALVIN'S LAST DAYS.—HIS PERSONAL TRAITS AND CHARACTER

AS has already been pointed out, Calvin's position in Geneva was absolutely assured from the time of the defeat of the Perrinists in 1555. Whatever dangers thenceforth threatened him and his system were from without the city, not from within. He had triumphed within its walls. His conception of a city obedient to the will of God in Church and State, served by an educated body of ministers, disciplined by ecclesiastical watch and strict magisterial supervision, and taught by excellent schools had been largely realised. Not but that there was much for the Consistory to reprove and for the Little Council to punish in the lives of the citizens. The iron discipline and drastic inquisitionary inspection of Genevan morals were now given their fullest development; but the ideal of a perfected society for which Calvin had striven was now clear, and, to many, seemed to have been more fully realised than at any previous time in Christian History. Geneva stood in the thought of a large section of Evangelical Christendom as a model Christian commonwealth.[1]

[1] Calvin's last days are well described by Colladon and Beza, who were contemporary witnesses, *Opera*, xxi 95–118, 160–172 A careful, though too critical, estimate is that of Kampschulte, ii 354–387;

Calvin was now almost universally honoured by the inhabitants of the city not only as its most eminent resident, but as a well-nigh infallible interpreter of that Word of God which the new generation of citizens had been taught by him to regard as the ultimate law of public and private conduct and belief. By his critics outside of Geneva he was called its "pope," "king" or "calif." A simple-minded refugee, who spoke of him as "Brother Calvin," was quickly reminded that in Geneva "Master Calvin" was the only fitting form of address.[1] His voice oftenest spoke the disciplinary sentences of the Consistory. It was he who expressed the wishes and the criticisms of the ministers to the Little Council. He was largely consulted in affairs of State. His advice greatly influenced the political relations of the city.

Yet Calvin's ripened fame and power brought no change in title or in official position. He was still simply one of the city pastors, a preacher at Saint-Pierre, and a teacher of theology. His clothing was very plain, his house scantily furnished for one in his station.[2] Though considerable sums of money passed through his hands, especially in the form of gifts for needy refugees, his administration was to the utmost scrupulous, he refused presents even from the city government, and his

and full, though over-laudatory, accounts are those of E Stähelin, *Johannes Calvin*, ii 365–471, and Adolf Zahn, *Die beiden letzten Lebensjahre von J Calvin*, Leipzig, 1895

[1] Kampschulte, ii 376, 387

[2] Colladon, *Opera*, xxi 113. An inventory of the furniture allowed him by the city, made in 1548, may be found, *Ibid.*, xiii 135 The whole matter is carefully discussed by Doumergue, iii. 491–508

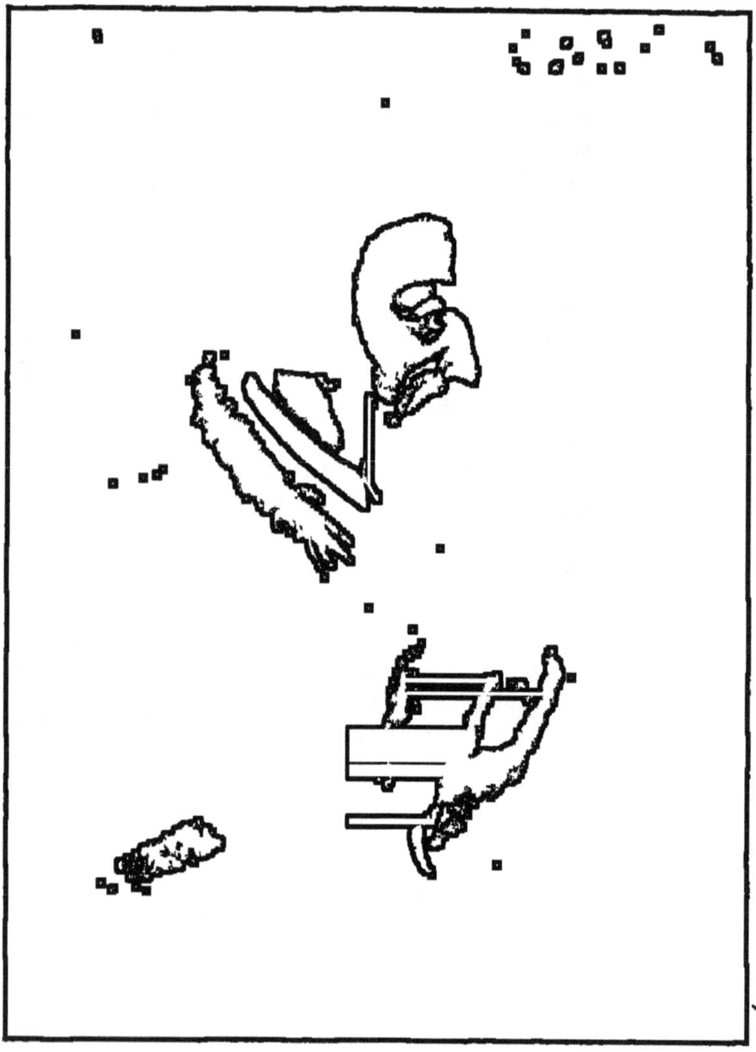

CALVIN PREACHING OR TEACHING.

salary barely sufficed to meet the very modest demands of his own living and the cost of a freely bestowed but exceedingly simple hospitality. His whole estate amounted to less than two hundred *écus*, the equivalent in value perhaps from fifteen hundred to two thousand dollars, including the worth of his library.[1] He had enough, however, for his modest wants and was satisfied with his thoroughly unostentatious *ménage*

In personal appearance, Calvin "was of medium height, of a rather pale and dark complexion, with eyes clear even to his death, which evidenced the sagacity of his mind." Greatly emaciated in later life by illness, his face was little changed to the last.[2] The slight figure, with the strongly marked features, broad, high forehead, bright eyes, and rather scanty beard, must always have carried an impression of scholarly refinement; but Calvin's chief graces were those of the intellect and spirit,—vivacity, clarity, impressive earnestness, keen penetration, felicitous and striking characterisation. Men felt an intellectual and moral masterfulness in him, perhaps the more strongly because its physical embodiment so imperfectly bespoke its greatness. Calvin's capacity for work was prodigious. When not in extreme ill-health,[3]—

he preached every day of each alternate week; he lectured three times each week on theology, he was at the Consistory

[1] Colladon, *Opera*, xxi 113, see also, the notes of the Strassburg editors, *Ibid.*, xx. 301, and Doumergue, iii. 481–483. Calvin's will named 225 *écus* of bequests

[2] Colladon, *Ibid*, xxi 105; Beza, *Ibid*, p. 169.

[3] Colladon, *Ibid.*, p. 66.

on the appointed day, and spoke all the remonstrances; what he added at the Conference on the Scriptures every Friday which we call the Congregation, . . was equal to a lecture; he was not neglectful in the visitation of the sick, in special remonstrances, and in other innumerable concerns having to do with the ordinary exercise of his ministry.

Beza reckoned his sermons at two hundred and eighty-six annually and his lectures as only a hundred less in number.[1] To these must be added his constant work on his *Institutes* and other theological treatises, his long and frequent consultations with those who sought his counsel, and above all his correspondence, some account of the voluminous extent of which has already been given.[2] Such a multiplicity of duties left scanty opportunity for special preparation. He worked with great rapidity, and, even in expository lectures, took nothing but the text of the Scriptures into the desk. Here his retentive memory stood him in good stead. All that he had ever read was at ready command. Nor was he less observant of men Though he mingled little in familiar intercourse with the people of Geneva, and must have been to most of them rather a remote and awe-inspiring figure, he constantly surprised his associates in the Consistory by his recollection of past offenders and his minute accuracy as to previous censures. A large proportion of his letters and of his scholarly writing was dictated, and interruptions seemed rarely to break the chain of his thought or compelled

[1] Kampschulte, ii. 376, from Beza, *Tract theol*, ii. 353.
[2] *Ante*, p. 378

him to read over what he had said before the visit or the new demand upon his attention compelled the suspension of his task.[1]

While he could at times display much oratorical skill, as in the crisis of December, 1547, of which some account has already been given,[2] Calvin in general spoke with great simplicity, brevity, and directness. He avoided rhetorical ornament. Clarity and logical strength added an intellectual impressiveness to the weight of his thought, while his evident earnestness of conviction lent an emotional force to his quiet delivery. He spoke slowly, and could therefore easily be followed by those who would take notes. Much of his work as a commentator owed its preservation to the zeal of his auditors, who wrote from his oral delivery what he afterwards prepared for the press.[3] His sermons and lectures always commanded a crowded congregation.

Calvin kept long hours in his study. "He slept little", by five or six in the morning his books were brought to him in bed and his amanuensis was ready. Much of the morning, even on days on which he preached, he lay on his couch, believing a recumbent position better for his weak digestion; but always at work. After the single meal which constituted his daily repast in the latter part of his life, he would walk for a quarter of an hour, or at most for twice that time, in his room and then return to the labours of the study. Sometimes, chiefly when urged by his friends, he would

[1] Colladon, *Opera*, xxi. pp. 108, 109

[2] *Ante*, p 309

[3] *Opera*, xxi. 70, 132, xxix 238, Kampschulte, ii. 376–378.

play a simple game, quoits in his garden, or "clef" on the table in his living-room.[1] He was not indisposed to good-humoured chaffing. He was not insensible to a pleasant garden or a cheerful outlook from his windows. But his few recreations were briefly enjoyed.

Calvin's acquaintance was vast, but his intimate friends were few. With Farel, Viret, and Bullinger he remained for years in constant correspondence. Beza was to him as a son in his last days.[2] His brother Antoine, the Colladons, Trie, des Gallars, Michel Cop, Laurent de Normandie, a few of the refugees and magistrates, enjoyed his full confidence. His fascination of manner for his friends was always marked. If he had none of the genial *bonhomie* of Luther, he was no misanthrope. His comparative isolation of spirit was that of a man oppressed with multitudinous burdens, compelled to husband his strength to the utmost, of aristocratic tastes, and with little leisure or inclination for anything which did not bear on the accomplishment of his task. With his few familiar friends, however, he stood on terms of cordial intimacy

From the time of his prolonged illness in the autumn and winter of 1558–59, Calvin's health, never vigorous at best, and long undermined by overwork, anxiety and want of exercise, was evidently gravely impaired. That illness left its mark in a lameness that at times involved

[1] Colladon, *Opera*, xxi pp 109, 113 Doumergue, iii 527–563, has made the utmost possible of this side of Calvin's character In the game of "clef" the keys were pushed on a table, the aim being to bring each contestant's nearest to the further edge without falling off

[2] "*Optimus ille meus parens*," Beza styled him Letter to Bullinger, March 6, 1564, *Opera*, xx 261

distress; and a yet more serious sequence was manifest in pulmonary hemorrhages. The severe indigestion from which he had suffered since the days when he was an unsparing student at Paris and Orléans now increased so as to compel the rigidly abstemious diet, the long hours on the bed, and the semi-invalid life of which some account has been given. His old enemy, protracted headaches, doubtless the result of his digestive weakness, often attacked him.[1] By 1563, Calvin's feeble frame was rapidly breaking. In the autumn he was for two months confined to the house. His indigestion was now marked by severe attacks of colic. He suffered from renal calculus and gout; and other distressing symptoms appeared.[2] He still laboured at his books and correspondence, he still preached and lectured; but with increasing difficulty. The brave spirit was master of the feeble body and he was carried to the familiar pulpit in a chair, when no longer able to walk But a shortness of breath that seemed to his contemporaries an indication of advancing pulmonary tuberculosis was now manifest. On February 2, 1564, he lectured for the last time in the Academy; four days later he preached his last sermon. For a little longer he attended the Friday "Congregation" where he was not obliged to speak at length. On March 27th, he was carried to the City Hall and appeared before the Little

[1] *E g* letter of October 14, 1560, to Bullinger, *Opera*, xviii. 217, Colladon, *Opera*, xxi 89, 94

[2] Calvin himself gave a minute account of his symptoms in a letter of February, 1564, to the physicians of Montpellier, *Ibid.*, xx 252, see, also, Colladon, *Ibid*, xxi 94 Doumergue discusses them fully, iii. 509–526.

Council to present his friend, Nicolas Colladon, as rector of the School. At the April communion, which fell on the second, he was present, borne in a chair, and not only partook of the consecrated elements, but joined in singing the psalm as much as his feeble voice would permit.[1]

Calvin felt that his end was near. He was ready and even eager to go. "Lord, how long!" was the exclamation constantly on his lips. He seemed continually in prayer.[2] On April 25th, he made his will, leaving most of his little property to his brother, Antoine, and Antoine's children, but remembering the School and the relief of poor strangers.[3] Two days later, the Little Council appeared before him in his sick-room, and heard from the familiar voice a characteristic exhortation, expressive of gratitude for what they had done for him, of friendship, and of desire for forgiveness for any faults and excess of vehemence on his part; but pointing out clearly their short-comings, since "each has his imperfections," and urging humble dependence upon God.[4] The day following he received the Genevan ministers, and spoke to them a farewell remarkable for its biographic allusions:[5]—

When I first came to this Church it had well-nigh nothing There was preaching and that is all. The idols were sought

[1] Colladon, *Opera*, xxi pp 96–98, Beza, *Ibid*, p 161.

[2] *Ibid.*, pp. 96, 104

[3] In French, *Opera*, xx 298, in Latin, *Ibid.*, xxi. 162, in English trans, Schaff, vii 828

[4] *Opera*, ix. 887, xxi 164, Schaff, vii 831

[5] *Opera*, ix. 891; xxi 166, Schaff, vii 833

out and burned; but there was no reformation. All was in confusion. That good man Master Guillaume [Farel] and the blind Coraud were indeed here. . . . I have lived in marvellous combats here I have been saluted in mockery of an evening by fifty or sixty gun-shots before my door. Fancy how that could shock a poor student, timid as I am and as I confess I have always been. After that I was hunted from this city and betook myself to Strassburg. Having dwelt there some time, I was recalled, but I had no less difficulty than before in seeking to fulfil my office. They set dogs on me, crying, "Scoundrel," and my cloak and legs were seized. I went to the Council of Two Hundred when they were fighting,[1] . . . and when I entered they said to me, "Sir, withdraw, it is not with you we have to do." I said to them, "No, I shall not! Go on, rascals, kill me and my blood will witness against you, and even these benches will require it." . . . I have had many faults which you have had to endure, and all that I have done is of no value. The wicked will seize upon that word, but I repeat that all that I have done is of no value, and that I am a miserable creature. But, if I may say so, I have meant well, my faults have always displeased me, and the root of the fear of God has been in my heart. You can say that the wish has been good; and I beg you that the ill be pardoned, but if there has been good in it that you will conform to it and follow it.

As concerns my doctrine· I have taught faithfully, and God has given me grace to write. I have done it with the utmost fidelity, and have not to my knowledge corrupted or twisted a single passage of the Scriptures; and when I could have drawn out a far-fetched meaning, if I had studied subtilty, I have put that [temptation] under foot and have

[1] He refers to the tumult of December, 1547, *ante*, p. 309.

always studied simplicity. I have written nothing through hatred against any one, but have always set before me faithfully what I have thought to be for the glory of God.

These are the words of one already much broken by illness, dwelling in memory on the perils of the past, which had burned their bitterness into his soul; but they speak forth Calvin's characteristic humility before God, his conscious rectitude toward men, and his ruling motive to exalt the divine will. The sensitive, easily wounded spirit, and the unbending determination of purpose, so curiously combined in him, equally appear in them.

From this farewell address to his ministerial associates to his death nearly a month elapsed. On May 2d, Calvin wrote to his well-tried friend Farel the last letter he was ever to send to any correspondent.[1]—

Farewell, best and truest brother. If God wills that you remain the survivor, live mindful of our union, which has been useful to the Church of God, so that its fruit abides for us in heaven. I am unwilling that you weary yourself for my sake, for I draw breath with difficulty, and constantly await its failing me. It is enough that I live and die unto Christ, who is gain to those who are His in life and in death. Again, farewell, [to you] together with the brethren.

In spite of the infirmities of age,[2] of which Calvin showed such tender consideration in this letter, Farel

[1] *Opera*, xx. 302

[2] Farel was seventy-five; but seemed older to his friends, *e.g.* Colladon, *Opera*, xxi. 103.

could not let his younger associate pass from earthly companionship without looking upon Calvin's face once more. He hastened from Neuchâtel, visited and supped with Calvin, and preached, under the burden of his grief, to the people of Geneva. But the sands of Calvin's life had not yet quite run out. On May 19th, the day when the Genevan ministers fulfilled the curious quarterly duty of mutual criticism which Calvin had made part of the ecclesiastical constitution, he had them assemble at his house, was carried to them in a chair, spoke briefly with them, and feebly tried to join in the common meal with which it was the amicable custom to close the trying session. It was a final effort to discharge his ministerial duty and to express his fraternal regard. He never rose from his bed again.

On Saturday, May 27, 1564, about eight in the evening, the end came. Conscious and intelligent to the last, he fell peacefully asleep. The next day, as the *Ordonnances* provided,[1] they buried his body about two in the afternoon, wrapped in a shroud and encased in a plain wooden coffin, without pomp or elaborate ceremony "in the common cemetery called Plain-palais," his grave being marked by a simple mound like that of his humbler associates in death. It was his wish that his burial should be thus modest, and that no gravestone should mark his resting-place; but he could not prevent, nor would he have desired to prevent, the spontaneous outpourings of the inhabitants of Geneva, pastors, professors, magistrates, and citizens, to do him

[1] *Opera*, xa. 27.

honour at his burial.[1] And there in some now undeterminable spot in the ancient Genevan acre of God rests all that was mortal of the reformer.

Calvin was not fifty-five years of age. The thought is natural that his career was prematurely cut short, and that had he lived he might have done much more. Yet, to a degree unusual even in the experience of long-lived men, his was already a completed work, and it may well be doubted whether a score of years of added life would have increased materially its power and significance. His theological system had long been complete. His conceptions of the Church and of its relations to the State had not merely long been familiar to the public, but had been as fully realised in Genevan practice as it was possible to anticipate that they would ever be. His system of discipline was in high efficiency. The Genevan schools had been crowned by the Academy. His ideal of the Reformation had become that of a large part of western Europe, and had extended to Germany, Poland, and Hungary; but its guidance had passed beyond the control of any one man, however gifted. Even in Geneva, it was probably desirable that the further direction of the ecclesiastical life of the city should come under more conciliatory leadership. The battle had been fought, as he alone could fight it. Another, devoted to his ideals but less warlike, such as Beza, could now better maintain what had been won. Calvin's work was essentially finished.

Calvin's character is one of lights and shadows. He

[1] Colladon, *Opera*, xxi 106; Beza, *Ibid.*, p 169 A comparatively modern stone bearing the letters J C. has been placed as a memorial.

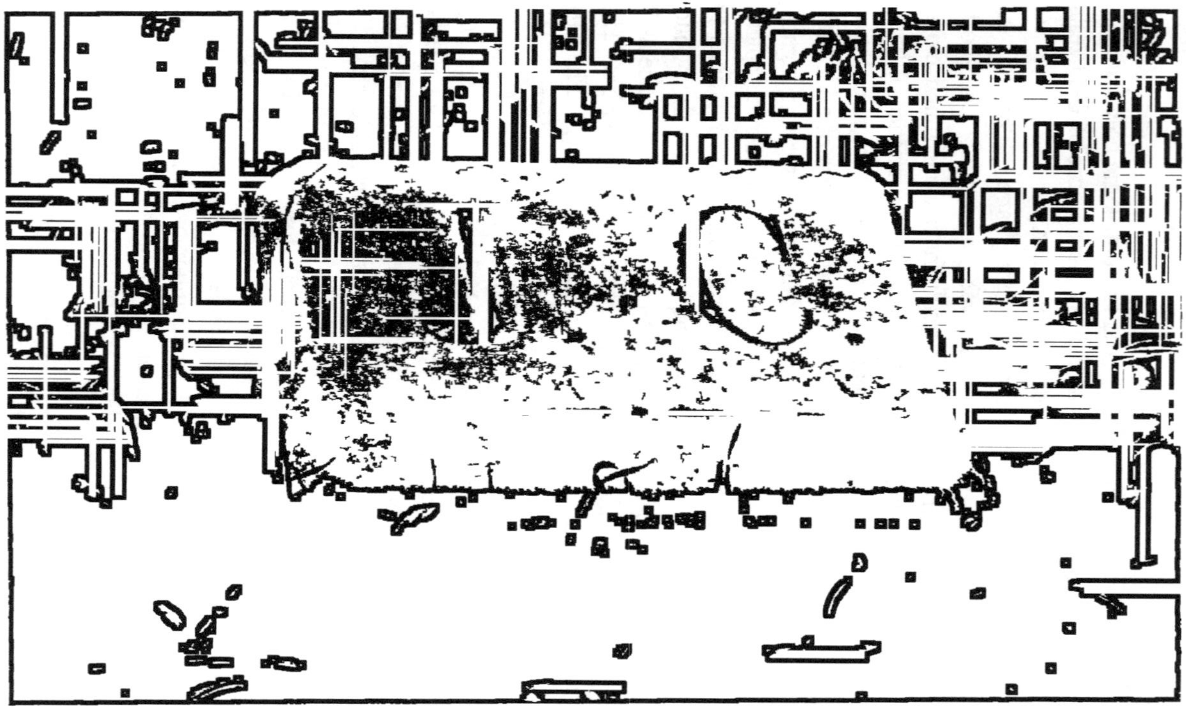

STONE COMMEMORATIVE OF CALVIN IN THE CEMETERY OF PLAIN-PALAIS.

(The exact place of his burial is unknown.)

was the
was a
native
advoca
made a
develop
him:[1]—

Few
oped m
and so
showed
phasise
and th
virtues
an exe
incisive
nation.
through
of theo
to orga
the pr
the rel
while
the reg
sinning
able a
and es
substitu
that cl
of Chri

[1] A. M

was the son of his age and of the land of his birth. He was a lawyer by training. With the clarity of mind native to the Frenchman, he combined the skill of the advocate and the reverence for system of the jurist. He made all his experiences and learning tributary to his development. As a recent biographer has well said of him.[1]—

> Few men may have changed less; but few also have developed more. Every crisis in his career taught him something, and so enhanced his capacity His studies of Stoicism showed him the value of morals; and he learned how to emphasise the sterner ethical qualities as well as the humaner, and the more clement by the side of the higher, public virtues His early Humanism made him a scholar and an exegete, a master of elegant Latinity, of lucid and incisive speech, of a graphic pen, and historical imagination. His juristic studies gave him an idea of law, through which he interpreted the more abstract notions of theology, and a love of order, which compelled him to organise his Church. His imagination, playing upon the primitive Christian literature, helped him to see the religion Jesus instituted as Jesus Himself saw it; while the forces visible around him—the superstitions, the regnant and unreproved vices, the people so quickly sinning and so easily forgiven, the relics so innumerable and so fictitious, the acts and articles of worship, and especially the Sacraments deified and turned into substitutes for Deity—induced him to judge the system that claimed to be the sole interpreter and representative of Christ as a crafty compound of falsehood and truth.

[1] A. M. Fairbairn, in *The Cambridge Modern History*, ii. 363.

That he was a creative theologian of the highest rank may well be questioned. He owed much to Augustine, and to the type of thought which Scotus had impressed on the later middle ages. His debt to Bucer was large. Without Luther his work could not have been done. But as a systematiser of Christian truth he stood without a rival in his century. He best taught men the answer to make to Roman claims, and, under his logic, theology attained once more a classic presentation. Yet he was much more than a theologian. As an organiser he was at his best, at least in intention. To quote Fairbairn's happy phrase, he sought to answer the question: "How could the Church be made not simply an institution for the worship of God, but an agency for the making of men fit to worship Him?"[1] His answer had its evident faults His methods were largely those of inquisitorial discipline, of State support, of force; but his answer was the best given in his age.

Calvin's own judgment of himself was that he was shy and timid by nature. To this opinion he often gave expression;[2] and there is no reason to doubt its truth as an analysis of his inward feeling. But his moral, and even his physical, courage is beyond doubt. Once convinced of the rightfulness of a course of action, no perils led him to swerve from its pursuit. The spirit was master of the flesh and of the mind. His chief faults were a supersensitive self-consciousness which led him to feel slights and criticisms far too keenly, and a quickness of temper which often overcame him to the loss of

[1] *The Cambridge Modern History*, ii p. 364

[2] *E g Opera*, xxi 102, xxxi. 21–24.

self-control. Of this infirmity a characteristic example has already been cited.[1] He was himself fully conscious of the weakness, and it was no less clearly recognised by his friends.[2] His nerves, racked by constant struggle and by long illness, were easily rasped. In his lightly aroused exasperation, he often expressed himself, even to his intimates, with acerbity. To his enemies, for example to Castellio and Servetus, he was hard and vindictive. Much of this asperity was the result of semi-invalidism; but much, also, was the fruit of the conviction—a source, indeed, in no small degree of his strength—that his work was fully that of God. So intense was this identification of his own interests with those of the Master he would serve, that he thanked his physician for aid in recovery from illness less on his personal account than as a service rendered to the Church; and he regarded attacks upon himself as a danger to the cause of the Gospel[3] It was easy for such a temperament to see in a criticism a serious offence and in an opponent an enemy of God.

Calvin undoubtedly appeared in different aspects to his contemporaries, and this diversity has led ever since his time to widely various estimates of his character. To his opponents he was the stern, unrelenting enemy,—the "king," "pope" or "calif." To the majority of his supporters he was the admired leader, the matchless logician, the wise commander in a great cause, the inspirer of courage and of martyr-zeal; but a figure

[1] *Ante*, p 232

[2] *E g* Colladon, *Opera*, xxi. 117, Beza, *Ibid*, p 170.

[3] *Opera*, xi 68, xiii 598; compare Kampschulte, ii. 383.

somewhat distant and awesome. To his intimates, he was the affectionate, if quick-tempered and sometimes censorious friend—a man to be loved as well as reverenced.

But whether friend, disciple, or foe, none could fail to recognise Calvin's transcendent ability. He might be slandered, the worst of motives might be imputed to him by traducers, but none who knew him could doubt his devotion to his cause. With all his frequent arrogance towards men, Calvin's spirit was humble towards God. To do and to teach His will was undoubtedly his prime intention; and if Calvin too often identified the divine purpose with his own wishes the error does not detract from the sincerity of his consecration. He submitted to his long bodily enfeeblement as from the wise hand of God. In the crises of his life, his conversion, his first settlement in Geneva, and in his return to the difficult ministry in that turbulent city, he sacrificed ease, scholarly honours, and personal inclination to what he deemed the imperative voice of God. He put God first. In the strength of the conviction that God had chosen his task, he fought his battles and did his work. It is this crowning trait that was expressed in the declaration of the Genevan Little Council, standing under the shadow of his recent death. "God gave him a character of great majesty,"[1]—and that must ever remain Calvin's highest claim to personal regard.

[1] R. Stähelin, in Hauck's *Realencyklopädie*, iii 683.

# INDEX

## A



## B

## C

CPSIA information can be obtained
at www.ICGtesting.com
Printed in the USA
LVHW081318040621
689374LV00005B/136

9 780343 20